FINANCIAL CONTAGION

The *Robert W. Kolb Series in Finance* provides a comprehensive view of the field of finance in all of its variety and complexity. The series is projected to include approximately 65 volumes covering all major topics and specializations in finance, ranging from investments, to corporate finance, to financial institutions. Each volume in the *Kolb Series in Finance* consists of new articles especially written for the volume.

Each volume is edited by a specialist in a particular area of finance, who develops the volume outline and commissions articles by the world's experts in that particular field of finance. Each volume includes an editor's introduction and approximately thirty articles to fully describe the current state of financial research and practice in a particular area of finance.

The essays in each volume are intended for practicing finance professionals, graduate students, and advanced undergraduate students. The goal of each volume is to encapsulate the current state of knowledge in a particular area of finance so that the reader can quickly achieve a mastery of that special area of finance.

Please visit www.wiley.com/go/kolbseries to learn about recent and forthcoming titles in the *Kolb Series*.

FINANCIAL CONTAGION

The Viral Threat to the Wealth of Nations

Editor

Robert W. Kolb

The Robert W. Kolb Series in Finance

WILEY

John Wiley & Sons, Inc.

Library of Congress Cataloging-in-Publication Data:

Financial contagion : the viral threat to the wealth of nations / Robert W. Kolb, editor.
     p. cm. – (Robert W. Kolb series in finance)
  Includes bibliographical references and index.
  ISBN 978-0-470-92238-5 (hardback)
 1. Financial crises.   2. International finance.   3. Financial risk management.
I. Kolb, Robert W., 1949–
  HB3722.F528 2011
  332′.042–dc22

                                                                   2010043305

Printed in the United States of America

10 9 8 7 6 5 4 3 2 1

To the next generation,
Katherine Ann Kolb and Rafael A. Quinn

Contents

Introduction

By its very name, *financial contagion* invokes a metaphor. Like all metaphors, this one requires interpretation and like all metaphors, the metaphor of financial contagion can both illuminate and mislead. This book places flesh on the bare bones of the contagion metaphor. In the discussion of financial contagion, key themes emerge and appear in many contexts, and the chapters in this book follow these themes into various markets and countries.

If any idea is ubiquitous in the analysis of contagion it is the idea of correlation between or among affected domains—financial instruments, firms, markets, economies, countries, regions, or the world economy. Economists have long noted that in certain crisis situations, different markets or economies in different countries suddenly start behaving much more similarly than they typically have done. Thus, this sudden increase in correlation of economic behavior is a prime symptom of contagion.

A second key issue explored in this book focuses on the channels of contagion—the avenues by which financial difficulty is transmitted. Imagine a physician who suddenly sees several patients all exhibiting similar symptoms. Given a germ theory of illness, it is easy to conclude that a disease is being transmitted from person to person through the physical exchange of germs, perhaps by exchange of bodily fluids or via some airborne mechanism. In cases of highly correlated economic symptoms, there is no such well-established theory about how an economic malady can be transmitted. Some channels of transmission seem clear: Economic upheaval in one nation can cause economic difficulties in another through interruptions in trade, for example. Similarly, financial distress in one nation can affect another via reduced financial flows, an interruption that can be a result of those same diminished volumes of trade. Yet in some cases the method of transmission is not apparent. For example, the Asian financial crisis originated in Thailand and spread rapidly to other nations. However, this rapid transmission of financial difficulties stunned policy makers in the United States, who never anticipated that such a small economy with limited linkages to other nations could foment such a widespread economic crisis.

A third key conceptual issue in understanding contagious episodes concerns the speed of transmission. For some economists spreading economic distress is an instance of financial contagion if and only if it is rapid. For these scholars, a slowly spreading economic malaise is regarded as a spillover of financial or economic distress. Within this framework, the two types of economic problems have different sources and may require different correctives. The chapters in this book trace these three issues, and others, into many markets and countries.

ABOUT THE TEXT

All of the chapters in this volume represent the cutting edge of thinking about financial contagion. The contributions stem from the authors' deep expertise in the subject matter. Almost all of the contributions are based on formal academic research conducted in the past two years. Accordingly, this book spreads before the reader the best thinking on financial contagion by specialists drawn from top universities and key international financial institutions including central banks, the International Monetary Fund, and the World Bank. All of the contributions in this volume have been especially written for the intended reader—a nonfinance specialist interested in understanding the vital importance of financial contagion for the world's economic future. The book is divided into six sections, and each is preceded by a brief essay describing the chapters in that section:

Part One. Contagion: Theory and Identification
Part Two. Contagion and the Asian Financial Crisis
Part Three. Contagion and Emerging Markets
Part Four. Contagion in the Financial Crisis of 2007–2009
Part Five. Regional Contagion
Part Six. Contagion within an Economy

Acknowledgments

No one creates a book alone. In the first instance, this book was created by the many contributors who lent their wisdom and knowledge to the project. In addition, Ronald MacDonald at Loyola University Chicago served as an extremely capable editorial assistant, while Pooja Shah, also at Loyola, provided immediate and expert research assistance. At John Wiley & Sons, I have benefited from working closely with my editor Evan Burton, who encouraged me to undertake this project. Also at Wiley, Emilie Herman has managed the production of this volume with her typically high level of expertise.

To these approximately 100 people I extend my sincere gratitude for making this book possible.

ROBERT W. KOLB
Chicago
September 2010

PART ONE

Contagion: Theory and Identification

T he chapters in this section begin the exploration of financial contagion with a conceptual overview of the nature of contagion and the methods for identifying contagious episodes. The section begins with a discussion of "what is financial contagion?" Perhaps, surprisingly, there is not a simple answer to this question. However, there does seem to be a widespread view that the key to understanding contagion lies in the concept of correlation.

Contagious episodes seem to be characterized by a change in the correlation between affected domains, whether those are particular financial instruments, markets, or economies. For some scholars, there is no contagion without an increase in correlation. However, the problem of identifying contagion is more complicated than merely identifying an increase in correlation.

An increase in volatility of prices will cause correlations to increase generally. So a mere increase in volatility should not count as proof of contagion according to many experts working in this area. On this view, the problem of identifying contagion then turns on measuring the jump in correlation that is not merely a function of heightened volatility, but that depends on linkages between the affected domains. Further, some experts on contagion want to distinguish between genuine contagion and what they would characterize as mere interdependence.

This section also inaugurates an examination of the particular mechanisms that allow economic problem to spread. One of the clearest channels of contagion is a trade relationship between two nations, such that economic difficulty in one nation quickly becomes a problem for its trading partner.

A conceptual treatment of contagion and the identification of contagious episodes ultimately requires a particular context for its full analysis. Accordingly, some chapters in this section consider the problem of contagion in a variety of concrete episodes, episodes that are the subject matter of many subsequent chapters: the Russian default of 1998, the Brazilian crisis of 1999, the dot-com crisis at the beginning of the twenty-first century, the long-lived Argentine crisis from 2001 to 2005, and, of course, the financial crisis of 2007–2009.

CHAPTER 1

What Is *Financial Contagion*?

ROBERT W. KOLB
Professor of Finance and Considine Chair of Applied Ethics,
Loyola University Chicago

The phrase *financial contagion* draws on a concept whose root meaning lies in the field of epidemiology. Like almost all metaphors, this one has the power to illuminate and to mislead. Its referent is the spread of financial distress from one firm, market, asset class, nation, or geographical region to others. But, *contagion* carries with it other burdens of meaning. First, to refer to *contagion*, instead of merely to an *epidemic*, is to implicitly assert that there is a mechanism of transmission from one infected victim to other potential victims. For example, bubonic plague and malaria may give rise to epidemics, but these diseases are not contagious, being transmitted by the bite of a flea and the sting of a mosquito, rather than being spread from one infected party to another. By contrast, some epidemics may be the result of truly contagious diseases in which the disease spreads directly from one victim to another through the direct transmittal of a pathogen, such as is the case with tuberculosis and AIDS. Second, because a contagious disease spreads from one infected host to others by some mechanism, the key to understanding such a malady is to comprehend the method of transmission. Finally, by invoking a metaphor of illness, *financial contagion* implies an economic disorder, dislocation, or disease.

Contagion is a fairly new concept in the economics literature—before 1990, it was scarcely mentioned (Edwards 2000, p. 1). Early interest in the concept stemmed from international finance, particularly the finance of emerging economies, and concern about contagion was exacerbated by the Asian financial crisis of 1997–1998 (Hunter, Kaufman, and Krueger 1999). Because concern originated in the international arena, the idea of transmission of financial difficulties across national borders has always had a prominence in discussions of contagion. But the financial crisis of 2007–2009, which inaugurated the subsequent Great Recession, provided powerful evidence that contagion was not a phenomenon limited to emerging markets or the arena of international finance.

Although there is little agreement about the meaning of *contagion*, much has been written about the channels of contagion, or the mechanisms by which financial distress originating in one source spreads to other victims. The problem here is to identify the channels of contagion or the means by which financial distress spreads from one arena to others. In some instances, financial difficulties percolate slowly and only gradually affect other markets or nations. In other situations, financial distress spreads like the most virulent of infectious or contagious diseases. Notice also that the so-called *channels of contagion* matter both for the spread of financial distress when the transmission is conceived on the epidemic model (like bubonic plague and malaria) or on the truly contagious model (like tuberculosis or AIDS).

There is some danger of conflating contagion with the evidence of contagion. That is, there is a risk of taking evidence of contagion as the malady itself. According to many studies, a contagious episode in finance typically results in a particularly heightened correlation among the affected domains. For example, if a financial crisis arises, the stock returns of two financial firms may suddenly start behaving more similarly than they did in the pre-crisis period. Although increased correlations may provide a method for identifying the occurrence of a contagious episode, the jump in correlations is hardly contagion per se.

These issues—alternative conceptions of contagion, the channels of contagion, and methods for identifying contagion—are key to understanding financial contagion. This chapter addresses each of these fundamental problem areas in turn.

THE CONCEPT OF CONTAGION

There is no settled meaning for *contagion* in finance. Some scholars fully embrace the disease metaphor: "One theory is that small shocks which initially affect only a few institutions or a particular region of the economy, spread by contagion to the rest of the financial sector and then infect the larger economy" (Allen and Gale 2000, p. 2). For others, contagion is merely the diffusion of financial stress, without connotations of disease: "the spread of financial difficulties from one economy to others in the same region and beyond in a process that has come to be referred to as 'contagion'" (Caramazza, Ricci, and Salgado 2004, p. 51).

In "A Primer on Financial Contagion," Marcello Pericoli and Massimo Sbracia consider five definitions of contagion that reflect the wide variety of meanings ascribed to this term: "1. Contagion is a significant increase in the probability of a crisis in one country, conditional on a crisis occurring in another country. . . . 2. Contagion occurs when volatility of asset prices spills over from the crisis country to other countries. . . . 3. Contagion occurs when cross-country comovements of asset prices cannot be explained by fundamentals. . . . 4. Contagion is a significant increase in comovements of prices and quantities across markets, conditional on a crisis occurring in one market or group of markets. . . . 5. Contagion occurs when the transmission channel intensifies or, more generally, changes after a shock in one market" (Pericoli and Sbracia 2003, pp. 574–575). These five definitions exhibit substantial conceptual differences. For example, the first is defined as a change in probabilities of a crisis, while the second focuses on a change in volatilities. Similarly, the first seems to pertain only to international financial contagion, while the third speaks of markets or groups of markets.

On some understandings, the speed with which financial distress spreads is critical. For Kaminsky, Reinhart, and Végh (2003), contagion is "an episode in which there are significant *immediate* effects in a number of countries following an event—that is, when the consequences are *fast and furious* and evolve over a matter of hours or days" (p. 55). They also acknowledge that there are similar events in which the spread is gradual, but these they regard as *spillovers*, not instances of contagion.

For many scholars, a change in the correlations among economic variables is a key. This is reflected in the third and fourth definitions listed by Pericoli and Sbracia. For their part, Kaminsky, Reinhart, and Végh (2003) make this an explicit additional condition in their definition of contagion, saying "Only if there is 'excess comovement' in financial and economic variables across countries in response to a common shock do we consider it contagion" (p. 55).

Kristin J. Forbes and Roberto Rigobon (2002) make this idea of correlation or changes in correlation the centerpiece of their understanding of contagion. Acknowledging a widespread disagreement over the meaning of contagion, they note that increased correlation has been taken as evidence of contagion. But for Forbes and Rigobon the matter is more complicated. Consider a major economic shock affecting one country or market. Such an event can raise volatility in financial markets generally, and heightened volatility, *by itself*, can cause an increase in measured correlation. For Forbes and Rigobon, such an increase in measured correlation is not an indicator of contagion. Instead, they regard contagion as reflected by an increase in correlation among asset returns, after discounting any such increased correlation that is due to an increase in volatility.

The core idea is that such an increase in correlations, properly measured, reflects an increase in linkages across markets or countries, and a change in the economic linkages are the key in their definition: "This paper defines contagion as a significant increase in cross-market linkages after a shock to one country (or group of countries)" (Forbes and Rigobon 2002, p. 2223). If the episode is truly one that exemplifies contagion, there will be an increased correlation among returns of the affected entities, even after discounting the measured correlation for the increased correlation due to heightened volatility. On this definition, Forbes and Rigobon argue that there was virtually no contagion during the 1997 Asian crisis, the 1994 Mexican peso devaluation, or the market crash in U.S. markets in October of 1987, all episodes that many others had identified as contagious episodes.

Others have followed or even extended the intuition of Forbes and Rigobon. Geert Bekaert, Campbell Harvey, and Angela Ng (2005) define contagion as "excess correlation, that is, correlation over and above what one would expect from economic fundamentals," and they assert that "Contagion is a level of correlation over what is expected" (pp. 40, 65). For those who adopt this framework of thought, the idea is that a model of asset returns provides a gauge of how an asset should behave based on other variables. Thus, the model gives an expected return for the asset being modeled. If we have special confidence in our model, we might even be tempted to think (even if we are not bold enough to say) that the model tells us how returns of the asset ought to behave, or what the rational behavior of those returns would be. In this framework of thought, contagion occurs when correlations jump to a level that is beyond what the model tells us to expect regarding correlation or what the model tells us is the rational level of correlation. Contagion, viewed as a departure from the normal, the expected, or the rational, taps the disease dimension of the contagion metaphor. This line of thought has seemed attractive to quite a few researchers, but it threatens implicitly to define contagion as that which is inexplicable on our ordinary understanding.

Thus, requiring heightened correlation not due to an increase in overall volatility and/or not due to economic fundamentals sets a high evidentiary bar for identifying contagion. On such criteria, many episodes that seem to have been instances of contagion are disqualified. Corsetti, Pericoli, and Sbracia (2005) attack this literature exactly on the grounds of setting an unrealistically difficult test for finding correlation. These findings of interdependence, but no contagion, they assert "follow from arbitrary assumptions on the variance of the country-specific noise in the markets where the crisis originates—assumptions that bias the test towards the null hypothesis of interdependence" (p. 1178).

In many cases, people who live through crises experience these financial episodes as exemplifying contagion. Against this background, a definition of contagion that disqualifies almost of all of these events fails to be useful in understanding people's experience. By the same token, it must be possible for people to experience a financial crisis as exemplifying contagion and for them to be mistaken. Otherwise, the effort to define *contagion* would be pointless. To truly identify some financial catastrophe as a contagious episode really turns on being able to specify the mechanism by which financial distress is propagated. Understanding how financial distress spreads will throw additional light on the concept of contagion and will be important in distinguishing true from merely apparent instances of financial contagion.

CHANNELS OF CONTAGION

It is at least possible to imagine widespread financial distress that is not the result of contagion. For example, if a large asteroid were to strike the earth, the economic consequences would be extremely large and widespread. But this would not be an episode of contagion on many definitions, because there would not be a transmission of financial distress from one stricken domain to another. Instead, in this example, all of the distress stems from an exogenous common source. Similarly, the outbreak of widespread war might cause dramatic financial losses in many markets, but it would hardly constitute an example of contagion. Thus, widespread financial distress that results from some event external to the economy will not be seen as an instance of contagion, generally speaking.

Some channels of contagion seem clear and easy to understand. For example, a trade link between two countries stands as the most obvious avenue of transmission for financial difficulties from one country to another. Consider two adjacent countries with strong trade links. If one of these countries experiences an internally generated economic crisis, due perhaps to a coup or civil war, that country will suffer large economic effects on the production of export goods and on the demand for goods from its trading partner. This disruption in trade can have profound and virtually immediate effects on its trading partner, and such a situation seems to be a clear instance of contagion. Here financial difficulties in one country arise, and we can understand quite readily how those difficulties can be transmitted to another country through trade linkages.

Although financial ties are not as directly palpable as a trade linkage, they also provide a fairly clear means by which financial difficulties in one country (or firm) can be transmitted to another. Assume that country A is a large creditor of country B. Country B experiences internally generated economic difficulties that make it apparent that it will not be able to pay its creditors as promised. In this case, country A sustains large losses and experiences its own financial distress. The financial difficulties in country B are then transmitted to country A through these financial linkages.

These examples rest on changes in real economic activities or changes in cash flows from financial assets. By contrast, much financial distress can arise more or less immediately from a change in perceptions, no matter whether those perceptions are grounded in reality. For example, consider a situation in which the public witnesses a run on a particular bank without knowing anything about the true condition of the bank suffering the run. Observing the run on this bank might make depositors at other banks fear the soundness of their own banks. Faced with this new uncertainty about the soundness of other banks, depositors might run to withdraw funds from their own accounts, even though they have no independent reason to question the soundness of their own banks. In this example, the financial difficulties at the first bank led to financial difficulties at other banks, but the transmission mechanism was due entirely to a shift in public perceptions. There may well have been no real difficulty at the first bank, and there may have been no financial linkages between the first bank to suffer a run and the other banks. Yet, financial difficulties at the first bank can lead to financial difficulties at other banks through a mechanism that can be specified quite clearly.

Closely allied to the bank run example is a situation in which investors see a variety of countries, firms, or assets as similar. Assume that investors in one particular asset realize that the value of that asset is much lower than previously thought. Further, assume that this information becomes public. Given the reduced value of the first asset, one may quickly come to view other similar assets as overpriced. This can lead to a rapid reassessment of the value of these other assets. In some sense, the financial difficulty in the first asset is transmitted to others through the medium of changed investor perceptions. In this example, the information about the first asset was true. This kind of potentially contagious event is referred to as a *wake-up call*. The perception of a lower value for the first asset awakens investors to the true economic value of other assets. It seems that part of the Asian financial crisis of the late 1990s stemmed from such a wake-up call when a realization that the Thai baht was overvalued led investors to question the value of other Asian currencies. As a result, financial difficulties in Thailand were quickly replicated in other Asian countries.

A sudden reassessment of asset values played an important role at a crucial juncture in the financial crisis of 2007–2009. Many financial firms had long been under suspicion and had suffered major depreciation in their stock prices. In a single week, from September 15 to 21, 2008, all major investment banking firms left the industry: Lehman Brothers filed for bankruptcy on September 15, and Bank of America absorbed Merrill Lynch on the same day. The week before, Fannie Mae and Freddie Mac had become explicit wards of the federal government, driving their share prices nearly to zero. On September 16, AIG, formerly the only triple-A financial firm in the United States, received a federal guarantee of support to the tune of $85 billion. After these events, it was clear to many that the financial difficulties just experienced by all of the largest financial firms in the United States would now focus on the only two significant investment banks still surviving, Goldman Sachs and Morgan Stanley. Fearing their own demise, both firms petitioned the Federal Reserve to become bank holding companies to secure a virtually bottomless pool of financing, while succumbing to increased regulation.

Widespread financial distress often has many sources. For example, the origins of the Great Depression remain a subject of continuing debate—in part because it had so many disparate causes. In many instances, various sources of financial distress and contagion operate together. In their book *The Panic of 1907*, Robert F. Bruner and Sean D. Carr explain how financial difficulties began with a purely external event, the great San Francisco earthquake and fire of 1906. This catastrophe led to economic dislocations in the real economy, leading to financial effects by affected companies and individuals. Troubles were furthered by an attempted stock market manipulation, which itself had widespread consequences. Before long, financial difficulties engulfed the world.

The financial crisis of 2007–2009 had many causes that will be debated for a long time, and the role of contagion in transitioning from a subprime real estate problem in the United States to a worldwide recession and widespread financial distress will long be debated. However, most accounts of the financial crisis and ensuing Great Recession acknowledge the role of long-standing U.S. policies to promote homeownership, an enduring policy of easy money and low interest rates at the macro level, along with corruption, dishonest mortgage practices, and a hubris with respect to very complex financial instruments, among still other factors (Kolb 2010 and Kolb 2011, especially Chapters 9–13).

The complexity of large-scale and widespread financial dislocations makes it almost certain that many observers will find a role for financial contagion in explaining how the disaster spread so quickly, widely, and completely. But the very size and complexity of these financial crises also makes it extremely likely that much more was in play besides a merely contagious episode. The fact that contagious financial distress is often embedded in a more complex context makes it difficult to identify and isolate the contagion that appears to be a central part of the story.

IDENTIFYING CONTAGIOUS EPISODES

Those who live through large-scale financial dislocations, and especially those leaders charged with responding to them have no trouble in identifying the episode as being one of contagion, but sometimes they are not seen until they already have an effect. Laura Tyson, former Chair of the Council of Economic Advisors, speaking on the role of Thailand in the Asian financial crisis, said: "Thailand is a very small economy. It didn't have a lot of links, and it's not exactly in your backyard. So in any event, the U.S. chose not to intervene in Thailand [while the baht was under pressure in 1997], thinking it was not going to spill over. Why would it? The contagion effects were not apparent to anybody, not just the administration" (Yergin and Cran 2003).

Yet the contagion was soon apparent to policy makers in this episode and we find William McDonough, then President of the Federal Reserve Bank of New York saying: "From about the first of February until the beginning of August [1998], there was a period in which financial markets essentially decided that risk didn't exist anywhere," but then Russia defaulted in August 1998 and McDonough continues: "All these people who in the previous seven months had decided there was no risk anywhere literally panicked and decided there's got to be massive risk everywhere. Behind each fence and barnyard wall there must be a risk that we hadn't thought of, you know, like the redcoats retreating from Lexington" (Yergin and Cran 2003). One could hardly ask for a clearer account of contagion conceived as a "wake-up call" exemplified by rapidly shifting investor perceptions. Thus, the contagion was clearly evident to these policy makers faced with responding to the Asian financial crisis, as it was to the new set of policy makers forced to deal with the financial crisis of 2007–2009.

However, economists tend to believe that actual contagion should be discernible in economic data. We have already discussed the main tool that economists use—the examination of changing correlations among asset return behaviors, sometimes adjusting those correlations by using sophisticated econometric techniques.

Yet one must wonder if the economists' toolkit is adequate to the challenge of identifying contagion. First, contagion is often examined against the background of larger crises, a context that may make the identification of contagion particularly difficult. Further, there seem to be many avenues for the spread of financial difficulty. Although some, like direct trade and financial links, may be fairly easy to trace, a sudden widespread shift in investor perceptions may be virtually instantaneous and leave few traces in the historical data. For example, there can be little doubt that Goldman Sachs and Morgan Stanley terminated their existence as investment banks as a direct result of the financial difficulties that took Lehman Brothers to oblivion and induced Merrill Lynch to throw itself into the arms of Bank of America. Yet those events were separated by barely a week, hardly enough time to create an economic record that would statistically show the contagion that economists labor to discern.

REFERENCES

Allen, Franklin, and Douglas Gale. 2000. "Financial Contagion," *Journal of Political Economy* 108:1, 1–33.

Bekaert, Geert, Campbell R. Harvey, and Angela Ng. 2005. "Market Integration and Contagion." *Journal of Business* 78:1, 39–69.

Bruner, Robert F., and Sean D. Carr, (2007). *The Panic of 1907: Lessons Learned from the Market's Perfect Storm*, Hoboken, NJ: John Wiley & Sons.

Caramazza, Francesco, Luca Ricci, and Ranil Salgado. 2004. "International Financial Contagion in Currency Crises." *Journal of International Money and Finance* 23:51–70.

Corsetti, Giancarlo, Marcello Pericoli, and Massimo Sbracia. 2005. "'Some Contagion, Some Interdependence': More Pitfalls in Tests of Financial Contagion." *Journal of International Money and Finance* 24:1177–1199.

Edwards, Sebastian. 2000, March. "Contagion." *Working Paper*.

Forbes, Kristin J., and Roberto Rigobon. 2002, October. "No Contagion, Only Interdependence: Measuring Stock Market Comovements." *Journal of Finance* 57:5, 2223–2261.

Hunter, William C., George G. Kaufman, and Thomas H. Krueger. 1999. *The Asian Financial Crisis: Origins, Implications, and Solutions*. Dordrecht: Kluwer Academic.

Kaminsky, Graciela L., Carmen M. Reinhart, and Carlos A. Végh. 2003, Fall. "The Unholy Trinity of Financial Contagion." *Journal of Economic Perspectives* 17:4, 51–74.

Kolb, Robert W. 2010. *Lessons from the Financial Crisis: Causes, Consequences, and Our Economic Future*. Hoboken, NJ: John Wiley & Sons.

Kolb, Robert W. 2011. *The Financial Crisis of Our Time*. Oxford: Oxford University Press.

Pericoli, Marcello, and Massimo Sbracia. 2003. "A Primer on Financial Contagion." *Journal of Economic Surveys* 17:4, 571–538.

Yergin, Daniel, and William Cran. 2003. *The Commanding Heights: The Battle for the World Economy* 3 DVDs, PBS.

ABOUT THE AUTHOR

Robert W. Kolb received two PhDs from the University of North Carolina at Chapel Hill (philosophy 1974, finance 1978), and has been a finance professor at the University of Florida, Emory University, the University of Miami, the University of Colorado, and currently at Loyola University Chicago, where he also holds the Frank W. Considine Chair in Applied Ethics.

He has published more than 50 academic research articles and more than 20 books, most focusing on financial derivatives and their applications to risk management. In 1990, he founded Kolb Publishing Company to publish finance and economics university texts, built the company's list over the ensuing years, and sold the firm to Blackwell Publishers of Oxford, England in 1995. His recent writings include *Financial Derivatives, 3e*, *Understanding Futures Markets, 6e*, *Futures, Options, and Swaps, 5e*, and *Financial Derivatives*, all co-authored with James A. Overdahl. Kolb also edited the monographs *The Ethics of Executive Compensation*, *The Ethics of Genetic Commerce* and *Corporate Retirement Security: Social and Ethical Issues*, and (with Don Schwartz) *Corporate Boards: Managers of Risk, Sources of Risk*. In addition, he was lead editor of the *Encyclopedia of Business Society and Ethics*, a five-volume work.

Two of Kolb's most recent books are *Lessons From the Financial Crisis: Causes, Consequences, and Our Economic Future*, an edited volume published by Wiley, and *The Financial Crisis of Our Time*, published by Oxford University Press in 2011. He is currently writing: *Incentives in Executive Compensation*, to be published by Oxford University Press. In addition, to the current volume, he is also editing *Sovereign Debt: From Safety to Default*, also forthcoming from Wiley.

CHAPTER 2

Correlation Analysis of Financial Contagion[*]

GIANCARLO CORSETTI
University of Cambridge

MARCELLO PERICOLI
Bank of Italy

MASSIMO SBRACIA
Bank of Italy

INTRODUCTION

The outbreak of the Greek crisis in 2009–2010 and the transmission of financing strains to other countries—such as Portugal, Ireland, and Spain—have once more turned the spotlight on financial contagion. The term *contagion*, generally used in contrast to *interdependence*, conveys the idea that during financial crises there might be breaks or anomalies in the international transmission mechanism, arguably reflecting switches across multiple equilibria, market panics unrelated to fundamentals, investors' herding, and the like.

There is still wide disagreement among economists about what contagion is exactly, and how it should be tested empirically. Pericoli and Sbracia (2003), for instance, list five different definitions and related measures of contagion that are frequently used in the literature.[1] A common approach, however, consists of identifying breaks in the international transmission of shocks *indirectly*, inferring from them a significant rise in the correlation of asset returns across markets and countries. In practice, analysts compare cross-country and cross-market correlations of asset returns in *tranquil* and *crisis* periods, under the maintained assumption that a significant rise in the correlation of returns can be attributed to a break in their data-generating process. Of course, the importance of the correlation statistics for financial investors provides a strong and direct motivation for this type of analysis. As Engle (2009) puts it, the correlation structure of financial assets is the key ingredient to a portfolio choice, because it is instrumental in determining the risk.

---

[*]The views expressed in this chapter are those of the authors and do not necessarily reflect those of the Bank of Italy or of any other institution with which the authors are affiliated.

11

Still, these studies share a basic problem. Crises are typically identified as periods in which return volatility is abnormally high. Suppose that a crisis is driven by large shocks to a common factor, affecting all asset returns across the world. Other things equal, a higher variance of the common factor simultaneously causes higher-than-usual volatility *and* stronger comovements in all markets. In other words, holding the parameters of the data-generating process constant (other than the variance of the common factor), so that by definition there is no break in the international transmission of financial shocks, a rise in the magnitude of the common shock mechanically increases cross-country correlations. Consistently with most definitions, however, this would provide no evidence of financial contagion. Meaningful tests of contagion should thus net out the effect of changes in volatility from changes in cross-country correlations.

In this chapter, we first document a small set of stylized facts that motivates the construction of tests of contagion based on correlation analysis (Section 2). Second, drawing on Corsetti et al. (2005), we present a general correlation test for contagion addressing the issue discussed above, and illustrate its properties with an application to the Hong Kong stock market crisis of October 1997 (Section 3). Section 4 concludes.

STYLIZED FACTS

We start by documenting a set of four stylized facts characterizing the transmission of shocks across stock markets. The first two are well understood in the literature: (1) sharp drops in stock prices tend to cluster across countries, and (2) the volatility of returns rises during financial crises. The other two are often confused in formal and informal discussions of contagion: (3) financial crises are frequently associated with a rise in the cross-country *covariances* of returns; (4) cross-country *correlations* of returns increase often during financial turbulences, but there are many crisis episodes in which correlations fall or remain invariant, relative to tranquil periods.

We document these facts, using weekly stock prices and returns in local currency for 20 countries: the G-7, Argentina, Brazil, Mexico, Greece, Spain, Russia, Hong Kong, Indonesia, South Korea, Malaysia, Philippines, Singapore, and Thailand. The sample period runs from January 1990 to May 2010. The data source is Thomson Reuters Datastream.

Sharp Falls in Stock Prices Tend to Occur in Clusters Across National Markets

Crises are not independently distributed. As noted by Eichengreen et al. (1996), for instance, long phases of tranquillity in foreign exchange markets are interrupted by waves of speculative attacks, simultaneously hitting different currencies. Similar patterns characterize stock markets. This is apparent in the two decades spanning the period 1990–2010 (Exhibit 2.1). In five episodes of financial turmoil, at least three quarters of the countries in our sample recorded a decline in stock market prices by 20 percent or more. These episodes are the U.S. recession in 1990–1991, occurring contemporaneously to the First Gulf War; the Russian financial crisis and

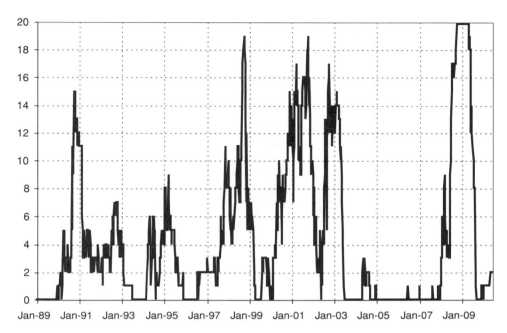

Exhibit 2.1 Number of Countries Experiencing Stock Market Distress (Values, Weekly Data)

Source: Elaborations on Thomson Reuters Datastream. The figure shows the number of countries in our sample in which weekly returns on the stock market index recorded a decline of 20 percent or more with respect to the peak achieved over the previous year.

the associated collapse of the U.S. hedge fund LTCM in 1998; the U.S. recession in 2001 and the terrorist attacks on September 11; the period preceding the Second Gulf War; the Great Recession of 2008–2009. In the other three episodes, the financial turmoil was somewhat less widespread: the crisis of the European Exchange Rate Mechanism (ERM) in 1992 (which nonetheless affected stock prices in Europe, Asia, and Latin America); the crisis in Mexico in 1994–1995; and the stock market crash in Hong Kong in October 1997. It is worth emphasizing that the last two crises severely affected stock prices all over the world, even though they originated in two peripheral economies.

The Volatility of Stock Market Returns Rises During Crisis Periods

The major crisis episodes in our sample are characterized by a sharp increase in the volatility of returns (Exhibit 2.2). Among them, the Great Recession of 2008–2009 stands out for both its virulence and global nature. In fact, following a period of low volatility in asset prices between 2004 and 2007 (below 15 percent), volatility rose to unprecedented levels (up to more than 40 percent for the cross-country median), affecting most countries, as shown by the small interquartile difference.

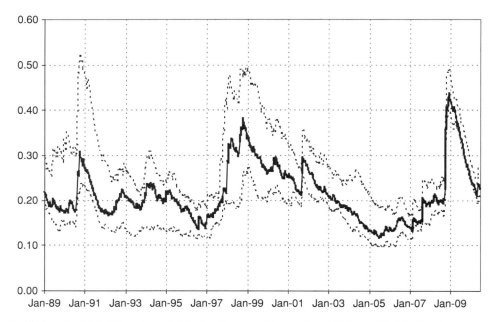

Exhibit 2.2   Volatility of Stock Market Returns (Annualized Values, Weekly Data)
Source: Elaborations on Thomson Reuters Datastream. The bold line shows the median volatility of weekly stock market returns in local currency; the thin-dotted lines show the first and the third cross-sectional interquartile. Volatilities are computed as exponential moving averages with a decay factor equal to 0.96.

Covariances between Stock Market Returns Frequently Increase during Crisis Periods

The covariances of returns display a somewhat different pattern relative to volatility (Exhibit 2.3). A sharp rise in the covariances is apparent during the crisis episodes in 1990–1991, in 1998, in 2001, and especially during the Great Recession. A clear rise in covariances also occurred during the collapse of the Hong Kong stock market in 1997, as well as during the burst of the dot-com bubble in March 2000. But there is virtually no rise in covariances during the ERM crisis or during the Mexican crisis in 1995. Note that covariances remained on a descendent path after September 11, until the eruption of the global crisis in 2007.

Correlations Often Rise during Crises, But Are Not Always Higher Than in Tranquil Periods

Looking at the major crisis episodes listed earlier, a clear rise in correlations can be detected in 1990–1991, during the Mexican crisis in 1995, during the Hong Kong stock market crash in October 1997, in 1998, and during the Great Recession (Exhibit 2.4). Correlations instead declined in 1992, during the ERM crisis. In 2001, they rose only after the terrorist attacks of September 11, although many countries had already recorded sharp falls in stock prices since the beginning of the U.S. recession in March. By the same token, there was no rise in correlation before the

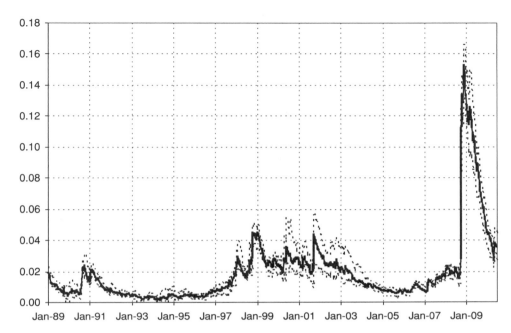

Exhibit 2.3 Covariances between Stock Market Returns (Annualized Values, Weekly Data)
Source: Elaborations on Thomson Reuters Datastream. The bold line shows the median of 190 (10 × 19) bivariate covariances of weekly stock market returns in local currency; the thin-dotted lines show the first and the third cross-sectional interquartile. Covariances are computed as exponential moving averages with a decay factor equal to 0.96.

Second Gulf War, even if at the end of 2002 more than half of the stock markets in our sample had already recorded sharp price falls; correlations only started to rise in February 2003, during the last phase of stock price adjustment, and continue to increase through the spring of 2004—at a time in which stock prices were already on a rising path.

Note that during the tranquil period 2004–2007, characterized by rising stock prices and low return volatility, the median correlation is often above the peaks observed in crisis episodes, such as those recorded in 1998 and in 2001.

CORRELATION ANALYSIS OF CONTAGION: THEORY AND AN APPLICATION

Can we interpret a significant increase in the comovements of asset returns during financial crises as evidence of contagion? More specifically, can we infer contagion via a straightforward application of standard statistical tests for differences in correlation coefficients? As already mentioned, a key problem with this approach is that the correlation between returns is affected by their volatility, which is typically higher during crises. This point was acknowledged early on by seminal contributions on contagion, such as King and Wadhwani (1990).[2]

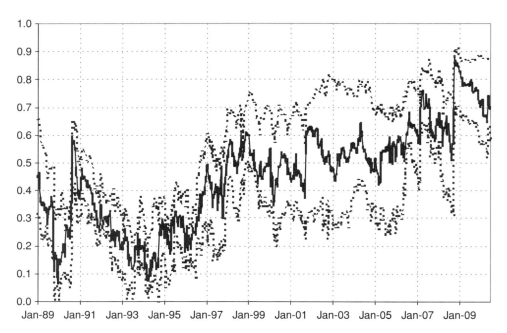

Exhibit 2.4 Correlations between Stock Market Returns (Annualized Values, Weekly Data)
Source: Elaborations on Thomson Reuters Datastream. The bold line shows the median of 190 (10×19) bivariate correlation coefficients of weekly stock market returns in local currency; the thin-dotted lines show the first and the third cross-sectional interquartile. Correlation coefficients are computed as exponential moving averages with a decay factor equal to 0.96.

To illustrate the problem in detail, assume that returns are generated by a standard factor model:

$$r_j = \alpha_0 + \alpha_1 f + \varepsilon_j$$
$$r_i = \beta_0 + \beta_1 f + \varepsilon_i$$

where r_j and r_i denote stock market returns, respectively, in countries j and i; f is a global factor affecting all countries (usually, the market return); ε_j and ε_i are idiosyncratic factors independent of f and of each other; α_0, β_0, α_1, and β_1 are constants, with the last two parameters measuring the strength of cross-country linkages: the higher α_1 and β_1, the stronger the correlation between r_i and r_j. The expressions above can be derived from several models in finance, including the capital asset pricing model and the arbitrage pricing theory.

From the factor model above, the correlation between r_i and r_j, hereafter denoted with ρ, can be written as:

$$\rho = \left[1 + \frac{Var(\varepsilon_j)}{\alpha_1^2 Var(f)}\right]^{-1/2} \left[1 + \frac{Var(\varepsilon_i)}{\beta_1^2 Var(f)}\right]^{-1/2}$$

Here is the problem: ρ depends on the importance of the terms $\alpha_1^2 Var(f)$ and $\beta_1^2 Var(f)$, capturing how movements in the common factor affect returns, relative to the terms $Var(\varepsilon_j)$ and $Var(\varepsilon_i)$, reflecting country idiosyncratic noise. Suppose we observe a crisis in country j, associated with an increase in the volatility of the returns r_j. Holding the parameters α_1 and β_1 constant, the effect of the crisis on the cross-country correlation of returns will depend on the extent to which the rise in the variance of r_j is driven by the variance of the common factor f, as opposed to the variance of the country-specific factor ε_j. If movements in the common factors are relatively large, the correlation rises; otherwise, it falls. Two points are worth stressing: Correlations may increase or decrease during a crisis, and change with the variance of r_j, *even if the intensity of the cross-country linkages α_1 and β_1 does not change at all*. These observations suggest that, according to the standard definition of contagion, some fluctuations in correlation are actually consistent with simple interdependence, in the sense that they can occur absent changes in the parameters of the model. To provide evidence in favor of contagion, changes in correlation should be large enough, to point to breaks in the transmission mechanism, that is, to changes in the structural parameters α_1 and β_1, affecting the intensity of the cross-border transmission of shocks (note that α_0 and β_0 do not affect ρ).

Thus, proper tests of contagion should at least distinguish between breaks due to shifts in the variance of the common factors, and changes in the values of α_1 and β_1. Using the factor model described above, in Corsetti et al. (2005) we have shown that, under the null hypothesis of no contagion, the correlation between r_i and r_j corrected for the increase in the variance of r_j, takes the following form:

$$\phi = \rho \left[\left(\frac{1+\lambda^T}{1+\lambda^C} \right) \frac{1+\delta}{1+\rho^2\psi\,(1+\lambda^T)} \right]^{1/2}$$

where

$$\lambda^T = \frac{Var(\varepsilon_j|T)}{\alpha_1^2 Var(f|T)} \quad \lambda^C = \frac{Var(\varepsilon_j|C)}{\alpha_1^2 Var(f|C)}$$

$$1+\delta = \frac{Var(r_j|C)}{Var(r_j|T)} \text{ and } \psi = (1+\delta)\frac{1+\lambda^T}{1+\lambda^C} - 1$$

and T and C denote, respectively, the *tranquil period* (a regime characterized by the absence of crisis) and the *crisis period* (a regime of turmoil initiated by the crisis in country j). The correlation statistic ϕ depends on the correlation in the tranquil period (ρ), the change in the variance of r_j during the crisis (δ), as well as the relative importance of the idiosyncratic factor relative to the global factor during the tranquil and the crisis period (λ^T and λ^C). Note that, in the special case in which λ^T and λ^C are identical, $\lambda^T = \lambda^C = \lambda$ (i.e., in country j, the variance of the country-specific factor relative to that of the common factor remains constant during the crisis), ϕ further simplifies as follows:

$$\phi' = \rho \left[\frac{1+\delta}{1+\delta\rho^2\,(1+\lambda)} \right]^{1/2}$$

Now, by construction, ϕ is the correlation under the assumption of interdependence; that is, the assumption that the intensities of the cross-country links α_1

and β_1 do not change between tranquil and crisis periods. Testing for contagion requires verification as to whether the correlation observed during the crisis, call it ρ^c, is significantly larger (or smaller) than ϕ. In other words, instead of comparing ρ^c to ρ (a comparison biased by the increase in the variance of r_j), a proper test for contagion should compare ρ^c to ϕ.

It is important to stress that biases in correlation tests of contagion occur not only if one fails to correct, but also if one *overcorrects* the influence of changes in the variances across regimes. An example of overcorrection can be illustrated as a special case of ϕ (or ϕ'), by setting $\lambda^T = \lambda^C = 0$—that is, by arbitrarily and unrealistically imposing that in the country where the crisis originates there is no idiosyncratic shock. In this case, the factor model collapses to an *ad hoc* linear model $r_i = \gamma_0 + \gamma_1 r_j + \upsilon_i$, and the test statistics is $\rho[\frac{1+\delta}{1+\delta\rho^2}]^{1/2}$. This framework—again, a special case of our model for $Var(\varepsilon_j) = 0$—implies that correlation always increases with the variance of r_j; that is, it always increases during crises. This prediction is clearly inconsistent with the evidence discussed in Section 2. Most importantly, because of *overcorrection*, tests derived from this biased framework tend to always yield the same result of no contagion across crisis episodes.

To illustrate our methodology, we reproduce results from early work (see Corsetti et al. 2005), in which we study contagion from the market crisis in Hong Kong in October 1997—an archetype example in the literature. Based on a subset of 18 of the 20 countries in our sample (excluding Spain and Greece), we compute two-day rolling averages of daily returns in U.S. dollars between January 1, 1997, and October 17, 1997, (the tranquil period), as well as between October 20, 1997, and November 30, 1997, (the crisis period).[3] The latter period starts with the crash in the Hong Kong stock index, which lost 25 percent of its value in just four days from October 20 onward. Hong Kong stock prices then continued to decline until the end of November, seemingly influencing returns in several other markets.

The parameter δ is estimated by computing the variance of Hong Kong stock returns in the tranquil and the crisis period. The ratios λ^T and λ^C are obtained by regressing returns on the Hong Kong stock market on a common factor, which can be proxied by returns on the world stock market index produced by Thomson Reuters Datastream—a weighted average of the stock indices of several countries. As an alternative, we also use a cross-sectional average return from the full sample, the G7 countries, or the United States only, and further verify our results using principal components and factor analysis.

Results are quite striking. Ignoring the need to correct the correlation coefficient, a standard statistical test of the hypothesis $\rho^c \leq \rho$ would reject the null in favor of the alternative $\rho^c > \rho$ for 8 out of 18 countries. Our correction makes a difference: Using the world stock market index as a benchmark, the hypothesis of interdependence ($\phi \leq \rho$) is rejected for only five countries under the maintained assumption $\lambda^T = \lambda^C$, and for six countries in the general case $\lambda^T \neq \lambda^C$.[4] Overcorrection can be quite misleading though. A test assuming $\lambda^T = \lambda^C = 0$, still popular among practitioners, would reject interdependence for just one country (Italy).

CONCLUSION

Correlation analysis provides a useful tool for testing for financial contagion. Yet, no correlation measure of interdependence can be derived independently of a model of asset returns. Analysts should note their preferred model, and verify its implications for correlation analysis. Specifically, different models may prescribe different corrections of the standard correlation coefficient in order to check for changes in the variance of returns across tranquil and crisis periods. Our results, however, strongly suggest that country-specific noise should not be arbitrarily ignored in testing for structural breaks in the international transmission of shocks.

NOTES

1. Pericoli and Sbracia (2003) discuss the fact that some studies do not distinguish between contagion and interdependence, but focus on the channels through which negative shocks propagate. In these studies, contagion is defined as an increase in the probability of a crisis following the crisis in another country or as a volatility spillover. More recently, a new wave of studies has made the distinction between contagion and interdependence central, and has developed tests of contagion based on regime switching models or on changes in correlation.

2. In the first major paper using the correlation approach, King and Wadhwani (1990) acknowledged that volatility affects correlation (see p. 20), but implemented no correction for this effect in their empirical tests.

3. This application uses U.S. dollar returns because they represent profits of investors with international portfolios and two-day rolling averages in order to account for the fact that stock markets in different countries are not simultaneously open. Results are robust, however, to these choices.

4. Due to the rapid convergence to the normal distribution, tests for correlation coefficients are generally performed by using their Fisher z-transformation (see Corsetti et al., 2005, for details).

REFERENCES

Corsetti, Giancarlo, Marcello Pericoli, and Massimo Sbracia. 2005. "Some Contagion, Some Interdependence: More Pitfalls in Tests of Financial Contagion." *Journal of International Money and Finance* 24:1177–1199.

Eichengreen, Barry, Andrew Rose, and Charles Wyplosz. 1996. "Contagious Currency Crises: First Tests." *Scandinavian Journal of Economics* 98:463–494.

Engle, Robert. 2009. *Anticipating Correlations: A New Paradigm for Risk Management*. Princeton, NJ: Princeton University Press.

King, Mervyn A., and Sushil Wadhwani. 1990. "Transmission of volatility between stock markets." *Review of Financial Studies* 3:5–33.

Pericoli, Marcello, and Massimo Sbracia. 2003. "A Primer on Financial Contagion." *Journal of Economic Surveys* 17:571–608.

ABOUT THE AUTHORS

Giancarlo Corsetti (PhD Yale, 1992) is professor of macroeconomics at the University of Cambridge. He has been Pierre Werner Chair and professor of economics at the European University Institute, and professor of economics at the University of Rome III. He has previously taught at Bologna and Yale. He is a fellow of CEPR and CESifo, and has been a regular visiting professor at the Bank of Italy, the European Central Bank, the Federal Reserve Bank of New York, and the International

Monetary Fund. His articles have appeared in the Brookings Papers on Economic Activity, Economic Policy, *Journal of International Economics*, *Journal of Monetary Economics*, *Quarterly Journal of Economics*, and the *Review of Economic Studies*, among others. His contributions include studies of the international transmission mechanism, monetary and fiscal policy, as well as currency and financial crises. He is currently co-editor of the *Journal of International Economics* and the *International Journal of Central Banking*.

Marcello Pericoli holds a PhD in economics from the University of Rome La Sapienza (1996), an M.A. in economics from the University of Pennsylvania (1995), and a B.A. in economics and business from the University of Rome La Sapienza (1991). He worked as economist for a private research institute in Rome and as country strategist for an investment bank in London. He joined the Bank of Italy in 1997, where he is currently head of the financial market unit of the economics, research, and international relations area. In 2002–2003, he was visiting fellow at the Bendheim Center for Finance of Princeton University. He has conducted research in the fields of asset pricing and international finance, with articles published in several refereed journals, including the *Journal of International Money and Finance*, *Journal of Money, Credit and Banking*, *Economic Modelling*, the *Journal of Economic Surveys*, and *International Finance*.

Massimo Sbracia received an M.A. in economics from the University of Pennsylvania (1997) and a B.A. in statistics and economics from the University of Rome La Sapienza (1994). He joined the Bank of Italy in 1998, where he is senior economist in the international finance and advanced economies division of the economics, research, and international relations area. He held visiting or temporary appointments at the New York University, the IMF, the Einaudi Institute for Economics and Finance, the International Institute for Applied Systems Analysis, the Italian National Institute of Statistics, and the Institute for Studies on Economic Planning. He has done extensive work in the fields of finance and international trade, and has published articles in many refereed journals, including the *Journal of Monetary Economics*, the *Journal of International Money and Finance*, *International Finance*, *The World Economy*, *Economic Modelling*, the *Journal of Economic Surveys*, and *International Economics and Economic Policy*.

CHAPTER 3

Uncertainty and Contagion

PRAKASH KANNAN
International Monetary Fund

FRITZI KOEHLER-GEIB
World Bank

The spread of financial crises, or contagion, reemerged as a pressing issue following the succession of financial and economic crises around the globe that began with the unraveling of the subprime crisis in the United States in 2007. Contagion also featured prominently in several other episodes of financial crises. Emerging market crises that started in Mexico in 1994–1995, Thailand in 1997, and Russia in 1998 entailed subsequent crises in neighboring and faraway economies. A similar accumulation of crises occurred in industrialized countries in the context of the European Exchange Rate Mechanism (ERM) crisis in 1992. However, several other episodes, such as the crises in Brazil in 1999, Turkey in 2001, and Argentina in 2001–2002, remained primarily local. These differential patterns raise the question of why some crises have a contagious effect on other economies while others do not.

A common theme arising from several recent papers is that contagion depends on the nature of the crisis in the "initial-crisis" country. In particular, a distinction has been drawn between "surprise crises"—crises that were unexpected by market participants—and "anticipated crises"—crises that were largely expected well before they actually occurred.[1] The consensus from this literature is that the earlier crises—Mexico, Thailand, and Russia—were largely unanticipated events, while the more recent set of crises—Brazil, Turkey, and Argentina—were anticipated. The link between the degree of anticipation and the occurrence of contagion has led some authors to regard the surprise element as a necessary condition for contagion.[2] The literature thus far, however, has not come up with a satisfying mechanism to explain the differential occurrence of contagion.[3]

This chapter proposes a new channel for the international transmission of crises and provides empirical evidence that supports it.[4] The mechanism at play is a straightforward one: Investors have a view on particular economies based on information signals that they obtain from time to time. Based on these signals, they make investments in a particular country. The signals also inform them on the likelihood of a crisis materializing. When an unexpected crisis occurs, investors begin to doubt the accuracy of their signals and question their views on other economies. In equilibrium, this change in beliefs will increase the aggregate uncertainty regarding fundamentals in other countries in which the investor is invested. As this uncertainty increases, so does the cost of financing faced by the firm, which in turn increases the probability of a crisis in the other country. The mechanism operates symmetrically in the opposite direction—an anticipated crisis event will reduce the aggregate uncertainty in other countries and, therefore, reduce the probability of a crisis. The proposed mechanism thus explains the differential pattern of contagion between surprise and anticipated crises. The empirical analysis provides insights based on a panel dataset including 38 countries from 1993 to 2005, covering six pronounced crisis periods.

THE MECHANISM BEHIND THE UNCERTAINTY CHANNEL OF CONTAGION

Investors continuously receive information about the economies in which they invest. This information takes on a variety of forms—new economic data, political events, policy announcements—but they all serve toward providing the investor insight into the "state" of the economy. If the economy is expected to enter a crisis, there is a high likelihood that returns on investments in that country will be low. Likewise, if an economic boom is expected, returns on investments will likely be high. Processing this information, however, requires an investment of resources. For example, an investor may set up a research department staffed by analysts who translate the various pieces of information into a final "buy–sell" recommendation.

Extracting information regarding the state of an economy from these different pieces of information, however, is an inexact science. Returning to the analogy of a research department, the investor who ultimately uses the recommendation from her analysts always attributes some degree of uncertainty to the interpretation of the information. This degree of uncertainty can change over time as the investor gains or loses confidence in the ability of the analysts in the research department. One such metric used to verify the degree of uncertainty that is relevant to understand the uncertainty channel of contagion is whether the models used by the analysts are able to predict crises. As mentioned earlier, whether the models are able to predict crises is an important concern for investors as crises have large negative consequences on their investment returns. If the predictions based on the models turn out to be correct, investors place more confidence in the quality of their information. Likewise, if the information turns out to be wrong, investors will lose confidence in their research team, and subsequently invest less resources in the information-analyzing technology.

The belief that investors have in the quality of their information is not without consequences to the firms and countries in which they invest. As investors attribute a lower precision to the quality of their information, they rationally become more cautious and invest less than they would, given the same information, were they more confident. In the aggregate, information becomes more noisy resulting in securities trading below their fundamental values. From the point of view of the firms that issue these securities, the resulting behavior of investors results in an increase in their cost of funding. This makes the firm vulnerable to other shocks that it may experience during the period, such as liquidity shocks specific to the firm or larger shocks that affect the whole economy.

This interaction between the behavior of investors—who are uncertain about the quality of their information—and the firms in which they invest, forms the core of the mechanism that underlies the uncertainty channel of contagion. The mechanism works as follows: Suppose a crisis happens that was unexpected by the investor based on the information that she received prior to the event. This "surprise" crisis leads the investor to doubt the ability of whatever technology she has employed to process the information, and thus to spend less resources in the technology. The resulting cautiousness exercised by the investor leads to an increase in the cost of funds for firms in other countries in which she invests, thus making those economies also vulnerable to crises. Analogously, if instead the crisis was one that was anticipated, investors will feel more assured by their information-analyzing technology, influencing their investment behavior in such a way as to make crises less likely in other economies.

EVIDENCE

The described mechanism yields two testable hypothesis: First, surprise (anticipated) crises result in an increase (decrease) in uncertainty, as measured by the dispersion of beliefs regarding fundamentals, in other countries. And second, an increase in uncertainty is associated with a higher probability of the incidence of a financial crisis.

A broad data set serves to verify the suggested mechanism. It comprises 38 countries with monthly data spanning the period from December 1993 to September 2005. The sample of countries together with the associated time frame allow for the analysis of the following six significant crisis periods: Mexico (1994–1995), Thailand (1997), Russia (1998), Brazil (1999), Turkey (2001), and Argentina (2001–2002). These crises cover currency crises as well as episodes of sovereign debt default. In both cases, however, these episodes featured significant drops in stock market returns in the respective economies. Therefore, drops in stock market returns serve to date the crises events. Based on our model, uncertainty is defined as the variance of private signals around the true value of the fundamentals that affect the rate of return on investments. Such data, however, is not directly observable. The return on investment typically correlates strongly with the growth rate of output, we follow Prati and Sbracia (2002) and use the standard deviation of GDP growth forecasts from Consensus Economics as a reasonable proxy.

The empirical strategy is designed as a two-step procedure following the two testable hypotheses: The first step estimates the effect of the crisis in an initial crisis country on uncertainty in other countries. Uncertainty in all sample countries—with the exception of the six initial crisis countries—is regressed on crisis dummies for the months of stock market crisis in the six initial crisis countries in a fixed effects panel estimation controlling for other potential domestic and external drivers of uncertainty. Potential domestic drivers of uncertainty are the mean of growth expectations, stock market volatility, and proxies for economic, financial, and political risks, and past stock market crisis in the country itself. The strong variation in uncertainty across countries points to systematic differences that are accounted for through country-fixed effects in the regression. As an external factor, the interest rate in advanced economies is included (see Fernandez-Arias 1996).

The second step estimates the effect of uncertainty about the fundamentals in the potentially affected countries on the probability of a crisis there. In these discrete-dependent variable regressions the most important control variables account for alternative contagion channels, such as trade links, common creditors, overexposed fund investors, and the market size of the initial crisis country.[5] Additionally, the estimations control for domestic and external drivers of crises, namely, the mean of growth expectations and stock market volatility, country fixed effects, and interest rates in advanced economies.

The estimation results suggest robust effects of the initial crisis on uncertainty in other countries in the direction predicted by the model. The Mexican, Thai, and Russian crises—identified by the literature to be surprise crises—increase the level of uncertainty regarding fundamentals in other countries. However, in the case of the three other crises, the Brazilian, Turkish, and Argentine crises—identified as anticipated crises in the literature—the panel analysis shows a different pattern: The Turkish and Argentine crises significantly *decrease* the level of uncertainty in potentially affected countries. These results are robust to the choice of regional or emerging markets subsamples and the inclusion of a large number of control variables. The effect of the Brazilian crisis is less clear, turning out insignificant in the estimations.

Both surprise crises and anticipated crises prompt stronger effects on uncertainty in emerging markets than in all countries. This finding might reflect higher costs of information gathering in emerging markets that are, on average, less transparent than advanced economies.[6] This could explain a higher disincentive to investors to bear the cost of acquiring information about emerging markets if surprised by a crisis. The estimations also show strong positive effects of surprise crises within their own region. Of the three surprise crises, the Thai crisis had the strongest impact on uncertainty in other countries. Viewed through the lens of the model, this observation suggests that the Thai crisis shattered the confidence in information-gathering technology more than the other two surprise crises.

The second step of the estimation strategy shows a significant and robust effect of uncertainty on the probability of a crisis. Importantly, this effect is robust to the inclusion of various alternative channels of contagion, domestic, and external crisis drivers.

To summarize, these results suggest that uncertainty about fundamentals in a country increases with the occurrence of a surprise crisis in another country. The uncertainty, in turn, leads to an increase in the probability of a crisis. Conversely, in the case of an anticipated crisis in the first country, uncertainty in the second country is reduced, thereby decreasing the probability of a crisis in the second country. Calculating marginal effects makes clear that the effect of the uncertainty on the probability of crises in the potentially affected countries is not negligible.

IMPLICATIONS

Can we learn anything from the development of the suggested measure of uncertainty and stock market returns in terms of the transmission of financial stress during the current downturn? Exhibit 3.1 shows the evolution of a weighted average of our uncertainty measure for the G-7 countries plus Brazil, India, Mexico, and China from 2001 up to the most recent episode. Aggregate uncertainty in the world

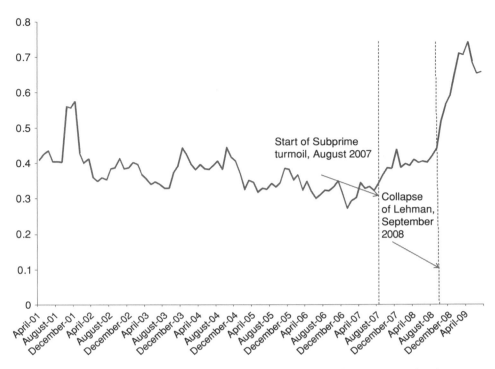

Exhibit 3.1 Standard Deviation of One-Year Ahead Forecast for GDP (Weighted Average G-7 plus Brazil, India, Mexico, and China)
Source: Authors' calculation, Consensus Economics.

economy nudged upward in August 2007 when the subprime crisis first came to light. The collapse of Lehman Brothers, however, marked a distinct increase in the aggregate measure.

In terms of stock market returns, an interesting picture presents itself: Beginning in August 2007, stock market returns worldwide increased, rather than dropped and only in September 2008 and the following months fell significantly. As illustrated in Exhibit 3.2, this pattern is even more pronounced in emerging than in industrialized economies, reflecting the initial discussion of decoupling of emerging markets from the financial center. The strong drop in stock returns after September 2008 is a piece of evidence in favor of the type of contagion that we analyze in our paper.

Taken together, the surprise element of the crisis, the development of uncertainty and of stock market returns seem to suggest that the uncertainty channel of contagion may well have been at work in spreading the current crisis around the globe.

WHAT COMES NEXT?

One implication arising from our paper is that surveillance activities have to be an important element in any effort to promote international financial stability. Apart

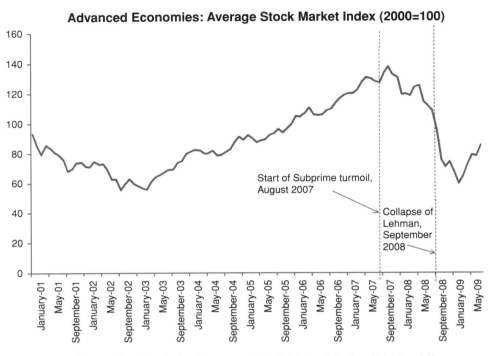

Exhibit 3.2 Stock Market Returns (MSCI GDP-Weighted Aggregate Indices)
Source: Authors' calculation, MSCI.

from helping prevent crises in the first place, closer monitoring of the fundamentals of a country can minimize the risk of a surprise crisis in one country resulting in harmful spillovers to other countries.

The still elevated level of uncertainty or disagreement about the state of the various economies leaves us with a note of caution. With fiscal deficits rising, in some cases coupled with concerns about long-term affordability, this uncertainty might reflect concerns about inflation, looming interest rate increases, or sovereign defaults—all affecting the cost of financing.

NOTES

1. A variety of measures have been used to identify the degree of anticipation. Kaminsky, Reinhart, and Vegh (2003) use changes in domestic bond spreads, and revisions to sovereign credit ratings, as a measure of the degree to which markets anticipate a crisis. Didier, Mauro, and Schmukler (2006), instead, use net sales or purchases by mutual funds in the period leading up to a crisis. Finally, Rigobon and Wei (2003) and Mondria and Quintana-Domeque (2007) use the number of news articles about a particular country as a measure of anticipation.
2. Kaminsky, Reinhart, and Vegh (2003), for example, consider it as one of the three necessary elements in their "unholy trinity."
3. An exception is Mondria (2006) where, in the event of a surprise crisis, investors reallocate their limited attention to the crisis country, which induces them to liquidate positions in other countries. If a crisis were anticipated instead, the investor can take the time necessary to increase her information processing resources, thus reducing the impact of the attention reallocation on other countries.
4. For more detail see Kannan and Koehler-Geib (2009).
5. To ensure the robustness of the results, pooled logit and linear probability estimations are added to the initial pooled probit estimations.
6. See Gelos and Wei (2005) for a thorough discussion of the role of transparency in investment decisions of emerging market mutual funds.

REFERENCES

Didier, T., P. Mauro, and S. L. Schmukler. 2006. "Vanishing Contagion?" *IMF Policy Discussion Papers* 06/01, International Monetary Fund.
Fernandez-Arias, E. 1996. "The New Wave of Private Capital Inflows: Push or Pull?" *Journal of Development Economics* 48:389–418.
Gelos, G., and S. Wei. 2005. "Transparency and International Portfolio Holdings." *Journal of Finance* 60:6, 2987–3019.
Kaminsky, G., C. Reinhart, and C. Vegh. 2003. "The Unholy Trinity of Financial Contagion." *Journal of Economic Perspectives* 17:4, 51–74.
Kannan, P., and F. Koehler-Geib. 2009. "The Uncertainty Channel of Contagion." *IMF Working Papers* 09/219, International Monetary Fund.
Mondria, J. 2006. "Financial Contagion and Attention Allocation." *Working Papers* 254, University of Toronto, Department of Economics.
Mondria, J., and C. Quintana-Domeque. 2007. "Financial Contagion through Attention Reallocation: An Empirical Analysis." Mimeo.
Prati, A., and M. Sbracia. 2002. "Currency Crises and Uncertainty About Fundamentals." *IMF Working Papers* 02/3, International Monetary Fund.
Rigobon, R., and S.-J. Wei. 2003. "News, Contagion and Anticipation," Mimeo.

ABOUT THE AUTHORS

Prakash Kannan is an economist at the research department of the International Monetary Fund. He has a PhD in economics from Stanford University, and a bachelor's degree in economics from MIT. His research interests fall in the general field of international macroeconomics. He has published in the *European Economic Review*, and has written several book chapters including NBER Conference volumes and the IMF's World Economic Outlook. Prior to his career at the IMF, he was an economist at the Central Bank of Malaysia.

Friederike (Fritzi) Koehler-Geib is an economist in the Poverty Reduction and Economic Management group in the Latin America Department of the World Bank in Washington, DC. Her prior work experience includes the Economic Policy and Debt department of the Poverty Reduction and Economic Management network of the World Bank, the monetary and capital markets department (MCM) and the research department of the International Monetary Fund.

Her research interests fall in the area of international finance and economics. She has published articles in the areas of sudden stops of capital flows, contagion of financial crises, economic growth, and asset management.

She holds a PhD in Economics from Ludwig Maximilians University (Munich) with extended research stays at Universidad Pompeu Fabra (Barcelona) and two master's degrees from the University of St. Gallen, HEC Paris, and University of Michigan.

CHAPTER 4

Contagion Dating through Market Interdependence Analysis and Correlation Stability

MONICA BILLIO
Department of Economics, University Ca' Foscari, Venice, Italy
GRETA Associati, Venice, Italy
Advanced School of Economics, University Ca' Foscari, Venice, Italy

MASSIMILIANO CAPORIN
Department of Economics, University of Padova, Italy
GRETA Associati, Venice, Italy

In the financial literature, the concept of contagion captures the phenomena of one country's reactions to shocks affecting other countries to which the former may not be linked from a strict economic point of view. Despite the large agreement on the existence of contagion occurrences, there is no consensus on its definition or on its causes. In this chapter, we build on the restrictive definition of contagion, as defined by the World Bank, which is used in many studies such as that of Forbes and Rigobon (2000): Contagion is the change in the information transmission mechanism that takes place during periods of turmoil, and that could be associated with significant increases in cross-market correlations.

Within this definition, many authors have proposed models, approaches, and statistical tests to determine if a given event could be associated with a contagion occurrence. Examples of possible contagion events are the Asian crisis of 1997, the Russian default of 1998, or the technology market bubble of 2000. The surveys and references in Rigobon (2002), Dungey et al. (2005), and Dungey and Tambakis (2005a, 2005b) provide a first guidance to this growing literature.

We mention two of the most followed approaches. Note that both of them associate contagion with the presence of common shocks, and analyze contagion events in specific time ranges of market turbulence. The first approach assumes that contagion occurrences could be identified by means of observable quantities or variables, which are considered as proxies of common shocks (see Bae, Karolyi, and Stulz 2003, among others). The second method assumes that shocks are not observable and tries to identify them by means of statistical models, such as in Pesaran and Pick (2007). Both approaches suffer from a number of possible draw-backs: the choice of variables, the time zone in which markets operate, and, more relevantly, the knowledge of the time range in which the contagion took place (see also Billio and Pelizzon 2003, for an analysis of misspecification due to the wrong choice of the time range).

In Billio and Caporin (2010), we consider a quite different approach. By focus-ing on the returns of a set of international stock market indices (from Asia and America), we directly introduce time-zone effects in an econometric model. Fur-thermore, we explicitly take into account the interdependence across markets, both on the market return levels and on their risk (thus, modeling the interdependence through variances).

Once existing relations across markets are taken into account and filtered out, the resulting "filtered" stock market returns (the model residuals) are used for two further main steps: First, we define a testing procedure for the identification of changes in the correlation levels across markets, which considers also the use of graphical procedures; and, second, we introduce a Concordance Index and a Strength Index for contagion occurrences.

The model we propose allows capturing of both interdependence and inte-gration across markets. Although the former is explicitly introduced in the model, the latter is summarized in the correlation of the "filtered" stock market returns. We thus follow the World Bank's restrictive definitions of contagion and associate contagion with changes in market integration, or, in other words, with changes in the long-term correlation across the "filtered" stock market returns. Such a choice allows us to create a model with contagion occurrences and short-term changes in the correlation levels following, for instance, the Dynamic Conditional Correlation model proposed by Engle (2002).

It is important to underline that the approach in Billio and Caporin (2010) should be considered as a tool for the identification of contagion occurrences. It could be then used to identify and evaluate the appropriate reactions to contagion events, thus allowing determination of how to immunize an economic system from the effects of a disease that is spreading across financial markets.

THE MODEL AND THE TESTING PROCEDURE

The main contribution provided in Billio and Caporin (2010) is the testing pro-cedure for contagion occurrences. This result is the by-product of a model that captures market interdependence.

More precisely, given a set of international stock markets index returns, we first specify an innovative simultaneous equation model: Each equation is market-specific, and the system is simultaneous because stock markets opening and closing times are not synchronized within the same day (due to time-zone effects), and contemporaneous relations may exist (for instance, when one market closes before other markets open). We also introduce variance spillovers in our model. Follow-ing Ling and McAleer (2003), we specify a Multivariate GARCH model for the simultaneous equation system innovations. Each stock market equation residual is conditionally heteroskedastic, where time t variance depends on the previous period variance (as in standard GARCH models) and on the residuals of all equations. Therefore, a shock affecting a specific market has an impact on the variance of all markets. This second element of the model captures the interdependence across market risks. Once the model parameters have been estimated (see Billio and Caporin 2010, for details on the estimation approach), both the market mean and variance interdependences are filtered out. The model residuals contain only the information that refers to the correlations across the financial markets, because mean and variance dynamics have already been captured.

The "filtered" stock market returns are then analyzed to detect changes in their correlation levels. In order to provide a statistically robust approach, we considered the tests for changes in the correlation coefficient proposed by Fisher (1915), and have extended them to the multivariate case by Rao (1979). This statistical test evaluates the equivalence of the correlation matrix across a number of variables (in our case the "filtered" stock market returns) computed on two different nonoverlapping samples.

The test has maximum power if we know the period of market turbulence. However, because the turbulence period is not known, we provide a tool for its identification. First, we consider a rolling approach and estimate correlations using samples of 120 observations (roughly equivalent to six months). Furthermore, to exclude transitory changes in the correlation levels, we suggest that test statistics are computed using two samples, which are at first contiguous and then separated by a window of days ranging from 1 to 120. The resulting 121 test statistics are then aligned such that the window used for the evaluation of the second correlation matrix starts at the same point in time (for all the 121 test statistics). Finally, we build two indices with the aim of dating contagion events: a Concordance Index equal to the number of test statistics indicating a significant increase in the correlation level of the second window, and a Strength Index equal to the cumulated values of the Concordance Index over the last 120 days. In addition, we standardize the two indices to ensure that they assume values between zero and one. By construction, both indices are time varying, and could be easily analyzed through a graphical representation. The Concordance Index could be employed to determine if, at a given date, the analyzed markets are experiencing contagion events. The Strength Index allows for evaluation of the severity of these events on the economic system. Using this framework, we associate contagion events with values of the Concordance Index greater than 0.5 for at least one week. Therefore, the evaluation of this index over time could be used to determine the length of contagion events.

Finally, we note that a Concordance Index and a Strength Index could be created for flight to quality events, which are associated with a decrease in the average correlation levels in the second sample compared to the first one.

AN EMPIRICAL EXAMPLE

In Billio and Caporin (2010), we verified the performances of our approach with a set of American and Asian markets: Brazil, Mexico, United States, Japan, Singapore, and Hong Kong. This choice allows the time-zone effect that exists between these two areas to be taken into account: Asian markets close before American markets open, thus creating a contemporaneous flow of information from Asian to American markets (beside the contemporaneous relationships among markets operating in the same area).

We considered data ranging from June 1995 to November 2005. Therefore, we worked on a time span including the Asian crisis, the technology market bubble, and September 11. Finally, we analyzed the indices over a common currency (the United States dollar, USD), and over local currencies. The availability of local currency analysis and its comparison with the USD currency allows the identification of a crisis that spread over markets affecting both exchange rates and stock indices, or just one of the two.

The empirical results show evidence of contemporaneous effects within the Asian and American markets, and of a significant transmission from Asian to American markets. Relevant interconnections also exist in terms of variance spillovers, but these are less evident. These findings are substantially equivalent in both common and local currencies.

According to empirical estimates, we filtered out the mean and variance dynamics from the stock market indices and analyzed the correlation across residuals with the Concordance and Strength indicators previously outlined. Note that, in order to avoid distortive effects, we removed the September 11 innovation, because this event could be safely interpreted as a global shock and not as the start of a contagion event.

In Exhibits 4.1 and 4.2, we report the Concordance and Strength indices for contagion in both the common and the local currencies cases. Both graphs focus on events lasting for at least five days. Similar graphs for flight to quality are not shown.

In analyzing Exhibit 4.1, we note that just one contagion event appears in the Strength Index computed over local currency data: the Asian crisis. In fact, the

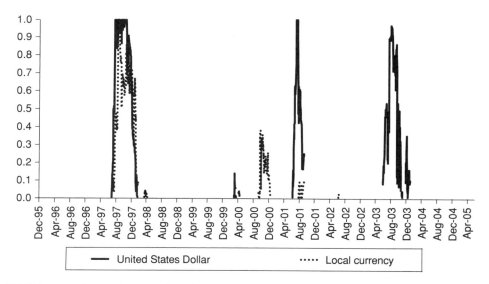

Exhibit 4.1 Concordance Index of Contagion in Common and Local Currency among the Brazilian, Mexican, United States, Japanese, Singapore, and Hong Kong Stock Markets

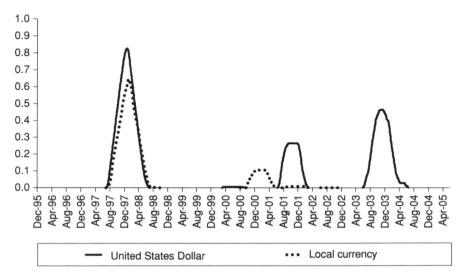

Exhibit 4.2 Strength Index of Contagion in Common and Local Currency among the Brazilian, Mexican, United States, Japanese, Singapore, and Hong Kong Stock Markets

other two peaks are associated with maximum values lower than the 0.5 threshold that we used to define a change in the correlation level as a contagion event.

However, if we consider the analysis in a common currency, the United States dollar, three main turmoil periods appear, all of which are identified as contagion occurrences (they all peak at values close to one): again, the Asian crisis, and two periods in 2001 and 2003. We interpret this result as evidence of contagion events absorbed mainly by the exchange rate market (when converting stock market returns in a common currency, we are basically mixing the stock market return and the exchange rate return dynamics).

With respect to the time span of contagion occurrences, we note that in following our approach (Strength Index larger than 0.5), the Asian crisis period starts from the end of July 2007 and lasts up to the end of December 2007. This period is perfectly consistent with that proposed by Forbes and Rigobon (2002), but, differently to these authors, our range is completely data-driven. The other two contagion events lasted from June to August 2001, and from June to September 2003; the second one could be associated with the Iraq war.

Moving to the analysis of the Strength Index in Exhibit 4.2, we note that the Asian crisis was the most severe one, as the index is associated with higher values. The other two turmoil periods had a minor impact on the markets, with the 2003 event being more severe than the 2001 one. Moreover, both the common and local currency lines confirm the impact of the Asian crisis, which, as expected, is more relevant if we take into account the exchange rates (the USD line is higher than the local currency line).

Finally, a similar analysis for the flight to quality case provides evidence of an event from September to November 2004, which we can associate with a number of elements: the long-term effects of the Iraq war, the Argentinean default, the increase of oil price, and the increased expansion of China and India compared to the stagnation in South America.

Building on these results, in Billio and Caporin (2010) we show how changes in the unconditional correlation levels could be easily included in a dynamic conditional correlation GARCH model (see Engle 2002). The empirical estimates demonstrate that taking into account the breaks in correlations improves the performances of standard models that are currently used in the risk management process, with possible implications on the market risk capital requirements.

CONCLUDING REMARKS

According to the restrictive definition of contagion based on changes in the unconditional correlation across a number of stock market indices, we show how it is possible to date contagion occurrences by using statistical approaches. This dating procedure can be helpful in identifying contagion occurrences, and could then be used to identify and evaluate the appropriate reactions to contagion events. Moreover, the identified changes in the unconditional correlation levels can be easily included in a dynamic conditional correlation GARCH, allowing the improvement of models that are currently used in risk management processes. The method we have outlined in this chapter has the advantage of being robust to time-zone effects and interdependence across markets.

REFERENCES

Bae, K. H., G. A. Karolyi, and R. M. Stulz. 2003. "A New Approach to Measuring Financial Contagion." *Review of Financial Studies* 16:3, 717–763.

Billio, M., and M. Caporin. 2010. "Market Linkages, Variance Spillovers, and Correlation Stability: Empirical Evidences of Financial Contagion." *Computational Statistics and Data Analysis* 54:11, 2443–2458.

Billio, M., and L. Pelizzon. 2003. "Contagion and Interdependence in Stock Markets: Have They Been Misdiagnosed?" *Journal of Economics and Business* 55:5/6, 405–426.

Dungey, M., R. Fry, B. Gonzalez-Hermosillo, and V. L. Martin. 2005. "Empirical Modelling of Contagion: A Review of Methodologies." *Quantitative Finance* 5:1, 9–24.

Dungey, M., and D. Tambakis. 2005a. *Identifying International Financial Contagion: Progress and Challenges.* New York: Oxford University Press.

Dungey, M., and D. Tambakis, D. 2005b. "International Financial Contagion: What Do We Know?" In M. Dungey and D. Tambakis, eds. *Identifying International Financial Contagion: Progress and Challenges* Chapter 1. New York: Oxford University Press.

Engle, R. F. 2002. "Dynamic conditional correlation: a new simple class of multivariate GARCH models." *Journal of Business and Economic Statistics* 20:339–350.

Fisher, R. A. 1915. "Frequency Distribution of the Values of the Correlation Coefficient in Samples of an Indefinitely Large Population." *Biometrika* 10:507–521.

Forbes, K., and R. Rigobon. 2000. "Measuring Contagion: Conceptual and Empirical Issues." In S. Claessens and K. Forbes, eds. *International Financial Contagion*. Alphen aan den Rijn, the Netherlands: Kluwer Academic.

Forbes, K. J., and R. Rigobon. 2002. "No Contagion, Only Interdependence: Measuring Stock Market Comovements." *Journal of Finance* 57:5, 2223–2261.

Ling, S., and M. McAleer. 2003. "Asymptotic Theory for a Vector ARMA-GARCH Model." *Econometric Theory* 19:278–308.

Pesaran, H., and A. Pick. 2007. "Econometric Issues in the Analysis of Contagion." *Journal of Economic Dynamics and Control* 31:1245–1277.

Rao, D. C. 1979. "Joint Distribution of z-Transformations Estimated from the Same Sample." *Human Heredity* 29:334–336.

Rigobon, R. 2002. "Contagion: How to Measure It?" In S. Edwards and J. Frankel, eds. *Preventing Currency Crises in Emerging Markets*. Chicago: University of Chicago Press.

ABOUT THE AUTHORS

Monica Billio is Full Professor of Econometrics at the University Ca' Foscari of Venice. She holds a doctorate in Applied Mathematics obtained at the University Paris Dauphine in 1999. Her main research interests include financial econometrics, with applications to risk measurement and management, volatility modeling, financial crisis and hedge funds; business cycle analysis; dynamic latent factor models; simulation based inference techniques. Her research projects have appeared in peer-refereed journals including *Journal of Econometrics, Journal of Statistical Planning and Inference, European Journal of Finance, Journal of Empirical Finance, Journal of Financial Econometrics, Computational Statistics and Data Analysis* and *Journal of Forecasting*.

Massimiliano Caporin is assistant professor of econometrics at University of Padova. He holds a PhD in quantitative economics and a degree in economics received from the University Ca' Foscari Venice. His research interests cover univariate and multivariate volatility modeling, conditional correlation models, financial contagion, high-frequency data analysis, active portfolio management strategies, performance evaluation, long-term investment strategies, and weather and energy derivative pricing. He is author of papers appeared that in *Econometric Reviews, Journal of Time Series Analysis, Journal of Financial Econometrics, Computational Statistics and Data Analysis, Journal of Forecasting*, and *Journal of Economic Surveys*.

CHAPTER 5

Contagion or Interdependence[*]

Does the Speed of the Transmission of Shocks Matter?

STEFANIE KLEIMEIER
Maastricht University, School of Business and Economics

THORSTEN LEHNERT
University of Luxembourg, Faculty of Law, Economics and Finance,
Luxembourg School of Finance

WILLEM F. C. VERSCHOOR
Erasmus University Rotterdam, Erasmus School of Economics

T he financial crisis that started in 2007 and spread from the United States to global banking markets and finally to real economies is just the latest—though arguably one of the most severe—in a series of crises including the Latin American debt crisis in the mid-1980s, the U.S. stock market crash in 1987, or the Asian and Russian crises in 1997–1998. Researchers at the IMF have recorded 124 banking crises, 208 currency crises, and 63 sovereign debt crises since 1970 (Laeven and Valencia 2008). In 42 cases, countries experienced a twin crisis in their banking and currency markets and in 10 cases even a triple crisis in their banking, currency, and debt markets.

Considering the high frequency of crises but also the potentially substantial adverse impact of a crisis on a country, policy makers are looking for ways to protect their economies against crises that are "imported" from abroad. In order to find the right policy responses, a fundamental question that needs to be answered is exactly how a crisis is transmitted from one country to another: Is a crisis contagious or is it transmitted interdependently? If speculative attacks, financial panic, or herd behavior are the transmission forces then crises are contagious and will spread further. National policy makers will find it difficult to protect their markets from such crises. In contrast, if crises are transmitted to interdependent countries through real and stable linkages, then the spread of a crisis can be limited. In this case, countries with good economic fundamentals will be protected. Stable

---

[*]This chapter is based on Kleimeier, Lehnert, and Verschoor (2008).

linkages between countries can have their roots in the international financial system or in the economic relationships among countries. Consider financial institutions that pledge their stock portfolios as collateral for leveraged transactions. When the stock market in a given country falls due to a country-specific shock, collateral values drop and institutions face margin calls. In order to be able to meet these margin calls, institutions need to raise cash. As the shares in the affected market have already dropped in price, institutions sell their still valuable stocks from yet unaffected markets and thereby transmit the initial shock to other countries.

One way to answer the contagion-versus-interdependence question is to look at the comovements between markets and their prices. An increase in cross-market correlations during the crisis is typically seen as an indicator of contagion while stable correlations indicate interdependence. Thus, for markets that exhibit a low degree of comovement during stable periods, a significantly higher degree of comovement during a crisis period indicates contagion. In contrast, for markets that exhibit a high degree of comovement already during stable periods, an equally high degree of comovement during a crisis points toward interdependence. Here the permanently high degree of comovement suggests the existence of real linkages between the two countries.[1] By showing the levels of different national stock market indices, Exhibit 5.1 illustrates how stock markets behaved relative to each other during the Asian crisis of 1997. Thailand is typically considered the ground-zero country from which this crisis originated. Before the crisis, markets moved rather independently. For the indices shown in Exhibit 5.1, the closing-price correlation with Thailand can be calculated: It is lowest for Japan with -0.71 and highest for France with -0.30. During the crisis, the picture changes dramatically. Prices drop in all markets and markets appear to be much more volatile. The correlations with Thailand increase for all markets and now range from 0.06 for the United Kingdom to 0.96 for Indonesia.

The picture presented in Exhibit 5.1 is representative of many crises. Cross-market correlations increased substantially during the U.S. stock market crash (King and Wadhwani 1990; Lee and Kim 1993), the 1994 Mexican peso crisis and the 1997 Asian crisis (Baig and Goldfajn 1999; Calvo and Reinhart 1996). Exhibit 5.1, however, also shows that stock market volatilities increased during the Asian crisis. This is important for the contagion-versus-interdependence question because higher volatility leads to higher correlations. In this sense, correlation is *conditional* upon volatility. This linkage is a statistical artifact that has no economic meaning and should thus have no implications for contagion or interdependence. However, as crises are typically periods of high volatility, they are consequently also periods of high correlation. In order to draw the correct conclusions about contagion and interdependence, the volatility-driven component has to be excluded from the crisis-period correlation. Forbes and Rigobon (2002) are the first to recognize this problem and propose the use of *unconditional* correlation coefficients. When applying their method to the 1987 U.S. stock market crash, the 1994 Mexican peso crisis, and the 1997 Asian crisis they find *no contagion, only interdependence*: The large cross-market linkages during a crisis are simply a continuation of strong transmission mechanisms that already exist during noncrisis periods.

One further issue that must be addressed when answering the contagion-versus-interdependence question is that of *time-zone alignment*. For the stock markets affected by the Asian crisis, the market indices shown in Exhibit 5.1 are based

Panel A: Pre-crisis period

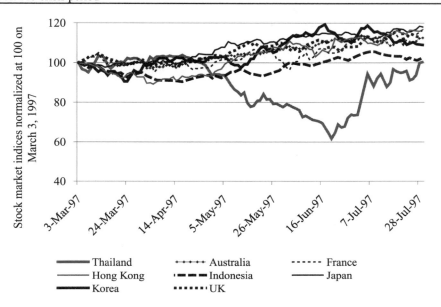

Panel B: Crisis period

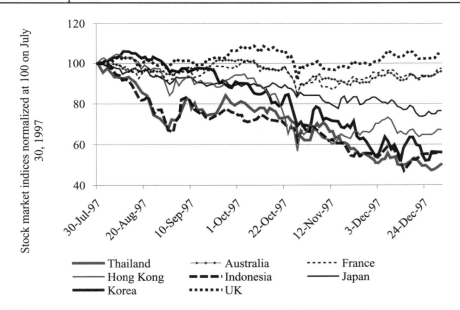

Exhibit 5.1   Selected Stock Markets before and during the Asian Crisis
Note: This exhibit shows the development of local-currency, daily closing prices of stock markets for ground-zero country Thailand and five selected countries in the periods surrounding the Asian crisis. Closing prices are set to 100 on March 3, 1997, and July 30, 1997, respectively.

on the closing-prices in each market. When testing for contagion in equity markets using correlations, most researchers employ synchronized data based on just such closing prices. However, closing prices are taken at different points in time because trading hours differ from market to market and, more importantly, time zones and the application of daylight saving time differ, too. Thailand's market closes at 5 PM local time. No other market closes at exactly the same point in time, not even those in the same geographic region or time zone. What do these time differences imply for the transmission of shocks during a crisis from one market to the other? If we assume that global financial markets are not fully and equally efficient, then shocks are not instantaneously transmitted but need time to be transmitted from one market to the other. This speed of transmission of shocks might well be specific to each market. One can imagine that the speed of transmission is potentially faster in a more efficient market than in a less efficient one. Thus, contagion studies using synchronized data make strong as well as differing assumptions about the speed of transmission of shocks. The effective time difference of closing prices between Thailand and other markets range from five or six hours for European markets (depending on daylight savings time), five hours for Taiwan, four hours for Japan, Korea, and the Philippines, three or four hours for Australia (depending on daylight savings time) to two hours for China and only one hour for Indonesia, Malaysia, and Singapore. For the Asian crisis the assumed speed of transmission of shocks toward Singapore is five times faster than the assumed speed of transmission of shocks toward Taiwan. If such differences affect the answer to the contagion-versus-interdependence question, then any documented variations in results across countries might well be caused by the differences in the speed of transmission implicitly assumed when using synchronized data. Putting it differently—is the answer to the contagion-versus-interdependence question robust to changes in the assumed speed of transmission of shocks?

One response to the problem inherent in synchronized data is to solve it methodologically by using moving average returns (Forbes and Rigobon 2002), lags (Bae et al. 2003), or dummy variables (Kaminsky and Reinhart 2008). These solutions are, however, less than optimal as the true effects of synchronized data on correlations are not fully understood. A first step to be better understanding of these effects is to investigate the sensitivity of correlations—and thus of the contagion-versus-interdependence conclusion—to the assumed speed of transmission of shocks. In Kleimeier, Lehnert, and Verschoor (2008) we set out to do just that by developing a new method that we call *time alignment of data*. We apply this method to two phases of the Asian crisis: The shocks transmitted from Thailand to other markets from July 30 to October 16, 1997, during the Thailand crisis phase and the shocks transmitted from Thailand to other markets from October 17 to December 30, 1997, during the Hong Kong crisis phase. As potentially affected markets we consider the 14 stock markets from Australia to Europe, including those shown in Exhibit 5.1.

Our method proceeds in three steps:

1. We match the stock market price in Thailand to the price in another country at exactly the same point in time. This point in time corresponds to the closing prices in the Asian markets. European markets close at a time when the Thai market is not open and closing prices cannot be used. However,

the Thai market is still open at 10 A.M. U.K. time and we can use prices at this time to generate pairwise *exactly time-aligned* stock market data for the European markets.

2. We calculate conditional and unconditional correlation coefficients for our crises periods and for corresponding stable noncrisis periods, respectively. We use both synchronized and exactly time-aligned data. This allows us to assess whether the answer to the contagion-versus-interdependence question is sensitive to the use of synchronized data. Recall that in our terminology, an exact time-alignment of data implies that shocks are immediately transmitted. An immediate transmission of shocks might, however, not be the appropriate one that can be considered contagious.

3. We extend our analysis in a third step and allow for time differences between observations to account for a slower speed of transmission.

When using synchronized data we find evidence for contagion for only one of our 14 countries (Indonesia) during the Thailand crisis phase. In contrast, exactly time-aligned data indicates contagion for five additional countries: Australia, Hong Kong, Japan, Malaysia, and Singapore. For the Hong Kong crisis phase synchronized data indicate contagion only for Korea, Philippines, and Taiwan while exactly time-aligned data indicate contagion for Germany, Switzerland, Korea, Malaysia, Philippines, and Taiwan. Exhibit 5.2 illustrates these results in the last and first column, respectively. Thus synchronized data seems to favor the conclusion of interdependence while exactly time-aligned data seems to favors contagion. However, it is not generally true that exactly time-aligned correlations indicate contagion for markets with large time differences in closing times relative to Thailand. Evidence to the contrary can be found in the lack of contagion for many of the European markets. We conclude that if the transmission of shocks is immediate and exactly time-aligned correlations reveal the true nature of crises, there is more evidence for contagion than is so far believed. The under-identification of contagion for the synchronized results can, however, not be predicted based on closing time differences.

As we do not know what speed of transmission between markets should be considered contagious, we generate results for differently time-aligned data assuming a speed of transmission of 5, 30, 60, and 120 minutes. Exhibit 5.2 shows the results for both crisis phases. For the Thailand crisis we find that some markets are interdependent with Thailand at all time alignments. These are the European markets, Korea, the Philippines, Taiwan, and China. As the assumed speed of transmission decreases, the evidence for contagion weakens for Indonesia but strengthens for the remaining markets. For the Hong Kong crisis, similar patterns can be found for some markets: France, the United Kingdom, Australia, Hong Kong, Indonesia, Japan, Singapore, and China are always interdependent with Thailand. With decreasing speed of transmission, the evidence for contagion weakens for Germany, Switzerland, and Malaysia but strengthens for Korea. For the remaining markets, however, the Hong Kong crisis reveals new patterns: The evidence of contagion is stable for Taiwan and weakest for a 60-minute time alignment for the Philippines.

In sum, we conclude that a higher assumed speed of transmission generally leads to more evidence for contagion. A careful identification of the proper

Exhibit 5.2 Contagion versus Interdependence with Time-Aligned and Synchronized Data

Panel A: Thailand phase

Country	Time-Aligned Data (assumed speed of transmission in minutes)					Synchronized Data
	0	5	30	60	120	
France	I	I	I	I	I	I
Germany	I	I	I	I	I	I
Switzerland	I	I	I	I	I	I
U.K.	I	I	I	I	I	I
Australia	C	C	C	C	I	I
Hong Kong	C	C	C	C	I	I
Indonesia	I	I	C	C	C	C
Japan	C	C	C	C	I	I
Korea	I	I	I	I	I	I
Malaysia	C	C	C	C	I	I
Philippines	I	I	I	I	I	I
Singapore	C	C	C	I	I	I
Taiwan	I	I	I	I	I	I
China	I	I	I	I	I	I

Panel B: Hong Kong phase

Country	Time-Aligned Data (assumed speed of transmission in minutes)					Synchronized Data
	0	5	30	60	120	
France	I	I	I	I	I	I
Germany	C	C	C	C	I	I
Switzerland	C	C	C	C	I	I
U.K.	I	I	I	I	I	I
Australia	I	I	I	I	I	I
Hong Kong	I	I	I	I	I	I
Indonesia	I	I	I	I	I	I
Japan	I	I	I	I	I	I
Korea	I	I	I	C	C	C
Malaysia	C	C	C	C	I	I
Philippines	C	C	C	I	C	C
Singapore	I	I	I	I	I	I
Taiwan	C	C	C	C	C	C
China	I	I	I	I	I	I

Notes: C indicates contagion, I indicates interdependence. Adapted from Table 4 in Kleimeier, Lehnert, and Verschoor (2008).

time-alignment is essential before starting any study on crisis contagion or interdependence.

NOTE

1. Forbes and Rigobon (2002) propagate this concept of contagion but acknowledge that alternative definitions and measures exist. More information is available from the World Bank's Macroeconomics and Growth Research Program on "Financial Crises and Contagion" available at http://go.worldbank.org/V89G77PGW0. According to the World Bank, this is the restrictive definition of contagion.

REFERENCES

Bae, K., G. A. Karolyi, and R. M. Stulz. 2003. "A New Approach to Measuring Financial Contagion." *Review of Financial Studies* 16:3, 717–763.

Baig, T., and I. Goldfajn. 1999. "Financial Market Contagion in the Asian Crisis." *IMF Staff Papers* 46:2, 167–195.

Calvo, S., and C. M. Reinhart. 1996. "Capital Flows to Latin America: Is There Evidence of Contagion Effects?" In G. A. Calvo, M. Goldstein, and E. Hochreiter, eds. *Private Capital Flows to Emerging Markets After the Mexican Crisis*, 151–171. Washington, DC: Institute for International Economics.

Forbes, K. J., and R. Rigobon. 2002. "No Contagion, Only Interdependences: Measuring Stock Market Comovements." *Journal of Finance* 57:5, 2223–2261.

Kaminsky, G. L., and C. M. Reinhart. 2008. "The Center and the Periphery: The Globalization of Financial Turmoil." National Bureau of Economic Research Working Paper 9479. In C. M. Reinhart, C. A. Végh, and A. Velasco, eds. *Capital Flows, Crisis, and Stabilization: Essays in Honor of Guillermo A. Calvo*, 171–216. Cambridge, MA: MIT Press.

King, M. A., and S. Wadhwani. 1990. "Transmission of Volatility Between Stock Markets." *Review of Financial Studies* 3:1, 5–33.

Kleimeier, S., T. Lehnert, and W. Verschoor. 2008. "Measuring Financial Contagion Using Time-Aligned Data: The Importance of the Speed of Transmission of Shocks." *Oxford Bulletin of Economics and Statistics* 70:4, 493–508.

Laeven, L., and F. Valencia. 2008. "Systemic Banking Crises: A New Database." *IMF Working Paper* No. 08/224, www.imf.org/external/pubs/ft/wp/2008/wp08224.pdf.

Lee, S. B., and K. J. Kim. 1993. "Does the October 1987 Crash Strengthen the Comovements Among National Stock Markets?" *Review of Financial Economics* 3:1, 89–102.

ABOUT THE AUTHORS

Stefanie Kleimeier received her PhD in 1993 from the University of Georgia (U.S.) and currently holds the position of associate professor of finance at the Maastricht University in the Netherlands. Through her affiliation with the Maastricht School of Management from 1993 to 2002, she has been involved in education and educational development in Azerbaijan, Bulgaria, China, India, Indonesia, and Singapore. Her research focuses on financial market linkages and banking with specializations in banking market integration, retail banking, syndicated lending, and project finance. Her research has been published in academic journals, including the *Oxford Bulletin of Economics and Statistics, Journal of Banking and Finance,* and *Journal of International Money and Finance.*

Thorsten Lehnert is a professor of finance at the Luxembourg School of Finance at the University of Luxembourg. He is a graduate from the department of economics at Bonn University and obtained a PhD in finance from Maastricht University. Dr. Lehnert has published several articles on international finance, behavioral finance, and financial risk management in leading academic journals, including *Management Science*, the *Oxford Bulletin of Economics and Statistics*, the *Journal of International Money and Finance*, and the *Journal of Derivatives*.

Willem F. C. Verschoor is a professor of finance and director of the department of business economics at the Erasmus University Rotterdam. He received a PhD in international finance from Maastricht University. Before entering his academic career, he was employed as a chief economist at Kempen & Co, Amsterdam, and at the National Investment Bank, The Hague. Verschoor has done extensive work in the area of international finance and risk management, and has published in leading academic journals, including the *Journal of Banking and Finance*, *Journal of Business*, *Journal of Economic Dynamics and Control*, *Journal of Empirical Finance*, and *Journal of International Money and Finance*. He has taught extensively in executive programs and served as a consultant to various financial institutions. He is a member of the supervisory board of Optimix Investment Funds N.V. in Amsterdam, and a member of the advisory board for the Global Finance Forum in Chur.

CHAPTER 6

Modeling International Financial Markets Contagion

Using Copula and Risk Appetite

SICHONG CHEN
Investment Analyst, Bocom Schroders Fund, Shanghai

SER-HUANG POON
Professor of Finance, Manchester Business School, United Kingdom

F inancial market contagion is a hot issue at all times. Forbes and Rigobon (2002) define financial contagion as a significant increase in cross-market linkages triggered by a shock. Using a volatility-adjusted Pearson correlation estimator, Forbes and Rigobon (2002) conclude that many claims of contagion during the Asian crisis are simply spurious statistical artifact. Our study replicates the tests in Forbes and Rigobon (2002) but with a more robust methodology. Using a dummied t-copula and two versions of time varying t-copula, we find clear evidence of contagion among volatility-filtered stock returns in the same data set used in Forbes and Rigobon (2002). Another novelty in our chapter is the use of world and regional risk appetite indices to study financial crisis and contagion. These risk appetite indices are constructed from 34 equity indices and 32 bond indices over a 10-year period. The behavior of these regional risk appetite indices during the Asian crisis is consistent with the findings we obtained earlier from our copula models. The movements of regional risk appetite indices during six different crisis events show that developed financial markets are more sensitive and vulnerable than emerging markets to extreme events. Latin American markets are hardly affected by extreme events originated outside its region. Moreover, the impact of terrorist attacks is small and short lived when compared with the impact of fundamental changes in economic conditions, which took much longer for investors and markets to restore confidence.

We first review the literature of financial market contagion studies and the use of risk appetite to analyze contagion, and then we explain the copula models and present the results of copula estimation. The next section discusses the dataset used in the construction of risk appetite indices, and explains how these risk appetite indices can be used to detect contagions, while the final section concludes the discussion.

LITERATURE ON CONTAGION AND RISK APPETITE

For a long time, stock return dependence was measured by using the Pearson correlation, which is inherently biased if heteroskedasticity is not taken into account (Forbes and Rigobon 2002). To correct for this bias, the authors propose a new correlation estimator that adjusts for heteroskedasticity in returns. Using stock market return data covering the Asia financial crisis, the Mexico crisis, and the 1987 crash, they find that the unadjusted Pearson correlation coefficients increased significantly during these crisis periods, but not the heteroskedasticity adjusted correlation. Therefore, they concluded that contagion did not take place during these crisis periods. In another study, Bekaert, Harvey, and Ng (2005) define contagion as an increase in the level of correlation over and above what is expected. They propose a two-factor model whose parameter values depended on a collection of macroeconomics factors, such as the sum of total import and export, and the difference between long and short term bond yields. Bekaert et al. did not find evidence of contagion during the Mexican crisis but report an economically significant increase in correlations among the residuals during the Asia financial crisis. Bae, Karolyi, and Stulz (2003) use logistic regression to link international stock returns co-exceedances (i.e., several stock market returns drop below a threshold simultaneously) to regional macroeconomic variables, such as regional volatility, exchange rates, and interest rates. Bae et al. conclude that stock market shocks originated from Latin America are more contagious than those originated from Asia. The authors also find that the U.S. stock market appeared to be largely insulated from the Asian financial crisis. This finding is supported by our empirical tests. So it is clear that studies in contagion reached different conclusions with different methodologies.

Here we propose the use of copula method despite its negative reception in recent subprime crisis. Patton (2006) uses Clayton copula and reports finding a structural break in dependence among currency markets after the introduction of the euro. Bartram, Taylor, and Wang (2007) use Gaussian copula to find that dependence of European equity markets increased in anticipation of the markets joining the Eurozone. Jondeau and Rockinger (2006) report similar findings by using t–copula. Rodriguez (2007) uses regime switching copula and finds stronger dependence in the high volatility state. The copula method is far more superior to Pearson correlation, which is based on multinormal distribution. For example, student-t copula can capture extremal tail dependence whereas Pearson correlation cannot. Copula also allows a greater choice of marginal distribution beyond Normal distribution. Thick tail distributions such as the student-t or the skewed student-t distribution are commonly used to model financial time series.

Both practitioners and academia have considered the possibility that financial crisis is not purely driven by worsening macroeconomic fundamentals. Kumar and Persaud (2002), for example, find that the Asian financial crisis was associated with a substantial drop in the so-called *risk appetite*. The term risk appetite is referred loosely to the *willingness of investors to bear risk* and is to be distinguished from *risk aversion* and the *riskiness of assets*. During a stable economy, investors are willing to bear more risk, as characterized by high risk appetite. The literature has the tendency to mask the distinctions between risk appetite and risk aversion. Gai and Vause (2004) argue that risk appetite is a function of the aversion to uncertainty as well as the level of market uncertainty conditioned on the macroeconomic environment. Risk aversion is thought to be relatively stable, moving very slowly with aggregate wealth and business cycle. On the other hand, perception of macroeconomic uncertainty could change more quickly and frequently, which in turn causes risk appetite to change frequently.

Many investment banks and central banks have developed their own risk appetite indices to reflect investors' perceptions of risk. Examples of these risk appetite indices include the JPMorgan's liquidity, credit, and volatility index; the UBS's investor sentiment index; the Merrill Lynch's Financial stress index; the Westpac's risk appetite index; the Tarashev, Tsatsaronis, and Karampatos's (2003) risk appetite index developed at the Bank for International Settlements; the Gai and Vause's (2004) risk appetite index developed at the Bank of England; the Kumar and Persaud's (2002) global risk appetite index used by both the IMF and JPMorgan; Wilmot, Mielczarski and Sweeney's (2004) global risk appetite index developed at the Credit Suisse First Boston; the State Street Investor Confidence Index and Goldman Sachs Risk Aversion Index.

Not all risk appetite measures are practical or appropriate for the study of international stock market contagion. The rank correlation method used in Kumar and Persaud (2002) and Misina (2003, 2006) can detect change in risk appetite but not the level of risk appetite when there is no change. Both Tarashev, Tsatsaronis, and Karampatos (2003) and Gai and Vause (2004) calculate risk appetite by extracting risk neutral probability densities from stock option data and use the GARCH model to estimate the subjective probability densities. Such method is data intensive, which its use to a handful of developed markets. Here, we compile our risk appetite indices following the CSFB's approach. Illing and Aaron (2005) compared 11 risk appetite indices and concluded that the CSFB's index is the only index that captured most important financial events. The implementation of the CSFB approach is easy and straightforward, and can easily be modified for regional and global risk appetite indices.

EMPIRICAL STUDY

We use daily returns on stock market indices from 28 markets available in Datastream. The data period from January 1, 1996, to December 31, 1998, is exactly the same as that in Forbes and Rigobon (2002). The sample period is subdivided into stable period (January 1, 1996, to October 16, 1997), crisis period (October 17, 1997, to November 17, 1997), and post-crisis period (November 18, 1997, to December 31, 1998). Forbes and Rigobon argue that in October 1997, the Asian financial crisis hit Hong Kong the hardest. Hence, for this particular crisis period, we will focus on the pair-wise dependence between Hong Kong and the other 27 markets following Forbes and Rigobon (2002). Copula model can be estimated based on maximizing likelihood function following Joe (1997), McLeish and Small (1988), and Xu (1996). Here, we adopt the more efficient two-step approach whereby, in the first step, the log-likelihood function for each of the univariate margin is maximized individually. The estimated parameter values are used to transform the marginal distribution into uniform margins. In the second step, the density function of the copula with uniform marginal is maximized to obtain the dependence parameter.

Marginal Distribution

We model the marginal distributions as univariate $AR(p)$–$GARCH(q, r)$ with $p = 10$ and $q = r = 1$ assuming that the standardized residuals follow a skewed student-t distribution with constant parameter values.[1] The results of the marginal distribution estimation show that most markets have a low degree of freedom average 9.029 confirming that stock market returns are not Gaussian. The skewness parameter of the marginal distribution is negative for 21 markets, which shows that most markets have negative tails even after adjusting for stochastic volatility. For diagnostic tests, we implement the Ljung-Box (L-B) test to check if the marginal probability is serially correlated, and the Kolmogorov-Smirnov test to check if the transformed standardized residuals is uniform (0, 1) distributed. Of the 27 markets, only Canada and Malaysia failed the L-B test. We have estimated other AR-GARCH specifications for the Canadian and Malaysian stock returns with no improvement. Hence, the original specification is kept. All markets passed the K-S test.

Dependence

If the marginal distribution is skewed student-t, the dependence parameter estimated using the Gaussian copula will not be the same as the Pearson correlation coefficient. For South Africa, Singapore, Indonesia, and Australia, their stock returns' Pearson correlation with Hong Kong stock returns is higher than the Gaussian dependence value and, in turn, both are greater than the dependence parameter estimated using t-copula. After we have filtered the volatility effect, the Gaussian and t-copula dependence values decrease further. This highlights the potential overestimation and distortion of the degree of dependence if heteroskedasticity, marginal distribution and the copula function are not controlled properly.

To check the fit of the copula model, we adopt the goodness-of-fit test introduced by Breymann, Dias, and Embrechts (2003), which is based on probability integral transform and is valid for any copula family. The test results cannot reject both Gaussian copula and t-copula (except for Thailand). From the findings by Rodriguez (2007), there is no loss of likelihood value when specified Gaussian copula as t-copula. Hence, we use the t-copula in the following sections and for all market pairs.

Testing for Increased Dependence Using Time-Varying t-Copula

Here, we introduce two sets of dummies in the dependence parameter in order to test if there is a change in dependence during the crisis and the post-crisis periods. In addition, we apply time-varying t-copula following two different specifications used in Jondeau and Rockinger (2006) and Patton (2006) respectively. From the 27 dependence parameters estimated by three different copula dynamics, we found a significant increase in stock markets dependence in the Asian crisis and post-crisis periods; 14, 15, and 20 cases tested show evidence for contagion for the dummied copula, JR dynamic copula, and Patton's dynamic copula model respectively. There are only seven markets that do not show the evidence of contagion in any of the three tests. The other eight markets with contagion signs are all European markets;

the U.S. and Japanese markets do not show any sign of increase in dependence. None of four Latin American markets has signs of contagion.

Finally, 17 markets show stronger dependence with Hong Kong in the post-crisis period than the stable pre-crisis period for all three tests, and 25 markets show stronger dependence with Hong Kong in at least two tests. This increase can possibly be explained as the integrated world economy after crisis because the international stock markets are more dependent on each other than ever.

RISK APPETITE INDICES AND CONTAGION

In this chapter, we follow the method of CSFB to construct our own global and regional risk appetite indices. The dataset used to construct the risk appetite indices includes 36 stock market indices and 32 bond market indices, covering the period ranging from January 1, 1993, to December 31, 2005. We categorize markets into developed Asian and Latin markets when estimating the regional risk appetite indices. For each day t, we estimate the daily risk appetite measure β_t by using equity indices and bond indices returns through the following cross section regression: (see Exhibit 6.1).

$$R_{t,i}^{ex} = \alpha + \beta_t \times volatility_{(t-125),i}$$

$$volatility_{t,i} = \sqrt{variance(X)}$$

$$R_{t,i}^{ex} = \frac{\log P_{t,i}}{P_{(t-125),i}} - R_f$$

$$X = \left(R_{t,i}^{ex}, \ R_{(t-1),i}^{ex}, \dots, R_{(t-125),i}^{ex} \right)$$

where $P_{t,i}$ is the value of index i in day t and R_f is the cash market return proxied by the U.S. treasury bill. As highlighted in Kumar and Persaud (2002), the period covered by $R_{t,i}^{ex}$ and the period used to estimate risk should not overlap. Hence, $R_{t,i}^{ex}$ and $volatility_{(t-125),i}$ have a gap of 125 days (or six months). CSFB use value-weighted regression, which takes market capitalization into account, so the U.S. equity and bond market have the biggest impact on the risk appetite measurement. Here,

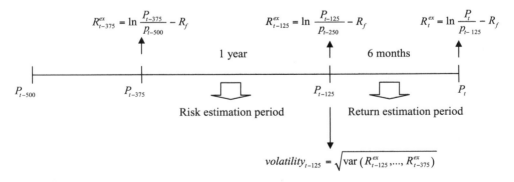

Exhibit 6.1 Risk Appetite Estimation Method

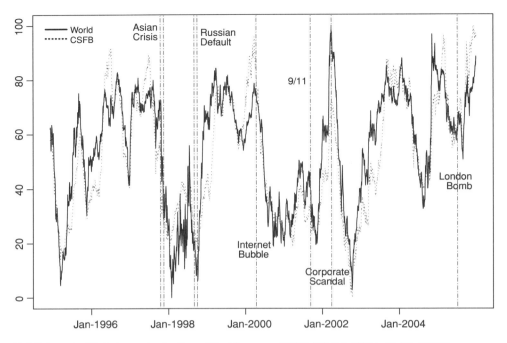

Exhibit 6.2   Risk Appetite Indices: World versus CSFB (02/12/1994–12/31/2005)

we use equally weighted regression similar to the method used by the Deutsche Bundesbank (2005) because our objective here is to capture global contagion.

The risk appetite index estimated covers the period from December 2, 1994, to December 31, 2005. We scale both our risk appetite estimates and CSFB's index to aid comparison. Exhibit 6.2 plots our world risk appetite index (solid line) and that estimated by CSFB (dotted line). The difference is due to different dataset and different regression methods used. However, we can see from Exhibit 6.2 that our estimates are very close to CSFB's and the two risk appetite indices have a correlation of 0.89.

In Exhibit 6.2, we highlighted six big events that took place in our sample period. The first is the Asian financial crisis, from October 17, 1997, to November 17, 1997, the same data period used in Forbes and Rigobon (2002). The second event is the Russian debt default crisis, from September 1, 1998, to September 30, 1998. The third event is the NASDAQ bubble burst around April 2000. The fourth event is the terrorist attack on September 11, 2001. The fifth event is the American corporate scandal around March 2002. The sixth and last event is another terrorist attack in London on July 7, 2005. From Exhibit 6.2, both risk appetite estimates capture these events quite well.

Exhibits 6.3, 6.4, and 6.5 plot world risk appetite indexes alongside the regional indices for Asian, developed, and Latin American financial markets respectively. The regional indices are plotted as solid lines and world index as dotted lines. For the Asian financial crisis, we can see from Exhibit 6.3 that the Asian risk appetite index dropped significantly and did not recover until the beginning of 1998. The risk appetite index of developed markets plotted in Exhibit 6.4 was also affected

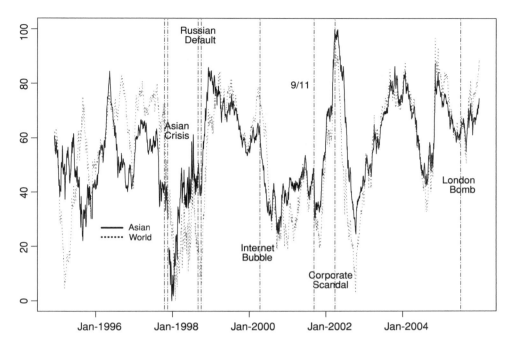

Exhibit 6.3 Risk Appetite Indices: Asian versus World (02/12/1994–12/31/2005)

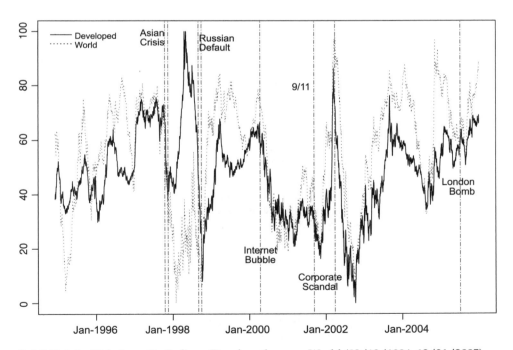

Exhibit 6.4 Risk Appetite Indices: Developed versus World (02/12/1994–12/31/2005)

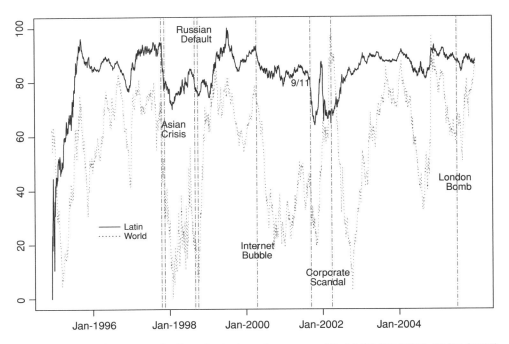

Exhibit 6.5　Risk Appetite Indices: Latin American versus World (02/12/1994–12/31/2005)

by this crisis and dropped significantly but the impact is not as severe as that experienced in the Asian markets in Exhibit 6.3. It recovered quickly at the end of November. The risk appetite index for Latin American plotted in Exhibit 6.5 behaves less dramatically than the Asian and developed regional risk appetite indices. These findings are consistent with our previous findings, where we found four Asian markets and eight developed European markets showed clear evidence of contagion during the Asian financial crisis. However, none of the Latin American markets was affected by the Asian crisis.

For the period of Russian debt crisis and the default of LTCM, we find that the Asian and Latin American risk appetite indices experienced only small movements. But the index for the developed markets had decreased quite a lot; clear evidence that developed markets were severely affected by this event. For the September 11 terrorist attack in New York, we find a small drop for all three regional risk appetite indices but it was not a long-term impact and all three regional indices recovered within a week. For the July 7 London bombing, we observe a similar but smaller impact. The Internet bubble burst and U.S. corporate scandals had severe and prolonged impact. Both the Asian and the developed market risk appetite indices had decreased dramatically and did not recover in the following six months. Compared with the impact of terrorist attacks, which have only a small and short-term shock to the global and regional financial markets, the Internet bubble burst and American corporate scandals appeared to fundamentally change the economics environments and investors' confidence. These changes have a more serious and longer-term impact to the world financial markets.

Another interesting finding not shown in Exhibit 6.5 is that the risk appetite for Latin American markets only dropped dramatically at the end of 1994. It coincides with the period of the Mexico currency crisis. For this particular crisis, the Latin American risk appetite index reached the bottom of the whole estimation period. Since then, it remained relatively stable and was hardly affected by the big events elsewhere. In contrast, we find that the developed markets are more sensitive to extreme events than emerging markets as the developed market index has reacted to just about all six events. Moreover, the Asian markets are much more sensitive than Latin American markets. A possible explanation for this could be financial market integration; the more integrated and open the financial market, the more sensitive and vulnerable it is to the external events.

CONCLUSION

In this chapter, we examined the dependence structure and contagion among 28 stock markets during and after the Asian crisis by using copula. After applying the AR-GARCH model to filter the marginal distribution, we find that at least half of the 28 markets we examined show strong evidence of contagion. We also find that the dependence among markets has increased since the Asian crisis. Another novelty of this chapter lies in our risk appetite estimation for world and regional financial markets. We find that the Asian crisis has seriously impacted the Asian and the developed financial markets, and the European markets in particular. It has little impact on the Latin American markets. These findings are consistent with findings produced from our copula estimation. We find, during major crisis events, the developed financial markets are more sensitive and vulnerable to these extreme events. The impact of terrorist attacks is small and short-lived and the financial markets recovered quickly after the incidents. The Internet bubble burst and corporate scandals, on the other hand, have longer-term and more severe impact. It took a much longer time for investors to restore their confidence and for the market to recover. The risk appetite indices have been shown here to be useful for modeling contagion and comovement of financial markets.

NOTE

1. Patton (2006) uses time-varying skewed student-t distribution, Rodriguez (2007) uses normal distribution. Jondeau and Rockinger (2006) test four density functions, viz. Gaussian, standard student-t, skewed student-t with constant skewness and kurtosis and a student-t distribution with time-varying skewness and degree of freedom; they are not able to reject all four distributions statistically.

REFERENCES

Bae, Kee-Hong, G. Andrew Karolyi, and René M. Stulz. 2003. "A New Approach to Measuring Financial Contagion." *Review of Financial Studies* 16:717–763.

Bartram, Sohnke M., Stephen J. Taylor, and Yaw-Huei Wang. 2007. "The Euro and European Financial Market Integration." *Journal of Banking and Finance* 31:5, 1461–1481.

Bekaert, Geer, Campbell Harvey, and Angela Ng. 2005. "Market Integration and Contagion." *Journal of Business* 78:39–69.

Breymann, Wolfgang, Alexandra Dias, and Paul Embrechts. 2003. "Dependence Structures for Multivariate High-Frequency Data in Finance." *Quantitative Finance* 3:1–16.

Deutsche Bundesbank. 2005. "Risk Appetite in a Dynamic Financial Market Environment." Deutsche Bundesbank Monthly Report.

Forbes, Kristin, and Roberto Rigobon. 2002. "No Contagion, Only Interdependence: Measuring Stock Market Co-movements." *Journal of Finance* 57:5, 2223–2262.

Gai, Prasanna, and Nicholas Vause. 2004. "Risk Appetite: Concept and Measurement." *Bank of England Working Paper*.

Illing, Mark, and Meyer Aaron. 2005. "A Brief Survey of Risk-Appetite Indexes." *Bank of Canada Working Paper*.

Joe, Harry. 1997. *Multivariate Models and Dependence Concepts*. London and New York: Chapman Hall.

Jondeau, Eric, and Michael Rockinger. 2006. "The Copula-GARCH Model of Conditional Dependencies: An International Stock Market Application." *Journal of International Money and Finance*, 25: August 5, 827–853.

Kumar, Manmohan S., and Avinash Persaud. 2002. "Pure Contagion and Investors' Shifting Risk Appetite: Analytical Issues and Empirical Evidence." *International Finance* 5:401–436.

McLeish, Don L., and Christopher G. Small. 1988. *The Theory and Applications of Statistical Inference Functions*. London and New York: Springer-Verlag.

Misina, Miroslav. 2003. "What Does the Risk-Appetite Index Measure?" *Bank of Canada Working Paper*.

Misina, Miroslav. 2006. "Benchmark index of risk appetite." *Bank of Canada Working Paper*.

Patton, Andrew. 2006. "Modelling Asymmetric Exchange Rate Dependence." *International Economic Review* 47:2, 527–556.

Rodriguez, Juan Carlos. 2007. Measuring financial contagion: A Copula approach. *Journal of Empirical Finance* 14:June 3, 401–423.

Tarashev, Nikola, Kostas Tsatsaronis, and Dimitrios Karampatos. 2003. "Investors' Attitude Towards Risk: What Can We Learn from Options." *BIS Quarterly Review*, 57–65.

Wilmot, Jonathan, Paul Mielczarski, and James Sweeney. 2004. Global Risk Appetite Index, Credit Suisse First Boston: Global Strategy Research: Market Focus.

Xu, James J. 1996. Statistical modelling and Inference for Multivariate and Longitudinal Discrete Response Data, Working Paper, Department of Statistics, University of British Columbia.

ABOUT THE AUTHORS

Sichong Chen is an investment analyst at Bocom Schroders Fund, Shanghai. He has a degree in economics from Fudan University and a PhD degree in finance from Manchester Business School. He works as an economist in this mutual fund, which is a top 10 mutual fund in China and has 10 billion USD assets under management. His PhD research work focused on financial crisis and liquidity, both strongly featured in his current job and asset allocation strategy.

Ser-Huang Poon is a professor of finance at Manchester Business School, United Kingdom. She received her B.Acc. degree from the National University of Singapore, and M.A. and PhD degrees from Lancaster University. She is the founder of the U.K. ESRC Advanced Doctoral Training Programme in Finance and has contributed to the training program since its inception in 2002. Since 2009, she has been leading a consortia of 19 university and industry partners on a 3.7 million euro project on research training under the theme, Risk Management and Risk Reporting. Dr. Poon is the author of three books, *Forecasting Volatility in Financial Markets*, *Asset Pricing in Discrete Time*, and *Financial Modelling Under Non-Gaussian Distribution*, and more than 25 published articles. Her volatility survey co-authored with Clive Granger, 2003 (Economic prize, Nobel Laureate) has more than 3,000 downloads and was cited on the Nobel web site as a reference reading for volatility research.

CHAPTER 7

The Origins and Resolution of Financial Crises[*]

A Policy Dilemma

LARS OXELHEIM
Lund University, Lund Institute of Economic Research, Stockholm, Sweden

CLAS WIHLBORG
Chapman University, Orange, CA

FINN ØSTRUP
Copenhagen Business School, Copenhagen, Denmark

The crisis that began as the so-called *subprime crisis* in the United States in mid-2007 developed into a worldwide deep recession by the end of 2008. Halfway through 2010, the fear that economic activity will remain depressed for years in Europe and the United States is widespread. At this time, it is not clear to what extent the depth and the length of the recession are caused by a fragile financial sector or whether it depends on a shift in consumption-savings behavior in Europe and the United States, in particular. Such a shift may have been induced by the perceived need of firms and households to reduce leverage. In the first case, the low level of economic activity would be explained by a decline in the supply of credit while, in the second case, a low level of demand for credit would be explained by the low level of real activity. Disagreements among economists about the appropriate response to the crisis reflect differences in opinion about the main source of current problems as well as the ability of fiscal and monetary authorities to stimulate the economy without prolonging adjustment.

There are a number of theories, hypotheses, and stories about the origin of financial crises. Although not mutually exclusive, we can distinguish among five types of explanations:[1] (1) macroeconomic developments and leverage; (2) behavioral factors and speculation; (3) shift to liquidity and safety; (4) management failure; and (5) institutional weaknesses. All these factors seem to have played a role in the current crisis (Wihlborg 2009). For example, the expansionary, low-interest

---

[*]This chapter summarizes arguments from Østrup, Oxelheim, and Wihlborg (2009).

rate policies of the Fed may have contributed to the run-up in housing prices since 2001 but they do not explain why the system could not handle the decline. Often cited "short memories" and other behavioral characteristics of financial market participants may also have contributed to the development of a real estate pricing bubble but explanations for the systemwide effects of the decline in prices must be sought elsewhere.

We argue that the root of a financial crisis lies in inappropriate legal and political institutions. Severe recessions are possible and occur in the best of institutional settings as a result of, for example, deleveraging after a period of great optimism and perceived low risk. However, for a crisis to be classified as a financial crisis in our terminology the decline in economic activity must be caused by financial system failures. In a financial crisis, an event affecting a part of the financial system spread throughout the financial system as a whole through contagion effects and the crisis in the financial system must have real consequences through, for example, a credit crunch. We argue that systemic failures in the financial sector are generally caused by inappropriate legal and political institutions.

The existing literature on financial crises rarely distinguishes between factors that create the original losses in the financial sector and factors that explain why these losses led to systemwide contagion and a possible credit crunch. To illustrate this point, it can be noted that the bursting of the "tech bubble" in 2001 caused a greater wealth loss in the United States than the bursting of the residential property price bubble in 2007. The economic consequences of the tech bubble were relatively mild. Why did the much smaller wealth losses associated with the decline in real estate values in 2007 have such severe worldwide economic consequences?

The factor that immediately comes to mind as an explanation of the difference between the two cases is *leverage*. Equity investment is leveraged to a much lower degree than real estate investment. The financial firms supplying real estate financing are also highly leveraged. Thus, in the case of real estate investment, a relatively modest decline in asset values threatens the solvency of a number of financial firms. Insolvency or threat of insolvency of banks and other financial institutions does not necessarily lead to a systemic financial crisis, however.

In markets functioning without much friction, the leverage and insolvency of firms should not cause a substantial problem. After all, there are contracts specifying how losses are to be allocated. Once the equity of the financial firms is wiped out, the additional losses should be borne by their creditors. Some of these creditors are households, others are other financial firms. Insolvency procedures would allocate the losses in accordance with the prespecified contractual arrangements or in accordance with rules as specified in insolvency law. Assets of the failing firms would be purchased at reduced values by other financial and nonfinancial firms or households. The indirect ramifications for the real economy need not be severe if appropriate institutions for allocation of losses are in place.

In the following, we argue that policy makers face a dilemma when designing policies to reduce the incidence of and severity of financial crisis. Fear of systemic effects of failures of large banks and other financial firms creates incentives for policy makers to provide a safety net for banks in particular and for bailouts of financial institutions considered "too big to fail." The safety net increases the risk of bank failures because explicit and implicit protection of depositors and other stakeholders in financial institutions create incentives for excessive risk-taking.

The safety net also creates frictions in the allocation of losses, which worsens the systemic effects of shocks to the financial system. Thereby, the incentives for bailouts are strengthened further.

One way to break the vicious-circle dilemma described in the previous paragraph would be to strengthen legal, regulatory, and political institutions that contribute to the reduction of frictions in the allocation of losses and, thereby, reduce the need for bailouts and other forms of protection of financial firms and their stakeholders. One institutional reform of this kind would be the implementation of specific legally binding insolvency procedures for banks and other systemically important financial institutions.

To expand the argument for an improved institutional framework for the financial sector, we discuss different types of contagion as sources of systemic risk in Section 2. Thereafter, we turn in Section 3 to frictions in loss allocation and institutional reform that could reduce such frictions and, thereby, systemic risk. We conclude in Section 4 with a brief assessment of alternative approaches to financial stability.

NEW VIEWS OF SYSTEMIC RISK: ARE BANKS REALLY SPECIAL?

In the traditional view, banks were special as a result of their participation in payment systems and as suppliers of liquidity. Also, the interconnectedness of banks implies that there is a substantial difference between the failure of a bank and the failure of, for example, a car manufacturer. One car manufacturer's failure improves the profitability of others. One bank's failure can lead to losses for other banks with claims on the failing bank. The opaqueness of banks in combination with their long maturity assets relative to very short maturity liabilities make them vulnerable to runs as soon as there is some uncertainty about their solvency.

The subprime financial crisis has led to increased awareness that failures of nonbank financial institutions can create contagion effects as well. Thus, in addition to bank contagion mentioned earlier, there are channels of contagion we can call *price contagion* and *liquidity contagion*.

> *Price contagion* occurs through securities markets when a large financial institution must sell assets quickly resulting in a decline in asset values throughout the financial system. This type of contagion has increased in importance as a result of increased reliance on mark-to-market valuation and higher, relatively rigid capital requirements.
>
> *Liquidity contagion* refers to lack of liquidity in securities markets with the consequence that financial institutions wanting to or having to sell securities have difficulties finding buyers at prices corresponding to conventional economic values. The lack of liquidity may arise as a result of uncertainty about the solvency of opaque financial institutions. If there is fear of a liquidity squeeze, financial institutions may also hoard liquidity out of fear that they may not be able to sell when needed. In this case, the financial institution may look liquid on the balance sheet but this liquidity could contribute to lack of liquidity in securities markets.

These types of contagion have in common that they affect nonbank financial institutions as well as traditional banks, and that they are likely to have repercussions on the real economy when the financial institutions reduce the supply of credit in order to retain or build up capital or retain or build up liquidity. The contagion effects are particularly severe for financial institutions with substantial mismatch of maturities of assets and liabilities. As the crisis has demonstrated, nonbanks often financed the purchase of long-term securities in the markets for short-term securities such as commercial papers. Cohan (2008) reported that Bear Sterns funded much lending activity through overnight borrowing.

Price and liquidity contagion are likely to reinforce each other because the market value of securities can drop dramatically when buyers require a substantial liquidity premium and, therefore, bid below the traditional economic value. Mark-to-market valuation clearly plays an important role in the process.[2]

There are important implications for the legal and regulatory framework of the expanded view of contagion as a source of systemic risk. One is that special insolvency law may have to cover nonbank financial firms as well as banks. A second implication is that flexibility in the required capital ratio can reduce the need for fire sales of assets. "Structured early intervention" prior to insolvency along the lines of Prompt Corrective Action (PCA) procedures is one way of achieving flexibility while reducing the probability that a financial institution will reach the default point. A third implication is that principles for valuation of assets must be transparent and clear because they affect points of intervention and insolvency. Finally, it must be recognized that the procedures for dealing with a financial institution in distress affect the incentives for risk-taking and liquidity planning (including mismatch of maturities) prior to insolvency. Similarly, valuation principles affect these incentives.

LOSS ALLOCATION AND INSTITUTIONAL FAILURES

The task at hand in this section is to identify the sources of frictions that cause great delays in the loss allocation and to ask why these frictions exist. The tragedy in a financial crisis is that the friction can cause additional losses in wealth and income. These losses must be allocated as well. Therein lies the systemic failure of contagion among financial institutions and the decline in real activity that we are now experiencing.

Looking for explanations for frictions in financial markets, four candidates come to mind:

- The individuals and firms facing and taking losses are reluctant to accept these losses and may try to cover them up in order to, for example, not lose creditworthiness or to avoid runs.
- Lack of transparency in valuation of assets allows financial firms, in particular, to delay loss recognition.
- Uncertainty and asymmetric information about asset values create a liquidity problem in markets when potential buyers suspect that sellers try to unload relatively low-quality assets (adverse selection).

- Insolvency procedures for many financial firms are time-consuming and costly in themselves. Allocation of losses requires assets of the firms to be valued without well-functioning markets and exact contractual relationships must be identified.

Many potential losers are protected by explicit or implicit insurance schemes created by expectations of bailouts in different forms. The coverage of explicit deposit insurance schemes and other creditors of banks are often expanded in times of crises. In the current crisis, creditors of nonbank financial firms have also obtained protection. Even shareholders and managers of large entities facing losses obtain a degree of protection when the survival of their firms is more or less guaranteed. The greater the share of the ex ante contractual losers that gain protection the greater are the losses potentially faced by others. In the end, losses must be borne by someone. The taxpayers are obviously the "loss-takers of last resort."

Political conflicts about the allocation of value losses create uncertainty about the final allocation of losses. This uncertainty about the political process creates disincentives for those contractually responsible for losses to take private initiatives to deal with them. Firms hold out in order to first see where the political process leads and they lobby to influence the political process with the objective of shifting losses to others.

The listed factors contribute not only to delays in the allocation of the original losses but potentially to an amplification of them, as well as to contagion among financial institutions and from financial institutions to firms. Contagion is created by lack of liquidity in markets for securities, delays in settlement of claims, possibly runs on banks, and the withholding of new credit.

Legal, regulatory, and political institutional factors are not linked one-to-one to the listed factors but a specific institutional characteristic of a country can influence friction in financial markets as well as ex ante incentives in several ways. Relevant institutions affecting frictions in the allocation of losses are those influencing the incentives of firms and individuals to recognize losses, enforcement of contracts, liquidity of securities, transparency of valuation, and transparency of risk factors for securities as well as financial firms. Relevant institutions affecting ex ante incentives are those influencing risk-taking incentives of managers of financial firms and their incentives and ability to provide relevant information in the markets for securities including markets for their creditors and shareholders. The institutional features discussed below affect frictions as well as ex ante incentives in financial markets.

We do not claim to present an exhaustive list of institutional features that contribute to frictions in loss allocation and systemic effects of shocks to the financial system but focus of a few key institutional features. Østrup, Oxelheim, and Wihlborg (2009) discuss in more detail the following institutional features of financial systems: (1) explicit and implicit insurance of stakeholders in financial institutions; (2) procedures for resolution of distress and insolvency; (3) corporate governance in financial institutions; and (4) uncertainty about the political process in times of crisis. In this chapter, we discuss briefly the key issue of distress and insolvency procedures for banks and other financial firms.

The European Shadow Financial Regulatory Committee (1998) expressed the objective of a special insolvency law for banks in the following way: "The implementation of insolvency law for banks . . . should achieve an acceptable, low risk of runs and low risk of contagion while inefficient owners and managers exit. The contractual predictability of claims and the predictability of bankruptcy and PCA-costs should provide efficient ex ante incentives. By achieving these objectives the government's and the regulator's fear of a system crash should be alleviated. Thereby, non-insurance of groups of creditors and shareholders would be credible."

To reduce the fear of systemic consequences of a bank's insolvency, the procedures must be speedy and allow important functions of the insolvent bank to continue with a minimum of disruption. This can be accomplished by a "bridge bank" that retains asset and liabilities of the failing bank. The value of the liabilities are reduced by means of "haircuts" that specify a rapid reduction of creditors' claims on the bank.[3]

Few countries have special insolvency law for banks and other financial firms, however.[4] The main exception is that the United States has implemented bank-specific insolvency procedures through the FDIC through the enactment of FDICIA (Federal Deposit Insurance Corporation Improvement Act) in 1991. A bank that reaches a capital ratio of 2 percent is put under the receivership of the FDIC. Specific rules for merging or allocating the assets of the bank exist. A number of small- and medium-size banks have been closed this way since the beginning of the subprime crisis. However, the procedures were set aside for large banks in the current crisis based on an exception clause in the FDICIA. Also, the procedures do not apply to investment banks.

Several economists have discussed the potential contribution of bank insolvency law in enhancing market discipline in Europe, where specific bank crisis resolution procedures have not been implemented.[5] Without predictable rules for the allocation of losses, resolution will be delayed and, in the meantime, management and shareholders of distressed firms are likely to avoid the realization of losses in various ways.[6] To be truly predictable and credible the insolvency procedures must be mandatory and not leave great scope for exceptions.

CONCLUDING REMARKS ON APPROACHES TO FINANCIAL SECTOR REFORM

We have argued that a lack of appropriate institutional features for the financial sector contribute to systemic consequences of substantial losses in one part of the financial system. At the center stands the lack of operational and credible insolvency procedures for financial firms.

The lack of specific insolvency procedures for financial firms implies that governments are compelled to issue far-reaching guarantees to creditors and even to shareholders of financial firms. These implicit guarantees affect risk-taking incentives of financial institutions, thereby increasing the likelihood of crises, as well as the incentives of financial institutions to resolve problems without government bailouts. The risk-taking incentives can also contribute to the existence of executive compensation schemes that favor short-term earnings and discourage consideration of risk in the longer term. Most likely, failures of corporate governance system go deeper, however, and depend on corporate law more generally.

Valuation and transparency issues have not been addressed at any depth in spite of their importance for crisis resolution. It can be argued, however, that transparency and incentives for information revelation are to a large extent endogenous relative to explicit and implicit protection of creditors of financial institutions, as well as to compensation schemes. Weak incentives of creditors to monitor risk taking create weak incentives for information revelation. In times of crisis, information revelation is discouraged as long as the political process for support is uncertain and subject to lobbying efforts.

If mandatory, credible and predictable insolvency procedures for financial firms cannot be implemented and the reform process for the financial sector is likely to be a "band-aid" approach. This approach is characterized by regulatory measures aimed directly at weaknesses observed during the crisis. Both the G-20 proposals and the recently approved U.S. financial reform package can be viewed this way. There are a large number of proposed reforms and most of them require stricter direct oversight by regulators and supervisors. There are strong reasons to be skeptical about the effectiveness of a large regulatory bureaucracy to control risk taking as long as financial institutions have incentives to shift risk to taxpayers and deposit insurance funds.

NOTES

1. This categorization is based on Østrup, Oxelheim, and Wihlborg (2009) and Østrup (2007).

2. Brunnermeier et al. (2009) discuss the process of contagion through securities markets. They describe a potentially serious systemic "loss spiral" for financial institutions caused by price effects in securities markets. They base their analysis on M. Brunnermeier and L. Pedersen (2009). Adrian and Shin (2007) present evidence of this spiral based on a strong positive correlation between change in leverage and change in assets.

3. See, for example, Bollard (2005), Eisenbeis and Kaufman (2007), Harrison, Anderson, and Twaddle (2007), Huertas (2007), Krimminger (2005), and Mayes (2004).

4. In addition to the United States, Canada, Italy, New Zealand, and Norway have specific insolvency laws for banks. The existence of a law does not necessarily mean that it is successful in the sense that it achieves its objectives. If not, as in Norway, the law is typically not put to use. In Sweden, a law for public administration of distressed banks was proposed in 2000. The law has only been partially implemented in 2008.

5. See Angkinand and Wihlborg (2006), Eisenbeis and Kaufman (2007), Goldberg, Sweeney, and Wihlborg (2005), Huertas (2007), Hüpkes (2003), Krimminger (2005), Lastra and Wihlborg (2007), Mayes (2004), Schiffman (1999).

6. The European Shadow Financial Regulatory Committee (ESFRC) (1998) and Lastra and Wihlborg (2007) discuss characteristics of special bank insolvency procedures.

REFERENCES

Adrian, Tobias, and Hyun S. Shin. 2007. "Liquidity, Financial Cycles and Monetary Policy." In *Current Issues in Economics and Finance*. Federal Reserve Bank of New York, Vol. 14, No. 1.

Angkinand, A. Penny, and Clas Wihlborg. 2006. "Bank Insolvency Procedures as Foundation for Market Discipline" in Gerard Caprio, Douglas Evanoff, and George Kaufman, eds.

Cross-border Banking, Proceedings from Federal Reserve Bank of Chicago-The World Bank Conference, World Economic Publishers, 2006

Bollard, Alan. 2005. "Bank Regulation and Supervision in New Zealand: Recent and Ongoing Developments." *Reserve Bank of New Zealand Bulletin* June, Vol. 68, 2.

Brunnermeier, Markus, Andrew Crocket, Charles Goodhart, Martin Hellwig, Avi Persaud, and Hyun S. Shin. 2009. "The Fundamental Principles of Financial Regulation." *Geneva Report on the World Economy* 11, January 6.

Brunnermeier, Markus, and Lasse Pedersen (2009) "Market Liquidity and Funding Liquidity," *Review of Financial Studies* 22:6, 22-1-38.

Cohan, William D. 2008. "Why Wall Street Has to Alter Its Financial Incentives." *Financial Times*, March 17.

Eisenbeis, Robert A., and George G. Kaufman. 2007. "Cross-Border Banking and Financial Stability in the EU." *Journal of Financial Stability* 4:3, 168–204.

European Shadow Financial Regulatory Committee. 1998. "Resolving Problem Banks in Europe." Statement No 1, London, June 22, available on www.esfrc.eu.

Federal Deposit Insurance Corporation Improvement Act (FDICIA). 1991.

Goldberg, Lawrence, Richard. J. Sweeney, and Clas Wihlborg. 2005. "Can Nordea show Europe the way?" *The Financial Regulator* 10:2, 9–16.

Harrison, Ian, Steve Anderson, and James Twaddle. 2007. "Pre-positioning for Effective Resolution of Bank Failures." *Journal of Financial Stability* 13:4, 324–341.

Huertas, Thomas F. 2007. "Dealing with Distress in Financial Conglomerates." In Harald Benink, Charles Goodhart, and Rosa Lastra, eds. *Prompt Corrective Action and Cross-border Supervisory Issues in Europe*. Financial Markets Group Special Paper 171, London School of Economics.

Hüpkes, Eva. 2003. "Insolvency—Why a Special Regime for Banks." In *Current Developments in Monetary and Financial Law* Vol. 3. Washington, DC: International Monetary Fund.

Krimminger, Michael. 2005. "Deposit Insurance and Bank Insolvency in a Changing World: Synergies and Challenges." In *Current Developments in Monetary and Financial Law* Vol. 4. Washington, DC: International Monetary Fund.

Lastra, Rosa, and Clas Wihlborg. 2007. "Law and Economics of Crisis Resolution in Cross-border Banking." In Harald Benink, Charles Goodhart, and Rosa Lastra, eds. *Prompt Corrective Action and Cross-border Supervisory Issues in Europe*. Financial Markets Group Special Paper 171, London School of Economics.

Mayes, David. 2004. "Who Pays for Bank Insolvency." *Journal of International Money and Finance* 23:515–551.

Østrup, Finn. 2007. *Finansielle kriser*, CBS Press, Copenhagen.

Østrup, Finn, Lars Oxelheim, and Clas Wihlborg. 2009. "Origins and Resolution of Financial Crises; Lessons from the Current and Northern European Crises." *Asian Economic Papers* 8:3, 2009.

Schiffman, Henry. 1999. "Legal Measures to Manage Bank Insolvency." In Rosa Lastra and H. Schiffman, eds. *Bank Failures and Bank Insolvency Law in Economies in Transition*. The Hague: Kluwer Law International.

Wihlborg, Clas. 2009. "Can Market Discipline Be Restored: Lessons from The Subprime Crisis." In David Mayes, Robert Pringle, and Michael Taylor, eds. *Towards a New Framework for Financial Stability*. London: Central Banking Publications.

ABOUT THE AUTHORS

Lars Oxelheim holds a chair in international business and finance at the Lund Institute of Economic Research, Lund University, and is affiliated with the Research Institute of Industrial Economics (Institutet för Näringslivsforskning), Stockholm, and with the Fudan University, Shanghai. Lars Oxelheim is chairman of the Swedish Network for European Studies in Economics and Business (SNEE). He has authored or edited some 35 research monographs and authored or co-authored a number of research articles published in international business, finance, and economic journals. His recent research monographs include *How unified is the European Union?* (Springer-Verlag), *Corporate decision-making with macroeconomic uncertainty* (Oxford University Press), *Markets and Compensation for Executives in Europe* (Emerald Group), *National Tax Policy in Europe—To Be or Not to Be* (Springer-Verlag), *Corporate and Institutional Transparency for Economic Growth in Europe* (Elsevier), *European Union and the Race for Inward FDI in Europe* (Elsevier) and *Money Markets and Politics—A Study of European Financial Integration and Monetary Policy Options* (Edgar Elgar). Lars Oxelheim is a frequently invited keynote speaker and adviser to corporations and government agencies.

Clas Wihlborg is the Fletcher Jones Chair of International Business at the Argyros School of Business and Economics, Chapman University. After receiving his PhD at Princeton University in 1977, he held positions at New York University, the University of Southern California, Gothenburg University in Sweden, and the Copenhagen Business School in Denmark. Clas Wihlborg's teaching and research focus on international finance, corporate finance, and financial institutions. Publications include numerous articles in scientific journals and books; most recently *Corporate Decision Making with Macroeconomic Uncertainty, Performance and Risk Management* (Oxford University Press, 2008, with Lars Oxelheim) and *Markets for Compensation and Executives in Europe* (Emerald Publishers, 2008, co-edited with Lars Oxelheim). He received an Honorary Doctorate at Lund University in 2008 and is a member of the Royal Swedish Academy for Engineering Sciences and the European Shadow Financial Regulatory Committee.

Finn Østrup is professor at Copenhagen Business School. He has a master's in economics from the University of Copenhagen and doctorate of economics from Copenhagen Business School. He has written extensively in the area of capital markets and financial institutions. He has published a number of books, including books on the Danish financial system, on financial crises, and on European monetary integration.

CHAPTER 8

Runs on Chartered and Shadow Banks

The Mechanics and Implications

ROBERT R. BLISS
Wake Forest University

GEORGE G. KAUFMAN
Loyola University Chicago

R uns on banks (depository institutions) have been a hallmark of financial crises in the United States and most other countries since the introduction of banks. Until 1933, bank runs were primarily by depositors who doubted the ability of their banks or any other banks in their market area to redeem their claims in full and on time. These depositors ran into currency (specie). This drained reserves out of the banking system and caused a contraction in bank deposits. As banks sought to accommodate this drain by selling securities, often at fire-sale prices, interest rates or interest rate spreads on securities increased. If the runs and the accompanying losses from fire-sale asset sales were sufficiently great, the solvency of the banks involved was threatened.

Runs can be triggered by problems originating in the macroeconomy, which cast doubts on the value of bank assets and the solvency of the banks, or by problems that may originate in the banking system, such as excessive risk taking. Whatever the initial cause of the run, the resulting contraction in money and credit and rise in interest rates triggered an adverse feedback loop to the macroeconomy, intensifying the damage.

Runs to currency primarily involved only smaller, retail depositors, who could conduct their financial transactions in currency. Runs into currency reduce both the amount of reserves and deposits, unless the Federal Reserve acts to offset the drain of reserves, as it failed to do at the beginning of the Great Depression. The introduction of the FDIC and limited deposit insurance in 1933 effectively ended runs into currency in the United States. Some large depositors and other large creditors were unlikely to be able to conduct most of their transactions in currency and thus did not run into currency. Instead, they would run to safe (Treasury) securities or to safer banks. In either case, the deposits and reserves stayed in the banking system. Runs into safe securities will not change the amount of deposits in the banking system. It will, however, change the relative structure of interest rates for risky and safe loans and securities. Interest rates on safe securities will decline as their prices are bid up and interest rates will increase on risky securities as their prices are bid down. Hence, spreads will widen.

Banks may also fear credit losses during a financial crisis and "run" from risky loans to safe securities or to excess reserves in the form of deposit balances at the Federal Reserve Banks. If banks increase their desired levels of excess reserves, the deposit multiplier will decline triggering contractions in both bank deposits and bank loans. Bank runs into excess reserves took place in the 1930s, but did not occur again until 2008. In the 1930s, as noted above, the Federal Reserve did not act to offset the decline in either reserves or the multipliers and deposits and credit declined sharply.

Although in the 2007–2009 financial crisis retail depositors did not run on their banks into currency, another new form of run developed. Large suppliers of short-term funds have increasingly provided these funds to both bank and nonbank financial institution counterparties only on a fully collateralized basis through short-term repurchase agreements (repos). Nonchartered bank financial institutions that increasingly funded themselves on this basis include dealers and brokers (investment banks), finance companies, insurance companies, and hedge funds. These institutions are often individually referred to as *shadow* banks and as a group referred to as the *shadow* or *parallel* financial system.[1] The collateral pledged by the borrowing institution is in the form of marketable securities. The market value of the collateral generally exceeds the amount borrowed to protect the creditor if the debtor institution defaults. The difference between the value of the collateral and the amount of the borrowing is referred to as the *haircut* and is expressed in terms of the percentage below the collateral value that can be borrowed.

During the recent crisis, large collateralized creditors, who feared the ability of their debtor counterparties to repay their loans in full and on time or doubted the value of the collateral backing their loans increased the haircuts they demanded to protect their claims. Thus, the debtor institutions were required either to put up additional securities to collateralize the funding or to reduce their funding. This action by the creditors has been viewed as being analogous in its effects to a traditional depositor currency run on banks.[2]

Although retail depositor runs into currency and chartered bank runs into excess reserves have been thoroughly analyzed in the literature, large creditor runs on chartered banks and shadow banks in the form of higher haircuts have been less so. We do so below and derive the implications for bank credit extension. We then compare the implications of these runs on credit extension by shadow institutions with credit extension effects of currency and excess reserve runs on chartered banks. We employ a simple, highly stylized static equilibrium analysis to develop the signs and magnitudes of the derivatives of bank credit extension with respect to each of the three types of runs. We find that under reasonable assumptions, increases in haircuts decrease credit extension by both chartered and shadow banks that finance themselves in part or totally through repos, just as increases in currency holdings by the public and excess reserves by banks decrease lending.

THE MODELS

We begin our analysis with a simple traditional stylized model of the banking system. We then introduce a simple stylized nonbank financial institution sector. Last, we expand the traditional bank model to incorporate elements of the nonbank funding model. Using these models, we examine how credit provision responds to various exogenous factors and show how the introduction of the nonbank financial sector complicates the credit channel of traditional monetary policy theory.

A Simple Bank

Our stylized simple banking system holds reserves (R) in the form of cash in bank vaults and deposits at the central bank and makes loans (L). The assets are "funded" with deposits (D) and equity (E). Loans include all earning assets but cash reserves. In terms of a T-account:

$$\begin{array}{c|c} R & D \\ L & E \end{array}$$

We assume that the banking system is subject to several constraints, which are defined in terms of ratios. One is the leverage ratio defined as $e \equiv \frac{E}{R+L} = \frac{E}{D+E}$. Regulators impose a hard constraint, $\bar{e}$, on bank leverage. Banks may, for various reasons, desire to operate with more equity capital than regulators require, $\tilde{e} \geq \bar{e}$. We will refer to constraints arising from the banks' own endogenous preferences, rather than exogenous regulatory diktat, as soft constraints, designated by a tilde. It is possible that the actual leverage ratio, e, will differ from both $\bar{e}$ and $\tilde{e}$, though in equilibrium it cannot be less. Another constraint is on the reserve ratio, which is defined as $r \equiv \frac{R}{D}$. Reserves are the sum of required and excess reserves. Regulators impose a hard reserve requirement, $\overline{rr}$, so that required reserves $RR = \overline{rr} \times D$. Excess reserves are then $ER = R - RR$, and the excess reserve ratio is defined as $er \equiv \frac{ER}{D} \geq 0$. Thus, $r = \overline{rr} + er$. Banks may target a positive level of excess reserves, $\tilde{er}$, which together with the hard regulatory minimum of required reserves, produces a soft target level of reserves, $\tilde{r} = \overline{rr} + \tilde{er}$.

If we consider R and E as exogenously determined and the level of loans as the choice variable, banks face two balance sheet constraints on the level of credit they can create:

$$L + R \leq \frac{E}{\tilde{e}} \rightarrow L \leq \frac{E}{\tilde{e}} - R$$

and

$$L + R = D + E, \ R \geq \tilde{r} \times D \rightarrow L \leq R\frac{1 - \tilde{r}}{\tilde{r}} + E$$

Which of these constraints is binding depends on the levels of R, E, $\tilde{r}$, and $\tilde{e}$.[3]

Suppose banks are holding no more reserves than required by the required reserve ratio plus their desired liquidity buffer. Then $R = \tilde{r}D$, where $\tilde{r} = \overline{rr} + \tilde{er}$. A run to currency reduces both reserves and deposits. The reduction in reserves will force banks to further reduce their deposits to bring the ratio of deposits to reserves back to the desired level. In the process, the banks reduce loans by not rolling them over loans or by not lending out new funds when loans are repaid.

A run by banks into excess reserves, that is an increase in $\tilde{er}$, will also require banks to reduce deposits and loans. In this case, the amount of reserves is unchanged, but the higher desired reserve ratio reduces the deposit multipliers.

The sensitivity of bank lending to changes in reserves resulting from withdrawal of deposits from the banking system in the form of currency or from an increase in the desired level of excess reserves, can be expressed in terms of partial derivatives as follows:

$$\frac{\partial L}{\partial R} = \frac{1 - \tilde{r}}{\tilde{r}} > 0$$

and

$$\frac{\partial L}{\partial \tilde{er}} = -R\frac{1}{\tilde{r}^2} < 0$$

The magnitude of the change in loans depends on the values of both r and R.

A Simple Nonbank Financial Institution

Our stylized simple shadow financial institution system funds itself through secured borrowing, B, using the loans, L, that it holds as collateral.[4] It does not take deposits. The nonbank financial institution holds precautionary balances of cash or equivalents, M, to meet liquidity needs and has equity, E.

M	B
L	E

We define the leverage and liquidity ratios as $e \equiv \frac{E}{M+L} = \frac{E}{B+E}$ and $m \equiv \frac{M}{M+L} = \frac{M}{B+E}$. In our stylized world, nonbank financial institutions are unregulated. In addition to the desired self-imposed leverage and liquidity constraint, $\tilde{e}$ and $\tilde{m}$, the market imposes a hard constraint in the form of a haircut on secured borrowing. This takes the form of a restriction on the amount of borrowing that a given quantity of loans can support. This may be written as $L(1 - \overline{h}) \geq B$, where $\overline{h}$ is the market-determined haircut.

When the combined effects of the m and h prevent the shadow sector from expanding to the level it might otherwise reach, given its level of equity and desired leverage ratio, changes in the desired liquidity ratio, m, will have an effect analogous to that of changes in desired excess reserves in the banking sector—both result from changes within the system. Similarly, a run to cash in the banking system is analogous, in the same circumstances, to an increase in the required haircut, h—both are changes arising outside the system. The sensitivity of shadow bank financial sector lending to changes in the demand for liquidity within the sector, or changes in required haircut from outside the sector, can be expressed as partial derivatives as follows:

$$\frac{\partial L}{\partial m} = -E \frac{1}{(m + h - mh)^2} < 0$$

and

$$\frac{\partial L}{\partial h} = -E \frac{1 - m}{(m + h - mh)^2} < 0$$

Thus, runs by creditors in the form of increases in haircuts reduce loans similar to the effect of runs to currency by creditors of chartered banks. The magnitude of the change depends on the values of m and h.

The Hybrid Banking System

Large chartered banks also raise funds by borrowing or issuing secured debt in addition to attracting deposits. Thus:

$$
\begin{array}{c|c}
R & D \\
L^S & B \\
L^F & E
\end{array}
$$

where L^S are loans and securities that have been pledged as collateral against secured borrowing, B, so that $L^S(1 - \bar{h}) = B$; and $L^F \geq 0$ are free loans and securities that have not been pledged.

Secured borrowing by banks increases the balance sheet without necessarily affecting the amount of deposits in the system. The use of secured funding by banks is ultimately constrained by the equity ratio requirement. In equilibrium $R + L^S + L^F = D + B + E = E/\bar{e}$. In this situation, a run to currency will reduce reserves and force a proportionately greater reduction in deposits. However, as long as there are free assets, $L^F \geq 0$, the banking system can compensate by new secured borrowing and further lending. Similarly, a run by banks to excess reserves need not shrink lending as the resulting decrease in deposits can be offset by increased secured borrowing. Within limits, an increase in the required haircut can be accommodated by pledging free assets and not lead to a reduction in borrowings and loans.

It follows that the hybrid banking system is, within limits, more robust to changes in desired currency holdings, desired excess reserves, desired liquidity, and required haircuts than either the simple banking system or the simple shadow bank financial sector. But when free, unassigned assets are exhausted, the hybrid banking system becomes vulnerable to the joint and reinforcing effects of simultaneous changes in the desire for liquidity and larger haircuts. In this situation, the contraction in lending may be sharper than for simple bank or nonbank financial institutions.

CONCLUSIONS

The recent financial crisis has seen a new type of creditor run on large financial institutions. In contrast to previous runs by depositors of chartered banks into currency and by the banks themselves into excess reserves, the newer runs were in the form of increases in the haircuts that creditors demanded on the securities that large chartered and shadow banks used as collateral for borrowings. We show that, although substantially different in form, these haircut runs have the same implications for bank lending as the traditional runs. Nevertheless, the Federal Reserve is likely to encounter greater difficulties in offsetting the effects of runs into either higher haircuts or greater liquidity in the shadow banking system than runs into currency and excess reserves in the traditional chartered banking system.

NOTES

1. For a description of shadow banking see Pozsar et al. (2010).
2. This was first suggested by Gary Gorton (Gorton and Metrick 2010).
3. Bliss and Kaufman (2003) explore the interaction of reserve requirements and leverage ratios and their impact on monetary policy.
4. The secured lending market we are modeling is the repo market. In this market, "good collateral" takes the form of securities rather than bank loans. We note in passing that restrictions on what constitutes "good collateral" would constrain expansion of credit in the nonbank sector and narrow the range of sectors that could access this source of funds. For the present purpose we will abstract from this issue.

REFERENCES

Bliss, Robert R., and George G. Kaufman. 2003. "Bank Procyclicality, Credit Crunches, and Asymmetric Effects of Monetary Policy: A Unified Model." *Journal of Applied Finance* 13:2, Fall–Winter, 23–31.
Gorton, Gary B., and Andrew Metrick. 2010. "Securitized Banking and the Run on Repo." *Yale ICF Working Paper* No. 09–14.
Pozsar, Zoltan, Tobias Adrian, Adam Ashcraft, and Hayley Boesky. 2010. "Shadow Banking." *Staff Reports* No. 458 (Federal Reserve Bank of New York), July.

ABOUT THE AUTHORS

Robert R. Bliss is the F. M. Kirby Chair in Business Excellence at the Schools of Business at Wake Forest University, where he teaches courses in derivatives, financial engineering, and capital markets. Prior to returning to academia, Dr. Bliss served as a senior financial economist at Federal Reserve Bank of Chicago and held research positions at the Bank of England and the Federal Reserve Bank of Atlanta. Previously, Dr. Bliss taught finance at Indiana University. Professor Bliss's research interests include fixed income securities and derivatives, structured finance, risk management, financial regulation, and the law and economics of insolvency. Professor Bliss earned his doctorate in finance from the University of Chicago.

George G. Kaufman is the John F. Smith Professor of Economics and Finance at Loyola University Chicago and consultant to the Federal Reserve Bank of Chicago. Earlier, he was an economist at the Federal Reserve Bank of Chicago and the John Rogers Professor of Finance at the University of Oregon. He has been a visiting professor at Stanford University, University of California at Berkeley, and the University of Southern California. He has published widely on financial markets and institutions. Kaufman is co-editor of the *Journal of Financial Stability* and a founding editor of the *Journal of Financial Services Research*. He is former president of the Western Finance Association, the Midwest Finance Association, and the North American Economic and Finance Association. He serves as co-chair of the Shadow Financial Regulatory Committee. Kaufman holds a PhD in economics from the University of Iowa.

CHAPTER 9

Debt and Currency Crises

CHRISTIAN BAUER
University of Trier

BERNHARD HERZ
University of Bayreuth

VOLKER KARB
Sal. Oppenheim

The threat of bankruptcy for the Eurozone member Greece was followed by a significant devaluation of the euro against the U.S. dollar in 2010. While rigorous saving and restructuring of the budget as well as the economic pickup especially in Germany seems to have banned this threat, the $1 trillion fund (750 billion €) and a dramatic change in the European Central Bank's (ECB) policy are still a painful reminder for taxpayers.

While international financial crises and their costs are on everyone's lips again, the focus of public debate remains on the current case and the question, whether the actions taken have been appropriate. A neglected issue in this discussion, however, is the multiplicity of financial crises in the form of public debt and/or currency crises. Over the past 10 years, the Paris Club recorded 122 intergovernmental debt rescheduling agreements, while about as many currency crises have occurred. The vast majority of these crises has occurred in developing and transition countries and remains unnoticed by the general public, despite the sometimes dramatic consequences.

Sovereign debt crises and currency crises are two sides of one coin—both may be viewed as a solution to a government budget problem—and can occur both individually or together in the form of twin crises. The last important twin crises took place in Russia in 1998 and in Argentina in 2001. If a permanent budget deficit constantly increases the debt burden, a state can try to stop or even reverse this process either by spending cuts or by increased revenues (taxes). If both options are not feasible—for example, due to local political pressure—there remain two other alternatives: printing money or refusing to repay the debt.

Printing money creates *seigniorage* (the difference between the costs of printing and the nominal value) but also induces inflationary pressure and a devaluation of the currency. In case of a sovereign default, there is no international institution legally obliging a government to pay. Unlike in the case of private individuals or companies in default, there is no legal restraint against sovereigns in this regard.

This relationship between debt and currency crises serves as a starting point for a theoretical and empirical analysis. After a brief overview of each type of crisis, the underlying politic-economic calculus is introduced and then supported empirically. Our main conclusions are:

Double crises; that is, simultaneous debt and currency crises should theoretically and empirically be understood as separate types of crisis. The economic cost in terms of reduced growth and high inflation are extremely high for twin crises. Contagion from one crisis type to the other is possible. Finally, a sound fiscal policy has a twofold beneficial effect, reducing the likelihood of both a debt crisis and a currency crisis.

CURRENCY CRISES

A specialty of the foreign exchange market is the central bank as an exceptional and especially powerful market participant. The central bank may, by changing the interest rate, affect the expected net return of internationally traded financial assets, and thus influence supply and demand for foreign currencies. It can also offer its own currency in any amount (by printing money) and typically owns a large amount of foreign currency reserves and gold, which might be used for interventions to support the domestic currency. This asymmetry (limited foreign exchange reserves versus unlimited capacity to print money) is the starting point of speculative attacks.[1] Finally, as ultima ratio the central bank often has the power to introduce capital controls; that is, to alter the legal framework of the foreign exchange market.

A credibly fixed exchange rate has a number of advantages: It can reduce inflation and inflation expectations. It lowers the costs of transactions between home and the anchor country and simplifies and stabilizes the valuation of foreign liabilities. Benefits of flexible exchange rates include the possibility of active monetary policy, avoiding distortions of international trade by either over- or undervaluation, and to not have to fear sudden devaluations (currency crisis).[2] Successfully fixing an exchange rate requires that the monetary policy balances out supply and demand of the currency in the long run and remains a stable financial system. In the long run, this means domestic inflation meets the inflation rate of the anchor country in order to keep deviations from purchasing power parity low and that debt ratios and composition are sustainable. The monetary policy of a country with a fixed exchange rate is therefore not arbitrary, but must mimic to the anchor country.

Currency crises can occur when a potential free market price differs strongly from the current exchange rate. This is usually the case when a central bank enforces a fixed rate for a long time, while the shadow exchange rate of the fixed exchange rate (e.g., due to high inflation rates) moved away. If a central bank wants to impose a higher than the shadow exchange rate, one way to do so is to rebuy its own currency and sell foreign exchange reserves, thus increasing the demand of domestic currency and supporting the price. If speculators realize this strategy, they may take a loan in the domestic currency and exchange it against foreign exchange reserves. Once the central bank's reserves are depleted (or it gives up the fight), the currency revalues to the price that would have formed without any central bank intervention and the speculators can cheaply repay their loan.[3]

The macroeconomic consequences of a currency crisis and the associated sharp depreciation are quite heterogeneous. Both can provide a positive impact and negative effects on economic growth and other key economic variables through different channels. Increasing exports, for example, create a positive effect on economic growth, as after the devaluation domestically produced goods can be offered cheaper abroad. Likewise, monetary policy can boost demand with low interest rates after the restrictions of a fixed regime are lifted. Negative effects of a devaluation on the economy may arise from higher prices for imports of raw materials and intermediate products and from terms of trade losses. Additionally, a sharp fall in the exchange rate is virtually always accompanied by a rise in inflation (either in advance or as a result), which distorts the relative prices and leads to misallocations of resources, increased information and transaction costs, and arbitrary wealth redistribution. Finally, a devaluation also implies the increase of the value of government debt denominated in foreign currency. The government must therefore increase tax earnings to pay back debt. This problem also affects all other players in the economy, which have liabilities in foreign currency. In case the banking sector is refinanced mainly abroad and short term, the result of a devaluation will most likely be a banking crisis, as was the case with the Asian crisis.

The theoretical approaches to explain currency crises are usually divided into three generations. These models embed the currency crisis in a macro model of one or two economies. In addition, there are so-called coordination games, which model the dynamics of the attack itself.

The first-generation models follow the seminal work of Krugman (1979) and Flood and Garber (1984), which are inspired by the crises in Latin America in the 1970s. They explain how permanent unsound fiscal and/or monetary policies lead to a breakdown of a fixed exchange rate regime.

These models were able to convincingly explain the Latin American crises, but were not suitable to reflect the crisis of the European Monetary System, in particular the devaluation of England and Sweden in the 1990s. This gave rise to the second-generation based on Obstfeld (1994), who internalizes the decision problem of the central bank. For intermediate fundamental states of the economy there may exist multiple equilibria and self-fulfilling prophecies. The equilibrium outcomes "all speculators attack and devaluation" and "no attack and a stable regime" solely depends on the expectations of the speculators. The main rationale is that defensive measures are costly and these costs vary with the fundamentals.

Third-generation models extend previous models by a further policy dimension or another economic component to crises like the Asian crisis to explain the developments in the late 1990s. Typical examples are models of banking and currency crises (Chang and Velasco 2000 a-c, 2001), debt and currency crises (Bauer, Herz, and Karb 2003, 2007), contagion models (Drazen 2000; Masson 1999), "sudden stop" and "balance sheet "models (Aghion et al. 2001; Kaminsky and Reinhart 1999), in which a currency crisis is at least partially attributed to another policy or another country.

In addition, global games analyze the attack process in detail. Starting with Morris and Shin (1998), the dynamics and in particular the influence of large speculators like George Soros are analyzed in a series of works in more detail (e.g.,

Bauer 2005; Corsetti et al. 2004). The coordination problem of the speculators in the second generation models is solved by introducing incomplete information.

DEBT CRISES

There are fundamental differences between private and public debtors. The first and probably most important fundamental difference between a sovereign state and a private debtor is the fact that there are no legal means to force a sovereign state to repay its debts. Any creditor of a state, for example the owner of a treasury bill, is dependent on the fairness of the government to repay the debt as agreed.[4] The reason for this situation is the lack of an international insolvency law for states.[5] Although a government could print its own currency to meet demands (at the cost of increasing inflation and devaluation), it can't repay debt that is denominated in foreign currency. This is particularly a problem in developing and transition countries, because their borrowing is virtually limited to foreign currency ("original sin" problem).

A high proportion of short-term debt may lead to self-fulfilling expectations: Rising default expectations among financial market participants increase the risk premium; that is, the refinancing costs, so that the state is actually more likely to decide against a repayment of the debt.

Second, the question arises why a state pays its debts at all. The literature typically uses reputation loss and the accompanying increase in the cost of future liabilities as arguments. However, both arguments only apply to those countries that have never defaulted. Countries that have defaulted in the past experience no increasing effects of further defaults on the risk premium. On the contrary, after a default, a country's debt burden is much smaller than before, implying a reduced default risk, unless the debt crisis was accompanied by a significant recession. Such potential negative impacts on the economy during the crisis are more important than the loss of reputation. In case of a state bankruptcy, there usually is a liquidity squeeze in the credit market implying a decline in investment and consumption, a reduction of government expenditures and a decline of external trade (Rose 2005; Rose and Spiegel 2004), all fostering a recession. The strength of this effect depends in particular on the distribution of creditors from home and abroad. The more debt held by the state's own citizens, the larger the negative effect at home. The higher the share of foreign creditors, the easier the state can pass on negative effects to the international markets.

Third, political-economy-driven motives influence the default decision. Instead of a default, the government could also cut spending or raise additional taxes, both having a negative impact on citizens and the economy. Again, the optimal solution (for the government) depends in particular on the creditors' structure and reputation costs.

Developed countries are to a high degree indebted in their own currency, and much of the debt is directly or indirectly (e.g., through pension funds) held by domestic citizens. They mostly have a good reputation, have never defaulted, and pay a low-risk premium. These countries thus have almost no incentive not to repay their debts. First, default costs are high with respect to future growth, higher risk premiums and losses due to problems in the credit markets, and a decline in

Exhibit 9.1 Default and Devaluation

	No Devaluation	**Devaluation**
No default	No crisis	Currency crisis
Default	Sovereign debt crisis	Twin debt and currency crisis

consumption. Second, to a large extent the default hurts domestic citizens, who make up a majority of creditors.

However, the situation in developing and emerging countries is typically reversed. They are particularly indebted to foreign creditors in foreign currency and pay a higher risk premium. The costs of a default for domestic citizens are relatively low if a recession can be avoided or moderated.

DEBT AND CURRENCY CRISES

With respect to the government budget problem, sovereign defaults and currency crises are two sides of the same coin. From the choice of the government there are three different crisis scenarios (see Exhibit 9.1), which were already analyzed extensively in the literature.

The empirical literature almost exclusively studies these crises types separately: for example, IMF (1998), Glick and Hutchison (1999), Kaminsky and Reinhart (1999), DeLargy and Goodhart (1999), Bordo, Eichengreen, Klingebiel and Martinez-Peria (2001), Eichengreen (2002) and Bordo and Eichengreen (2003). Bauer, Herz, and Karb (2003) show that a joint consideration of all three types of crisis provides much more stable results, particularly in the field of early warning systems.

Debt and currency crises can be positively correlated due to common causes and "internal contagion effects" between both types of crises or negatively correlated due to substitution effects (see Exhibit 9.2).

An example of a common cause is a negative shock to GDP growth, which reduces the government's tax base. As the public budget situation deteriorates, default becomes more likely. At the same time, a slowdown in GDP growth also raises the government's incentive to devalue in order to stimulate economic activity. Other important variables that can be interpreted in the sense of common causes are the volume, the currency structure, and the maturity structure of sovereign debt.

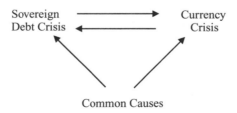

Exhibit 9.2 Links between Debt and Currency Crises

These debt variables are all essential to determine the sustainability not only of the public debt burden but also of a country's balance of payments position.

There are also direct links between both kinds of crises ("internal contagion effects"). Devaluation can, for example, directly trigger a debt crisis as it increases the real value of foreign currency denominated debt[6] or as it leads to credit rating downgrades, which increase the country's interest rate risk premium.[7] The opposite causality, which runs from debt to currency crises, has already been stressed, for example, by the first-generation currency crisis models, which imply that excessive fiscal and debt policies can trigger speculative attacks.

However, sovereign defaults and currency devaluations can also be negatively correlated due to budget financing aspects. If a government faces a deficit and is neither able to increase its tax revenues nor to reduce its spending, it can still choose among three options of financing: (1) issuing new debt, thus raising both the overall debt burden and the risk of a future debt repudiation; (2) printing money, which induces inflation and currency pressure and thus increases the risk of a currency crisis; or (3) default on debt coming due. From this perspective, a government that finances its budget via a monetary expansion lowers the pressure to default and vice versa.[8]

Bauer, Herz, and Karb (2003, 2007) combine several of these factors into an integrated framework. Their approach includes the characteristic properties of the second generation currency crisis literature, but extends this framework to a government that—weighing the costs and benefits of its policy options—decides whether to abandon a fixed exchange rate peg and/or whether to default on its maturing debt service payments at the same time.

Exhibit 9.3 visualizes the optimal decisions of the government to devalue and/or default. The debt level—inverse fundamentals plane (good fundamentals are resembled by low values on the abscissa)—consists of seven sectors in which different devaluation and default decisions are optimal. A binary pair of

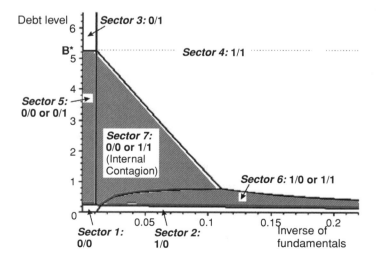

Exhibit 9.3 Optimal Policies Depending on the Investors' Default Expectations (see Bauer, Herz, Karb 2003)

Exhibit 9.4 Optimal Policies Depending on the Investors' Default Expectations

	Decision		Description
Sector 1	0/0	No devaluation No default	Fundamentals are very good and debt low.
Sector 2	1/0	Devaluation No default	Debt is low, fundamentals are bad. The devaluation will be large and the associated costs are lower than the benefits.
Sector 3	0/1	No devaluation Default	The fundamentals are good, but the debt is very high. It's optimal to default.
Sector 4	1/1	Devaluation and default (Twin crisis)	Fundamentals are bad and debt is high. It's optimal to both devalue and to default.
Sector 5	0/0 or 0/1	No devaluation default as a self-fulfilling expectation	Fundamentals are good, but debt is high. With moderate interest rates, defaulting is suboptimal for the government, because the saved interest is low. However, if investors expect a default and deny the rollover of the debt, the incentive for the government not to repay the old debt is large enough to default.
Sector 6	1/0 or 1/1	No devaluation default as a self-fulfilling expectation	Fundamentals are bad and debt is moderate. The situation is analogous to Sector 5 but for the devaluation, which is optimal due to the bad fundamentals.
Sector 7	0/0 or 1/1	Devaluation only in connection with a default Default as a self-fulfilling expectation Internal contagion	For medium fundamentals and moderate indebtedness there also are self-fulfilling expectations as in Sectors 5 and 6. However, the devaluation decision also depends on the default decision. After a default the cost of depreciation is lower, therefore a devaluation becomes optimal, too. There will be a transmission of the crisis between the policy areas ("internal contagion").

numbers yields the optimal decision, the first denoting devaluation, the second the default event. Thus the pair "1/1" stands for a twin crisis. In the three sectors that are marked gray, the result depends on investors' expectations and leads to self-fulfilling expectations and multiple equilibria. In the other areas (white), the optimal decision doesn't depend on investors' expectations. Exhibit 9.4 summarizes the results.

Four main results of the model should be emphasized here again. (1) There may be a transfer of the crisis between different policy fields; that is, a crisis in the fiscal or, alternatively, in the monetary policy may spread to the other field ("Internal Contagion"). In contrast to the well-known transmission channels of currency crises between countries (contagion), we propose a spread of the problems from one policy field to other areas within a country. (2) Improved fundamentals can compensate for higher debt levels and, conversely, worse fundamentals lower the level of sustainable debt. This is evident from the diagonal line between Sectors

4 and 7. (3) The model leads to self-fulfilling expectations and multiple equilibria in the debt sector. The analysis is analogous to the currency crisis models of the second generation. (4) There is a debt ceiling B*, which can't be exceeded by the government. Higher debt levels would imply defaults regardless of the remaining fundamental economic situation, so that creditors would not fund such a high level of debt.

EMPIRICS AND STYLIZED FACTS

Finally, we take a look at the empirical facts. Bauer, Herz, and Karb (2007) analyze a sample of 62 middle-income countries (GDP per capita 766–9,360 U.S. dollars) in the period from 1975 to 2002. The data is drawn from the World Bank World Development Indicators (WDI) 2004 database and focuses on the distinction between pure debt crises (65 events), pure currency crises (59 events), and twin debt and currency crises (44 events).

Exhibit 9.5 shows debt and monetary fundamentals of various past crises. The ellipses represent two-dimensional confidence intervals within ± 1 standard deviations around the average. The upper parts of the ellipses are dotted to clarify that of course crises are more likely to occur in situations with poor fundamentals and high debt levels than under better economic conditions.

Exhibit 9.5 reflects the model predictions on the occurrence of various crises very well. Pure debt crises occur particularly in situations with high debt levels but good monetary fundamentals. Pure currency crises tend to take place at relatively low debt levels but poor monetary conditions. Twin crises occur particularly in countries with poor fundamentals and high debt. In addition, there are

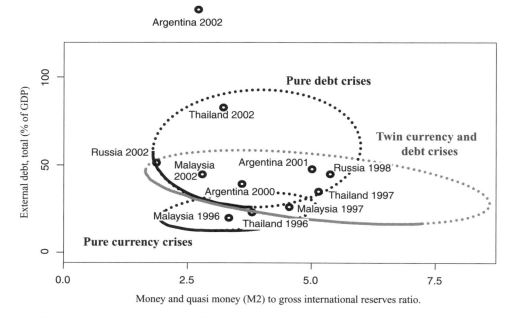

Exhibit 9.5 Occurrence of the Different Crisis Types (see Bauer, Herz, and Karb 2007)

overlaps, which can be viewed as multiple equilibria. It should be noted also that the inclination of the twin crisis ellipse corresponds exactly to the model prediction.

Furthermore, pre- and post-crises data are shown for some well-known crises. In 2001, when it experienced a twin crisis, Argentina was located at the center of the twin crisis ellipse. The extremely high debt ratio in 2002 is the result of the devaluation and yet again reflects the unilateral reduction of the debt by about 70 percent. Russia was lying amid the twin crisis ellipse at the outbreak of the double crisis in 1998. The situation in 2002, and the fact that a part of the debt was repaid prematurely, document the good economic condition four years after the crisis. Finally, Thailand and Malaysia, which had a banking and currency crisis in 1998, are shown as representatives of the Asian crisis.

Finally, the separate treatment of twin crises also significantly improves the power of early warning systems (see Bauer, Herz, and Karb 2007). In addition, the macroeconomic explanations are specific for each type of crisis.

The differentiated analysis of each type of crisis significantly improves the predictability of pure debt and twin crises, but not the predictability of pure currency crises. The predictability of twin crises is the best among all crisis types. More than half of the twin crises in the sample can be predicted with only a negligible number of false alarms.

With respect to internal contagion effects, we find that the maturity structure, in other words, the share of short-term debt, seems to be a significant factor in traditional empirical studies of debt crises only because it is relevant for twin crises. Although it is not relevant for pure debt crises, it has a rather strong impact only on twin crises as it promotes currency crises, which can trigger debt crises via contagion. This impact influences estimations of mixed pure debt and twin crisis samples.

We also encounter preselection bias effects. Foreign exchange reserves, for example, have a significant negative influence on the probability of pure debt crises, but a positive influence on twin currency and twin crises; that is, pure debt crises are associated with comparatively low reserve ratios, while twin crises are connected with comparatively high reserve ratios. This finding can be due to a preselection bias with regard to the exchange rate system: A need for high reserve ratios typically arises only in countries with fixed exchange rate regimes. Fixed exchange rate regimes are, however, more likely subject to a speculative attack than floating exchange systems. Thus, in countries with high reserve ratios (i.e., fixed exchange rate regimes) debt crises are more likely to be associated with simultaneous currency crises than in countries with low reserve ratios (i.e., flexible exchange rates).

CONCLUSION

The theoretical and empirical evidence strongly suggests that twin debt and currency crises should be classified as a specific type of crisis, which should be analyzed separately from pure currency and pure debt crises. Such a classification helps to better understand the interrelations between fiscal and exchange rate crises, as well as the different crises types themselves being characterized by unique sets of causes and consequences. Theory suggests a number of possible interrelations between debt and currency crises, which include common causes, contagion effects from one crisis to the other, and complementary budget financing aspects. The empirical analyses indicate internal contagion effects, that is, the transmission from one crisis type to the other. More sound fiscal policies not only reduce the threat of a default but also of a currency crisis and thus yield a double dividend.

NOTES

1. De facto a central bank is also limited in offering domestic currency, because an expansion of the monetary base usually creates an unwanted inflationary pressure or the economy might be in the liquidity trap as the Bank of Japan in the past decades.
2. Although recent crises—as in Iceland—show that debt crises may induce currency crises even in flexible exchange rate regimes.
3. In general, this exchange rate is significantly lower than the rate that would have formed without the crises due to the negative macroeconomic effects of the crises themselves.
4. In fact, even if a government defaults, this typically does not imply that it denies any payment. Typically the repayment is restructured; that is, prolonged with a lower nominal interest rate. This implies a recovery rate of 30 percent to 40 percent on average (see Bauer, Herz, and Hoops 2008).
5. Some countries have regulations for illiquid public entities, for example, Chapter 9, U.S. Bankruptcy Code. Under certain circumstances, it is possible to obtain a title against a foreign sovereign country that entitles the owner to claim money or funds owned by the debtor in the country in which the title was granted. A number of financial institutions have specialized in this business of exploiting junk bonds.
6. On the causes, implications, and possible cures to this so-called original sin phenomenon see Eichengreen, Hausmann, and Panizza (2004).
7. See Calvo and Reinhart (2000) and Reinhart (2002) for empirical evidence and possible explanations of credit rating downgrades in the aftermath of devaluations.
8. For a comprehensive overview of theoretical and empirical links between currency and debt crises also see Herz and Tong (2003).

REFERENCES

Aghion, P., P. Bacchetta, and A. Banerjeef. 2001. "Currency Crises and Monetary Policy in an Economy with Credit Constraints." *Economic Review* 45:1121–1150.
Bauer, Christian. 2005. "Solution Uniqueness in a Class of Currency Crisis Games." *International Game Theory Review* 7:4, 1–13.
Bauer, Christian, and Bernhard Herz. 2006. "Monetary and Exchange Rate Stability at the EU-Mediterranean." *Revue Economique* 57:4, 899–917.
Bauer, Christian, Bernhard Herz, and Stefan Hoops. 2008. "A Free Lunch for Emerging Markets: Removing International Financial Market Imperfections with Modern Finance Instruments." *Word Development* 36:9, 1514–1530.
Bauer, Christian, Bernhard Herz, and Volker Karb. 2003. "The Other Twins: Currency and Debt." *Review of Economics* 54:3, 248–267.
Bauer, Christian, Bernhard Herz, and Volker Karb. 2006. "How Likely Are Macroeconomics Crises in the CIS." *Research in International Business and Finance* 20:227–238.
Bauer, Christian, Bernhard Herz, and Volker Karb. 2007. "Are Twin Currency and Debt Crises Something Special?" *Journal of Financial Stability* 3:1, 59–84.
Bauer, Christian, and Michael Seitz. 2007. "Empirical Determination of Currency Baskets—A new de facto Classification." Mimeo.

Bordo, Michael D., and Barry Eichengreen. 2003. "Crises Now and Then: What Lessons from the Last Era of Financial Globalization?" In Mizen, Paul ed., *Monetary History, Exchange Rates and Financial Markets. Essays in Honour of Charles Goodhart*, Cheltenham and Northampton: 52–91.

Bordo, Michael D., Barry Eichengreen, Daniela Klingebiel, and Maria S., Martinez-Peria. 2001. "Is the Crisis Problem Growing More Severe?" *Economic Policy*, 16:(32), 51–82.

Calvo, Guillermo A., and Reinhart Carmen M. 2000. "Fixing for Your Life." In Calvo, G. ed., *Emerging Capital Markets in Turmoil: Bad Luck or Bad Policy?* Cambridge, MA: MIT Press 2005.

Chang, Roberto, and Andrés Velasco. 2000a. "Financial Fragility and the Exchange Rate Regime." *Journal of Economic Theory* 92:1, 1–34.

Chang, Roberto, and Andrés Velasco. 2000b. "Exchange Rate Regimes for Developing Countries," *American Economic Review* 90:2, 71–75.

Chang, Roberto, and Andrés Velasco. 2000c. "Banks, Debt Maturity and Financial Crises." *Journal of International Economics* 52:1, 169–194.

Chang, Roberto, and Andrés Velasco. 2001. "A Model of Financial Crises in Emerging Markets," *Quarterly Journal of Economics*, 116:489–517.

Corsetti, Giancarlo, Amil Dasgupta, Stephen Morris, and Hyun Song Shin. 2004. "Does One Soros Make a Difference? A Theory of Currency Crisis with Large and Small Traders." *Review of Economic Studies* 71, 87–114.

DeLargy, Robert P.J., and Charles Goodhart. 1999. "Financial Crises: Plus ça Change, Plus c'est la Meme Chose" *LSE Financial Markets Group Special* 108.

Drazen, Allan. 2000. "Political Contagion in Currency Crises." In Paul Krugman, ed. *Currency Crises*. Chicago, IL: University of Chicago Press.

Eichengreen, Barry. 2002. "International Financial Crises: Is the Problem Growing?" *Jahrbuch für Wirtschaftsgeschichte* 1, 89–104.

Eichengreen, Barry, Ricardo Hausmann, and Ugo Panizza. 2002. "Original Sin: The Pain, the Mystery, and the Road to Redemption." Paper prepared for the conference. *Currency and Maturity Matchmaking: Redeeming Debt from Original Sin*. Washington, DC: Inter American Development Bank, 21–22.

Eichengreen, Barry, Ricardo Hausmann, and Ugo Panizza. 2004. "The Mystery of Original Sin" in Barry Eichengreen and Ricardo Hausmann, eds. *Other People's Money: Debt Denomination and Financial Instability in Emerging Market Economics*. University of Chicago Press.

Flood, Robert P., and Peter M. Garber. 1984. "Collapsing Exchange-Rate Regimes: Some Linear Examples." *Journal of International Economics* 17, 1–13.

Glick, Reuven, and Michael Hutchison. 1997. "Banking and Currency Crises: How Common Are Twins?" Federal Reserve Bank of San Francisco, Center for Pacific Basin Monetary and Economic Studies, *Working Paper* No. 99–07.

Herz, Bernhard, Volker Karb, Axel Dreher. 2006. "Is There a Causal Link between Currency and Debt Crises?" *International Journal of Finance and Economics*, Band: 11, Nr. 4, 305–325.

Herz, Bernhard, and Hui Tong, "Debt and Currency Crises - Complements or Substitutes?" *Review of International Economics*, Band: 16, Nr. 5, 2008, 955–970.

IMF-Inernational Monetary Fund. 1998. "Financial Crises: Causes and Indicators." *World Economic and Financial Surveys, World Economic Outlook* 5.

Kaminsky, Graciela L., and Carmen M. Reinhart. 1999. "The Twin Crises: The Causes of Banking and Balance-of-Payments-Crises." *American Economic Review* 89:3, 568–592.

Krugman, Paul R. 1979. "A Model of Balance-of-Payments Crises."*Journal of Money, Credit and Banking* 11:3, 311–325.

Levy-Yeyati, Eduardo, and Frederico Sturzenegger. 2004. "Classifying Exchange Rate Regimes: Deeds vs. Words." *European Economic Review* 49:6, 1603–1635.

Masson, Paul. 1999. "Contagion: Macroeconomic Models with Multiple Equilibria." *Journal of International Money and Finance* 18, 587–602.

Morris, Stephen, and Hyun Song Shin. 1998. "Unique Equilibrium in a Model of Self-Fulfilling Currency Attacks." *American Economic Review* 88:587–597.

Obstfeld, Maurice. 1994. "The Logic of Currency Crisis, Banque de France." *Cahiers economiques et monetaires* 43, 189–213.

Olivier, Jeanne. 2005. "Why Do Emerging Economies Borrow in Foreign Currency?" *Other People's Money*, B. Eichengreen and R. Hausmann eds., Chicago: University of Chicago Press, 190–217.

Reinhart, Carmen, and Kenneth Rogoff. 2004. "The Modern History of Exchange Rate Arrangements: A Reinterpretation." *Quarterly Journal of Economics* 119:1, 1–48.

Reinhart, Carmen. 2002. "Default, Currency Crises, and Sovereign Credit Ratings," *World Bank Economic Review*, Oxford University Press, vol. 16 (2), 151–170.

Rose, Andrew K. 2005. "One Reason Countries Pay Their Debts: Renegotiation and International Trade," *Journal of Development Economics*, 77, June 1, 189–206.

Rose, Andrew K., Spiegel, M. M. 2004. "A Gravity Model of Sovereign Lending: Trade, Default and Credit." *IMF Staff Papers Vol. 51, Special Issue*.

ABOUT THE AUTHORS

Christian Bauer is a professor of monetary economics at the University of Trier. He received diploma degrees in mathematics and economics as well as a PhD from the University of Bayreuth. His research focuses on international finance, monetary policy, and uncertainty. Christian Bauer's book *Partial Information in Currency Crises Models* connects the formal underpinning of economic decisions with policy-relevant questions in crises. He has published in several leading economic journals, including *World Development* and *Journal of Economic Dynamics and Control*. He is also editor of the free online textbook Dynamic Economics (http://gxt.cbauer.de) which provides more than 100 interactive graphics to allow an easy understanding of many economic concepts. He can be reached at Bauer@uni-trier.de.

Bernhard Herz is a professor of monetary economics at the University of Bayreuth. He received a diploma degree in economics as well as a PhD from the University of Tübingen. He has done extensive work in the area of international finance and financial crises. In this context, he has been a visiting researcher at several international organizations, among others the European Commission and the International Monetary Fund. He is also co-editor of the *Journal of International Economics and Economic Policy*. The third edition of his book *Geld, Kredit und Banken* (*Money, Credit and Banking*), co-authored with Horst Gischer and Lukas Menkhoff, will be published in late 2010 by Springer Verlag.

Volker Karb has focused on international macroeconomics and international financial crises. He received a diploma degree as well as PhD in economics from the University of Bayreuth. In the past years, he worked for a German investment bank in the field of strategic equity research. Currently, he works for a large German private health-care provider.

CHAPTER 10

A Fixed-Time Effects Model of Contagion

DIRK G. BAUR
School of Finance and Economics, University of Technology

RENÉE A. FRY
Centre for Applied Macroeconomic Analysis, Australian National University

There has been a surprising number of financial market crises evident over the past decade, from the East Asian financial crisis in 1997–1998 to the latest financial crisis affecting most developed economies particularly in the United States and Europe. Understanding crisis transmission has been the subject of a substantial body of research coming from regulatory bodies and the academic sector. One element is in working out if comovements in financial markets change significantly during periods of financial market crisis. If comovements are larger in crisis periods than in normal periods, there is contagion. Often contagion is thought to be the addition of a factor common to all financial markets. Economic theorists often explain this factor as reflecting the role of investors and the nature of the financial services sector, whether it be herding of investor decisions, information asymmetries or cascades, portfolio rebalancing, or wealth or borrowing constraints.

Finding an empirical basis for modeling these factors that theorists raise as being important is difficult given the data available for input. However, economists can still measure the existence and nature of this common factor, and can glean some clues to its foundations. Decisions in modeling contagion require empiricists to make assumptions about their models, including which asset markets should be included in the sample; how to control for interdependencies that always exist between markets; when to define a crisis period as occurring; and which asset market should act as the source of a crisis. In most models of contagion, these assumptions can impact substantially on the results, even if the assumptions are only slightly misspecified. In Baur and Fry (2009) we propose a simple model in terms of specification, computation, and interpretation to analyze contagion. This model avoids the need to make most of these decisions listed above and provides a time series of *joint* or systemwide contagion where all markets in the sample are simultaneously affected by this additional factor.

Our chapter applies a panel data fixed-time effects model to equity market returns in Asia during the East Asian financial crisis. Eleven equity markets are

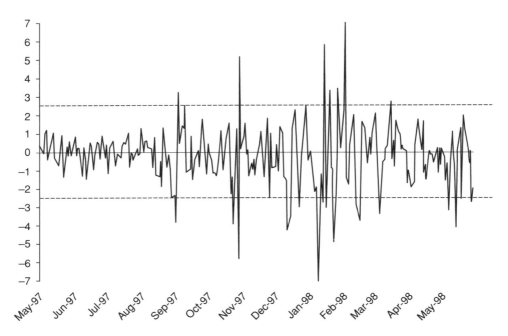

Exhibit 10.1   Incidences of Joint Contagion for Asian Equity Markets during the Asian Crisis

The plot presents the estimated test statistic of the fixed-time effect. The fixed-time effects sample period is from May 2, 1997, to May 29, 1998. The dashed lines indicate the threshold for the statistical significance (99 percent confidence interval) of joint contagion. The results illustrate that contagion clusters, is short-lived, and is equally split between joint positive and negative shocks.

included in the sample. Most of these markets are directly involved in the crisis, are major financial centers through which a crisis would be likely to transmit within Asia, or are included to help measure contagion that is systemwide rather than affecting only a small subset of markets. Test statistics of the fixed-time effect estimates are provided in Exhibit 10.1. The figure presents the values of the test statistic that indicates the significance of contagion for each day of the estimated fixed-time effect window. When the statistic exceeds a threshold indicated by the dashed lines, there is significant evidence of an additional factor affecting all markets in the sample labeled *contagion*. The statistical significance is determined by the ratio of the estimated magnitude of the effect in each country and the estimated standard error of the effect. Most contagion studies are not able to present a time-series of contagion or to identify the existence of contagion on a particular date. An exception is Diebold and Yilmaz (2009).

The main conclusion of the analysis in Baur and Fry (2009) is that interdependence through regional and global relationships (coefficient estimates are not reported here) remains the dominant reason for comovements in the equity markets throughout the crisis, with equity markets predominantly determined by systematic relationships on 90 percent of days during the fixed-time effect window. This is an important result. Interdependencies are controlled for by including global and regional equity market variables. The results show that the regional risks are important for all asset markets in the sample, while the global risks are more important for the developed countries of Hong Kong, Japan, and Singapore, and two of the emerging countries in the sample, namely China and Malaysia.

For comparison to these results and for this chapter, a simple version of the model in Baur and Fry (2009) has been applied to the Global Financial Crisis. A model of weekly asset returns for Australia, Canada, France, Germany, Greece, Ireland, Italy, Japan, Netherlands, New Zealand, Norway, Portugal, Spain, Switzerland, the United Kingdom, and the United States is estimated, conditioning on the MSCI World Index as a control for interdependence. The World Index is assumed to capture systematic or common interdependencies among these countries. In contrast to the application for Asia, the model for the Global Financial Crisis is modeled by using weekly data. This is to avoid complications in the estimation procedure due to trading hours occurring in different time zones. Daily data are appropriate for the Asian crisis because all countries are in the same region and are not subject to time-zone distortions.

Exhibit 10.2 presents the test statistic of the fixed-time effect measuring joint contagion during the Global Financial Crisis. The figure shows the statistics for each point in time, with the dashed lines again representing the threshold over which

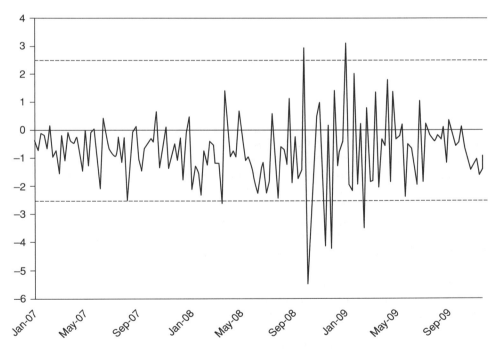

Exhibit 10.2 Incidences of Joint Contagion for Major Developed Markets during the Global Financial Crisis
The plot presents the estimated test statistic of the fixed-time effect. The fixed-time effects sample period is from January 1, 2007, to December 31, 2009. The dashed lines indicate the threshold for the statistical significance (99 percent confidence interval) of joint contagion. The results illustrate that contagion clusters around October and November 2008, is short-lived, and is predominantly characterized by joint negative shocks.

there is contagion. The results of the model for the Global Financial Crisis are similar in substance to those for the Asian crisis. That is, the relationships between the asset returns in most of the developed countries are driven by interdependence rather than contagion with few cases of the fixed-time effect statistic exceeding the critical thresholds indicating contagion. This outcome and also that for the East Asian financial crisis, echo the result of the dominating role of interdependence over contagion in crises of Forbes and Rigobon (2002).

Although we find that interdependence is more important for asset returns than contagion during crises, it remains of interest to examine the time-series indicating contagion. As pointed out earlier, many studies on contagion are forced to assume dates on which the crisis period is defined. Our model has the advantage of defining a large window that is able to encompass the crisis period and to detect the crisis start and end dates, as it is not a feature of the model that contagion needs to exist on every day or week over the sample period. There are calm episodes within the windows of the fixed-time effects period where no contagion is detected, for example, in the Asian crisis model in Exhibit 10.1, the first 80 observations corresponding from May to September 1997 do not show any evidence of contagion. This demonstrates the biggest advantage of the model where the crisis period encompasses noncrisis observations to no detriment, and that the model can be used to determine the temporal location of the crisis period.

For the East Asian crisis, the fixed-time effect window shown in Exhibit 10.1 extends for 281 trading days from May 2, 1997, to May 29, 1998. There is evidence of joint contagion on 28 dates, representing 10 percent of all observations in the fixed-time effects window, which tend to cluster around four periods. The four periods of contagion detected are: (1) September 2 to September 4, 1997; (2) October 24 to October 30, 1997; (3) December 12, 15, and 23, 1997; and (4) January 8 to January 28, 1998, along with several dates in February, March, and May 1998. The analysis of these periods found that Hong Kong, Indonesia, and Korea, three of the key crisis countries, were prominently in the headlines corresponding to days on which contagion is important. Further examination in Baur and Fry (2009) confirmed the importance of Hong Kong in particular in contributing to asset market volatility at that time.

The Global Financial Crisis extends over a relatively long period of time compared to other crises that are often much shorter in duration (for example, the Russian crisis in 1998 lasted for around three months while the U.S.-based Long Term Capital Management crisis also of 1998 lasted for about 17 days). For the recent crisis the window in which we allow contagion to appear if it is present extends for three years, from the first week of January 2007 to the last week of December 2009, which is some 156 weeks. Over the three-year period there are 20 weeks in which joint and systemwide contagion is evident. That is around 12 percent of weeks in the crisis period sample, like the results for the Asian crisis, contagion clusters, with the strongest incidences of contagion in October and November 2008. The model picks up the worst of the crisis in 2008 as central banks, governments, and financial markets attended to the resolution of financial institutions under duress. The evidence for contagion in 2007 is relatively weak and there is no significant incidence of contagion in the second half of 2009.

Another important result coming out of the original paper and often overlooked in the literature on this topic is that contagion does not have to be a negative occurrence. Concern is always evident when markets simultaneously fall. However, for obvious reasons, there is less concern voiced when markets simultaneously rise. Evaluating whether markets simultaneously rise for reasons other than interdependence has implications for investor diversification and optimal portfolio allocation, as portfolio diversification decisions are made based on measures of the strength of the common movement of asset prices. Portfolio diversification opportunities are likely to change with the appearance of significant systemwide contagion. For the crisis in Asia, one third of the observations on which there is contagion is actually positive contagion, and often these are quite large movements in absolute terms. For the case of the Global Financial Crisis, 17 of the 20 cases of contagion are weeks in which stock markets simultaneously fell, as we would traditionally expect in a crisis period. However, in the other three cases of contagion, stock markets simultaneously rise above the threshold. This asymmetry of contagion clarifies that the phenomenon of contagion is mostly related to market turmoil and financial crisis.

The main message from Baur and Fry (2009) is that the analysis of contagion does not have to be done using complicated techniques and invoking a substantial number of assumptions. There is a simple method in which to analyze contagion by using a fixed-time effects model as we demonstrate in that paper. The analysis provides a clear picture of the development of a crisis, documenting periods of time of interdependence where relationships between markets are no different to those that occur normally, but also episodes of contagion where there is the joint occurrence of (usually negative) market extremes. The method presents both the magnitude and the significance of the joint market movements. This means that sample selection bias problems are reduced, and identification of the model does not depend on the *ex post* selection of the crisis period. Episodes of contagion are determined endogenously.

Understanding in detail the nature of crisis transmission and contagion is important in forming policies to minimize crisis transmission once a crisis occurs, for designing an internationally coordinated regulatory system to prevent the occurrence in the first place as is the current thinking, and for investors to better understand the financial system in which they make their portfolio selection decisions. The analysis of our model is able to provide some evidence on these issues.

REFERENCES

Baur, D. G., and R. A. Fry. 2009. "Multivariate Contagion and Interdependence." *Journal of Asian Economics* 20:353–366.

Diebold, F. X., and K. Yilmaz. 2009. "Measuring Financial Asset Return and Volatility Spillovers, with Application to Global Equity Markets." *Economic Journal* 119:158–171.

Forbes, K., and R. Rigobon. 2002. "No Contagion, Only Interdependence: Measuring Stock Market Co-Movements." *Journal of Finance* 57:2223–2261.

ABOUT THE AUTHORS

Dirk G. Baur is a senior lecturer in finance at the School of Finance and Economics, University of Technology, Sydney. Dirk obtained a M.Sc. in economics and a PhD in financial econometrics from the University of Tübingen, Germany. Dirk worked for the Joint Research Centre of the European Commission from 2002 to 2005 where his main tasks were the execution of economic impact assessments of changes in the regulatory framework of the financial system within the European Union. In 2005, Dirk assumed a post-doc position at Trinity College Dublin and became a lecturer in finance at Dublin City University in 2007. Dirk joined the School of Finance and Economics in November 2009. His main research interests are the modeling and estimation of dependence, financial crises, financial contagion, and the role of gold in the global financial system. His papers have been published in the *Journal of Money and Finance*, *Japan and the World Economy*, *Journal of Multinational Financial Management*, *Journal of Financial Stability*, *Journal of International Financial Markets, Institutions and Money* and the *Journal of Banking and Finance*.

Renée A. Fry is the deputy director of the Centre for Applied Macroeconomic Analysis at the Australian National University where she is also the co-director of the finance and macroeconomy program. She is a research associate at the Centre for Financial Analysis and Policy, University of Cambridge, and has worked extensively on models of financial market contagion.

CHAPTER 11

Contagion or Interdependence in the Financial Markets of Asia, Latin America, and the United States

From Tequila Effect to the Subprime Crisis

EMERSON FERNANDES MARÇAL
Universidade Presbiteriana Mackenzie (UPM) and EESP-FGV

PEDRO L. VALLS PEREIRA*
CEQEF-FGV and EESP-FGV

DIÓGENES MANOEL LEIVA MARTIN
Universidade Presbiteriana Mackenzie (UPM)

WILSON TOSHIRO NAKAMURA
Universidade Presbiteriana Mackenzie (UPM)

WAGNER OLIVEIRA MONTEIRO
EESP-FGV

This chapter concentrates on determining the degree to which it is possible to state that contagion arose from the financial events that occurred from the mid-1990s onward. A series of simultaneous crises occurred, and given the synchronicity and intensity of them, we may conjecture the existence of a breakdown in the traditional pattern of propagation of events. The crises hit a wide range of countries with such severity and simultaneity that the suggestion of a more systemic pattern to these crises is a hypothesis that arises almost immediately.

*Pedro L. Valls Pereira would like to acknowledge the partial support from CNPq Grant n30229/2008–5.

A brief historical summary shows that over a decade, some nine major events with significant repercussions on markets may be listed: (1) the devaluation of the Mexican Peso in December 1994; (2) the devaluation of the Thai Baht in July 1997; (3) the collapse of Russia in August 1998; (4) the recapitalization of LTCM in September 1998; (5) the collapse of the Hong Kong stock market in October 1998; (6) the devaluation of the Brazilian Real in January 1999; (7) the collapse of the Argentine currency board in December 2001 and (8) the pre-electoral panic in Brazil in the second half of 2002; and (9) the subprime crisis in United States.

The precise definition of contagion is an open question in the literature and a consensus remains to be reached. In this way, not only is there no consensus on the definition of contagion, but also in the methodology for testing for the existence of contagion.

The objective is to investigate whether there was evidence of contagion and interdependence among the Asia, Latin America, and the United States financial markets during the 1990s and the subprime crisis, controlling for specific macro-economic fundamentals.

THEORETICAL BENCHMARK

The complexity of crises and their consequences result from the multiplicity of causes and the interaction of the various mechanisms of propagation in time and in space. This is aggravated by the difference between countries due to the degree of institutional, economic, and political development and the absence of mechanisms for international economic coordination. In this sense, a study of the crisis should begin by concentrating on a specific crisis and its consequences.

It may be stated that the literature on contagion begins with the models of currency crises. In generic terms, these are split into three generations of models. The first model by Krugman (1979) explains a currency crisis in the context of a fixed exchange rate regime. The crisis occurs in the balance of payments due to a speculative attack against the fixed exchange rate with the exhaustion of reserves, thus altering the currency regime. The rationality of agents and the macroeconomic fundamentals are relevant characteristics of this model, but the possibility of con-tagion does not exist. The second model by Flood and Garber (1984) and Obstfeld (1984) and Obstfeld and Rogoff (1996), considers the existence of multiple equilib-ria. The third model by Krugman (1998) explains the exchange rate crisis in terms of the existence of speculative bubbles and moral risk. The first two generations of models are inadequate for explaining the crises that began during the 1990s.

It was in the 1990s onward that the concept of contagion appeared. Allen and Gale (2007) affirm that the classical theory of risk considers this to be exogenous; that is, associated with conditions of nature, although what is observed is that the risks associated with globalization is endogenous, in other words, they result from its own dynamics. There is no consensus on the concept and measure of contagion, but it may initially be stated that the term expresses the international transmission of financial crises.

Dornbush, Park and Claessens (2000) adopt the definition of contagion as being the dissemination of market disturbances, most of the time with negative conse-quences, from one emerging market to another, observed through comovements in exchange rates, share prices, sovereign risk spreads, and capital flows.

Pritsker (2001) defined contagion as the occurrence of a shock in one or more markets, countries, or institutions that spread to other markets, countries, or institutions. Forbes and Rigobon (2002) defined contagion as the increase in the probability of a crisis in a country, given that there has been a crisis in another country, discounting the effects of interdependence or fundamentals; that is, the contagion refers to the residual character of the crisis, which befalls countries in an unpredictable way.

The existence of contagion should be seen as a structural shift that occurred during the crisis and not just as rising volatility throughout usual channels. In this way, in the event that the analyst has the information about crisis times, it is possible to test the hypothesis of contagion, comparing the structure of correlations between times. "In particular, contagion has the effect of causing a structural shift during the crisis period in the conditional covariance . . . and in conditional variance . . . " (Dungey, Fry, Gonzalez-Hermozillio, and Martin 2004). Pesaran and Pick (2003) criticize this kind of approach on the basis of three arguments: (1) the analyst is required to have a priori information on the moment of the crisis; (2) the duration of the crisis is not sufficiently great to allow comparisons of correlations, principally when there are more than two assets in question; (3) there is a selection bias in the sample, since crisis times are not known a priori.

An extensive literature has devoted its attentions to evaluating which are the determinants of the correlations in the case where contagion exists. After an intense debate, it was concluded that the existence of contagion cannot be considered to be a synonym of a high degree of correlation, but as some kind of structural instability associated with crisis events, with the implementation of such tests remaining an open question.

EMPIRICAL LITERATURE ON CONTAGION

Despite relatively extensive empirical literature on contagion in equity markets, the empirical results are divergent. Baig and Goldfajn (1998) considered daily exchange rate, interest rate, spreads on external debt securities, and stock indices for Thailand, Malaysia, Indonesia, South Korea, and the Philippines. In relation to the original correlation coefficient for the spreads, interest, and exchange rates, they noted the presence of contagion.

Forbes and Rigobon (2002) analyzed the impact of the Asian and Mexican crises and the 1987 crash of the New York stock exchange on the equity markets of emerging and developed countries, and concluded, with adjusted correlation tests, that most of the changes (16 out of 17 countries) were due to interdependence. The authors suggest that most of the events usually accepted in the literature as contagion are just interdependence.

Corsetti, Pericoli, and Sbracia (2005) used a factor model to estimate equity returns during the Asian crisis, checking the relationship between returns from the Hong Kong stock exchange, and the stock markets for 10 emerging countries and the G-7 countries. Rigobon (2003) applied the dynamic conditional correlation model (DCC) to the countries involved in the Mexican, Asian, and Russian crises. For the Mexican crisis, the mechanism for the transmission of crises remained relatively constant, providing evidence of interdependence.

Caporale, Cipollini, and Spagnolo (2005), in line with Rigobon (2003), after adjusting the model for heteroskedasticity, endogeneity, and omitted variables, concluded that there was evidence of contagion during the Asian crisis.

Boschi (2005) analyzed contagion effects between Argentina with Brazil, Venezuela, Uruguay, Mexico, and Russia. The author analyzed exchange rates, stocks, and bonds. The econometric methodology consisted in estimating a vector autoregression (VAR) and then analyzing the instant correlation coefficient corrected for heteroskedasticity as suggested by Forbes and Rigobon (2002). He was not able to find evidence in favor of contagion hypothesis.

Inchang, In, and Kim (2010) analyze the effects of the subprime crisis in the stock market for a sample of 38 countries. The sample was analyzed per region (Asia, Australia, Europe, Latin America) and per level of development in the two periods from 1996 to 2003 (Asian crisis) and 2005 to 2009 (subprime crisis). These samples were divided in tranquil and turmoil periods. The authors used the multivariate DCC-Garch of Engle (2002). The results suggest a significant rise of conditional correlation during the subprime period. The authors state this as evidence of contagion and they suggest the contagion effects were stronger during the subprime crisis compared to Asian crisis.

Santos and Valls Pereira (2010) analyze the effect of subprime crisis in stock market in the United States, Brazil, United Kingdom, and Japan. The sample used was from 2000 to 2009, divided in two periods, from 2000 to 2006—the stability period—and from 2007 to 2009—the crisis period. The authors use the theory of conditional copulas proposes by Patton (2002) and (2006). The results suggest evidence of shift contagion from the United States to Brazil using Gaussian and Clayton copulas, but there was no evidence of contagion from the United States to the United Kingdom and from the United States to Japan using both copulas.

TESTING CONTAGION USING MACROECONOMIC FUNDAMENTALS

The importance of fundamentals is highlighted by Pesaran and Pick (2003). Marçal, Valls Pereira, Martin, and Nakamura (2010) have made an effort to correct their analyses for fundamentals. The authors were able to find evidence in favor of contagion, particularly from the Asian crisis to Latin America. In this chapter, we extend the sample up to 2008 in order to deal with the subprime events. The methodology is similar to Marçal, Valls Pereira, Martin, and Nakamura (2010). The evidence of contagion persists but it's not clear whether the subprime crisis generated contagion effects.

On the basis of multivariate models of volatility, they tested for the existence of structural breakdowns in the structure of volatility propagation and whether these may be attributed to moments of crisis. This approach was also implemented by Marçal and Valls Pereira (2008) and Paula (2006), but in these studies due to the noncorrection of the fundamentals the results may be biased to the direction of finding evidence for contagion when this does not exist.

Marçal, Valls Pereira, Martin, and Nakamura (2010) collected daily stock index data for the following countries: Argentina, Brazil, South Korea, the United States,

Singapore, Malaysia, Mexico, and Japan. The frequency of the data is daily and for the period January 1, 1994, to December 31, 2003.

The importance of fundamentals was highlighted by the significance of the fundamentals to explain the dynamics of stock markets indices. The model with fundamentals consisted of a regression of returns against the variables listed above. In the model without fundamentals, they exclude all models corresponding to fundamentals, with only the lagged returns remaining. In general, the fundamentals used in the analysis add explanatory power to the returns. The exception is the United States, and to a lesser degree, Argentina. In the other countries, there is good evidence that the model corrected for fundamentals is superior to the uncorrected model.

Following this, they collected the residuals from the regression for the returns on the fundamentals. These variables are used as a starting point for the volatility models. This two-stage procedure is used in this literature on account of the complexity of the models used, although this procedure is only fully satisfactory if the returns are normal, which does not appear to be the case. In addition, the volatility models assume that the data are an innovation and do not show serial autocorrelation. This was tested for all countries and the results were satisfactory.

In modeling the volatility of returns, the authors used models in DCC-GARCH family. The hypothesis of contagion was tested by evaluating whether a negative surprise in one country can be a source of model misspecification in other countries. A first order of tests was carried out to evaluate whether the described indicator variables for each country are sources of misspecification in the equations of the other countries.

Their results suggest that (1) crises generated in Latin America countries had a strong regional impact, but the propagation to Asian countries was weak; (2) crises generated in Asian countries had a strong regional impact, and the propagation to Latin America countries was strong. In both previous cases, the crisis affected the U.S. market. Given that the fundamentals were not available for Russia, this country had to be excluded from the analysis, even though the period studied includes the Russian crisis, and hence the changes in the indices may be portraying the indirect effects of the Russian crisis. It follows that part of the contagion detected between the United States and Asia may be due to the propagation of the Russian crisis.

As a conjecture, the *collateral* effect was more intense in countries with more fragile fundamentals. In the case of the Asian crisis, Brazil and Argentina did not escape unscathed on account of more fragile fundamentals, in particular, because of a currency regime that maintained the exchange rate at a clearly overvalued level, and of poor fiscal fundamentals. An attempt to explain why the Asian countries succeeded in remaining immune to the Latin American crises perhaps lies in the temporal sequence of events. The Asian crisis occurred at a time when Brazil and Argentina had extremely fragile fundamentals with significant fiscal deficits and currency misalignments. The crises in these countries occurred at a point when the Asian countries were undergoing a clear recovery and already had more solid fundamentals, which made them "immune" to contagion. At the same time, this is a conjecture that remains to be demonstrated and that cannot be directly extracted from the analysis realized in this study. The negative surprise in U.S. stock markets during the subprime crisis did not cause significant effects of contagion on Asian countries, but generated effects on Latin America countries.

FINAL REMARKS

This chapter stresses the importance of correcting for fundamentals in the analysis of financial contagion. After correcting for fundamentals there is evidence favorable to the hypothesis of regional contagion in Latin America and in Asia. As a rule, there was contagion in the Asian crisis to Latin America, but not vice versa. The United States and Japan played the role of vectors for contagion, with the first basically to Latin America and the second to both regions. During the subprime crisis, there is evidence of contagions to Latin American countries but not to Asian countries.

A conjecture to explain the vulnerability of Latin America to the financial crises lies in its poor economic fundamentals during the periods of the crises in the 1990s, as well as the existence of a phase of transition to greater openness in trade and financial terms, through which Latin American countries were passing at the time.

REFERENCES

Allen, F., and D. Gale. 2007. *Understanding Financial Crises.* Oxford: Oxford University Press.

Baig, T., and I. Goldfajn. 1998. "The Asian Crisis." *Working Paper* 98/155. Washington, DC: International Monetary Fund.

Boschi, M. 2005. "International Financial Contagion: Evidence from the Argentine Crisis of 2001–2002." *Applied Financial Economics* 15:153–163.

Caporale, G. M., A. Cipollini, and N. Spagnolo. 2005. "Testing for Contagion: A Conditional Correlation Análisis." *Journal of Empirical Finance* 12:776–489.

Corsetti, G., M. Pericoli, and M. Sbracia. 2005. "Some Contagion, Some Interdependence: More Pitfalls in Tests of Financial Contagion." *Journal of International Money and Finance* 24:1177–1199.

Dornbush, R., Y. C. Park, and S. Claessens. 2000. "Contagion: Understanding How it Spreads." *The World Bank Observer* 15:177–197.

Dungey, M., R. Fry, B. Gonzalez-Hermozillio, and V. L. Martin. 2004. "Empirical Modeling of Contagion: A Review of Methodologies." *Working Paper* 04/78. Washington, DC: International Monetary Fund.

Engle, R. 2002. "Dynamic Conditional Correlation: A Simple Class of Multivariate Generalized Autoregressive Conditional Heterocedasticity Models." *Journal of Business and Economic Statistics* 20:339–350.

Flood, R. P., and P. M. Garber. 1984. "Collapsing Exchange Rate Regimes." *Journal of International Economics* 17:1–83.

Forbes, K., and R. Rigobon. 2002. "No Contagion, Only Interdependence: Measuring Stock Market Co-Movements." *Journal of Finance* 57:2223–2261.

Inchang, Hwang, Francis In, and Tongsuk Kim Kim. 2010. "Contagion Efects of the U.S. Subprime Crisis on International Stock Markets." *SSRN 1536349. 2009.*

Krugman, P. R. 1979. "A Model of Balance of Pyment Crises." *Journal of Money, Credit and Banking* 11:311–325.

Krugman, P. 1998. "Bubble, Boom, Crash: Theoretical Notes on Asia's Crises." *Working Paper.* Cambridge: MIT.

Marçal, E. F., and P. L. Valls Pereira. 2008. "Testing the Hypothesis of Contagion using Multivariate Volatility Models." *Brazilian Review of Econometrics* 28:2, 191–216.

Marçal, E. F., P. L. Valls Pereira, D. M. L. Martin, and W. Nakamura. 2010. "Evaluation of Contagion or Interdependence in the Financial Crises of Asia and Latin America Considering Macroeconomic Fundamentals." *Applied Economics* forthcoming.

Obstfeld, M. 1984. "Rational and Self-Fulfilling Balance of Payments Crises." *NBER Working Paper* 1486.

Obstfeld, M., and K. Rogoff. 1996. *Foundations of International Macroeconomics*. Cambridge, MA: MIT Press.

Patton, A. J. 2002. *Applications of copula theory in Financial Econometrics*. Unpublished Thesis (Ph.D.) San Diego: University of California.

Patton, A. J. 2006. "Modelling Asymmetric Exchange Rate Dependence." *International Economic Review* 47:2, 527–556.

Paula, Juliana de. 2006. "Contágio E Mercados Financeiros Emergentes." IMECC (Universidade de Campinas, Campinas). Working paper.

Pesaran, M. H., and A. Pick. 2003. "Econometric Issues in the Analisys of Contagion." *Cesifo Working Paper* 1176. Cambridge: University of Cambridge.

Pritsker, M. 2001. "The Channels of Finance Contagion." In S. Claessens, and K. Forbes, eds. *International Financial Contagion*. Norwell, MA: Kluwer Academic Publishers.

Rigobon, R. 2003. "On the Measurement of the International Propagation of Shocks: Is the Transmission Stable." *Journal of International Economics* 61:261–283.

Santos, R. P. de S., and Valls Pereira. 2010. "Modelando Contágio Financeiro através de Cópulas." Mimeo São Paulo School of Economics, FGV.

ABOUT THE AUTHORS

Emerson Fernandes Marçal is a professor of financial econometrics at the Applied Social Science Center at the Presbyterian Mackenzie University at São Paulo, Brazil. He also runs the Center for Applied Macroeconomics at São Paulo School of Economics at Getúlio Vargas Foundation. He received his doctoral degree in Economics at São Paulo University in 2004.

Pedro L. Valls Pereira holds a PhD from London School of Economics and Political Sciences and is full professor of financial econometrics and director of the Center for Quantitative Studies in Economics and Finance at São Paulo School of Economics of Getúlio Vargas Foundations. He was also a full professor at INSPER and associated professor at University of São Paulo. He has more than 40 articles in academic journals. He can be reached at pedro.valls@fgv.br.

Wilson Toshiro Nakamura received his master's and PhD degrees in management from Faculdade de Economia, Administração e Contabilidade of Universidade de São Paulo—FEA-USP (Brazil). He has been at Universidade Presbiteriana Mackenzie since 1993. He has published papers in many of the main journals of Brazil and Latin American.

Wagner Oliveira Monteiro is a PhD candidate at the São Paulo School of Economics of the Getulio Vargas Foundation and holds a master's degree in economics (2008) from the same institution. He works at the Centre for Quantitative Studies in Economics and Finance and the Center for Applied Macroeconomics, both at the São Paulo School of Economics. He is experienced in empirical and theoretical Finance modeling with an emphasis on time series, derivatives, GARCH and cointegration models.

PART TWO

Contagion and the Asian Financial Crisis

I n the 1990s, the economies of East Asia were roaring with growth as incomes and living standards surged across the region. Some of the nations in the region, such as Thailand, employed a currency regime in which the local currency was pegged to the U.S. dollar. In the summer of 1997, the Thai baht came under stress, largely as a result of excessive investment throughout the economy, particularly in real estate, which experienced a now too-familiar price bubble. In July 1997, the Thai government abandoned its policy of pegging the baht to the dollar, and it allowed the baht to float. Or, more exactly, the government allowed the baht to sink, as its value on world currency markets plunged. Before calm was restored, the implications of this painful event in one small Asian economy circled the world and humbled the mighty, leading to massive economic pain across much of Asia, a default by the Russian government, and the collapse of Long-Term Capital Management, a titanic hedge fund with its own contagious impact.

The Asian financial crisis was a dramatic episode in at least two major ways. First, it sent a powerful wake-up call to policy makers around the world—the financial market interlinkages that had developed in the era of globalization were much more important than anyone had previously imagined, so critical that an apparently small and localized financial problem in Thailand could quickly lead to a worldwide crisis. Second, the crisis led to interventions by world financial agencies, such as the International Monetary Fund and the World Bank, which enforced stringent economic policies on some Asian countries as a condition for financial assistance. These strong tactics convinced many in the Asian regions that the developed nations exercised an economic hegemony over their countries that amounted to a form of neo-colonization. The chapters in this section explore the question of contagion in the Asian financial crisis, tracing the agony of economic distress from the streets of Bangkok to the boardroom of banks and other corporations, to the halls of power in the Kremlin, and to the New York Federal Reserve Bank.

CHAPTER 12

Dynamic Correlation Analysis of Financial Contagion

Evidence from Asian Markets

THOMAS C. CHIANG
Department of Finance, Drexel University, Philadelphia

BANG NAM JEON
Department of Economics and International Business, Drexel University

HUIMIN LI
Department of Economics and Finance, West Chester University

This chapter examines empirical evidence on the contagion effect in the 1997 Asian financial crisis. By applying a dynamic conditional-correlation (DCC-GARCH) model (Engle 2002) to eight daily Asian stock-return data series for the period from 1990 to 2003, we present consistent evidence of contagion, which is followed by a herding phase during the later post-crisis period.[1]

The financial shocks and the contagion process in the 1997 Asian crisis were attributable to a variety of factors beyond economic linkages. Although many researchers have examined the financial contagion aspect of the Asian crisis, the existence of contagion in relation to the crisis remains a debatable issue. Some studies show a significant increase in correlation coefficients during the Asian crisis and then conclude that there was a contagion effect. Other researchers find that after accounting for different volatilities, there is no significant increase in the correlation between asset returns in pairs of crisis-hit countries, reaching the conclusion that there was "no contagion, only interdependence" (Basu 2002; Bordo and Murshid 2001; Forbes and Rigobon 2002).[2] However, in their tests for financial contagion based on a single-factor model, Corsetti et al. (2005) find "some contagion, some interdependence." Further, focusing on different transmission channels, Froot et al. (2001) and Basu (2002) confirm the existence of the contagion effect.[3] Thus, the evidence on financial contagion is not conclusive in the literature.

This chapter employs a cross-country, multivariate GARCH model (Engle 2002), which is appropriate for measuring time-varying conditional correlations among stock markets and detecting dynamic investor behavior in response to news and innovations. The major findings of this chapter are summarized as follows.

First, this chapter finds supportive evidence of contagion during the Asian-crisis period and resolves the puzzle of the "no contagion, only interdependence" argument supported by, for example, Forbes and Rigobon (2002). Second, two different phases of the Asian crisis—the contagion phase and the herding phase—were identified based on statistical analyses of correlation coefficients. Third, the correlation coefficients are time-varying and are affected by changes in sovereign credit ratings, implying that both market participants and financial credit-rating agencies have dynamic roles in shaping cross-country stock market correlations and the contagion process in the 1997 Asian financial crisis.

DATA AND DESCRIPTIVE STATISTICS

For our analyses, we use daily stock-price indices from January 1, 1990, through March 21, 2003, for selected Asian countries that were seriously affected by the 1997 Asian financial crisis. The data set consists of the stock indices of eight Asian economies: Thailand, Malaysia, Indonesia, the Philippines, South Korea, Taiwan, Hong Kong, and Singapore. In addition, two stock indices from industrial countries, Japan and the United States, are included. All of the national stock price indices are in local currency, dividend-unadjusted, and based on daily closing prices in each national market. Japan was affected by the Asian crisis, but at a much later stage and to a lesser extent. We also include the United States as a global factor in the Asian region. All of the stock index data are obtained from Datastream International.

As noted in various media reports, the Thai government gave up defending the value of its currency, the baht, on July 2, 1997, which triggered a significant depreciation of the Thai baht. This effect spread to the currencies of Thailand's neighboring nations. Therefore, we use this date to break the data set into two subperiods: pre-crisis and post-crisis. As shown in Exhibit 12.1, the average stock returns are generally higher during the pre-crisis period, while volatilities are higher for the post-crisis period. The data also show that for these markets, big positive and negative shocks are more likely to be present during the post-crisis period than the pre-crisis period. This market volatility clustering phenomenon has been recognized and successfully captured by the GARCH type of models in the literature (Bollerslev et al. 1992).

SIMPLE CORRELATION ANALYSES

Since correlation analysis has been widely used to measure the degree of financial contagion, it is convenient to start our investigation by checking the simple pairwise correlation between the stock returns for the countries under investigation. However, correlation coefficients across countries are likely to increase during a highly volatile period. That is, if a crisis hits Country A and results in increased volatility in its stock market, the crisis will be transmitted to Country B, which will also experience a rise in volatility and, in turn, the correlation of stock returns in both Country A and Country B. This spurious effect, however, does not imply closer comovement between the two markets.

To address this issue of rising volatility during a crisis, we calculate the heteroskedasticity-adjusted correlation coefficients proposed by Forbes and

Exhibit 12.1 Descriptive Statistics on Stock Returns (1/1/1990–3/21/2003)

	Average	Volatility	Extreme Values
Panel A: Before the Crisis			
HK	0.086	1.765	5.017***
Indonesia	0.031	0.984	19.141***
Japan	−0.034	2.093	5.098***
Korea	−0.009	1.965	2.799***
Malaysia	0.037	1.517	8.906***
Philippines	0.048	2.273	4.001***
Singapore	0.026	1.009	6.308***
Taiwan	−0.003	4.592	3.493***
Thailand	−0.026	2.741	5.294***
U.S.	0.047	0.535	2.249***
Panel B: After the Crisis			
HK	−0.034	4.112	8.524***
Indonesia	−0.041	4.182	5.973***
Japan	−0.06	2.474	1.864***
Korea	−0.018	6.611	1.949***
Malaysia	−0.045	4.03	22.882***
Philippines	−0.067	3.02	12.308***
Singapore	−0.025	2.818	8.241***
Taiwan	−0.045	3.329	1.755***
Thailand	−0.025	4.153	3.751***
U.S.	0.0004	1.808	2.148***

Notes: Observations for all series in the whole sample period are 3449. The observations for the pre-crisis and post-crisis subperiods are 1956 and 1493, respectively. ***, **, and * denote statistical significance at the 1%, 5%, and 10% levels, respectively. All variables are first differences of the natural log of stock indices times 100. Average, volatility, and extreme values refer to mean, variance, and kurtosis, respectively, in statistics.

Rigobon (2002; FR hereafter). A potential problem with this analysis is that the source of contagion has to be identified beforehand. For convenience of comparison with research in the literature, both Thailand (with a breakpoint at July 2, 1997) and Hong Kong (with a breakpoint at October 17, 1997) are considered as the source of contagion in this study.[4]

The results are reported in Exhibit 12.2. In both cases, although the contagion effects are not as significant as those being calculated without adjusting for rising volatility, evidence shows that about a quarter of correlation coefficients increase significantly after the crisis occurs.

This evidence also raises a question about whether the source country of contagion matters. To address this question, we recalculated the heteroskedasticity-adjusted correlation coefficients based on the order in which infected countries were affected during the crisis.[5] To do so, we calculated and tested 31 pair-wise correlation coefficients.[6] The results in Exhibit 12.3 show that, after the relative volatility is corrected, the contagion effect is moderate, appearing in only 16 out of 31 cases.

Exhibit 12.2 Test of Significant Increases in Correlation Coefficients (Thailand and Hong Kong as the Source of Contagion, Respectively)

	Correlation before Crisis	Correlation after Crisis	Adj. Correlation after Crisis
Thailand as the source:			
TH-HK	0.310	0.372	0.310
TH-IN	0.158	0.341	0.283
TH-JP	0.148	0.229	0.188
TH-KO	0.141	0.311	0.257
TH-PH	0.211	0.314	0.260
TH-SG	0.391	0.454	0.383
TH-TW	0.141	0.206	0.169
Hong Kong as the source:			
HK-TH	0.286	0.398	0.278
HK-PH	0.211	0.354	0.245
HK-IN	0.203	0.334	0.230
HK-SG	0.512	0.650	0.496
HK-TW	0.139	0.272	0.185
HK-JP	0.254	0.437	0.308
HK-KO	0.084	0.361	0.250

Notes: HK, IN, JP, KO, PH, SG, TH, and TW represent the stock returns of Hong Kong, Indonesia, Japan, Korea, the Philippines, Singapore, Thailand, and Taiwan, respectively. Malaysia is not included because of a decrease in correlation after the crisis.

The simple correlation analysis with correction for changing volatility highlights the significance of market volatility in a given window. However, market behavior and return volatility are expected to change continuously in response to ongoing shocks. Estimation of time-varying correlation coefficients will help us to capture the dynamics of the relationship between countries.

EVIDENCE FROM DYNAMIC CORRELATIONS FOR THE HARDEST HIT COUNTRY GROUP

We estimate time-varying correlations between stock index returns using a multivariate GARCH model proposed by Engle (2002). An advantage of using this model is the fact that all possible pair-wise correlation coefficients (45) for the 10 markets in the data can be estimated in a single-system equation and the dynamic correlations can be measured by using time-varying covariances and variances.[7] To simplify the presentation and reduce unnecessary parameterizations in calculation, we focus only on the hardest hit countries: Thailand, Indonesia, Malaysia, the Philippines, Korea, and Hong Kong.[8]

Exhibit 12.4 derived from a dynamic correlation coefficient GARCH (1,1) model (Engle 2002) presents pair-wise correlation coefficients between the stock returns of Thailand and those of Indonesia, Malaysia, the Philippines, Korea, and Hong Kong during the period 1996–2003. These time-series patterns show that the pair-wise correlations increased during the second half of 1997 and reached their highest

Exhibit 12.3 Test of Significant Increases in Simple Correlation Coefficients

	Correlation before Crisis	Correlation after Crisis	Adj. Correlation after Crisis
TH-HK	0.310	0.372	0.310
TH-IN	0.158	0.341	0.283
TH-JP	0.148	0.229	0.188
TH-KO	0.141	0.311	0.257
TH-PH	0.211	0.314	0.260
TH-SG	0.391	0.454	0.383
TH-TW	0.141	0.206	0.169
PH-HK	0.200	0.351	0.309
PH-IN	0.188	0.312	0.274
PH-JP	0.082	0.183	0.159
PH-KO	0.053	0.215	0.188
PH-SG	0.266	0.407	0.361
PH-TW	0.139	0.146	0.127
MA-IN	0.208	0.262	0.164
MA-KO	0.108	0.215	0.134
MA-TW	0.142	0.171	0.106
IN-HK	0.172	0.339	0.172
IN-JP	0.060	0.198	0.098
IN-KO	0.015	0.184	0.090
IN-SG	0.222	0.404	0.210
IN-TW	0.043	0.155	0.076
SG-HK	0.504	0.649	0.455
SG-JP	0.319	0.375	0.235
SG-KO	0.133	0.356	0.222
SG-TW	0.174	0.284	0.175
TW-HK	0.141	0.267	0.309
TW-JP	0.143	0.218	0.254
TW-KO	0.094	0.260	0.302
HK-JP	0.251	0.433	0.300
HK-KO	0.077	0.355	0.241
KO-JP	0.047	0.317	0.092

Notes: See notes in Exhibit 12.2. For the cases displaying a decrease in correlation, pair-wise correlations between the stock returns in Malaysia and those in Thailand, the Philippines, Hong Kong, Japan, and Singapore will not be reported.

level in 1998. Although all six countries were hit hard, the stock returns of Thailand during the early stages of the crisis showed very low, and even negative, correlations (as low as –0.055) with the stock returns of the other five countries.[9]

However, throughout 1998 the correlations became significantly higher and persisted at the higher levels, ranging from 0.30 to 0.47, before declining at the end of 1998.[10]

Consistent with the observations made by Bae et al. (2003) and Kallberg et al. (2005), our study provides evidence of contagion effects in these Asian stock markets in the early phases of the crisis and then a transition to herding behavior in the latter phases. Here contagion and herding behavior are distinguished in the sense that contagion describes the spread of shocks from one market to another with a

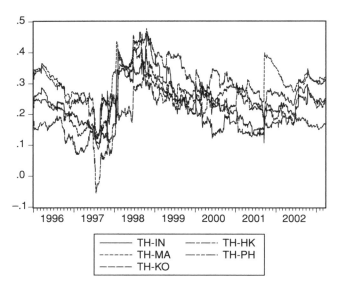

Exhibit 12.4 Dynamic Correlations between the Stock Returns of Thailand and Those of the Other Five Crisis Countries (1996–2003)

significant increase in correlation between markets, while herding describes the simultaneous behavior of investors across different markets with high correlation coefficients in all markets.[11] Our interpretation is that in the early phases of the crisis, investors focus mainly on local country information, so that contagion takes place. As the crisis becomes public news, investor decisions tend to converge due to herding behavior, creating higher correlations. Specifically, when Thailand devalued its currency, investors were focusing on asset management in Thailand's market, paying little attention to other countries' markets. As investors began to withdraw their funds from Thailand and reinvest in other countries in the region, this action resulted in decreased correlations at the beginning of the crisis. As more and more asset prices declined in neighboring countries due to the contagion effect spreading through various channels, investors began to panic and withdraw funds from all of the Asian economies.[12] During this process, the convergence of market consensus and the stock returns in these economies showed a gradual increase in correlation. This phenomenon is identified as the first phase of the crisis.

Given the increasing uncertainty in the markets, the cost of collecting credible information is relatively high during such a period, and investors are likely to follow major investors in making their own investing decisions. Any public news about one country may be interpreted as information regarding the entire region. That is why we see consistently high correlations in 1998; this phenomenon is a result of herding behavior and identified as the second phase. As observed, the second phase started when South Korea was affected and floated its currency, the won, on November 17, 1997. Thereafter, news in any country would affect other countries, representing the period of the most widespread panic.[13]

Based on these observations, there are two important implications from the investor's perspective. First, a higher level of correlation implies that the benefit from market-portfolio diversification diminishes, since holding a portfolio with diverse country stocks is subject to systematic risk. Second, a higher volatility of the correlation coefficients suggests that the stability of the correlation is less reliable, casting some doubt on using the estimated correlation coefficient in guiding portfolio decisions.

To further investigate the dynamic feature of the correlation changes associated with different phases of crises, we define the first phase of the crisis period as July 2, 1997, to November 17, 1997, when Korea floated the won; the second phase of the Asian crisis is November 18, 1997, to December 31, 1998, when most of these countries started to recover; the post-crisis period is January 1, 1999, to March 21, 2003. Another GARCH model was run to look at the differences in averages and volatilities of correlations at different phases defined above. The evidence (not reported) shows that the average correlation during the first phase of the crisis is not significantly different from that of the pre-crisis period. This may reveal the fact that there was a drop in the correlation coefficients at the beginning of the crisis because investors may have thought that the news involved only a single country and the crisis signal was not fully recognized.

However, as time passed and investors gradually learned the negative news affecting market development, they started to follow the crowd; that is, they began to imitate more reputable and sophisticated investors. At the moment when any public news about one country is interpreted as information about the entire region, the correlation becomes more significant. Indeed, as shown in our results and consistent with the comovement paths shown in Exhibit 12.4, correlation coefficients are consistently high across different pairs of countries in the second phase of the crisis and thus support the herding behavior hypothesis. Obviously, the herding phenomenon will negate the benefit of holding a diversified international portfolio in the region.

In the post-crisis period, the correlation coefficients decreased significantly in all cases except Korea and Hong Kong, where the stock markets might still have been experiencing some hangover effect. For the rest of the markets, as expected, investors became more rational in analyzing the fundamentals of the individual markets rather than herding after others. Thus, the correlations between market returns declined. The high correlation between the stock returns of Thailand and Korea as well as between Thailand and Hong Kong after the crisis is consistent with the wake-up call hypothesis, where investors realized that there was some similarity between the two markets' fundamentals after the crisis. Therefore, their trading strategy was based on related information from both markets.[14]

The results also indicate more volatile changes in the correlation coefficients in the first and second phases of the crisis; the explosive changes in volatility even extended into the post-crisis period. The evidence thus suggests that when crisis hits the market, the correlation coefficients could vary greatly, and this variability could be significantly prolonged. As a result, the estimates of risk models based on constant correlation coefficients can be very misleading.

A COMPARISON TO THE LITERATURE

It is of interest to compare our results with those presented by Forbes and Rigobon (2002). To elucidate, we depict both the dynamic Thailand-HK correlation coefficient series (reproduced from Exhibit 12.4) and the constant correlation coefficient series in Exhibit 12.5. The solid line shows the time-varying correlation derived

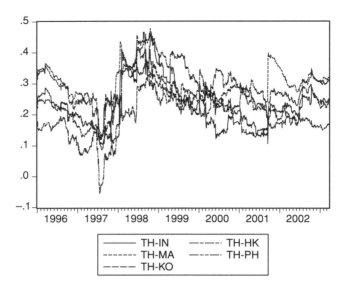

Exhibit 12.5 Dynamic and Constant Correlation Coefficients of the Stock Returns between Thailand and Hong Kong (1996–2003)

from our model for the period from January 1, 1996, to December 31, 1998. The broken lines show FR's adjusted correlation (AB and CD) for the Thailand-HK pair from January 1, 1996, to November 16, 1997, using October 17, 1997, as a breakpoint for defining periods of stability and turmoil. Two observations are immediately apparent by comparing the two models. First, the constant correlation model fails to reveal the time-varying feature and, hence, is unable to reflect the dynamic market conditions. Second, the estimate from the constant correlation model is conditional on the sample size of the regime or the length of the window for calculating. For instance, by estimating the correlation coefficients based on FR's sample periods, we obtain estimated values of 0.098 for the stable period (line AB) and 0.042 the turmoil period (line CD). By extending the turmoil period to a longer sample period, as we have done in this study, the correlation coefficient jumps to 0.244, as shown in the broken line (EF) in Exhibit 12.5. Thus, our finding is consistent with FR's analysis if a longer sample period is included. However, FR's analysis can only reflect average behavior for each subperiod; the dynamic correlation coefficient is able to capture the dynamic elements continually emerging from the markets.

It should be noted that the announcements of changes in foreign-currency sovereign credit ratings for a particular country in the region received substantial attention from policy makers and investors during the 1997 Asian financial crisis. We used a binary setting to capture rating changes and/or "outlook changes" and the on-watch or off-watch list of markets under investigation.

To provide an illustration of the influence of news about sovereign credit-rating changes in its own and foreign countries on cross-country correlation coefficients, we estimate another GARCH model with the news effect. The estimation results (not reported) show that all of the markets are negatively influenced by the previous day's changes in sovereign credit ratings in Thailand. However, a positive significant effect is found in the Indonesian and Hong Kong markets in the contemporaneous term, suggesting that the responses of investors in Indonesia and Hong Kong markets are more sensitive to announcements of rating changes in both domestic and foreign markets. The joint tests also find strong supporting evidence of the significant effect of sovereign credit-rating changes, domestic and foreign, on cross-country correlation coefficients of stock returns.[15]

CONCLUSIONS

This study examines the contagion effect during the 1997–1998 Asian financial crises with specific focus on the relationship between the stock returns of various crisis-hit countries. We conclude that there is evidence of contagion effects during the Asian financial crisis, a finding that does not agree with the "no contagion" argument presented by some researchers, for example, Forbes and Rigobon (2002).

By applying a dynamic conditional-correlation (DCC-GARCH) model to eight Asian daily stock-return data, this study further identifies two phases of the Asian crisis. In the first phase, the crisis displays a process of increasing correlations (contagion), while in the second phase, investor behavior converges and correlations are significantly higher across the Asian countries in the sample (herding). The contagion effect takes place early in the crisis, while the herding behavior dominates the latter stages of the crisis. The apparently high correlation coefficients during crisis periods imply that the gain from international diversification by holding a portfolio of diverse stocks from these contagion countries declines because these stock markets are commonly exposed to systematic risk.

An important finding that emerges from our investigation of the dynamic behavior of stock-return correlations is that the cross-country correlation structure of stock returns is subject to structural changes, both in level and in variability. The correlation coefficients are found to be significantly influenced by news about changes in foreign-currency sovereign credit ratings in its own and foreign countries. This study suggests that both investors and international rating agencies play significant roles in shaping the structure of dynamic correlations in the Asian markets.

NOTES

1. This is a shorter version of our earlier paper published in the *Journal of International Money and Finance*, 2007. A detailed specification of the model is available in Chiang, Jeon, and Li (2007).

2. Forbes and Rigobon (2002) define *contagion* as significant increases in cross-market comovement. Any continued high level of market correlation suggests strong linkages between the two economies and is defined as *interdependence*. Following this line of argument, contagion must involve a dynamic increment in correlation.

3. Pritsker (2001) summarizes four types of transmission channels: the correlated information channel (King and Wadhwani 1990; von Furstenberg and Jeon 1989) or the wake-up call hypothesis (Sachs et al. 1996), liquidity channel (Claessens et al. 2001; Forbes 2004), the cross-market hedging channel (Calvo and Mendoza 2000; Kodres and Pritsker 2002), and the wealth effect channel (Kyle and Xiong 2001). Many of the empirical research papers on the analysis of contagion effects turn to the investigation of asset-return

comovements, applying various forms of correlation analyses. Along this line, contagion is defined as a significant increase in correlation between asset returns in different markets.

4. FR argue that during the Asian crisis, the events in Asia became headline news in the world only after the Hong Kong market declined sharply in October 1997. Therefore, they use Hong Kong as the only source of contagion and October 17, 1997, as the breakpoint of the whole sample period.

5. The order of these countries is Thailand (managed float of the baht on July 2, 1997), the Philippines (wider float of the peso on July 11, 1997), Malaysia (floated the ringgit on July 14, 1997), Indonesia (floated the rupiah on August 14, 1997), Singapore (large decline in stock and currency markets on August 28, 1997), Taiwan (large decline in stock and currency markets on October 17, 1997), Hong Kong (large decline in the stock market on October 17, 1997), Korea (floated the won on November 17, 1997), and Japan (stock-market crash on December 19, 1997). Their respective breakpoints are also used, with similar results.

6. There are $(1 + 8) * 8/2 = 36$ pair-wise correlations with five correlation decreases in the case of Malaysia.

7. The contemporary correlation coefficients between U.S. stock returns and Asian stock returns may have less practical meaning due to time zone differences. The Asian stock returns in day t are expected to be the most affected by U.S. stock returns in day $t - 1$.

8. Hong Kong is added to the analysis because of its significance in relation to Asian markets and it is convenient for comparing our results with the study in a similar setting (Forbes and Rigobon 2002).

9. It should be noted that the low correlation in mid-1997 is not evidence against the contagion effect. Our explanation will be provided at a later point.

10. Most of the correlation coefficients started to decline around October 20, 1998. A similar model is run for the exchange-rate changes in these countries. However, relative to the stock markets, the currency markets had less activity and the estimated pairwise correlation coefficients could not explain all of the correlation changes in the stock markets. The evidence is consistent with results reported by Kallberg et al. (2005). One possible explanation is that the currency markets received more government intervention, setting a fixed parity relation with the U.S. dollar.

11. As noted by Hirshleifer and Teoh (2003), herding–dispersing is defined to include any behavioral similarity–dissimilarity brought about by actual interactions of individuals. Herding is a phenomenon of convergence in response to sudden shifts of investor sentiment or due to cross-market hedging. It should be mentioned that observation of others can lead to dispersing instead of herding if there are opposing preferences.

12. Kaminsky et al. (2000) indicate that bond and equity flows to Asia collapsed from their peak of US$38 billion in 1996 to US$9 billion in 1998. In particular Taiwan, Singapore, Hong Kong, and Korea experienced, respectively, 12.91 percent, 11.75 percent, 6.91 percent, and 6.49 percent average net selling (as a percentage of the holdings at the end of the preceding quarter) in the first two quarters following the outbreak of the crisis.

13. Applying the threshold-cointegration model to daily exchange rates, both spot and forward, Jeon and Seo (2003) identify the exact breakpoint as November 18, 1997, for the Korean won, and August 15, 1997, for the Thai baht.

14. Estimations are also conducted to investigate the possible existence of a contagion effect between Japan and the crisis countries. Our results (not reported) show that the impact of the Asian crisis on Japan is not as dramatic as events such as the 1990 Gulf War or the September 11, 2001, attacks. Starting from early 1998, the correlation coefficients rise

gradually and reach a high value of around 0.25 during the Russia crisis and the near-default of the U.S. hedge fund Long-Term Capital Management (LTCM) in the United States. Our evidence is consistent with the findings of Arestis et al. (2003) that contagion from the Asian crisis countries to Japan took place in early 1998. The contagion from the Asian-crisis countries to Japan was relatively slow and moderate compared with other events or factors.

15. The reported statistics are available in Table 5 in Chiang et al. (2007).

REFERENCES

Arestis, P., G. M. Caporale, and A. Cipollini. 2003. "Testing for Financial Contagion Between Developed and Emerging Markets During the 1997 East Asian Crisis." *Levy Economics Institute of Bard College, Working Paper* 370.

Bae, K-H., G. A. Karyoli, and R. M. Stulz. 2003. "A New Approach to Measuring Financial Contagion." *Review of Financial Studies* 16:3, 717–763.

Basu, R. 2002. "Financial Contagion and Investor 'Learning': An Empirical Investigation." *IMF Working Paper* 02/218.

Bollerslev, T., R. Y. Chou, and K. F. Kroner. 1992. "ARCH Modeling in Finance: A Review of the Theory and Empirical Evidence." *Journal of Econometrics* 52:5–59.

Bordo, M. D., and A. P. Murshid. 2001. "Are Financial Crises Becoming More Contagious? What Is the Historical Evidence on Contagion?" In S. Claessens and K. Forbes, eds. *International Financial Contagion*, 367–402. Norwell, MA: Kluwer Academic.

Calvo, G., and E. Mendoza. 2000. "Rational Contagion and the Globalization of Securities Market." *Journal of International Economics* 51:79–113.

Chiang, T. C., B. N. Jeon, and H. Li. 2007. "Dynamic Correlation Analysis of Financial Contagion: Evidence from Asian Markets." *Journal of International Money and Finance* 26:7, 1206–1228.

Claessens, S., R. Dornbusch, and Y. C. Park. 2001. "Contagion: Why Crises Spread and How This Can Be Stopped." In S. Claessens and K. Forbes, eds. *International Financial Contagion*, 19–42. Norwell, MA: Kluwer Academic.

Corsetti, G., M. Pericoli, and M. Sbracia. 2005. "Some Contagion, Some Interdependence: More Pitfalls in Tests of Financial Contagion." *Journal of International Money and Finance* 24:8, 1177–1199.

Engle, R. E. 2002. "Dynamic Conditional Correlation: A Simple Class of Multivariate Generalized Autoregressive Conditional Heteroskedasticity Models." *Journal of Business and Economic Statistics* 20:339–350.

Forbes, K. 2004. "The Asian Flu and Russian Virus: Firm-Level Evidence on How Crises Are Transmitted Internationally." *Journal of International Economics* 63:1, 59–92.

Forbes, K., and R. Rigobon. 2002. "No Contagion, Only Interdependence: Measuring Stock Market Comovements." *Journal of Finance* 57:5, 2223–2261.

Froot, K., P. O'Connell, and M. S. Seasholes. 2001. "The Portfolio Flows of International Investors." *Journal of Financial Economics* 59:2, 151–193.

Hirshleifer, D., and S. H. Teoh. 2003. "Herd Behaviour and Cascading in Capital Markets: A Review and Synthesis." *European Financial Management* 9:1, 25–66.

Jeon, B. N., and B. Seo. 2003. "The Impact of the Asian Financial Crisis on Foreign Exchange Market Efficiency: The Case of East Asian Countries." *Pacific-Basin Finance Journal* 11:509–525.

Kallberg, J. G., C. H. Liu, and P. Pasquariello. 2005. "An Examination of the Asian Crisis: Regime Shifts in Currency and Equity Markets." *Journal of Business* 78:1, 169–211.

Kaminsky, G., R. Lyons, and S. Schmukler. 2000. "Fragility, Liquidity, and Risk: The Behavior of Mutual Funds During Crises." A paper prepared for the World Bank, IMF, ADB conference on International Financial Contagion: How It Spreads and How It Can Be Stopped. Washington, DC, February 3–4.

King, M., and S. Wadhwani. 1990. "Transmission of Volatility Between Stock Markets." *Review of Financial Studies* 3:5–33.

Kodres, L. E., and M. Pritsker. 2002. "A Rational Expectations Model of Financial Contagion." *Journal of Finance* 57:2, 769–799.

Kyle, A., and W. Xiong. 2001. "Contagion as a Wealth Effect." *Journal of Finance* 56:4, 1401–1440.

Pritsker, M. 2001. "The Channels for Financial Contagion." In S. Claessens and K. Forbes, eds. *International Financial Contagion*, 67–97. Norwell, MA: Kluwer Academic.

Sachs, J., A. Tornell, and A. Velasco. 1996. "Financial Crises in Emerging Markets: The Lessons from 1995." *Brookings Papers on Economic Activity* 1:146–215.

von Furstenberg, G., and B. N. Jeon. 1989. "International Stock Price Movements: Links and Messages." *Brookings Papers on Economic Activity* 1:125–167.

ABOUT THE AUTHORS

Thomas C. Chiang is a professor of finance at the LeBow College of Business, Drexel University, where he holds the Marshall M. Austin Chair. Dr. Chiang has done extensive research in financial contagion, international finance, asset pricing, behavioral finance, and financial econometrics. His articles have appeared in the *Journal of Banking and Finance, Journal of International Money and Finance, Quantitative Finance, Journal of Money, Credit and Banking, Journal of Forecasting, Pacific-Basin Finance Journal, Journal of Financial Research, Weltwirtschaftliches Archiv*, among others. Dr. Chiang received his PhD from Pennsylvania State University, with a concentration in financial economics and econometrics.

Bang Nam Jeon is professor of economics and international business at Drexel University, Philadelphia. He holds a PhD degree in economics from Indiana University, Bloomington, Indiana. His research interests include international finance, international banking, FDI and international commercial policy, and regional economic integration among Asia-Pacific economies. He has published papers in economics and international business journals, such as *Brookings Papers on Economic Activity, Journal of International Money and Finance, Journal of Banking and Finance, Review of International Economics, Contemporary Economic Policy, Research in International Business and Finance, Pacific-Basin Finance Journal, East Asia Law Review* (University of Pennsylvania Law School), and *Journal of the Japanese and International Economies*. He has been invited to present his papers by Brookings Institution, Federal Reserve Bank of St. Louis, Soongsil University Brain Korea 21st Century (BK21) Program, and most recently, by Asian Development Bank (ADB) and the Bank of Korea.

Huimin Li is an associate professor of finance at West Chester University of Pennsylvania. She earned her PhD in business administration from Drexel University in 2004. Dr. Li has written articles on financial contagion, interlinkages among international stock markets and oil markets, and volatility of financial markets. She has been published in the *Journal of International Money and Finance, Quantitative Finance, Global Finance Journal, International Review of Financial Analysis, Journal of Economics and Business, Finance Letters, Energy Economics*, the *North American Journal of Economics and Finance*, and *Issues in Innovation*.

CHAPTER 13

Contagion Effects, Informational Effects, and Economic Fundamentals*

An Analysis of Exchange Rate Dynamics during the Asian Currency Crisis

KAM-HON CHU
Associate Professor of Economics, Memorial University of Newfoundland, Canada

W e apply regression and cluster analysis techniques to study the Asian currency crisis and find that short-run exchange-rate dynamics were largely unexplained by macroeconomic fundamentals alone. The collapse of the baht conveyed information about the stability of other Asian currencies and triggered both structural changes and warranted contagion, as the crisis spread from Thailand to economies with similar economic conditions.

INTRODUCTION

A central issue in international finance is whether currency crises are largely attributable to economic fundamentals or contagion. Baig and Goldfajn (1999), among many others, provide evidence suggesting that the Asian currency crisis was contagious. The various empirical findings and interpretations, however, are controversial because of lack of a consensus on the notion of contagion. For example, Eichengreen et al. (1996) define contagion as the occurrence of currency crises in at least two different countries in any given period. This definition is not universally accepted, however. Schwartz (1998) argues that, "to show that Thailand spread contagion, however, it would be necessary to demonstrate that otherwise sound economies suffered the Thai fate." Even if currency crises are contagious,

*This chapter is an abridged version of a paper with the same title by Chu, Chan, and Sin (2000), in which details of the theory, empirical procedures and results, and further references can be found. My sincere thanks to my former co-authors Bob Chan and Choryiu Sin for their contributions in the earlier paper, without which this chapter is impossible. All errors in this chapter are, however, entirely mine.

115

why and how contagion spreads out remain to be explained. Simply put, why did the collapse of the baht in 1997 impact adversely some but not all Asian currencies?

In this study, we measure contagion as excessive correlations across economies in exchange-rate returns after taking into account the impact of economic fundamentals on exchange rates. We also distinguish between warranted and unwarranted contagion (Gerlach and Smets 1995). Warranted contagion occurs when a currency crisis spreads to another currency or currencies with macroeconomic background similar to the original crisis country. By contrast, unwarranted contagion takes place when a crisis spreads to another currency that should not have suffered speculative attacks based on its economic fundamentals. Instead, the contagion can be due to speculation or herd behavior. This distinction sheds light on how and why some currencies are vulnerable to contagion.

A closely related concept is informational effects (Eichengreen et al. 1995), according to which the collapse of a currency conveys information about the stability of other currencies. The information leads to different possible outcomes, depending on how economic agents change their expectations and behaviors. The possible outcomes include structural change due to a varied impact of fundamentals, warranted contagion, and unwarranted contagion.

Our objective is to disentangle the effects of contagion, information, and fundamentals on exchange rates using the Asian currency crisis as a case study. More specifically, what was the role of economic fundamentals as determinants of exchange rates? Were there informational effects affecting exchange-rate dynamics? Was the Asian currency crisis contagious? And if so, was contagion warranted or unwarranted?

DATA AND METHODOLOGY

Based on data availability, our sample includes nine East Asian economies—Hong Kong, Indonesia, Japan, Korea, Malaysia, the Philippines, Singapore, Taiwan, and Thailand—with diverse economic structures and policies. To capture the short-lived contagious effects, if any, high-frequency (i.e., daily or weekly) data are preferred to low-frequency (annual or quarterly) data. However, high-frequency data are unlikely to reveal the laggardly effects of fundamentals. As a compromise, we use monthly data in order to obtain reliable regression results and meaningful interpretations. Data are collected from *International Financial Statistics* and other sources, and the sample period covers January 1991 to December 1998. When Thailand devalued the baht on July 2, 1997, the Asian currency crisis broke out and spread to other economies. For comparison and analysis, we divide the sample into a pre-crisis period (January 1991–June 1997) and a post-crisis period (July 1997–December 1998).

We postulate that the exchange-rate dynamics are simultaneously driven by economic fundamentals and other unspecified factors including contagious and informational effects. The impact of fundamentals on exchange rates can differ across economies because of diverse economic structures and policies. Furthermore, the estimated impact of fundamentals can be sensitive to the choice of theory of exchange-rate determination. Therefore, we adopt an eclectic model (Gandolfo 1995, 397–400), which encompasses four classes of model—the flexible-price monetary model of Frenkel (1976) and Bilson (1978), the sticky-price monetary model

Exhibit 13.1   Predicted Signs of Regression Coefficients

Macroeconomic Variable	Predicted Sign	Theory
Money Supply	+	All Four Theories
Interest Rate	+	FB
	−	DF, HM, HMR
Industrial Production	−	All Four Theories
Foreign Reserves	0	FB, DF, HM
	−	HMR
International Debt	0	FB, DF, HM
	+	HMR
Exports	0	FB, DF, HMR
	−	HM
Imports	0	FB, DF, HMR
	+	HM

Notes:
1. The "+", "−", "0" signs denote respectively currency depreciation, appreciation, and no impact (or not considered by the theory) as a result of an increase in the macroeconomic variable.
2. BF, DF, HM, and HMR denote respectively the Bilson-Frenkel approach, Dornbusch-Frenkel approach, the Hooper-Morton model without risk, and Hooper-Morton model with risk.

of Dornbusch (1976) and Frankel (1979), the sticky-price asset model of Hooper and Morton (1982) and their model with risk—as special cases (see Exhibit 13.1).

In the actual estimation we make two modifications to this model. First, one-period lagged macroeconomic variables instead of contemporaneous variables are used for analytical tractability and meaningful interpretations. Contemporaneous regression results can be difficult to interpret because economic fundamentals and the exchange rate interact with each other. The use of lagged variables allows us to identify the effects of fundamentals on the exchange rate. Second, we focus on the return rate (i.e., percentage change) of the exchange rate rather than its level. For each currency, the model is specified as:

$$\Delta e_t = b_0 + b_1 \Delta e_{t-1} + b_2 \Delta (m - m_{us})_{t-1} + b_3 \Delta (y - y_{us})_{t-1} + b_4 \Delta (i - i_{us})_{t-1}$$
$$+ b_5 \Delta exp_{t-1} + b_6 \Delta imp_{t-1} + b_7 \Delta res_{t-1} + b_8 \Delta fd_{t-1} + \varepsilon_t \qquad (13.1)$$

where the variables e, m, y, i, exp, imp, res, and fd, stands for the spot exchange rate, the money supply, industrial production (as a proxy for real GDP), short-term interest rate, exports, imports, foreign reserves, and foreign debt, respectively, and ε is a random disturbance term with the conventional assumptions. The subscripts us and t denote the variables for the U.S. economy and time respectively.

We apply ordinary least squares (OLS) technique to each currency as specified above and also seemingly unrelated regression (SUR) technique to a system of nine equations to account for the potential interrelationship of currency movements. The impact of fundamentals on exchange rates can be assessed by the econometric results, such as statistical significance and magnitudes of the regression coefficients, how good the model is in explaining the variations in exchange rates, and so forth.

Under the informational effects hypothesis, the collapse of a currency conveys information about the impending collapse of another currency or other currencies. The informational effects can be reflected in at least two ways. First, a structural change in the forces driving the currency that suffers a currency crisis is ensued by a structural change in another currency, as currency traders revise their expectations and portfolios accordingly based on the information revealed by the crisis. Empirically, we can compare the regression results for the pre- and post-crisis periods to verify any significant change in the impact of fundamentals.

Second, informational and contagion effects can coexist. Speculative attacks on a currency provide information about the instability of another currency or its monetary authorities' commitment to exchange-rate stability, which can in turn trigger speculative attacks. By our definition, contagion exists when there are excessive correlations among the currencies after controlling for the effects of fundamentals. Accordingly, the regression residuals can be interpreted as exchange-rate variations unexplained by fundamentals. The correlations of the SUR regression residuals reflect the extent of informational and contagious effects due to a currency crisis, because they capture the interrelationship among contemporaneous disturbances across different currencies *after controlling for the effects of the economic fundamentals*. Intuitively, in the presence of contagion the correlation coefficients for the post-crisis period are expected to be substantially positive and significantly higher in value than before the crisis.

To determine whether contagion is warranted, we apply cluster analysis to classify the economies into groups of similar economic structures or conditions based on changes in domestic interest rates and inflation rates and percentage changes in exports, imports, and the money supply during the post-crisis period. Two economies are similar in economic conditions if they have similar changes in these economic variables. The choice of these criteria is suggestive rather than definitive. Our objective is to explore whether the regression residuals are systematically related to those economic variables. In the Asian currency crisis, the collapse of the baht probably prompted currency traders to reassess the other economies' performance based on their economic conditions. In the case of warranted contagion, the currency crisis tends to spill over to another economy (or economies) with economic conditions similar to Thailand's. The closer the similarity, the more vulnerable is that economy to currency crisis. Empirically, the residuals for two similar economies tend to be positively and highly correlated with each other in the post-crisis period.

By contrast, in the case of unwarranted contagion the residuals tend to be positively and highly correlated across the board after the crisis. Irrational and herd behavior dominates economic fundamentals so much that contagion spreads out to other economies irrespective of the degrees of similarity in economic conditions.

EMPIRICAL RESULTS

The nine exchange rates were relatively stable before the Asian financial crisis but responded quite differently to the crisis (Exhibit 13.2 and 13.3). The currencies of Indonesia, Korea, Malaysia, and the Philippines depreciated sharply along with the baht, whereas the other currencies remained relatively stable. Except for the Hong Kong dollar, exchange rates became not only more volatile but also more

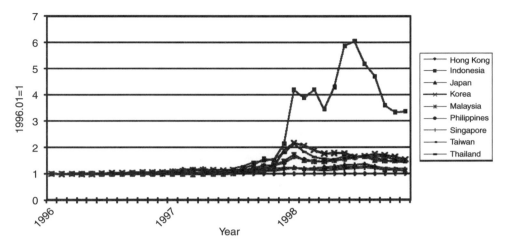

Exhibit 13.2   Asian Currency Crisis

positively correlated in the post-crisis period (Exhibits 13.3–13.5). The higher post-crisis correlations are prima facie evidence of contagion, but it is premature to conclude until we have accounted for the impact of economic fundamentals on exchange rates.

Similar to the findings of many other empirical studies, our regression results indicate that a large proportion of short-run variations in exchange rates are unexplained by economic fundamentals. Nonetheless, the fundamentals are not all immaterial in explaining exchange rates in the short run as some variables are statistically significant and have the correct signs as predicted by theory. For brevity, we report here only the OLS results for the pre-crisis period to let the reader have an idea about the impact of fundamentals on exchange rates (Exhibit 13.6).[1]

The statistical tests (Exhibit 13.7) formally confirm that all the economies except Hong Kong and Taiwan experienced a regime shift after the crisis. This is

Exhibit 13.3   Summary Statistics of Rates of Return on Exchange Rates

	Pre-Crisis				Post-Crisis			
Currency of	Mean	Std. Dev.	Min.	Max.	Mean	Std. Dev.	Min.	Max.
Hong Kong	−0.010	0.110	−0.515	0.258	0.007	0.070	−0.129	0.129
Indonesia	0.330	0.229	−0.617	1.259	6.407	22.491	−26.884	67.722
Japan	−0.201	2.801	−8.167	8.070	0.163	3.815	−10.397	4.043
Korea	0.279	0.782	−1.558	3.330	1.716	10.584	−8.857	36.954
Malaysia	−0.088	1.182	−3.403	5.304	2.282	6.979	−14.101	15.680
Philippines	−0.076	1.323	−4.553	3.504	2.182	5.379	−7.126	13.776
Singapore	−0.244	0.906	−2.091	2.299	0.795	3.028	−5.343	5.884
Taiwan	0.034	0.943	−2.305	3.665	0.817	2.748	−4.569	7.273
Thailand	0.030	0.426	−1.045	1.305	1.895	9.119	−15.378	17.237

Note: Positive (negative) rate of return means depreciation (appreciation) of the currency against the U.S. dollar.

Exhibit 13.4 Correlations of Exchange-Rate Changes for the Pre-Crisis Period

	Hong Kong	Indonesia	Japan	Korea	Malaysia	Philippines	Singapore	Taiwan	Thailand
Hong Kong	1.0000								
Indonesia	0.1261	1.0000							
Japan	−0.0179	0.1071	1.0000						
Korea	−0.0156	−0.0059	0.3731	1.0000					
Malaysia	−0.0014	0.0484	0.2272	0.0332	1.0000				
Philippines	0.0289	0.0550	−0.1443	0.0604	0.0910	1.0000			
Singapore	−0.0774	0.1498	0.6012	0.3311	0.2955	−0.1218	1.0000		
Taiwan	0.0851	−0.0337	0.4185	0.1614	0.0703	0.0170	0.4435	1.0000	
Thailand	0.0118	0.1588	0.9005	0.3224	0.2724	−0.0902	0.7306	0.4010	1.0000

Exhibit 13.5 Correlations of Exchange-Rate Changes for the Post-Crisis Period

	Hong Kong	Indonesia	Japan	Korea	Malaysia	Philippines	Singapore	Taiwan	Thailand
Hong Kong	1.0000								
Indonesia	0.2303	1.0000							
Japan	−0.0038	0.4237	1.0000						
Korea	0.1335	0.5204	0.2202	1.0000					
Malaysia	0.0507	0.6918	0.4688	0.4871	1.0000				
Philippines	0.1302	0.6957	0.3141	0.5385	0.7887	1.0000			
Singapore	0.0158	0.7590	0.6364	0.5440	0.8032	0.7537	1.0000		
Taiwan	−0.2392	0.5405	0.6540	0.4804	0.5808	0.5302	0.7569	1.0000	
Thailand	0.0035	0.6380	0.4051	0.6220	0.7935	0.8369	0.8197	0.6051	1.0000

Exhibit 13.6   OLS Results for the Pre-Crisis Period

Equation	Intercept	LDV	M2	INT	IP	RES	FD	EXP	IMP	R^2	Adj. R^2	DW
Hong Kong	-0.997×10^{-4} (−0.720)	−0.0106 (−0.087)	0.0011 (0.191)	-0.111×10^{-3} (−0.301)	0.850×10^{-3} (0.748)			−0.0060 (−1.979)*	0.0046 (1.625)†	0.060	−0.021	2.03
Indonesia	0.0021 (4.036)***	0.3017 (2.675)***	−0.0055 (−0.308)	-0.178×10^{-3} (−1.221)	−0.006 (−1.405)†	0.0173 (2.151)**	0.0017 (0.399)	−0.0019 (−0.622)	0.0013 (0.572)	0.213	0.119	1.97
Japan	0.0021 (0.634)	0.0805 (0.641)	−0.3655 (−1.220)	0.0256 (2.052)**	−0.2277 (−1.243)	−0.0278 (−0.260)	0.3814 (3.792)***	−0.0081 (−0.241)	0.0058 (0.134)	0.314	0.232	2.02
Korea	0.227×10^{-3} (0.199)	0.3840 (3.650)***	0.1670 (3.692)***	0.0011 (1.748)†	0.0391 (1.589)†	−0.0187 (−0.737)	0.0054 (0.213)	−0.0083 (−1.006)	−0.0259 (−1.901)*	0.385	0.312	1.79
Malaysia	−0.0025 (−1.506)†	0.3019 (2.581)**	0.1185 (1.583)†	−0.0020 (−0.494)	−0.0085 (−0.274)	0.0094 (0.411)	0.0216 (1.343)†	0.0183 (0.952)	−0.0262 (−1.129)	0.216	0.122	1.77
Philippines	−0.0020 (−1.147)	0.4357 (3.927)***	0.1286 (2.178)**	−0.0011 (−0.857)	−0.0265 (−1.147)	−0.0081 (−0.527)	0.0063 (0.281)	−0.0149 (−0.969)	0.0065 (0.374)	0.281	0.195	1.80
Singapore	0.633×10^{-3} (0.432)	−0.0111 (−0.082)	0.0612 (0.634)	0.0046 (2.304)**	0.0053 (0.342)	−0.2967 (−3.715)***	0.0913 (2.221)**	−0.0390 (−2.1910)**	0.0063 (0.355)	0.403	0.332	1.92
Taiwan	-0.918×10^{-4} (−0.070)	0.4383 (4.097)***	−0.0431 (−0.423)	−0.0016 (−1.289)	−0.0425 (−3.067)***	0.1107 (1.622)†	0.0414 (1.619)†	0.0297 (2.309)	−0.0098 (−0.777)	0.344	0.266	1.68
Thailand	0.201×10^{-3} (0.259)	0.3454 (3.078)***	−0.0238 (−0.441)	-0.450×10^{-3} (−2.093)**	0.0134 (1.439)†	0.0192 (0.957)	0.0019 (0.161)	0.245×10^{-3} (0.036)	−0.0129 (−1.882)*	0.217	0.123	1.86

Notes:

1. Figures in parentheses are t-statistics.
2. ***, **, *, and † denote statistical significance at the 1%, 5%, 10%, and 20% levels respectively.

Exhibit 13.7   Results of Tests for Structural Changes

	Chow	Likelihood Ratio
Hong Kong	0.238	1.952
Indonesia	7.962***	62.169***
Japan	3.158***	29.943***
Korea	8.840***	66.986***
Malaysia	10.684***	76.341***
Philippines	4.381***	39.302***
Singapore	2.426**	23.840***
Taiwan	0.601	6.522
Thailand	11.308***	79.298***

Note: ***, **, *, and † denote statistical significance at the 1%, 5%, 10%, and 20% levels respectively.

consistent with the informational effects hypothesis: The speculative attacks on the baht and its subsequent devaluation released information that affected traders' expectations about other currencies, thus causing structural changes. Our regression results also suggest that currency traders probably monitored and responded more closely to changes in economic fundamentals in the post-crisis period, although the exchange-rate dynamics remain largely unexplained by our model.[2]

Therefore, we cannot rule out the possibility of contagion in driving exchange rates. Exhibit 13.8 and Exhibit 13.9 show clearly that most regression residuals are positively related, reflecting that certain unspecified factors simultaneously affecting the currencies in the same direction. More importantly, there is evidence in support of contagion. First, the number of high correlation coefficients (a value of 0.5 or above) jumps from 6 before the crisis to 15 after the crisis. Second, 23 of these coefficients are higher in value. Third, the coefficients between the baht and almost all other currencies also increase in value, consistent with the notion that contagion spread out from Thailand to other economies. Finally, half of the 36 correlation coefficients record phenomenal increases (an increase in value of 0.25 or more). Noticeably, substantial increases are found between the baht and the currencies of Korea (+0.39), Malaysia (+0.45), the Philippines (+0.51), and Taiwan (+0.40), suggesting that these four economies were more vulnerable to contagion.

To determine if contagion is warranted, we examine the cluster analysis results. As a picture is worth more than a thousand words, let us interpret the results with reference to the dendrogram (Exhibit 13.10). Singapore and Taiwan have the closest similarity in economic conditions and form a group first, then joined by Japan to form a larger group. On the other hand, the three Tigers—Malaysia, the Philippines, and Thailand—form another group of similar economic conditions. Hong Kong lies between the above two groups, followed by Korea. Indonesia stands out on its own due to its dramatic developments in political and economic instability in 1998. Though imperfect, the cluster analysis results serve reasonably well in measuring the degree of similarity in economic conditions among these economies.

The cluster analysis results together with the correlation coefficients of the residuals lend support to the hypothesis of warranted contagion, according to

Exhibit 13.8 Correlations of Residuals for the Pre-Crisis Period

	Hong Kong	Indonesia	Japan	Korea	Malaysia	Philippines	Singapore	Taiwan	Thailand
Hong Kong	1.0000								
Indonesia	0.1860	1.0000							
Japan	0.0151	−0.0071	1.0000						
Korea	0.0734	−0.0072	0.3560	1.0000					
Malaysia	0.0148	0.0618	0.2495	−0.0733	1.0000				
Philippines	0.0053	−0.0284	−0.1883	0.1552	0.0732	1.0000			
Singapore	−0.0543	0.0299	0.5147	0.1756	0.2045	−0.3394	1.0000		
Taiwan	0.1681	−0.0016	0.5071	0.2649	0.1631	−0.0598	0.5298	1.0000	
Thailand	0.0094	0.0599	0.8822	0.3464	0.3100	−0.1091	0.6282	0.4010	1.0000

Exhibit 13.9 Correlations of Residuals for the Post-crisis Period

	Hong Kong	Indonesia	Japan	Korea	Malaysia	Philippines	Singapore	Taiwan	Thailand
Hong Kong	1.0000								
Indonesia	−0.4300	1.0000							
Japan	0.0617	0.6193	1.0000						
Korea	−0.1453	−0.4249	−0.7476	1.0000					
Malaysia	−0.0694	0.5238	−0.7350	0.5365	1.0000				
Philippines	0.1860	0.2654	−0.3378	0.6128	0.3613	1.0000			
Singapore	−0.1483	0.9068	−0.5888	0.6410	0.7837	0.6800	1.0000		
Taiwan	−0.3872	0.6438	−0.5100	0.5548	0.4418	0.2860	0.5549	1.0000	
Thailand	−0.1099	0.1975	−0.7853	0.7373	0.7600	0.4011	0.7092	0.8003	1.0000

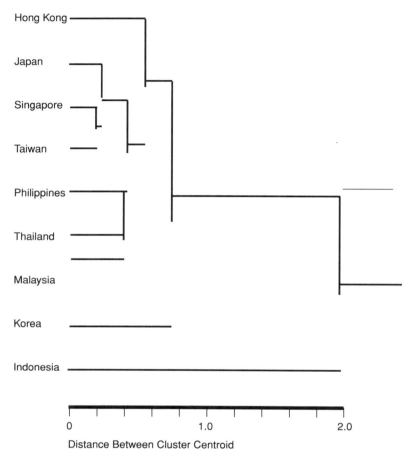

Exhibit 13.10   Dendrogram of Cluster Analysis

which the collapse of the baht in July 1997 should spill over to similar economies—namely Malaysia and the Philippines. Indeed, the three correlation coefficients are all noticeably high: 0.76 for Thailand–Malaysia, 0.44 for Malaysia–Philippines, and 0.40 for Thailand–Philippines (Exhibit 13.10). In general, a correlation coefficient for any two countries within the same group is higher than that between two different groups. The correlation coefficients within the three Tigers have not only the highest average value but also the largest increases (Exhibit 13.11).

CONCLUSION

We have applied regression and cluster analysis techniques to analyze exchange-rate dynamics in nine East Asian economies during January 1991–December 1998 with respect to contagion effects, informational effects, and economic fundamentals. Although the macroeconomic variables as specified in our theoretical model cannot adequately explain the short-run exchange-rate dynamics during that period, our empirical results suggest that currency traders paid more attention to changes in macroeconomic conditions after the outbreak of the crisis. More

Exhibit 13.11   Analysis of Correlation Coefficients

Description of Correlation Coefficients	Number of Observations	Average Value for the Post-Crisis Period	Average Increase over the Pre-Crisis Period
Between Malaysia, Thailand, and the Philippines themselves	3	0.5075	0.4161
Between the Above Three Countries and the Remaining Six Countries	18	0.2624	0.1239
Between All Countries Except Those Three in the First Row	33	0.1613	0.0024
Between All Countries	36	0.1902	0.0396

importantly, economic fundamentals clearly played a crucial role in the propagation of the crisis. The exchange-rate movements of many currencies showed excessive correlations even after controlling for the effects of economic fundamentals. Most of the correlations were positive and had increased significantly in value as a result of the crisis, reflecting the contagious nature of the Asian currency crisis. Such high correlations and significant increases were, however, more prominent among economies of similar economic conditions, notably Thailand, Malaysia, and the Philippines. Therefore, our findings provide evidence in favor of warranted contagion—the Asian currency crisis broke out in Thailand and spread to other countries with similar economic conditions rather than in a purely random way.

Our finding of warranted contagion has policy implications. When a currency crisis breaks out in a country, policy makers of countries with similar economic conditions should announce in time their commitment to credible policies so as to prevent warranted contagion. Of course, prevention is always better than cure. Sound macroeconomic policies in maintaining consistency between economic fundamentals and the external value of the currency are the best measures to avoid currency crises.

NOTES

1. The full set of regression results are reported in Chu, Chan, and Sin (2000).
2. Needless to say, our theoretical model excludes other important determinants of exchange rates. For instance, the post-crisis movements of the Indonesian rupiah were mostly driven by political instability.

REFERENCES

Baig, T., and I. Goldfajn. 1999. "Financial Market Contagion in the Asian Crisis," *International Monetary Fund Staff Paper* 46:167–195.

Bilson, J. F. O. 1978. "Rational Expectations and the Exchange Rate." In J. A. Frenkel and H. G. Johnson, eds. *The Economics of Exchange Rates: Selected Studies*, 75–96. Reading, MA: Addison-Wesley.

Chu, K., B. Y. Chan, and C. Sin. 2000. "Contagion Effects, Informational Effects, and Economic Fundamentals: An Analysis of Exchange Rate Dynamics during the Asian Currency Crisis," *HKIMR Working Paper* 2/2000. Hong Kong Institute for Monetary Research.

Dornbusch, R. 1976. "Expectations and Exchange Rate Dynamics." *Journal of Political Economy* 84:1161–76.

Eichengreen, B., A. K. Rose, and C. Wyplosz. 1995. "Exchange Market Mayhem: The Antecedents and Aftermath of Speculative Attacks." *Economic Policy* 21:249–296.

———. 1996. "Contagious Currency Crises: First Test." *Scandinavian Journal of Economics* 98:463–484.

Frankel, J. A. 1979. "On the Mark: A Theory of Floating Exchange Rates Based on Real Interest Rate Differentials." *American Economic Review* 69:610–622.

Frenkel, J. A. 1976. "A Monetary Approach to the Exchange Rate: Doctrinal Aspects and Empirical Evidence." *Scandinavian Journal of Economics* 78:200–224.

Gandolfo, G. 1995. *International Economics II: International Monetary Theory and Open-Economy Macroeconomics* (2nd edition). Berlin: Springer-Verlag.

Gerlach, S., and F. Smets. 1995. "Contagion Speculative Attacks." *European Journal of Political Economy* 11:5–63.

Hooper, P., and J. Morton. 1982. "Fluctuations in the Dollar: A Model of Nominal and Real Exchange Rate Determination." *Journal of International Money and Finance* 1:39–56.

Schwartz, A. J. 1998. "International Financial Crises: Myths and Realities." *Cato Journal* 17:251–256.

ABOUT THE AUTHOR

Kam Hon Chu is associate professor of economics at Memorial University of Newfoundland, Canada. He received his B.Soc.Sc. from the University of Hong Kong, M.Phil. from the Chinese University of Hong Kong, and PhD from the University of Toronto. Before obtaining his doctorate degree, he taught at Concordia University and was a bank economist with HSBC and Shanghai Commercial Bank in Hong Kong. He has been a consulting economist in the Finance and Growth project of the Asia-Pacific Economic Cooperation (APEC) and a visiting associate professor in the School of Economics and Finance of the University of Hong Kong. His main research interests are in the broad area of monetary economics, and free banking in particular. His research output appears in international journals like the *Journal of Money, Credit and Banking, Journal of Macroeconomics, Open Economies Review, Cato Journal*, and *Kredit und Kapital*, among others.

CHAPTER 14

Contagion and the Transmission of Financial Crises

MARDI DUNGEY
Professor of Economics and Finance, University of Tasmania

RENÉE A. FRY
Australian National University and University of Cambridge

BRENDA GONZÁLEZ-HERMOSILLO
Sloan School of Management, Massachusetts Institute of Technology (MIT)

VANCE L. MARTIN
Professor of Econometrics, University of Melbourne

CHRISMIN TANG
La Trobe University and Australian National University

Financial crises over the past 10 years have involved countries with highly developed financial markets as well as a number of emerging markets. Typical examples include the Russian crisis in August 1998, the near collapse of Long-Term Capital Management (LTCM) in September 1998, the Brazilian crisis in early 1999, the dot-com crisis in 2000, the Argentinian crisis beginning in 2001, and the recent Global Financial Crisis triggered by the turmoil in the U.S. subprime mortgage market in mid-2007.

Financial crises typically build from foundations of asset price inflation, banking crises, and eventually to debt default (Reinhart and Rogoff 2009), suggesting that the origins of financial crises as having common features. A logical question to ask is whether the transmission of shocks between markets during a crisis also have common features. Crises may transmit in a number of ways. Probably the most apparent is the transmission through the known relationships between economies and markets—when the Chinese stock market experiences a sudden downturn, as it did in February to March 2007, this shock flowed quickly to other regions of the world due to the strong trading and investment links known to exist between China and the rest of the world. During the same period, the ABX index of subprime mortgages also began a cascading price decline for the investment grade BBB tranches. Linkages based on fundamental relationships are generally labeled as spillovers (Dornbusch, Park, and Claessens 2000), however in many instances of crisis the transmission of a shock from one market to another vastly exceeds what could be reasonably considered a spillover. An example is the case of the announcement by the Russian government that it would not honor its payment on GKO sovereign debt bonds in August 1998. Not only were its immediate creditors, such as Germany, affected, but almost all emerging markets experienced large increases in risk premia, and some like Brazil were massively affected by the withdrawal of funds as portfolios were adjusted. These reactions in excess of the usual linkages are what is meant by contagion and are generally a result of externalities, such as information asymmetries and herding behavior.

The concern with crises for policy makers and others is to limit contagion by halting the spread from a crisis event to other markets. This event may be from a particular market, or segment of a market, such as the dot-com collapse, which began in information intensive stocks in the first quarter of 2001 and spread more generally to other equity markets. Or it may be in a particular country, such as Greece in 2010 when their fiscal problems prompted a debt crisis, which subsequently affected other economies. Alternatively, it may be in a particular asset class, such as the problems with U.S. mortgage backed securities, which are commonly seen as the originators of the global financial crisis in 2007, or can be triggered by the collapse of an institution such a Lehman in September 2008. That is, there are three distinct channels through which contagion may spread: (1) market channels associated with a particular asset type such as equities; (2) country channels from particular economies; and (3) idiosyncratic channels associated with links originating from an identified asset in a particular market and country.

In Chapter 5 of our 2010 book, *Transmission of Financial Crises and Contagion: A Latent Factor Approach*, we provide a formal technical analysis of five crisis episodes during the period 1998 to 2007 for six countries in order to establish whether contagion effects do have measurably similar effects in multiple crises, markets, and countries. The five crises examined are:

1. The Russian bond default of August 1998, which resulted in massive increases in emerging market bond spreads all round the world, and contributed to the near-failure of the U.S.-based hedge fund LTCM, which was rescued by a consortium of banks coordinated by the New York Federal Reserve. Lowenstein (2001) provides an excellent review of this period.
2. The Brazilian crisis of 1999, which begins with the effective devaluation of the real in mid-January 1999 and features a significant loss of reserves, the short tenure of several new Central Bank Governors and finally settles just prior to the agreement of a new IMF program in March 1999.
3. The dot-com crisis of 2001, when the bubble associated with the so-called *new economy* and IT stocks in the United States collapsed and spread rapidly to other segments of the U.S. equity market, and other geographically dispersed equity markets.
4. The Argentine crisis of 2001–2005. This was an extraordinarily long period of continued disruption, particularly associated with renegotiations of the Argentine sovereign debt position. It was only finally resolved with the agreement of a new package of debt rescheduling and the renewed ability of Argentina to participate in international debt markets in March 2005. As

this period was so long a number of robustness checks were carried out to be sure that the results were not unduly influenced by the length of this period.
5. Finally, the last crisis investigated is the beginning of the global financial crisis starting in mid-2007. At the time of writing the chapter, the sample period ended in December 2007, thereby the sample period captures the initial effects of the subprime mortgage shock on international asset markets, but ends before the other major shocks characterizing this crisis, including the collapse of the hedge fund Bear-Stearns and Lehman Brothers, and the rescues of Fannie Mae and Freddie Mac, as well as AIG.

Two asset classes are examined in these five distinct crisis periods, specifically equity index returns (expressed in U.S. dollars) and U.S. dollar denominated long-term debt yield spreads. The main results of the analysis are summarized in Exhibit 14.1. The first panel of the table shows what proportion of total volatility observed in each market during each of the individual crises is attributable to contagion. The channel of contagion is not specified here. Rather, an overall measurement of contagion is provided. The results show that contagion is present in every crisis. However, its contribution to observed volatility in the market varies considerably across countries and crisis events. In the Russian/LTCM crisis of 1998, contagion accounts for some 97 percent of the volatility observed in Brazil's equity markets, but 40 percent in Canada's equity market. In general, this crisis shows that the largest contribution of contagion effects to volatility in all five crises investigated.

Exhibit 14.2 delves into the details of Exhibit 14.1 by dividing the total contagion contribution to returns volatility into its various channels; namely, market,

Exhibit 14.1 The Percentage of Total Observed Volatility in Selected Asset Returns Attributable to Contagion during Crisis Episodes

Market/Country	Crisis				
	Russia/LTCM	Brazil	Dot-com	Argentina	GFC
Stock markets					
Argentina	61.02	62.70	93.75	11.33	67.03
Brazil	96.93	9.56	55.86	32.32	16.10
Canada	39.94	6.93	22.18	25.74	73.73
Mexico	46.97	13.48	88.36	6.89	68.08
Russia	12.68	89.80	1.36	8.78	22.67
U.S.	67.64	18.28	0.48	52.03	80.62
Bond markets					
Argentina	39.04	14.12	0.04	5.80	96.87
Brazil	92.71	18.02	7.60	0.13	16.77
Canada	45.47	7.68	18.41	7.23	14.53
Mexico	88.57	81.01	0.15	8.86	15.91
Russia	13.30	63.24	11.60	0.81	27.84
U.S.	31.02	8.24	11.27	7.00	34.31

Exhibit 14.2 Contagion via Market, Country, and Idiosyncratic Channels

Market/Country		Russia/LTCM	Brazil	Dot-Com	Argentina	GFC
				Crisis		
Stock markets						
Argentina	Market	0.90	2.24	0.01	9.70	28.33
	Country	44.86	51.04	88.03	n.a.	n.a.
	Idiosyncratic	15.27	9.42	5.71	1.64	38.70
Brazil	Market	12.14	2.49	21.19	25.77	5.06
	Country	0.71	n.a.	7.09	2.96	n.a.
	Idiosyncratic	84.09	7.07	27.58	3.60	11.04
Canada	Market	6.65	0.28	0.28	2.01	30.88
	Country	21.81	1.53	0.48	4.85	n.a.
	Idiosyncratic	11.49	5.12	21.42	18.88	42.85
Mexico	Market	9.00	0.00	75.90	1.23	28.59
	Country	30.70	12.40	2.04	0.58	n.a.
	Idiosyncratic	7.28	1.08	10.42	5.08	39.50
Russia	Market	0.09	55.33	0.17	0.17	8.33
	Country	n.a.	n.a.	0.01	1.69	n.a.
	Idiosyncratic	12.59	34.47	1.18	6.92	14.34
U.S.	Market	5.99	2.23	0.48	0.08	36.05
	Country	54.86	2.31	n.a.	6.16	n.a.
	Idiosyncratic	6.80	13.75	n.a.	45.79	44.57
Bond markets						
Argentina	Market	31.65	0.16	0.01	5.80	2.15
	Country	0.74	13.92	0.01	n.a.	n.a.
	Idiosyncratic	6.64	0.04	0.02	n.a.	94.72
Brazil	Market	9.30	18.02	4.13	0.01	0.14
	Country	29.55	n.a.	0.21	0.08	n.a.
	Idiosyncratic	53.87	n.a.	3.26	0.04	16.62
Canada	Market	9.15	0.80	9.62	4.76	0.02
	Country	4.61	6.26	0.49	2.33	n.a.
	Idiosyncratic	31.71	0.62	8.30	0.14	14.50
Mexico	Market	26.32	1.87	0.06	0.74	0.03
	Country	18.22	76.72	0.02	1.33	n.a.
	Idiosyncratic	44.02	2.42	0.07	6.79	15.89
Russia	Market	0.47	28.63	4.20	0.04	0.00
	Country	n.a.	5.62	0.06	0.03	n.a.
	Idiosyncratic	12.83	29.00	7.34	0.74	27.84
U.S.	Market	5.91	3.25	7.18	1.42	11.45
	Country	7.47	3.98	n.a.	0.28	n.a.
	Idiosyncratic	17.64	1.01	5.09	5.29	22.86

country and idiosyncratic channels. The main message from Exhibit 14.2 is that every channel in every crisis has a statistically significant impact—in no crises were any of these channels not apparent in transmitting the crises. However, each crisis is different in nature with the relative importance of the three channels varying. There is no stylized evidence suggesting that the market, country, or idiosyncratic channels are systematically important in comparison to the others.

The results in Exhibits 14.1 and 14.2 show that contagion is often not responsible for the majority of observed volatility in crises. Rather, other factors are dominant including general world market conditions. In many crises, there is simply an increase in volatility in all markets due to heightened uncertainty and liquidity problems. This general increase in market volatility is distinct from contagion, and as a policy issue deserves to be tackled separately. Other aspects may be country-specific policy or institutional problems. Examples of this type include poor banking infrastructure and uncertain bankruptcy laws in Thailand during the East Asian crisis of 1997–1998 and the unsustainable fiscal positions such as the situation in Greece in 2010.

The analysis of these five crises across multiple countries belies the evidence that volatility is always primarily domestically generated. Contagion is significant and important in a number of crises, and has identifiable channels. Crisis management can usefully consider that these channels exist and how to combat them. Crises originating from country conditions do perhaps indicate a policy-based problem, although they may also include substantial exogenous shocks to infrastructure such as in the case of the September 11, 2001, terrorist attacks in New York, the July 7, 2005, terrorist attacks in London and the discovery of fraudulent trading at Societe Generale in January 2008, each of which caused disruption in financial markets. Crises transmitted through market channels may indicate a necessity to examine the microstructure of that particular market and respond appropriately. For example, the credit problems in the early part of the global financial crisis in late 2007 were reflected in the drying up of previously liquid markets such as the Euribor and London interbank markets, where a short-term structure had previously been almost innocuous in using these instruments as substitutes for the money market but suddenly became prohibitively risky. Crises transmitted from an individual identifiable asset, such as the Russian bond market, may be best met by a tailored response, one example being the steps taken to address the speculative attack on the Hong Kong dollar in August 1998, which the Hong Kong Monetary Authority defeated by the novel mechanism of investing heavily to support the Hong Kong equity market. Goodhart and Dai (2003) provide an excellent review of these events.

Turning briefly to the events of the global financial crisis, the evidence presented here has a number of lessons for policy makers. First, contagion effects in this crisis have been relatively large contributors to observed volatility—to an extent not seen since the Russian–LTCM crisis. Second, there are clearly different channels of contagion, which are most active in the different asset classes. In equity markets, the market channel is the largest contributor to the transmission of the crises. This means that the observed increased volatility is being mainly sourced from a common increase in volatility for all of these markets. Increased volatility of this nature is not easily pursued at a policy level. Although a number of proposals exist to *slow* markets by inserting transactions taxes and short-selling bans, it is not clear to the authors that this would necessarily dampen periods of high volatility, while facilitating trade in more normal times. In general, taxes of this nature encourage avoidance through financial innovation.

The main source of contagion in the bond markets during the global financial crisis period is idiosyncratic—which in this case means it is directly associated with contagion from U.S. bond markets, acting as a proxy for the turmoil originating in the mortgage backed assets market. When contagion effects are directed from individual assets, the importance of portfolio incentives can provide a means of understanding and potentially slowing contagion effects. For example, in the global financial crisis the direct effect of reduced quality of mortgage-backed securities was to put stress on banks' capital. In particular, to meet their regulatory obligations many institutions needed to raise more capital. As often happens in a crisis the incentive structures facing many institutions became similar and there were sudden calls on scarce capital, forcing up the price and volatility in these markets. The response of policy makers and regulators to these conditions, in particular by widening the types of capital that they would accept, was a sensible response to stress emerging via a particular channel. Being able to identify such channels sufficiently early and with a clear indication of the strength with which they may prevail, is critical for effective crisis management. Regulatory policies, such as capital ratios, are good criteria for preventing crisis onset, but once a crisis has begun it may be counterproductive to adhere rigidly to these conditions. But relaxing them creates the further problem of time consistency and moral hazard into future conditions, meaning it is absolutely necessary for authorities to review arrangements after the crisis in order to retain credibility into the next episode.

The stylized fact established in this analysis of multiple financial crises is that all channels of contagion are present in every crisis, but in each case the comparative importance of the channels differs, in many cases in an economically significant way. Thus, for policy makers to have a set of rules on how to react in the presence of a crisis seems to constrain them in what is likely to be an extremely unproductive manner. Instead, having a range of potential responses, and the discretion to respond quickly and effectively as the different crisis scenarios present themselves is more appealing. The most critical tool that policy makers need to have available to mitigate crises is the ability to recognize the features of crises, with a solid understanding of their sources in order to respond appropriately. History shows that often the most successful responses are those that obey the principles of providing markets with security, certainty, and liquidity, but that the form these take needs to vary with the needs of particular crisis events.

REFERENCES

Dornbusch, R., Y. C. Park, and S. Claessens. 2000. "Contagion: How It Spreads and How It Can Be Stopped." *World Bank Research Observer* 15:177–197.

Goodhart, A. E. Charles, and Lu Dai. 2003. *Intervention to Save Hong Kong: The Authorities' Counter-Speculation in Financial Markets*. New York: Oxford University Press.

Lowenstein, Roger. 2001. *When Genius Failed: The Rise and Fall of Long-Term Capital Management*. London: Fourth Estate.

Reinhart, Carmen M., and Kenneth S. Rogoff. 2009. *This Time Is Different: Eight Centuries of Financial Folly*. Princeton, NJ: Princeton University Press.

ABOUT THE AUTHORS

Mardi Dungey is professor of economics and finance at the University of Tasmania, a senior research associate at the Centre for Financial Analysis and Policy at the University of Cambridge and adjunct professor at the Centre for Applied

Macroeconomic Policy at the Australian National University. Her research interests combine the empirical sides of finance and economics, particularly in the effects of financial crises on open economies and policy assessment. Mardi has published extensively on the transmission of financial crises, and has written numerous papers on measuring contagion, most recently including a forthcoming book from Oxford University Press in 2010. She holds a PhD in economics from the Australian National University.

Renée A. Fry is the deputy director of the Centre for Applied Macroeconomic Analysis at the Australian National University where she is also the co-director of the finance and macroeconomy program. She is a research associate at the Centre for Financial Analysis and Policy, University of Cambridge and has worked extensively on models of financial market contagion.

Brenda González-Hermosillo is a visiting professor at the Massachusetts Institute of Technology (MIT) Sloan School of Management, where she teaches finance and economics at the graduate level, including areas related to financial crises and systemic risk. Prior to her appointment at MIT, she was deputy division chief of the Global Financial Stability Division in the Monetary and Capital Markets Department at the International Monetary Fund (IMF), where she led several analytical chapters of the IMF *Global Financial Stability Report*. She also served at various institutions: the Bank of Canada; Canada's Department of Finance; several investment banks (Bank of Montreal, Bank of Nova Scotia, and Banamex); Mexico's Ministry of Finance; and the Central Bank of Mexico. In addition to her current position at MIT, she has taught at the University of Western Ontario, and the IMF Institute. Her current research interests include financial volatility and systemic risk; global systemic liquidity crises; macro–financial market dynamics during crises; global contagion and spillovers for advanced economies and emerging markets; effects of regulation and market structure on the performance of financial markets for both advanced and developing countries; and macroprudential regulation of systemic risks.

Vance L. Martin is a professor of econometrics at the University of Melbourne whose research interests include contagion and financial econometrics.

Chrismin Tang obtained her PhD from the Department of Economics at the University of Melbourne and is currently a lecturer at the La Trobe University and a research associate of the Centre for Applied Macroeconomic Analysis at the Australian National University. Her research interests are in the areas relating to financial market contagion, risk assessment, and systemic stability.

CHAPTER 15

The Russian Financial Crisis, U.S. Financial Stock Returns, and the International Monetary Fund

M. HUMAYUN KABIR
School of Economics and Finance, Massey University, New Zealand

M. KABIR HASSAN
Department of Economics and Finance, University of New Orleans

I n the 1990s, the world experienced financial crises one after another—the Mexican Peso crisis, the Asian crisis, and lastly, the Russian financial crisis. One of the concerns of such crises is their impact, or spillover effect, on other countries that may be linked through financial or trade flows. For Russia, the crisis was of a serious concern as the economy was in transition from a centralized economic system to a decentralized capitalist system. As an emerging economy, Russia presented an opportunity for investors around the world, and as such, attracted Western investors, banks, and other financial institutions to its market. As a result any domestic economic and financial policy or external shock that produced repercussions, or led to internal imbalances, were of great importance to investors in different countries. According to Bank for International Settlements (BIS; 1999), European countries, especially Germany, were affected the most at the culmination of Russian debt default, and devaluation of the currency in 1998. Many banks and financial institutions of those countries had sizable loan contracts or created positions through leverage, or other financing or hedging techniques in the Russian market that led to sizable losses when the moratorium and ruble devaluation were announced. This is in contrast to what has been found during the Asian crisis, which did not affect the European and U.S. market significantly, even though banks, both Western and Asian, were at the heart of the crisis (Kho and Stulz 2000).

The financial infrastructure of Russia was quite different from the West, as Exhibit 15.1 shows. In contrast to banks in the West, most of the banks in Russia performed little retail banking and instead served mostly for the business tycoons

Exhibit 15.1 Russian Economic Indicator, 1995–1998 (in Millions U.S. Dollar)

Year	1995	1996	1997	1998: Q1	1998: Q2	1998: Q3	1998: Q4	1998: Total
GDP	1,540,490	2,145,660	2,478,590	—	—	—	—	2,696,350
CPI (% chg. Over previous period)	197.47	47.73	14.74	3.17	1.50	16.14	39.85	27.67
Unemployment rate	8.9	9.9	11.3	11.6	11.5	11.6	12.8	13.3
Budget deficit	69,508	147,607	150,415	31,398	41,048	22.645	31,867	126,958
Exports	82,913	90,563 (+9.23%)	89,008 (−1.72%)	18,554	18,866	18,125	19,339	74,884 (−15.87%)
Imports	62,603	68,092 (+8.77%)	71,983 (+5.71%)	17,841	17,388	13,431	9,355	58,015 (−19.40%)
Trade Balances	20,310	22,471 (+10.64%)	17,025 (−4.24%)	713	1,478	4,691	9,984	16,869 (−.092%)
Exchange rate (per U.S. dollar)	4.65	5.56	5.96	—	—	—	—	20.65
Real effective exchange rate	100.00	122.10	128.96	132.78	131.98	114.96	77.18	114.23
Total debt by currency	787,689	1,122,320	1,302,050	—	—	—	—	3,786,110
Debt: ruble	226,505	427,323	565,992	—	—	—	—	750,556
Debt: other	561,184	695,000	736,060	—	—	—	—	3,035,550

Source: IMF, and the Central Bank of Russian Federation 2000.

that owned them. Due to a lack of appropriate monetary management, control over government spending, and deregulatory coordination, the country was facing economic instability from the early 1990s. Before the crisis kicked off, the symptoms began to surface on the economic front.

The foreign exchange market was facing instability, part of which was caused by the manipulation of banking chains, while the country was battling hyperinflation. Second, a huge payment crisis due to increasing budget deficits made the economy more susceptible to external shocks. The large fiscal deficits of 7 to $8\frac{1}{2}$ percent of GDP at the federal level had resulted in an explosive increase in the debt burden in 1996–1997. The budget deficit was only $69,508 million in 1995. In two years the deficit more than doubled to $150,415 million. Since the economy was subject to hyperinflation, the issuance of ruble denominated debt to finance the deficits with short maturities (less than one year), known as GKO resulted in refinancing the debt constantly. Foreign investors held one third of the short-term bonds, GKOs, and the rest were held by Russian private banks, whose assets were tied up with in the GKOs and currency trading operations. And the banks used those bonds as collateral to obtain foreign loans.

The stabilization policy pursued by the Russian government, reflected in Exhibit 15.2, broke down when the external environment deteriorated in 1997–1998. Both exports and imports by Russia continued to decline, and the trade balance went down by 24 percent in 1997. Under such economic turmoil, the long-serving Prime Minister Victor Chernomyrdin was removed in March 1998, and Sergei Kiriyenko was nominated as a reformist. The Central Bank tripled the discount rate to 150 percent on May 27, 1998, to try to stabilize the ruble after government bonds and share prices fell precipitously. Due to the sharp increase in interest rates, the cost of government borrowing ballooned. Investors continued to withdraw from the government debt market, and international reserves dropped sharply. Total portfolio investment in Russia declined by more than 50 percent in 1998, which can be mainly attributed to the decrease in investment in bonds from $647 million to $38 million in 1998. Foreign exchange reserves declined by more than 40 percent in 1998.

Exhibit 15.2 International Investment Position of Russia, 1995–1998 (in Millions U.S. Dollars)

	1995	1996	1997	1998
Direct Investment in Russia				
Equity capital and reinvestment earning	**345**	**426**	**970**	**373**
Portfolio Investment	150	280	887	389
Equity securities	**132**	**122**	**240**	**389**
Bank	*132*	*122*	*240*	*38*
Debt securities	**18**	**158**	**647**	**351**
Bonds and notes (banks)	*18*	*158*	*647*	*38*
Money market instruments (bank)	—	—	—	*313*
Net International Investment Position	11,426	3,767	−2,481	−7,293
Foreign Exchange Reserves	14,265	11,271	12,895	7,800

Source: IFS CD-ROM 2000, IMF.

Several times the International Monetary Fund (IMF) criticized the government for its failure to return to fiscal discipline, and at last came forward to help the country by announcing a massive bailout in July 1998. The deficits continued growing with rising interest rates, and through the refinancing of debts. In 1997, the yield on short-term bonds, GKOs, was 23.4 percent, which increased to 40.1 percent by the second quarter of 1998. As a result, bond prices started to fall quickly, causing the banks that had used the bonds as collateral for loans to be more vulnerable to margin calls, and as a result on the verge of collapse.

At the culmination of the crisis on August 17, the Russian government unilaterally announced a 90-day debt moratorium on certain kinds of foreign commercial debt payments (mostly those owned by banks). Along with a freeze in the domestic government bond market, they announced a restructuring of short-term bonds into securities with longer maturities, and devalued the ruble with some currency control to prevent the depletion of foreign exchange reserve. Although devaluation cut the value of ruble-denominated bond GKOs in hard currency, it increased the likelihood of banks with larger debt in hard currencies to default. With the surge in GKOs yield, the interbank rate increased substantially from 21 percent in 1997 to 44.4 percent, and 81.2 percent in the second and third quarters of 1998 respectively. The chronology of events, both economic and financial and political, is provided in Exhibit 15.3.

We identify the crisis period starting from May 27 to August 28, the critical dates being shown in Exhibit 15.3. We then divide the whole crisis period into three

Exhibit 15.3 Event Dates and Descriptions

Event Day	Event Description
May 27	Central Bank triples the discount rate to 150% after GKO yields soar and share market tumbles.
June 02	Russia considers euro dollar bonds offer to refinance ruble debt.
June 04	Central Bank cuts discount rate to 60% from 150% in a sign of growing confidence.
June 19	Request for additional IMF help.
June 23	Yeltsin and Kiriyenko present anti-crisis plan considering mainly tax reform.
June 25	IMF approval of preassigned loans.
July 07	Rescue of Russia's Tokobank founders, raising fears for sector, Western creditors likely to see losses.
July 14	IMF and World Bank announce bailout of $22.6 million.
July 15	The Duma fails to adopt most of anti-crisis plan. Kiriyenko vows to compensate through resolutions and presidential decrees.
Aug 13	Russian interbank lending stalls as crisis deepens—some FIs fail to make payments.
Aug 17	A 90-day moratorium is announced on some foreign debt servicing.
Aug 24	Kiriyenko's government is dismissed and Chernomyrdin is named acting prime minister.
Aug 26	The Central Bank revokes the license of Bank Imperial.
Aug 27	Moscow halts dollar trading, ruble drops 69% versus mark.
Aug 28	Russia cancels ruble trading indefinitely.

subperiods in our analysis: (1) subperiod 1: from May 25 to July 13, the day before the IMF bailout; (2) subperiod 2: from July 14 to August 16, the day before debt moratorium; and (3) subperiod 3: from August 17 to August to 28.

Many U.S. leverage institutions like commercial and investment banks and hedge funds had direct or indirect exposures to the Russian market by being counterparties through different loan, security, or derivative contracts in the Russian market. We explore the impact of the Russian financial crisis on U.S. bank (commercial bank and S&Ls) and nonbank (investment firms and insurance companies) financial stocks. Although some U.S. commercial banks and investment institutions are expected to have exposure to the Russian market due to their lending and investment and financial services related activities, it is unlikely that S&Ls institutions and insurance companies would have such exposure. Second, a spillover effect is also expected to hurt U.S. financial stock returns due to the heavy losses experienced by European banks. Third, the currency risk associated with Russian default and ruble devaluation in emerging markets, and simultaneous movement of markets around the world in the same direction heightened uncertainty that led to a sharp decline in liquidity in all markets. Diamond and Dybvig (1983) have shown long ago how a bank-specific event, which is an external shock to other banks, creates bank runs, and affects the whole financial sector. Swary (1986), and Lang and Stulz (1992) show that such bank-specific trouble can lead to contagion effects on the other FIs. Investors' expectations, beliefs, and memories of past crises (Masson 1998; Mullainathan 1998) can generate contagious effects through multiple equilibria. Valdes (1996) shows that portfolio recomposition in order to satisfy margin calls, or meet the regulatory requirements in response to a crisis can reduce the liquidity of investors. Calvo (1999) explains that it is information asymmetry between the informed and uninformed investors that create such contagion effects.

We also explore the ineffectiveness of IMF bailouts in light of the recent debate on IMF-induced moral hazard problem that distorts investors' incentives and deepens the crisis. Although some papers on the Mexican or Asian crisis (Lane and Phillips 2000; Willett 1999; Zhang 1999) find no evidence of moral hazard induced by IMF bailouts, Dell'Ariccia, Schnabel, and Zettelmeyer (2002) find evidence of investors' moral hazard due to IMF bailout in the Russian crisis by examining the bond spreads for a group of countries.

Our sample consists of 869 financial institutions, of which the commercial bank portfolio comprises 368, savings and loans (S&Ls) 270, insurance companies 155, and investment banks 76. The analysis is based on equally weighted daily portfolio returns of these four groups. We further divide each of the portfolios into quintiles based on total assets.

While the mean returns of portfolios during the pre-crisis period are all positive ranging from 1.26 percent to 2.08 percent, the crisis period mean returns are in the negative territory with the highest being for the investment bank portfolio (–4.17 percent), and the lowest being for the insurance company portfolio (–2.87 percent). Most of the losses incurred during the crisis period are driven by the losses in the third subperiod of the crisis after the debt moratorium. In fact, the portfolio returns declined at least twice as much as the decline in the second subperiod for all but the insurance company portfolio. Both commercial bank and S&L portfolios lost close to 10 percent while the investment bank portfolio declined by 18 percent during this period. The variability measured by standard deviations of returns increased substantially for commercial, S&L, and insurance portfolios during the crisis period, especially in the third period of crisis. When compared with pre-crisis period, the standard deviations of returns for commercial bank and S&L portfolios jumped from 5.36 percent and 4.79 percent to 9.5 percent and 8.1 percent during the crisis period, respectively.

The correlation has gone up during the crisis period, especially after the debt default in the third subperiod of the crisis. During the pre-crisis period the correlation ranges from 0.68 to 0.83, which jumps to 0.84 to 0.96 in the crisis period. As Forbes and Rigobon (2001) suggest that the variances of portfolio returns increase during a crisis period, potentially causing correlations to increase when the returns are not actually correlated. We attempt to estimate the adjusted correlation, and find that these correlations are significantly higher for most portfolios in the crisis period.

One way to capture the impact of the events on our portfolios is to estimate the average abnormal returns around the event dates. We use Seemingly Unrelated Regression method to estimate the parameters and their statistical significance.

For all of our portfolios, there is no significant impact of events before the Russian debt default in August 17, 1998. The central bank's decision to increase the key interest rate did not have any impact on any portfolio returns. However, when the Central Bank reversed its decision on the discount rate playing down the need for any Western help, all portfolios reacted adversely. On June 23, when the anti-crisis plan was presented as the recognition of a crisis, the S&L and commercial bank portfolios reacted negatively.

Events only started to have significant impact at the climax of the crisis with the announcement of debt moratorium on August 17. On August 24, when Prime Minister Kiriyenko was fired, all portfolios reacted negatively; but only the abnormal returns of the commercial bank and S&L portfolios are statistically significant. Again, when the Central Bank revoked the license of Bank Imperial, one of the biggest commercial banks in Russia on August 26, both commercial bank and S&L portfolios reacted adversely, and the S&L portfolio lost more than 2 percent. One of the significant events that had a profound impact on several portfolios, and for the first time on the investment bank portfolio, is the halt of dollar trading, and the news published in the *New York Times* about the IMF refusal to help Russian reform on August 27. The S&L portfolio lost 3.4 percent, followed by the investment bank portfolio (2.2 percent), and commercial bank portfolio (1.2 percent).

For all events following the debt moratorium on August 17, the impact across portfolios is not similar. The events belonging to third subperiod of crisis have a significantly different impact on each of the portfolios. The cumulative abnormal returns of all announcements show that S&L portfolio lost a significant 6.7 percent, followed by a significant 2.9 percent loss by the commercial bank portfolio. The investment portfolio lost around 2 percent. The net loss accrued to all portfolios is 11.6 percent on these events. The S&Ls, which are not supposed to have direct exposure to the Russian market, face significant abnormal returns following the debt moratorium on August 17. In fact, S&Ls lost 6.61 percent on four event days following the debt moratorium while the commercial bank portfolio lost only 2.34 percent. The investment bank portfolio shows a significant loss of only 2.2 percent when Moscow halted dollar trading. This suggests a contagion effect from the

Russian crisis on financial institutions. The net losses to S&Ls and commercial banks are significantly different from other portfolios.

We also address the size issue. The distribution of FIs is highly skewed towards smaller-size banks. As a result, abnormal return estimates based on SIC-based broader portfolios may not capture whether the results were due to the crisis or the size of the FIs. We examine whether the stocks of smaller and larger banks reacted similarly around crisis events. The average abnormal returns of smallest portfolios in the three sub-periods are significant in statistical sense. In the second and third sub-periods, smallest portfolios lost almost same magnitudes on average (0.38 percent). The losses faced by larger sizes are not significant.

Although portfolio formation considering all FIs may be effective in isolating nonexposed, relatively smaller banks (smallest quintile), as more than 95 percent of banks in our sample falls in this group, it may not be ideal for separating the exposed from the nonexposed banks. Larger S&Ls and insurance companies that are not supposed to have exposures may be included with larger more-likely-to-be-exposed commercial and investment banks in higher size quintiles. Second, all larger commercial and investment banks may not have exposures. As a result, higher size quintile portfolios may contain both exposed and nonexposed banks, canceling the impact if nonexposed banks are not affected by the events. In order to correct for this problem, we also form quintile portfolios for each type of FIs.

The smallest portfolios of types of FIs face significant losses in the second and third subperiods. The loss by the largest commercial bank portfolio in the last subperiod is a significant 0.94 percent. In fact, all size groups of commercial banks end up with losses in the last period. Most importantly, we find that the smallest portfolios of all types of banks lost significant market value in the three subperiods. The losses in the third subperiods are relatively higher. Even the loss of the smallest investment bank portfolio jumps from 0.32 percent in the second subperiod to 0.55 percent in the third subperiod. The losses faced by other FIs in the smallest quintiles are close to 0.45 percent with slight variations. Thus, our findings suggest significant losses by the smallest banking firms and by commercial and S&L institutions during the crisis. Although the losses are more pronounced in the third subperiod following the announcement of debt moratorium for commercial bank and S&L portfolios, they are significantly different only for the smallest size commercial banks. Thus, the results imply that while some of the largest commercial banks lost their market value in the last period, it is mostly the smaller commercial banks and S&L institutions that faced huge losses. Thus unlike the Kho, Lee, and Stulz (2000) study, which report no contagion, we find a form of contagion effect on the portfolio of smaller banks.

We identified three major IMF-related events in studying the Russian crisis: (1) June 19, when Russia requested for additional IMF help; (2) June 25, when IMF approved preassigned loans; and (3) July 14, when IMF and World Bank announced bailout of $22.6 million. We find that none of the events had a significant impact on any of the portfolios. When comparing each type of FIs over an event we still do not find any significant differences in abnormal returns across portfolios. Overall, on the three events, the net abnormal returns are negative for all FIs except investment banks, but statistically insignificant. When we compare the net abnormal returns of all three events, we do not find any significant results. Thus our results imply that IMF help in Russia could not ameliorate the troubled economy. This finding is consistent with the idea that the IMF intervention in the form of bailouts in the period of financial troubles over a series of cases in the last decade generated a moral hazard problem leading to ineffectiveness of such policy.

REFERENCES

Bank of International Settlement (BIS). 1999. "A Review of Financial Market Events in Autumn 1998." *Committee of the Global Financial System*, October 1999.

Calvo, Guillermo A. "Contagion in Emerging Markets: When Wall Street is a Carrier," AEA Conference Meetings, New York, 1999.

Dell'Ariccia, Giovanni, I. Schnabel, and J. Zettelmeyer. 2002. "Moral Hazard and International Crisis Lending: A Test." *IMF Working Paper* 181.

Diamond, Douglas W., and Philip H. Dybvig. 1983. "Bank Runs Liquidity and Deposit Insurance." *Journal of Political Economy*, 401–419.

Forbes, Kristin, and Roberto Rigobon. 2001. "Measuring Contagion: Conceptual and Empirical Issues." In Stijin Claessens and Kristin J. Forbes, eds. *International Financial Contagion*. Norwell, MA: Kluwer Academic.

Gelos, Geston, and Ratna Sahay. 2001. "Financial Market Spillovers: How Different Are the Transition Economies?" In Stijin Claessens and Kristin J. Forbes, eds. *International Financial Contagion*. Norwell, MA: Kluwer Academic.

Kho, Bong-Chan, and R. Stulz. 2000. "Banks, the IMF, and the Asian Crisis." *Pacific-Basin Finance Journal* 8:177–216.

Kho, Bong-Chan, L. Dong, and R. Stulz. 2000. "U.S. Banks, Crises, and Bailouts: From Mexico to LTCM." *American Economic Review* 90:2, 28–31.

Lane, Timothy, and S. Phillips. 2000. "Does IMF Financing Result in Moral Hazard?" *IMF Working Paper* 168.

Lang, Larry H. P., and Rene M. Stulz. 1992. "Contagion and Competitive Intra-Industry Effects of Bankruptcy Announcements." *Journal of Financial Economics* 32:45–60.

Masson, Paul. 1998. "Contagion: Monsoonal Effects, Spillovers, and Jumps between Multiple Equlibria." *IMF Working Paper* 98/142.

Mullainathan, Sendhil. 1998. "A Memory Based Model of Bounded Rationality." Mimeo.

Swary, Itzhak. 1986. "Stock Market Reaction to Regulatory Action in the Continental Illinois Crisis." *Journal of Business* July, 451–473.

Tornell, Aaron. 1999. "Common Fundamentals in the Tequila and Asian Crisis." mimeo.

Valdes, Rodrigo. 1996. "Emerging Market Contagion: Evidence and Theory." MIT mimeo.

Willett, Thomas D. 1999. "Did the Mexican Bailout Really Cause the Asian Crisis?" *Claremont Policy Briefs* 99–01.

Zhang, Xiaoming Alan. 1999. "Testing for 'Moral Hazard' in Emerging Markets Lending." Institute of International Finance, *Research Paper* No. 99–1, August.

ABOUT THE AUTHORS

M. Humayun Kabir is a senior lecturer of finance at the School of Economics and Finance at Massey University at Palmerston North in New Zealand. He received his PhD from University of New Orleans in financial economics. His main research area is international finance, investments, and risk management. His publication includes scholarly papers published in *Journal of Banking & Finance, Applied Financial Economics*.

M. Kabir Hassan is a financial economist with consulting, research, and teaching experience in development finance, money, and capital markets, Islamic finance, corporate finance, investments, monetary economics, macroeconomics and international trade and finance. Dr. Hassan received his BA in economics and mathematics from Gustavus Adolphus College, Minnesota, and MA in economics and PhD in finance from the University of Nebraska-Lincoln, respectively. He is now a professor in the Department of Economics and Finance at the University of New Orleans, Louisiana. He has more than 100 papers published in refereed academic journals to his credit. He is editor of *The Global Journal of Finance and Economics* and *Journal of Islamic Economics, Banking and Finance*, and co-editor of *Journal of Economic Cooperation and Development*. Dr. Hassan has edited and published many books along with articles in refereed academic journals. Dr. Hassan is co-editor (with M. K. Lewis) of *Handbook of Islamic Banking* and *Islamic Finance, The International Library of Critical Writings in Economics* (Edward Elgar 2007), and co-editor (with Michael Mahlknecht) *Islamic Capital Market: Products and Strategies* (John Wiley & Sons, 2010). He is co-author *Islamic Entrepreneurship* (Routledge U.K., 2010). A frequent traveler, Dr. Hassan gives lectures and workshops in the United States and abroad, and has presented more than 150 research papers at professional conferences.

PART THREE

Contagion and Emerging Markets

C hapters in this section explore the phenomenon of contagion in emerging markets. This section also addresses another key topic of emerging markets —the effect of contagion from large economies to emerging countries.

As the chapters in Part Two, "Contagion and the Asian Financial Crisis," attest, there have been spectacular episodes of contagion in emerging economies. However, focusing only on crisis periods ignores the potentially beneficial effects of contagion during times of economic prosperity. Good economic times in one domain seem to spread to others as well. This phenomenon raises the question of whether the mechanisms by which crises spread are the same as those for the spread of beneficial effects.

A familiar bromide used in a variety of situations suggest that when a large entity sneezes, a smaller and related one catches pneumonia. Some of the chapters in this section address the possibility of this relationship between a large economy and emerging economies. For example, can problems in debt markets in the United States spread to emerging countries, and can turmoil in stock markets of well-developed countries adversely affect stock markets in emerging nations?

Financial crises in emerging markets have often been related to problems with sovereign debt. Thus, this section also explores the relationship among sovereign risk and contagion among emerging economies. Finally, this section also explores the specific responses of emerging countries to the global financial crisis of 2007–2009.

CHAPTER 16

Measuring Bulls and Bears Synchronization in East Asian Stock Markets

BERTRAND CANDELON
Professor in International Monetary Economics, Maastricht University School of Business and Economics, The Netherlands

STEFAN STRAETMANS
Associate Professor in Finance, Maastricht University School of Business and Economics, The Netherlands

JAN PIPLACK
Risk Model Validator at Rabobank, The Netherlands, and Assistant Professor in Finance, Utrecht University, The Netherlands

In the past couple of years, economists extensively documented the empirical features of stock market returns such as clusters of volatility and heavy tails; see, for example, Embrechts et al. (1997). That stock prices typically exhibit periods of persistent rises or falls, that is, so-called *bulls and bears*, has been recognized by financial practitioners for a long time but has attracted much less attention from the academic community. Accordingly, the potential for stock markets to be simultaneously bullish or bearish across geographical borders has also stayed underexposed. This chapter provides a nontechnical summary of the bulls-bears synchronization analysis earlier performed in Candelon, Piplack, and Straetmans (2008). This previous paper provided a framework for measuring synchronization between stock market cycles and examining to what extent the degree of synchronization has evolved over time. Here, we mainly focus on the empirical results and possible implications rather than on the estimation methodology. For more details on the used estimation techniques we therefore refer to the original source paper. Section 2 discusses the potential importance/implications of measuring bulls and bears synchronization. Sections 3 to 4 describe the outcomes obtained in Candelon, Piplack, and Straetmans (2008), in terms of bulls and bears dating, synchronization and evolution of the comovements. Section 5 concludes.

ON THE RELEVANCE OF MEASURING BULLS AND BEARS SYNCHRONIZATION

Measuring stock market cycles and their cross-border synchronization is of potential interest for both investors and policy makers. First, investors try to rebalance their portfolios by purchasing "cheap" stocks during bearish periods and selling "expensive" stocks when stock markets are bullish. The question arises, however, how to optimally implement this portfolio rebalancing. A thorough statistical analysis of bulls and bears can help investors to improve the timing of their investment decisions. The duration of a stock cycle constitutes the natural time horizon for a "single-cycle" or "short-term" investor (or, alternatively, constitutes the natural time horizon for portfolio rebalancing in case of a "multicycle" or "long-term" investor). Thus, in order to assess the potential for risk diversification across stock market cycles, it seems natural to consider correlations over the duration of a typical stock market cycle and not on, say, daily or monthly raw return data. Raw return correlations might offer a misleading view on the potential for risk diversification if investors base their rebalancing decisions on stock market cycles (we found that this "discrepancy" between correlations is present in the data we use in the empirical application).

Also, persistent swings in stock market prices and the potentially destabilizing effects on the real economy raise the issue of how monetary authorities should respond. Indeed, bullish stock markets can induce large amounts of loan collateral, which can fuel private debt, aggregate demand, and goods price inflation. Moreover, when the stock market bulls turn into bears, this can result in widespread liquidity problems and a credit crunch (cf. the subprime and sovereign crisis from 2007 until today). Thus, monitoring the impact of stock market swings is also relevant for regulatory bodies caring about systemic risk and overall financial stability. Finally, if stock cycles have become more synchronized over time, the potential for financial system instability to spill over (also denominated as *shift-contagion*) to other countries has also increased, which suggests that a coordinated effort of policy makers and regulatory bodies is necessary.

Our research contributes to the stock market bulls and bears cum synchronization literature. More specifically, we extend the Generalized Method of Moments (GMM) approach to measuring business cycle synchronization due to Harding and Pagan (2006) toward estimating and testing for multivariate cyclical stock market synchronization.[1] First, we explicitly allow for a continuous value of the synchronization index between –1 and 1. Second, the estimation and testing procedure for multivariate synchronization is complemented with a stability test for detecting a change in cyclical stock market synchronization. Third, our stability testing procedure can be seen as extending a scant preceding literature on structural change in cyclical stock market synchronization see, for example, Edwards et al. (2003).

A Monte Carlo simulation reveals that the stability test is able to detect contagion-like processes but not gradual changes. In that sense, our paper complements a recent literature on Asian contagion identification; see, for example, Forbes and Rigobon (2002) or Dungey et al. (2006).[2]

EVALUATION OF THE SYNCHRONIZATION BETWEEN STOCK MARKET BULLS AND BEARS

We estimate full sample bivariate and multivariate synchronization indices for the stock market cycles of five East Asian countries. We also distinguish full sample and subsample results to identify temporal shifts in synchronization. The choice for Asian countries can be motivated by the fact that changes in the synchronization of stock market cycles are probably more likely to occur for emerging markets because of the larger intensity of financial liberalization and recurrent financial turmoil.

U.S. dollar-denominated and dividend-adjusted monthly stock market indices for Singapore, Thailand, South Korea, Taiwan, and Malaysia were downloaded from the IFS database over the period January 1985 until November 2005. As we are interested in measuring the comovement of medium-run fluctuations or cycles across stock markets, we first have to identify these bulls and bears. The cycle binary variables are obtained by implementing the Bry and Boschan (1971) dating algorithm over a six-month time interval.

We found that the first half of the sample almost primarily consists of bull periods, which illustrates why investors have been talking about "Asian Tigers" for a long time. Not surprisingly, the 1997 Asian crisis and its aftermath are identified as bear periods. Our bull-bear classification also replicates the earlier finding that financial crises seem to erupt several months into bear phases, see, for example, Edwards et al. (2003). However, as Edwards et al. (2003, p. 936) pointed out, it would be premature to conclude on the basis of this observation that bear markets are leading indicators of financial crises. Somewhat surprisingly, the dot-com bubble burst is also identified as a bear period despite the relative underrepresentation of technology companies in emerging markets. Last but not least, upon "eyeballing" the bull and bear periods in graphs, we found that cycle comovement or *synchronization* is indeed visible across East Asian markets. In order to assess the degree of synchronization and whether it changed over time, we have to resort to the more advanced statistical tools introduced in Candelon, Piplack, and Straetmans (2008).

We previously argued that cycle correlations are the more relevant risk diversification indicators, provided investors base their buying and selling decision on how stock cycles evolve (i.e., if investors look at cycle turning points to time their buying and selling decisions). Moreover, the conventional correlations based on return pairs are found to be quite different for the majority of considered stock market pairs. This shows that raw return correlations can indeed provide misleading information about the potential for risk diversification when investors' time horizon (and thus their portfolio rebalancing) coincides with the stock market cycle.

STABILITY OF THE SYNCHRONIZATION BETWEEN BULLS AND BEARS

It is interesting to know whether the cycle correlations are stable over the whole sample period. In Candelon, Piplack, and Straetmans (2008) bootstrapped versions of the stability test for unknown breaks are performed to eliminate the size distortion. Applying those tests to our East Asian data, it turns out that instability is generally present, both in bivariate and multivariate synchronization indices and that the majority of the breaks coincide with the Asian crisis period.

We show that one should be careful in interpreting the full sample correlations because they hide different subsample values. We therefore also calculated these corresponding subsample values in order to find out the direction of the change in synchronization (the two-sided stability test does not provide us with that information).

The most striking feature is that the synchronization index in the second sub-sample is significantly larger than its prebreak counterpart. The confidence intervals actually suggest that prebreak synchronization was often insignificantly different from zero whereas post-break synchronization was close to perfect for more than half of the cases. As expected, the full sample synchronization index lies somewhere in between the subsample values and can be considered as a rough average of the true subsample values. Turning to the outcomes of the subsample homogeneity test, we find only a limited number of rejections for the first subsample; but deviations from homogeneity all disappear in the second subsample. Thus, the multivariate synchronization index increases over time and heterogeneity—present in the first subsample on a limited scale—almost completely disappears after the breaks.

The observed increases in cyclical correlations suggest that the room for risk diversification drastically diminished after the Asian crisis. If the increased synchronization persists in the long run (i.e., a permanent change), then the investors' (long-run) "strategic" asset allocation will be affected, whereas if the rise is transitory, it will only affect their "tactical" or short-run asset allocation. Insofar as the rise in stock market synchronization is permanent, regulatory authorities in the different countries probably have to adjust financial regulation in order to preserve banking system stability in the Asian financial system. More specifically, a high cross-country stock market synchronization can lead to boom-bust credit cycles spilling over from one country to the other.

On the other hand, if the increased synchronization is a purely contagious and short run phenomenon, policy makers cannot do much more than (1) avoid these spillovers by preventing the development of boom-bust cycles in their domestic economies and (2) mitigate the financial and real effects of the contagion if bulls and bears spill over to other markets.

Whether the increase in Asian stock market synchronization has a permanent or transitory character is open to debate. Our current econometric framework is not able to disentangle whether the increase in stock market synchronization is permanent or transitory. The magnitude of the jump and the inability to detect gradual breaks suggest that the breaks and corresponding subsample results provide evidence against financial integration. However, the observed sudden rises in synchronization are not necessarily interpretable as evidence in favor of "financial contagion." The latter phenomenon would require, inter alia, that the jump in the correlations is only temporary.

CONCLUDING REMARKS

In Candelon, Piplack, and Straetmans (2008) we proposed a Generalized Method of Moments (GMM) framework to measure the degree of synchronization between stock market bulls and bears. We argued that an assessment of cycle duration and cycle comovement is potentially relevant for investors. More specifically, investors could base their investment decisions on the turning points of the stock market cycle. Moreover, policy makers and regulators might be interested to know the magnitude of stock market synchronization and whether it changed over time because of the potentially destabilizing effects for stock market bulls and bears on the real economy.

Prior to calculating a measure of cyclical synchronization, we classified stock prices into bull and bear periods using the Bry and Boschan (1971) dating algorithm. We subsequently extended the Harding and Pagan (2006) framework in several directions.

First, we allowed for a value of the common synchronization index between −1 and 1. Moreover, our approach also produced an estimate of the multivariate synchronization index.

Second, we proposed an endogenous stability testing procedure for detecting structural change in the cyclical stock market synchronization index. The stability test seems unable to pick up gradual structural breaks in synchronization, which means that a financial integration interpretation for breaks is likely to be wrong in our framework. It is then tempting to interpret the breaks as evidence for financial contagion. However, one should be cautious with that break interpretation because the stability test is unable to distinguish permanent shocks from transitory shocks and contagion is by definition a transitory phenomenon.

We selected a set of Asian stock markets for our empirical application. Upon applying the stability test, we detected an increase in synchronization (mainly after the Asian crisis) that is both economically and statistically significant. Furthermore, the pair-wise (bivariate) synchronization indices seem to converge even more toward each other after the break. Moreover, we were unable to find breaks for a control group of developed countries, which seems to confirm that forces like financial liberalization, institutional reform, and market turbulence like the Asian crisis—that have been less prominent in developed markets—might be responsible for the increased synchronization.

The observed rise in Asian stock market synchronization implies that there is less space for diversifying risk after the Asian crisis (at least for investors that solely invest in the considered Asian markets and whose portfolio rebalancing is dictated by the turning points of the stock market cycle). If the rise in stock market synchronization has a lasting character, regulatory bodies probably need to change their supervisory framework in order to preserve banking system stability in the Asian financial system. On the other hand, if the stronger comovements between bulls and bears is a purely transitory (and possibly contagious) phenomenon, policy makers cannot do more than (1) preventing these spillovers by reducing the potential for the build up of boom-bust cycles in their domestic economies and (2) reducing the financial and real effects of the transitory shock if bulls and bears spill over to other markets.

The post-break increase in synchronization possibly contains a permanent as well as a transitory component. First, one could imagine that the Asian crisis and its direct aftermath had a contagious character as many authors have claimed since then. Subsequently, policy makers and regulatory bodies implemented a myriad of measures but the recipes for both dampening the effects of the Asian crisis and reducing the potential of future crises to strike and spread across borders were pretty similar in all affected countries. This "convergence" in post-crisis policy measures might itself have had a long run impact on the synchronization correlation. Disentangling the observed rise on synchronization correlations into a permanent and a transitory effect makes part of our future research agenda.

NOTES

1. For the theoretical properties of the tests, see Candelon, Piplack, and Straetmans (2008).
2. For details on the methodology as well as on the accompanying Monte Carlo simulations, see Candelon, Piplack, and Straetmans (2008).

REFERENCES

Bry, G., and C. Boschan. 1971. Cyclical Analysis of Time Series: Selected Procedures and Computer Programs, NBER (New York).

Candelon, B., J. Piplack, and S. Straetmans. 2008. "On Measuring Synchronization of Bulls and Bears: The case of East Asia." *Journal of Banking and Finance* 32:6, 1022–1035.

Candelon, B., J. Piplack, and S. Straetmans. 2009. "Multivariate Business Cycle Synchronization in Small Samples." *Oxford Bulletin of Economics and Statistics* 71:5, 715–737.

Dungey, M., R. Fry, and V. Martin. 2006. "Correlation, Contagion and Asian Evidence." *Asian Economic Papers* 5:2, 32–72.

Edwards, S., J. Gomez Biscarri, and H. F. Perez de Gracia. 2003. "Stock Market Cycles, Financial Liberalization and Volatility." *Journal of International Money and Finance* 22:925–955.

Embrechts, P., C. Kluppelberg, and T. Mikosch. 1997. *Modelling Extremal Events*. Berlin: Springer.

Forbes, K. J., and R. Rigobon. 2002. "No Contagion, Only Interdependence: Measuring Stock Market Co-movements." *Journal of Finance* 57:5, 2223–2261.

Harding, D., and A. P. Pagan. 2006. "Synchronization of Cycles." *Journal of Econometrics* 132:1, 59–79.

ABOUT THE AUTHORS

Bertrand Candelon is a professor in international monetary economics. He received a PhD from Universite Catholique de Louvain. After a post-doctoral fellowship at the Humboldt Universität zu Berlin, he joined University Maastricht School of Business and Economics in 2001. Bertrand Candelon has written extensive works in the area of international finance, in particular on contagion and on the analysis of financial market comovements. He is one of the founders of the Methods in International Finance Network.

Stefan Straetmans is an associate professor of finance at the Maastricht University School of Business and Economics in the Netherlands. He received an M.A. in economics from the University of Leuven in Belgium and a PhD in economics from Erasmus University Rotterdam in the Netherlands. Before joining Maastricht University, he was an assistant professor at the Free University Amsterdam. Dr. Straetmans' research interests include, inter alia, exchange rate behavior, banking system stability and the modeling and measurement of systemic risk, financial risk and financial crisis management, the design of stress tests, financial market contagion, linkages, and integration. His work has resulted in numerous publications in international academic journals like *Review of Economics and Statistics*, *Journal of Applied Econometrics*, *Oxford Bulletin of Economics and Statistics*, *Journal of International Money and Finance*, and *Journal of Banking and Finance*.

Jan Piplack was born on December 15, 1976, in Hamburg, Germany. From high school he graduated in 1996. He then proceeded for one year with the military service in the German Navy on Submarine U-23. In 1997, he joined Deutsche Bank AG obtaining the banker's degree with distinction. In 1999, he started his study of international economics at Maastricht University, the Netherlands. In 2004, he obtained his master's degree with distinction writing a thesis about volatility contagion.

After graduation, Jan joined the Department of Economics at Maastricht University as a PhD candidate. In 2007, he also worked as a visiting researcher at the University of California in Santa Cruz. In September 2008, he obtained his PhD in economics.

Since November 2008, he has been working as a model validator for the risk management department at Rabobank and as an assistant professor for the economics department at the University of Utrecht.

CHAPTER 17

Linkages between Debt Markets in the United States and Emerging Economies*

GUILLERMO FELICES
Citigroup

CHRISTIAN GRISSE
Federal Reserve Bank of New York

JING YANG
Bank of England

International financial markets are tightly linked: Developments in one market can quickly spread across countries and asset classes. Understanding these spillovers is important for market participants and policy makers alike. How do developments in U.S. debt markets affect the borrowing costs faced by issuers in emerging markets? And how, if at all, do shocks to emerging economies in turn influence U.S. government and corporate debt markets? This chapter analyzes the intra-day comovements across debt markets in the United States and emerging economies, and attempts to identify through which channels shocks are transmitted across markets.[1] Most empirical studies consider only the effect of U.S. financial markets on emerging economies, but not the possibility of reverse feedback. In contrast, this chapter emphasizes that the influence runs both ways, and discusses how these effects can be estimated in a structural model. The results show that feedback from emerging economy debt markets to U.S. financial markets is quantitatively significant, possibly reflecting the existence of "flight to quality" effects and the importance of contagion across worldwide markets for risky debt.

Exhibit 17.1 summarizes the correlations between some key variables that summarize debt markets in the United States and emerging economies. For U.S. debt markets, we look at short-term (3-month) and long-term (10-year) government

---

*The views in this chapter are those of the authors and do not necessarily reflect the views of the views of Citibank, the Bank of England, the Federal Reserve Bank of New York, or the Federal Reserve System.

Exhibit 17.1   Comovements Across Debt Markets in the United States and Emerging Economies

(a) Long-run correlations, 1997–2008

	U.S. 3-Month	U.S. 10-Year	U.S. High Yield	EMBIG
U.S. 3-month	1.00			
U.S. 10-year	0.27	1.00		
U.S. high yield	−0.24	−0.60	1.00	
EMBIG	−0.12	−0.29	0.33	1.00

(b) Correlations during Russian crisis, August–October 1998

	U.S. 3-Month	U.S. 10-Year	U.S. High Yield	EMBIG
U.S. 3-month	1.00			
U.S. 10-year	0.49	1.00		
U.S. high yield	−0.26	−0.74	1.00	
EMBIG	−0.21	−0.45	0.55	1.00

Data in first differences.

bond yields; in addition, as a measure of the broad U.S. corporate debt market, we include the Merrill Lynch High Yield Master II index (U.S. high yield), which tracks debt with a credit rating below BBB. As a benchmark for sovereign debt markets in emerging economies, we look at the emerging market bond index global (EMBIG) compiled by JPMorgan. This index tracks the spread between yields on dollar-denominated sovereign debt issued by emerging economies and U.S. government debt of corresponding maturities. Panel (a) of Exhibit 17.1 shows the long-run correlations of daily changes of these variables, computed from 1997 to 2008. EMBIG spreads are negatively correlated with U.S. government bond yields, but positively correlated with U.S. high yield spreads. While the latter result is intuitive—for example, we often observe that a crisis in one market prompts a repricing of risk more generally and leads to a sell-off across markets for risky debt—the former results seem surprising. For example, one might think that lower risk-free rates might lead to a "search for yield" and thus higher prices and lower yields and spreads on risky debt—which would suggest a positive correlation. The comovement between markets in developed countries and emerging economies is especially pronounced during high-risk events such as financial crises in emerging markets. Panel (b) of Exhibit 17.1 summarizes the correlations for the period of the Russian/LTCM crisis in 1998. All correlations have the same sign as the corresponding long-run correlations, but the strength of the comovement increases. The strong positive correlation between EMBIG spreads and U.S. corporate spreads in that period reflects the contagion that occurred following the Russian default, while the negative correlation between U.S. government bond yields and EMBIG spreads could be an indication of a "flight to quality" that occurred as investors shunned any form of risked and moved into safe assets.

Of course, the simple correlation between two variables A and B cannot tell us whether the observed comovement arises because variable A is affecting variable

B, or B is driving A, or both are influenced by some third variable C. More sophisticated empirical techniques are required to determine through which channels shocks are transmitted across financial markets.

Estimating the role of various contemporaneous transmission channels is complicated by the presence of endogeneity. For example, emerging market bond spreads are likely to be affected by developments in the United States, but may also influence U.S. financial markets. In this case, a simple regression of U.S. government bond yields on emerging market bond spreads, for example, will yield biased coefficients. To get around this problem we use a methodology developed by Rigobon (2003), which exploits the changing volatility of the data to fully identify a structural econometric model. To describe the intuition behind this methodology, consider again the relationship between U.S. government bond yields and emerging market bond spreads. Times when emerging market spreads are very volatile—for example, periods of financial crises in emerging markets—are likely periods in which the influence of emerging market bond spreads dominates the comovement across markets. Such periods can therefore be used to identify the effect of developments in emerging economies on U.S. debt markets. An important assumption underlying this identification method is that while the volatility of the structural shocks hitting financial markets is allowed to change over time, the relationships between the variables are assumed to stay constant over time—a common assumption in the empirical literature on long-run relationships across financial markets.

Our empirical model is a structural vector autoregression (VAR). In such a model, each endogenous variable is regressed on its own lags, as well as on lags of the other endogenous variables. To identify the contemporaneous comovements between the endogenous variables, we then proceed as follows. First, the residuals from the regression are used to determine periods in which the underlying, unobserved structural shocks are particularly volatile. Following Ehrmann, Fratzscher, and Rigobon (2010) we use a simple threshold rule to do this: whenever the volatility of the residuals (computed as the standard deviation over rolling windows) is larger than the chosen threshold, the variable is classified as volatile for that period. Periods of unique volatility are then classed together in volatility regimes. In a second step, the residuals in each volatility regime are used to identify the structural parameters of the model. This is done by relating the unique elements of the variance–covariance matrices of the residuals, for each volatility regime, to their theoretical counterparts. This yields several equations from which the unknown structural parameters that represent the contemporaneous comovements can be estimated. We use daily data from January 1997 to May 2008. The VAR model is estimated in first differences, which ensures that the variables are stationary, and includes five lags (capturing one work week).

Exhibit 17.2 gives an example of how volatility periods are selected. It plots the rolling standard deviation of the residuals from the EMBIG spreads regression. As seen in Exhibit 17.2, this proxy for the volatility of the underlying structural shocks to EMBIG spreads exhibits spikes that correspond to times of major financial crises in emerging economies, including the Asian crisis of 1996–1997, the Russian crisis of 1998, and the Argentinean crisis of 2001. The EMBIG volatility regime periods chosen mostly lie within these crisis periods. Note that we class only those periods in the EMBIG volatility regime where EMBIG residuals are *uniquely*

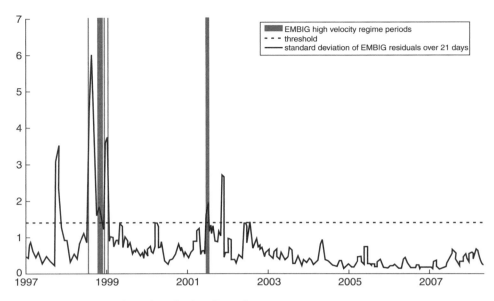

Exhibit 17.2 EMBIG High Volatility Periods

volatile. In line with the intuition outlined above, this classification scheme may help to robustly identify the underlying structural relationships by emphasizing those times in which one type of structural shock clearly dominates the observed comovements.[2]

Information is incorporated in financial markets very quickly, so that we are mainly interested in the spillovers that occur within the same day. The results from the benchmark estimation are shown in Exhibit 17.3. The coefficients correspond to the contemporaneous (intra-day) effect of a structural shock to the variables

Exhibit 17.3 Contemporaneous Comovements Across Debt Markets in the U.S. and Emerging Economies: Estimation Results from a Structural VAR Model

From . . . . . . to	U.S. 3-Month	U.S. 10-Year	U.S. High Yield	EMBIG
U.S. 3-month	1.0129***	0.1783***	−0.0086	−0.0805***
	[0.0000]	[0.0000]	[0.1450]	[0.0030]
U.S. 10-year	0.0823*	1.0952***	−0.1643***	−0.1392***
	[0.0840]	[0.0000]	[0.0050]	[0.0000]
U.S. high yield	−0.0408*	−0.5524***	1.0956***	0.1401***
	[0.0840]	[0.0000]	[0.0000]	[0.0000]
EMBIG	−0.0023***	−0.0923***	0.1986***	1.0239***
	[0.4920]	[0.0000]	[0.0000]	[0.0000]

The estimated model is $Ay_t = By_{t-1} + u_t$ where y_t is the vector of endogenous variables (U.S. 3-month, U.S. 10-year, U.S. high yield, EMBIG), u_t is a vector of structural shocks, and A and B are matrices of coefficients. The table shows the estimated coefficients of the matrix A^{-1}. The coefficient in row i and column j describes the intra-day effect of a structural shock to variable j on variable i. ***, ** and * denote significance at the 1%, 5%, and 10% level, respectively. Bootstrap p-values in brackets. For details, see Felices, Grisse, and Yang (2009).

listed in the columns to the variables listed in the rows. It is worth noting that the coefficients on the diagonal are greater than one: for example, the effect of a shock to EMBIG spreads will contemporaneously affect U.S. corporate spreads, which will feed back to EMBIG. As seen in Exhibit 17.3, the original impact of the shock is magnified as a result.

Consider first the effect of changes in U.S. government bond yields on emerging market and U.S. corporate bond spreads. What sign should we expect for the estimated coefficients? Risky debt is typically priced at a spread over riskless rates. Therefore, higher U.S. interest rates should raise the financing costs of risky borrowers, increase their default risk, and thus lead to higher spreads. Furthermore, lower riskless rates are often thought to be associated with a "search for yield," as investors shift into more risky assets in order to earn higher returns, thus driving the prices of these assets up and their spreads over riskless debt down. These "financing cost" and "search for yield" channels suggest that an increase (decrease) in U.S. government bond yields should lead to higher (lower) spreads on risky debt. However, from the first two columns of Exhibit 17.3, it is seen that the corresponding estimated coefficients are negative: the overall effect of shocks that raise U.S. interest rates—especially long rates—is to lower U.S. high yield and EMBIG spreads, although the effect of short-term yields on EMBIG spreads is not statistically significant. In particular, the effect of a shock to U.S. long-term interest rates on U.S. high yield spreads is estimated to be strongly negative and highly significant. One possible interpretation of these results is that the negative comovement reflects changes in investors' outlook for the U.S. economy following changes in interest rates, which have implications for the outlook for firm profitability and default risk. Economic booms are likely to be associated with higher profitability and lower default risk for the corporate sector compared to recessions. If an increase in U.S. interest rates goes together with or signals strong economic growth in the U.S., it could hence lead to a decrease in U.S. high-yield spreads. Furthermore, business cycles in advanced countries and emerging economies are connected through international trade. Therefore, announcements that change the economic outlook for the United States will also affect investors' expectations of economic developments and default risk in emerging economies. Thus, the negative coefficients may imply that this "growth effect" dominates the "financing cost" and "search for yield" channels.

Next, consider the effect of developments in emerging economies' debt markets on U.S. financial markets. From the last column of Exhibit 17.3, it can be seen that a shock to EMBIG spreads lowers both short- and long-term U.S. government bond yields. The coefficients are highly significant. This relationship can be interpreted as reflecting "flight to quality" associated with emerging market turmoil, as investors shift out of risky assets and into "safe-haven" assets such as U.S. government debt. From the last column, it is also seen that shocks that raise spreads on emerging market debt also tend to increase spreads on the U.S. corporate debt market: There is financial "contagion" from emerging economy debt to other high-risk markets. This is intuitive, as emerging market crises increases in investors' aversion to risk more generally, leading to a sell-off across markets for risky debt. What is the overall contemporaneous effect of a shock to emerging markets on the United States? On the one hand, mature economies might benefit from strong "flight to quality," which drives down the financing costs of low-risk borrowers. On the other hand, a shock to emerging market debt is not necessarily good news for U.S. bond markets because it is also associated with wider spreads on other risky debt, increasing the borrowing costs for corporate issuers. In the other direction, the last coefficient in the third row shows that shocks to the U.S. corporate debt market also tend to spill over to emerging economies. In particular, the effect of U.S. corporate spreads on EMBIG is stronger than the reverse effect.

In this chapter, we have discussed the intra-day comovements across bond markets in the United States and emerging economies. Using the estimated VAR model, it is also possible to trace the effect of structural shocks on the endogenous variables over time: But longer-term effects are rarely significantly different from zero, as relevant information is very quickly incorporated in asset prices. However, forecast error decompositions for the estimated structural VAR model show that emerging market and U.S. corporate bond spreads are mainly determined by shocks to U.S. government bond yields in the long run, while U.S. interest rates in turn are overwhelmingly determined by their own structural shocks.

NOTES

1. This chapter draws on Felices, Grisse, and Yang (2009).
2. Felices, Grisse, and Yang (2009) argue that the results are robust to alternative methods of volatility regime choice.

REFERENCES

Ehrmann, M., M. Fratzscher, and R. Rigobon. 2010. "Stocks, Bonds, Money Markets and Exchange Rates: Measuring International Financial Transmission." *Journal of Applied Econometrics*, forthcoming.

Felices, G., C. Grisse, and J. Yang. 2009. "International Financial Transmission: Emerging and Mature Markets." *Bank of England Working Paper* 373.

Rigobon, R. 2003. "Identification through heteroskedasticity." *Review of Economics and Statistics* 85:4, 777–792.

ABOUT THE AUTHORS

Guillermo Felices holds a PhD in economics from New York University. He is a Global Macro Strategist at Citigroup (London) and was previously a senior economist at the Bank of England.

Christian Grisse is an economist at the Federal Reserve Bank of New York, and received his PhD in economics from Cambridge University.

Jing Yang is a senior economist at the Bank of England. Prior to joining the Bank, she worked at the Bank of Canada and also had a short spell at the ECB. Jing holds a PhD in economics from Concordia University.

CHAPTER 18

Financial Spillovers and Contagion from Mature to Emerging Stock Markets

JOHN BEIRNE
European Central Bank

GUGLIELMO MARIA CAPORALE
Centre for Empirical Finance, Brunel University, London, U.K.

MARIANNE SCHULZE-GHATTAS
Financial Markets Group, London School of Economics

NICOLA SPAGNOLO
Centre for Empirical Finance, Brunel University, London, U.K.

The literature on financial contagion is vast. The October 1987 stock market crash in the United States and the 1992 Exchange Rate Mechanism (ERM) crisis gave rise to numerous empirical analyses of the transmission of shocks across *mature* financial markets. Research on financial contagion in *emerging* market economies (EMEs) was boosted by the crises of the 1990s, in particular the Asian crisis. Given the rapid propagation and large economic impact of these crises, contagion became virtually synonymous with turbulence in emerging markets and studies of different channels of contagion during these crises multiplied.

Although views on the precise definition of financial contagion differ, most empirical analyses distinguish between contagion during crises, and spillovers across asset markets during "normal" periods. Contagion is defined as a change in the transmission mechanism during crisis episodes. An important strand of this research focuses on conditional correlations to examine the extent of cross-country linkages in financial markets. However, changes in conditional correlations are influenced by special features of the data generating process such as heteroskedasticity, endogeneity, and the effect of common factors. Following the seminal paper by King and Wadhwani (1990), numerous studies addressed the implications of these features of financial time series for the analysis and interpretation of conditional correlations; these studies include King, Sentana, and Wadhwani (1994), Forbes and Rigobon (2002), Corsetti, Pericoli, and Sbracia (2005), Caporale,

Cipollini, Spagnolo (2005) and Caporale, Pittis, Spagnolo (2006). Other researchers have taken different approaches to examine the presence of contagion. Dungey, Fry, González-Hermosillo, and Martin (2002, 2003) estimate dynamic latent factor models to test for contagion in emerging bond and stock markets. Bekaert, Harvey, and Ng (2005) identify contagion as *excess correlation*, that is, cross-country correlation of the residuals from a factor model describing emerging market integration into global stock markets.

Empirical analyses of contagion and spillovers in *emerging* financial markets have primarily focused on the transmission of shocks originating in one, or several, emerging markets on other markets. Given the widespread repercussions of past emerging market crises, this is not surprising. In the literature on linkages between *mature* and *emerging* financial markets, contagion has not been a major theme. This literature has tended to focus on issues such as market liberalization and integration with global markets. Several episodes of turbulence in mature financial markets in the past decade, in particular the events of 2007–2009, suggest that this may be an important gap in the empirical research on contagion in emerging financial markets.

Our analysis attempts to help fill this gap. Although building on previous research, it differs from existing studies of emerging stock markets in three respects. First, we model variances and covariances using a multivariate GARCH framework that allows for volatility spillovers across markets. Although this method is common in the literature on mature financial markets, it is fairly rare in studies of emerging markets. Second, we test for shifts in the transmission of volatility during episodes of turbulence in mature markets. Third, we cover a large sample of 41 emerging market economies (EMEs) in Asia, Europe, Latin America, and the Middle East, which provides a rich basis for comparisons across countries and regions; most studies to date focus on smaller sets of countries in one or two regions.[1]

We employ a trivariate VAR-GARCH framework with the BEKK representation proposed by Engle and Kroner (1995) to model the means and variances of stock returns in local, regional, and global (mature) markets, with the latter defined as a weighted average of the United States, Japan, and Europe (Germany, France, Italy, and the United Kingdom). Although we are mainly interested in spillovers from mature global markets to local emerging markets, we include a regional market—defined as a weighted average of other emerging markets in the region—in each country model to control for the transmission of shocks originating in these countries. We modify the GARCH model by including a dummy variable that allows for shifts in the parameters capturing spillovers from mature to emerging markets during episodes of turbulence in the former. This approach accommodates multiple shifts between turbulent and tranquil periods. In the absence of an agreed definition of turbulence in mature financial markets, we use the Chicago Board Options Exchange index of implied volatility from options on the U.S. S&P 500 (VIX source: Datastream), a widely quoted indicator of market sentiment, to identify episodes of turbulence in mature stock markets.

Wald tests are carried out to examine various hypotheses concerning volatility spillovers from global mature stock markets to regional and local emerging markets, and from regional to local markets. Specifically, we consider the following possibilities: no volatility spillovers whatsoever from mature markets; no shift contagion, that is, no change in the transmission of volatility during turbulent periods in mature markets; no volatility spillovers during tranquil periods—a special case of volatility contagion if spillovers are present during turbulent episodes; and no volatility spillovers from regional to local markets.

We test for changes in conditional variances in local emerging stock markets during turbulent episodes in mature markets, analyze the behavior of conditional correlations between emerging and mature markets during these periods, and examine the conditional beta coefficients implied by the estimated variances and covariances to revisit the question of whether changes in correlations reflect primarily a rise in volatility in the turbulent market—as argued by Forbes and Rigobon (2002)—or "true" contagion, that is, changes in the transmission mechanism (beta coefficients).

The model for each EME consists of local stock returns, returns in the regional EME market, and returns in the global mature market. Weekly returns were calculated as log differences of local currency stock market indices for weeks running from Wednesday to Wednesday to minimize effects of cross-country differences in weekend market closures. The time series for the Asian EMEs start in September 1993 and the majority of the series for Latin America, emerging Europe, and the Middle East begin in 1996. All return series end in mid-March 2008. The regional market in each EME model was defined as a weighted average of all other sample EMEs in the region. Mature market returns were calculated as a weighted average of returns on benchmark indices in the United States, Japan, and Europe (France, Germany, Italy, United Kingdom). As complete time series on market capitalization are not available for all EMEs in our sample, weights are based on 104-week moving averages of US$-GDP data from the IMF's World Economic Outlook database.

The definition of the crisis window can significantly affect the results of contagion tests. Even though dating the start and end of financial crises is never straightforward, there is relatively broad consensus on the identification of major emerging market crises. By contrast, what may be considered a *crisis* in mature financial markets is less obvious, with the possible exception of the 1987 U.S. stock market crash, the 1992 ERM crisis, and the crisis that began in 2007. In the absence of a broad consensus on crisis events in mature financial markets, we define market turbulence as a period in which the VIX is either very high (30 or higher) or rising sharply (five-day moving average exceeding the 52-week moving average by 30 percent or more). Based on this definition, turbulent episodes are fairly rare events. Thirteen percent of the observations in the full data sample running from June 1993 to March 2008 fall into this category, with clusters in 1996–1998, 2001, 2002, early 2003, 2007, and 2008, which is in line with anecdotal evidence.

For most of the 41 EMEs in the sample, the estimated trivariate VAR-GARCH (1,1) models appear to capture the evolution of conditional means and variances of local stock returns, and their interactions with regional and mature markets, quite well. The parameter estimates for the conditional means of emerging market returns suggest statistically significant spillovers-in-mean from mature stock markets to local markets for half of the EMEs analyzed. These include all but one of the Asian emerging markets and nearly half of the countries in emerging Europe. By contrast, the estimates of the mean spillover parameter are insignificant (and negative) for all Latin American countries, except Brazil, and insignificant (though positive) for most countries in the Middle East and North Africa, except Egypt and Morocco. On the other hand, parameter estimates of spillovers-in-mean from regional to local emerging markets are insignificant for all of emerging Asia, but positive and significant for half of the countries in Latin America, close to half of emerging Europe, as well as Kuwait and Lebanon in the Middle East.

These differences in spillovers-in-mean are striking, particularly for Asia and Latin America. Common factors not explicitly included in our model may explain part of this variation. The estimated "own-market" coefficients of the conditional variances are statistically significant for all EMEs but one, and there is substantial evidence of spillovers-in-variance from mature stock markets to local emerging markets.

The results of the Wald tests strongly reject the null hypothesis of no volatility spillovers whatsoever from mature markets for well over three quarters of the EME sample, including all EMEs in Asia, except China, India, and the Philippines; all countries in Latin America, except Mexico and Venezuela; all EMEs in the Middle East and North Africa; and over two thirds of the countries in emerging Europe. These tests also suggest that in many EMEs the transmission of volatility changes during turbulent episodes in mature markets. Indeed, stock markets in some EMEs appear to be affected only during such periods. Although the hypothesis of no shift in the spillover parameters during turbulent episodes in mature markets is rejected for 60 percent of the sample, we reject the hypothesis of no volatility spillovers over the full sample period for just 40 percent of the EMEs covered. We find evidence of spillovers over the whole sample period but no shifts in the parameters for only four EMEs (Colombia, Estonia, India, and Taiwan). For well over a third of the countries, particularly in the Middle East and North Africa, the tests also point to spillovers-in-variance from regional to local emerging markets. In many of these cases, the regional markets are in turn affected by spillovers from mature markets and may thus act as a conduit for volatility transmission.

The average estimated conditional variances of local stock returns are higher during mature market turbulences than during nonturbulent periods in three quarters of the sample EMEs. Even though volatility in most emerging markets rises during turbulent episodes, volatility in mature markets tends to rise more. As pointed out by Forbes and Rigobon (2002), such increases in relative volatility may be the main source of increasing conditional correlations during crisis periods. This appears to be the case in many of the sample EMEs. Average conditional correlations between emerging and mature market returns rise during turbulent episodes in four out of five sample EMEs, but conditional beta coefficients are, on average, unchanged or lower during these episodes in well over half of the countries. We find a statistically significant increase in conditional betas in only four countries (Czech Republic, Latvia, Peru, and Romania).

The analysis provides a number of interesting insights. In particular, it suggests that spillovers from mature markets do influence the dynamics of conditional means and variances of returns in local and regional emerging stock markets. Moreover, there is evidence that spillover-in-variance parameters change during turbulent episodes in mature markets. This is the case in many EME stock markets. In four out of five of the EMEs in our sample, volatility spillovers from mature markets are present both during tranquil and turbulent times in mature markets, or at least during turbulent times. And where volatility spillovers are present, their nature often changes during turbulent times.

The analysis also adds an interesting nuance to the discussion on whether changes in conditional correlations are a reliable indicator of financial contagion. On the one hand, the estimated conditional variances and correlations confirm the view of Forbes and Rigobon (2002) that increases in conditional correlations during turbulent periods are often the result of a rise in volatility in the market where the turbulence originates relative to other markets. On the other hand, our results also indicate that in the presence of pervasive volatility spillovers across markets, it is not appropriate to correct for this effect by adjusting conditional correlations for the change in volatility in the turbulent market, and to assume that volatility in the other market remains unchanged. Our estimates suggest that this is generally not the case.

NOTE

1. Detailed results can be found in Beirne, Caporale, Schulze-Ghattas, and Spagnolo (2009).

REFERENCES

Beirne, J., G. M. Caporale, M. Schulze-Ghattas, and N. Spagnolo. 2009. "Volatility Spillovers and Contagion from Mature to Emerging Stock Markets." *ECB Working Paper* 1113.

Bekaert, G., C. R. Harvey, and A. Ng. 2005. "Market Integration and Contagion." *Journal of Business* 78:1, 39–69.

Caporale, G. M., A. Cipollini, and N. Spagnolo. 2005. "Testing for Contagion: A Conditional Correlation Analysis." *Journal of Empirical Finance* 12:476–489.

Caporale, G. M., N. Pittis, and N. Spagnolo. 2006. "Volatility Transmission and Financial Crises." *Journal of Economics and Finance* 30:3, 376–390.

Corsetti, G., M. Pericoli, and M. Sbracia. 2005. "Some Contagion, Some Interdependence: More Pitfalls in Tests of Financial Contagion." *Journal of International Money and Finance* 24:1177–1199.

Dungey, M., R. Fry, B. González-Hermosillo, and V. Martin. 2002. "International Contagion from the Russian Crisis and the LTCM Collapse." *IMF Working Paper* 02/74, International Monetary Fund, Washington DC.

Dungey, M., R. Fry, B. González-Hermosillo, and V. Martin. 2003. "Unanticipated Shocks and Systemic Influences: The Impact of Contagion in Global Equity Markets in 1998." *IMF Working Paper* 03/84. Washington, DC: International Monetary Fund.

Engle, R. F., and K. F. Kroner. 1995. "Multivariate Simultaneous Generalized ARCH." *Econometric Theory* 11:1, 122–150.

Forbes, K., and R. Rigobon. 2002. "No Contagion, Only Interdependence: Measuring Stock Market Co-Movements." *Journal of Finance* 57:5, 2223–2261.

King, M., and S. Wadhwani. 1990. "Transmission of Volatility between Stock Markets." *Review of Financial Studies* 3:1, 5–33.

King, M., E. Sentana, and S. Wadhwani. 1994. "Volatility and Links between National Stock Markets." *Econometrica* 62:901–933.

ABOUT THE AUTHORS

John Beirne attained his PhD in economics from Brunel University in the United Kingdom and is currently an economist at the European Central Bank. His academic interests focus on international finance, applied macroeconomics, applied econometrics, and emerging markets. His recent work focuses on volatility spillover effects in emerging stock markets, exchange rate and price dynamics in transition economies, and the equity premium and inflation. His research has been published in journals such as *Economics of Transition*, *Emerging Markets Review*, and *Applied Financial Economics Letters*.

Guglielmo Maria Caporale is professor of economics and finance and director of the Centre for Empirical Finance at Brunel University, London; he is also a visiting professor at London South Bank University and London Metropolitan University, a research professor at DIW Berlin, and a CESifo Research Network Fellow. Prior to taking up his current position, he was a research officer at the National Institute of Economic and Social Research in London; a research fellow and then a senior research fellow at the Centre for Economic Forecasting at the London Business School; professor of economics at the University of East London; professor of economics and finance as well as director of the Centre for Monetary and Financial Economics at London South Bank University.

His research interests include econometrics, macroeconomics, monetary and financial economics, international finance. Professor Caporale has published papers in numerous books and leading academic journals, such as *Journal of International Money and Finance*, *Economics Letters*, *Canadian Journal of Economics*, *Journal of Macroeconomics*, *Econometric Reviews*, *Oxford Bulletin of Economics and Statistics*, *Journal of Forecasting*, *Computational Economics*, *Computational Statistics and Data Analysis*, *Journal of Empirical Finance*, *Journal of Financial Econometrics*, *Southern Economic Journal*, *Eastern Economic Journal*, *Quarterly Review of Economics and Finance*, *Empirical Economics*, *Scottish Journal of Political Economy*, *Manchester School of Economic and Social Studies*, *International Journal of Finance and Economics*, *Review of International Economics*, *Review of Financial Economics*, *Review of Development Economics*, *Journal of Economic Surveys*, *Economic Modelling*, *Journal of Economics and Finance*, *Journal of Policy Modeling*, and *Review of World Economics*. He is a member of various professional bodies and of the Money, Macro and Finance Research Group (MMFRG) Committee, an active referee for several academic journals, a regular speaker at international conferences, and a consultant to leading companies and international organisations.

Marianne Schulze-Ghattas obtained a PhD in economics from the University of Hamburg, Germany and held various research, operational, and managerial positions at the International Monetary Fund from 1982 to 2008, covering advanced and emerging market countries. She is currently a fellow at the CASE Centre for Social and Economic Research, Warsaw; visiting fellow at the Financial Markets Group, London School of Economics; and a part-time lecturer in economics and finance at Kingston University, London. Research interests and publications focus on financial crises in emerging markets, financial market linkages, and contagion.

Nicola Spagnolo received his PhD from Birkbeck College, University of London in 2001. He is reader (associate professor) of economics and finance at Brunel University, London; he is also research associate at the Centre for Applied Macroeconomic Analysis, University of Canberra, Australia and research fellow at the Centre for

Empirical Finance, and at the Centre for the Analysis of Risk and Optimisation Modelling Applications, Brunel University, London.

His research interests include financial economics, international finance, macroeconomics, and time series analysis. Professor Spagnolo has published papers in books and leading academic journals, such as *Economics Letters, Emerging Market Review, Empirical Economics, International Journal of Finance and Economics, Journal of Economics and Behavioural Organization, Journal of Economics and Finance, Journal of Empirical Finance, Journal of Time Series Analysis, Review of International Economics,* and *Studies of Nonlinear Dynamics and Econometrics.*

He is a member of professional bodies, an active referee for several academic journals and a regular speaker at international conferences.

CHAPTER 19

Is There Any Contagion in Emerging Debt Markets?

IULIANA ISMAILESCU
Assistant Professor of Finance at Lubin School of Business, Pace University

HOSSEIN B. KAZEMI
Professor of Finance at Isenberg School of Management,
University of Massachusetts Amherst

On September 21, 1998, one month after the Russian government default, the Federal Reserve and 24 top investment banks, worried about a financial crisis in the U.S. markets, came up with a rescue package for Long Term Capital Management (LTCM), the fund that was most visibly affected by the Russian implosion and its aftermath. The Fed believed that if LTCM collapsed, other investment banks' trading losses might spin out of control, as many of these banks' trading desks had similar positions or were the counterparties in most of LTCM's transactions. Though LTCM had little direct exposure to emerging economies, the potential spillover effects of the Russian default and possible collapse of LTCM on U.S. capital markets provided the impetus for the Fed to intervene.

Crisis episodes, like the Russian default mentioned above, and their potential for financial contagion to other markets have received growing attention in recent years. As the most recent crises have shown, a powerful shock can no longer be restricted to the country of origin, and its effects can be equally destructive to healthy and financially stable economies.

Since the 1987 U.S. stock market crash, researchers have tried different techniques to test for the presence of contagion and to explain its transmission mechanisms. While focusing mostly on stock markets, previous studies have shown that contagion happens and can be propagated through banking centers, trade and financial linkages. Though stock markets represent a natural choice for studies of contagion, they represent only a small fraction of the global asset markets. Further, as the subprime mortgage crisis of 2007–2009 has shown, a financial crisis that reaches debt markets can spread farther and have more severe consequences than a crisis episode in stock or foreign exchange markets.

Using a sample of 15 countries from three different geographical regions—East Asia, Eastern Europe, and Latin America—Ismailescu and Kazemi (2008) provide one of the first and most comprehensive empirical analyses of contagion in emerging debt markets. Focusing on two government defaults, Russia's 1998 and Argentina's 2001, they consider three approaches that have been previously suggested for contagion tests in stock markets: the correlation framework, the volatility spillover, and the multinomial logistic model.

THE CORRELATION FRAMEWORK

Under this framework, an event is contagious if a significant post-event increase in cross-country correlations exists. Using this definition, Chakrabarti and Roll (2002), Bekaert et al. (2005), Chiang et al. (2007), among others, report that most national stock markets become more cointegrated after financial crises. Forbes and Rigobon (2002) argue that increased market correlations during financial crises are caused by volatility shocks. They show that when an adjustment to the correlation coefficient is applied, all evidence of contagion in equity markets during the 1987 U.S. market crash, 1994 Mexican peso crisis, and 1997 East Asian crisis disappears.

Using a data set of daily observations of JPMorgan's EMBI Global emerging country indexes, Ismailescu and Kazemi (2008) compute daily close-to-close index returns for each country in their sample. Then, for each region, arithmetic averages of correlation coefficients and standard deviations of EM bond index returns are calculated separately for the pre-crisis and crisis periods. As emerging market bond index returns have been found not to follow a normal distribution, one approach to test for differences in correlations (standard deviations) of returns is bootstrapping. Ismailescu and Kazemi (2008) test the statistical significance of the point estimates by bootstrapping for their confidence intervals. The point estimates are the actual differences in correlations (standard deviations) across periods.

Although not statistically significant at 10 percent confidence level, volatilities increase in all sample regions during the Russian crisis period. In contrast, Europe and Asia's average standard deviations are lower during the Argentine crisis period than they are in the pre-crisis period. Furthermore, changes in average correlation are also insignificant during both crises. This result differs from earlier research of Baig and Goldfajn (1999), and Chakrabarti and Roll (2002), where Asian bond markets, and Asian and European stock markets, respectively, become more correlated during the crisis period than before. Additionally, European and Asian markets become significantly less correlated with Latin American economies once the Argentine government default becomes imminent.

In summary, none of the regions in our sample becomes highly correlated during either crisis. Moreover, the average correlations of European markets during the Russian crisis and of Latin American markets during the Argentine crisis have both declined from the pre-crisis to the crisis period (see Exhibit 19.1a and Exhibit 19.1b). On average, the correlation of European bond returns is 8 percent lower in the crisis period than in the pre-crisis period. Likewise, the average correlation of Latin American bond returns declines by 27.60 percent from the pre-crisis to the crisis period. Under the correlation framework, this is evidence that neither of the two financial crises was a cause of contagion in emerging markets. Does this mean that an EM bond investor fares better than does a stockholder during crisis episodes? We have to answer negatively. Permanent high correlations in emerging debt markets reduce the diversification benefits of the international bond investor before as well as after a crisis.

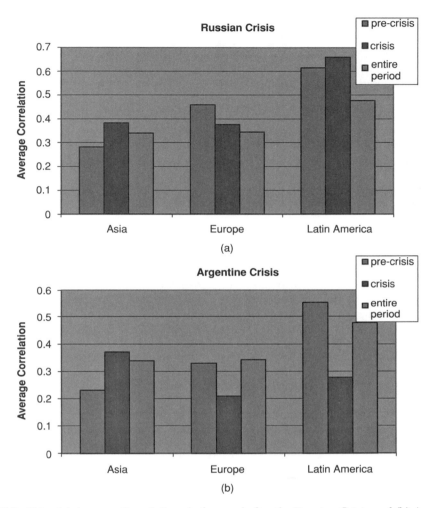

Exhibit 19.1 (a) Average Correlations before and after the Russian Crisis and (b) Average Correlations before and after the Argentine Crisis

EXTREME RETURNS

Results obtained under the correlation framework show that in times of crisis, country debt indexes do not co-move more than they do during periods that are more tranquil. This means that either the correlation framework is not an effective way to test for contagion in emerging debt markets, or financial crises are not a source of contagion in these markets. An argument that would undermine the validity of the correlation framework in contagion tests is that correlations do not differentiate between small and large returns. In times of turmoil, however, extreme negative returns rather than small negative returns are expected to be sources of contagion.

Ismailescu and Kazemi (2008) and Ismailescu (2010) examine contagion in extreme returns based on a methodology developed by Bae et al. (2003). They use

multinomial logistic regressions to predict occurrences of simultaneous large returns in one region given a high number of coexceedances (simultaneous large
returns) in another region. An exceedance is defined as an extreme return that
lies either above the 95th percentile or below the 5th percentile of the index daily
returns. The logit model is estimated separately for both tails of the return distribution.

To control for local and global contagion factors, the conditional volatility of
the regional index and the Eurodollar rate are both included in the multinomial
logit model. The conditional volatility is found to be a significant intraregional
contagion factor, but the effect of the Eurodollar rate on the probabilities of co-
exceedances is mixed.

After controlling for the local and global contagion factors, Ismailescu and
Kazemi (2008) and Ismailescu (2010) find evidence of contagion from Europe to
Asia and Latin America, and some evidence of contagion from Latin American
to European markets, but weak evidence that Asia has been contaminated by the
Argentine crisis. When the entire sample period is considered, once again they
find that contagion is as likely in periods of crisis as it is in the entire period. This
result confirms Ismailescu and Kazemi's (2008) earlier finding that financial crises
are not a source of contagion in emerging debt markets. They thus conclude that
contagion in emerging bond markets is more likely driven by their high correlations
(see Exhibit 19.1) than by crisis episodes.

VOLATILITY SPILLOVERS

Volatility spillover is another measure of contagion that has become critically important to international asset allocation, as it affects an investor's ability to diversify
globally. During periods of volatility spillover, market volatilities move in tandem,
as financial turmoil in one market spills over into other markets. In this regard,
two issues were studied in Ismailescu and Kazemi (2008): First, whether volatility
spillover exists in a period surrounding a credit event; second, whether it has the
same intensity in the period leading to and following the crisis.

Ismailescu and Kazemi (2008) find that volatility changes are highly serially dependent within countries, but, except for Latin America during the Argentine crisis,
they do not change significantly from pre-crisis to crisis periods. After controlling
for serial dependence, there is insignificant evidence of within-region spillover effects before each credit event, and equally weak support for a change in spillover intensity from the pre-crisis to the crisis period. The latter finding shows that an
increase in volatility contagion is not a general feature of financial crises.

They also test for cross-regional volatility spillover coming from Europe to
Asia and Latin America during the Russian crisis, and from Latin America to Asia
and Europe during the Argentine crisis. Their findings suggest that, except for
Asian markets that were sensitive to volatility spillovers coming from Europe, no
other spillover effects were found. This result differs from Diebold and Yilmaz
(2007), who find a substantial increase in volatility spillovers across stock markets
during and after the East Asia and Russian crises.

CONCLUSIONS

Previous studies have found evidence of contagion in foreign exchange and stock markets following a financial crisis. In contrast, Ismailescu and Kazemi (2008) and Ismailescu (2010) argue that transmission of information and contagion among emerging debt markets have a strong presence during both periods of financial crises as well as tranquil market conditions.

The existence of contagion among emerging debt markets may be explained by the presence of various economic as well as political factors. Foreign currency denominated debt can be serviced only if the emerging economy has enough foreign currency reserves. A decline in these reserves can take place during periods of economic crises and normal market conditions. Further, lack of foreign currency reserves in one emerging economy sends a signal to the markets that other emerging economies may face a similar predicament (e.g., because of a decline in commodity prices). Default or restructuring of emerging economies debt is to some degree a political event, which may be influenced by noneconomic factors. If the government of an emerging economy decides for political reasons to raise the possibility of default, it may lead other emerging economies to consider the cost and benefits of default or restructuring more seriously.

An important implication of the results described in this chapter for the emerging market investor is that the benefits from international diversification are far smaller for the bondholder than for the stockholder. Permanent high correlations of sovereign debt returns in emerging markets provide great rewards for the bondholders during tranquil periods, but also substantial losses in turbulent times.

REFERENCES

Bae, K.-H., G. A. Karolyi, and R. M. Stulz. 2003. "A New Approach to Measuring Financial Contagion." *Review of Financial Studies* 16:717–763.

Baig, T., and I. Goldfajn. 1999. "Financial Market Contagion in the Asian Crisis." *IMF Staff Papers* 46:167–195.

Bekaert, G., C. R. Harvey, and A. Ng. 2005. "Market Integration and Contagion." *Journal of Business* 78:39–69.

Chakrabarti, R., and R. Roll. 2002. "East Asia and Europe during the 1997 Asian Collapse: A Clinical Study of a Financial Crisis." *Journal of Financial Markets* 5:1–30.

Chiang, T. C., B. N. Jeon, and H. Li. 2007. "Dynamic Correlation Analysis of Financial Contagion: Evidence from Asian Markets." *Journal of International Money and Finance* 26:7, 1206–1228.

Diebold, F. X., and K. Yilmaz. 2007. "Measuring Financial Asset Return and Volatility Spillovers, with Application to Global Equity Markets." Unpublished Working Paper. Department of Economics, University of Pennsylvania.

Forbes, K., and R. Rigobon. 2002. "No Contagion, Only Interdependence: Measuring Stock Market Comovements." *Journal of Finance* 57:2223–2261.

Ismailescu, I. 2010. "Contagion and Its Sources: Evidence from Emerging Debt Markets." *Working Paper*. Pace University.

Ismailescu, I., and H. Kazemi. 2008. "Is There Any Contagion in Emerging Debt Markets?" *Working Paper*. University of Massachusetts Amherst.

ABOUT THE AUTHORS

Iuliana Ismailescu is an assistant professor of finance at Pace University, New York. She holds a PhD in finance from the University of Massachusetts Amherst (2008), an MBA from Pace University, and a degree in mathematics from the University of Bucharest. Her research interests include credit risk and credit derivatives, emerging debt and equity markets, and international finance. Her research has appeared or is forthcoming in *Journal of Banking and Finance, International Review of Finance*, and the *American Economist*. She co-authored a mathematics book in Romanian and contributed several book chapters to *Interest Rate Risk Modeling and Dynamic Term Structure Modeling*. Ismailescu is the recipient of the FMA 2007 Best Dissertation Proposal Award in International Finance.

Hossein B. Kazemi is a professor of finance at the Isenberg School of Management at the University of Massachusetts, Amherst. He is an associate director of Center for International Securities & Derivatives Markets (www.cisdm.org), a nonprofit organization devoted to research in the area of alternative investments and home to CISDM Hedge Fund/CTA Database, and he serves as the Associate Editor of the *Journal of Alternative Investments*. Dr. Kazemi the program director at Association for Chartered Alternative Investment Analysts (www.caia.org), where he oversees both examination and curriculum activities of CAIA. His research has been in the areas of valuations of equity and fixed income securities, asset allocation for traditional and alternative asset classes, and evaluation and replication of active management investment products. He is a managing partner of Alternative Investment Analytics, LLC, an investment and consulting firm offering investment products and services in hedge fund, CTA, and commodity areas. He has a PhD in finance from the University of Michigan.

CHAPTER 20

Measuring Contagion in Emerging Market Bonds

IRINA BUNDA[*]
A. JAVIER HAMANN
SUBIR LALL
International Monetary Fund

Other than foreign direct investment, emerging market (EM) bonds have been the largest source of financing to EMs since the beginning of the 1990s. International bonds have, however, been a volatile source of financing, vulnerable to external shocks and abrupt shifts in market sentiment.[1] Volatility in secondary markets has usually been associated with diminished appetite for primary market issuance (IMF 2001) and often with capital outflows and foreign exchange market pressures.

The sharp spikes in volatility of EM bond returns are often captured by increased cross-country market correlations in the now vast literature on contagion. In fact, correlation analysis represents one of the major strategies to measure the cross-country transmission of shocks. However, in the wake of the 1997–1998 Asian crisis, the inference of contagion drawn from increased cross-country correlation coefficients was challenged by several authors on grounds of being biased upward due to heteroskedasticity.[2] A more fundamental objection to the use of correlation coefficients to gauge contagion, which was raised much earlier, is the role of "third factors," particularly global financial factors, in driving market comovements. Excess comovement, free from the influence of third factors, was first quantified by Pindyck and Rotemberg (1990) and used as a measure of contagion in mature markets. After taking into account common fundamentals, they showed that there is a residual comovement across stocks from different industries and idiosyncratic fundamentals.

Contributing to the empirical literature on factor models, this article proposes a tractable three-factor specification to examine the comovement in emerging market bond returns and disentangle the influence of external and domestic factors. To capture the impact of external factors, we estimate correlations corrected for developments in U.S. markets for Treasury bonds, high-yield bonds, and equity. The

---

[*]The opinions expressed here are those of the authors and do not necessarily reflect those of the International Monetary Fund or IMF policy.

correlation coefficients of residuals are interpreted as measures of *excess comovement* or *true contagion* and are compared to simple correlations.

WHAT EXPLAINS EMERGING BOND MARKET RETURNS? A TRACTABLE MODEL

Comovements in emerging bond markets are often proxied by the average correlation of bond returns.[3] But these average correlations may be driven by a wide range of factors, some of which are internal to the asset class or to the issuing country, while others are not. Thus, we can classify these factors in the following two categories: (1) common external factors originating in developed countries; and (2) other factors that could account for the residual comovement of EM returns. These factors can be linked to international investors' behavior, as investors shift between asset classes and markets according to their expectations and attitudes towards risk.

We estimated a three-factor model of individual country returns for two countries i, j $(i \neq j)$:

$$R_i = \sum_{k=1}^{3} \beta_{ik} \cdot f_k + \varepsilon_i \qquad (20.1)$$

$$R_j = \sum_{k=1}^{3} \beta_{jk} \cdot f_k + \varepsilon_j \qquad (20.2)$$

where R_i and R_j are five-day returns of dollar-denominated EM bonds included in the EMBI Global, β_{ik} and β_{jk} are the country-specific loadings, f_k are the common external factors and ε_i, ε_j denote idiosyncratic country-specific factors.[4] The three main external factors driving the evolution of EM bond returns are (1) the return on U.S. Treasury bonds, commonly assumed to be the risk-free asset; (2) the return on the S&P 500 stock index, a proxy for a mature market stock portfolio; and (3) the performance of U.S. high yield corporate bonds. These three variables are intended to capture the impact of substitution between EM bonds and other classes of global assets.

To disentangle the roles of the common external and country-specific factors, we use the following two indicators of market comovement:

- A simple correlation coefficient of country specific returns or:

$$\rho_{i,j} = \rho(R_i, R_j) \qquad (20.3)$$

- And a correlation coefficient of residuals, henceforth the adjusted correlation coefficient:

$$\hat{\rho}_{i,j} = \rho(\varepsilon_i, \varepsilon_j) \qquad (20.4)$$

which is also the partial correlation coefficient of returns R_i and R_j, given f_k. The statistic $\hat{\rho}$ can be interpreted as a measure of the comovement of bond returns after removing the influence of common external shocks. A significant increase in this indicator during times of increased market volatility could then be viewed

Exhibit 20.1 Evolution of ρ and $\hat{\rho}$ in a Pre-Crisis Period and Potential Sources of Risk

ρ	$\hat{\rho}$	Source of Risk
$\uparrow$	$\approx;\downarrow$	Mature markets
$\approx;\downarrow$	$\uparrow$	Emerging markets
$\uparrow$	$\uparrow$	Mature or emerging markets
$\approx;\downarrow$	$\approx;\downarrow$	Potentially, from a subgroup of emerging markets

as evidence of excess comovement or "pure contagion." Notice, however, that an increase in the correlation of the residuals would also lead to an increase in ρ. For $\hat{\rho}$ to increase while ρ remains constant, the initial increase in excess comovement would have to be offset by a simultaneous decline in correlations driven by the common factor. As a result, it is essential to focus on the joint behavior of ρ and $\hat{\rho}$.

Let's consider now how ρ and $\hat{\rho}$ would behave in the run-up to a global or country-specific, negative event—Exhibit 20.1.[5] An increase in ρ, while $\hat{\rho}$ decreases or remains constant indicates that risks of a sell-off in EM stem mainly from a shock occurring in mature markets. A concomitant rise in both correlations during tranquil times indicates that the risk of a generalized selloff could come from either front: global factors as well as a given event in another EM.[6] Finally, low or decreasing values of ρ and $\hat{\rho}$ may be an indication of market tiering (i.e., the presence of two or more groups of countries characterized by high within-group correlation but low intergroup correlations) with risks potentially coming from the highly volatile group of emerging countries (Bunda, Hamann, and Lall 2005).

How could this framework be applied to provide an ex ante description of the shock propagation mechanisms and the behavior of global investors in the face of financial market instability? We follow the performance of ρ and $\hat{\rho}$, together with EM spreads, before and after the occurrence of a particular discrete, adverse event. As in the model described in (1) – (2), we focus on common external shocks affecting the EMs (the shock affects ε_i but not f_k) and on EM-specific shocks with potential spillover effects to other EMs (the shock affects f_k but not ε_i).

Generally, in the aftermath of the first event we would expect $\hat{\rho}$ to increase only to the extent that the shock to one EM is correlated to the idiosyncratic part of the return to bonds in the other EM (i.e., if it is capturing the true market comovement after controlling for the presence of global factors). But ρ would also rise, as the simple correlation measure is affected by both global and country-specific factors. A widening of EM spreads would be consistent with a generalized selloff across EMs. Conversely, a decrease in $\hat{\rho}$ and ρ would suggest that investors are discriminating within the EM asset class according to their country risk perception. Regardless of the changes in average spreads in EMs, these would be increasing for some countries and declining for others, consistent with the notion of selective sell-off.

In the aftermath of a negative event in mature markets, we would expect an increase in ρ driven by the common external factor and no change in $\hat{\rho}$; spreads would widen reflecting mainly a shift away from EM debt in general. A similar movement in ρ and $\hat{\rho}$, although with declining spreads, could also be observed following a positive global shock. The key message in this case would be that the main downside risk for EM debt going forward is a generalized sell-off triggered by a global event, rather than contagion following a negative event in a specific EM.

EMPIRICAL RESULTS

We present first the evolution of an aggregate measure of the two indicators of market comovement, namely the average of the rolling correlations across all 18 countries, and discuss the major emerging trends. We then analyze in detail the onset of the subprime crisis in the United States and the collapse of Lehman Brothers, which led to a global crisis.

Evolution of the Adjusted and Unadjusted Cross-Country Average Correlations

Exhibit 20.2 illustrates the evolution of average correlations as measures of the overall (ρ) and excess ($\hat{\rho}$) comovement in EM bond markets.[7] As a general feature, we note that the correlations are always positive, suggesting a tendency for individual country returns to move together. During the period 1997–2008, the annual average correlations fluctuated between a low of 0.24 in 2002 and a high of 0.59 in 1998, but exhibiting no clear trend.

The large spikes in global average correlations are usually associated with major episodes of financial markets turmoil and suggest a relatively low degree of investor discrimination during sell-offs compared with more normal times. The main rises in correlations take place during the Hong Kong SAR stock market crash of October 1997, the 1998 Russian sovereign default, the 2000 sell-off of Argentinean bonds and speculative corporate bonds in the U.S. high-yield market, and, more recently, during the summer 2007 and at the end of October 2008. These

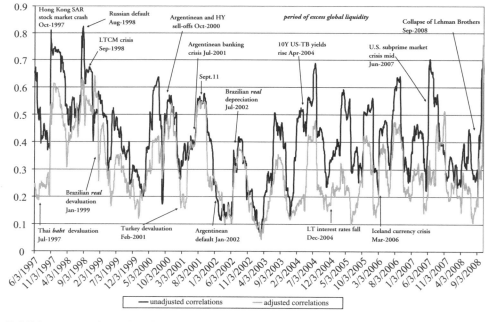

Exhibit 20.2   Adjusted and Unadjusted Rolling Average Correlations

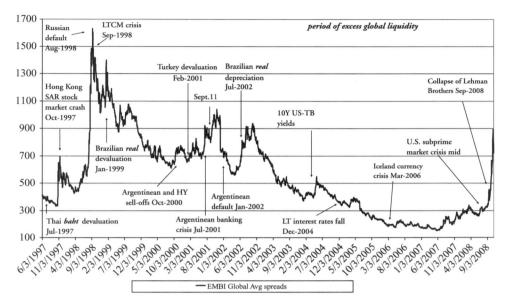

Exhibit 20.3   EMBI Global Spreads

episodes highlight the importance of "crossover" investors, who tend to unwind their open positions in EMs during times of turmoil. At the same time, while the earlier episodes affecting the EMs mentioned above can be classified as cases of "pure contagion," partial correlations and spreads declined systematically from 1997 through early 2003.[8] In fact, comovements in EM bond returns appear to be increasingly less specific to EMs and mainly driven by events taking place in mature markets, as showed by the widening gap between $\hat{\rho}$ and ρ since early 2003 and until the fall of 2008. This could be due to the general increase in liquidity and lower interest rates in global financial markets through early 2007, as well as the improved fundamentals in many EMs.

The evolution of sovereign spreads (Exhibit 20.3) provides additional insights as to the sources of comovement in bond returns. The all time high, of more than 1,600 bps, was reached during the 1998 Russian crisis and the LTCM collapse, whereas the peaks of intermediate size were associated with events taking place in EMs (1,100 bps during the 1999 Brazilian *real* devaluation, 900 bps during the 2001 Argentinean banking crisis, or 800 bps at the height of the 2002 Brazilian *real* depreciation). These trends seem to confirm the view that investors may have differentiated better the risks carried by EM bonds over the last decade as compared with the 1990s. It is only during the fall of 2008, when the financial turmoil accelerated dramatically turning into a more acute crisis of confidence, that the downward trend in spreads was reversed.

Recent Bouts of Financial Volatility

Next we look in more detail at the events that began in the summer of 2007. In the run-up to the U.S. subprime market crisis—between early May and mid-June

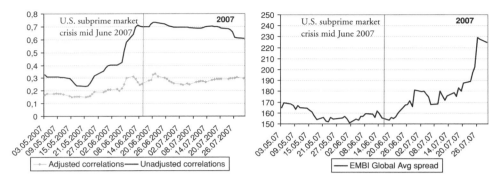

Exhibit 20.4   U.S. Subprime Market Crisis: Evolution of Correlations and EM Spreads

2007—we notice a steep increase in ρ but only a moderate one in $\hat{\rho}$ (Exhibit 20.4, left panel) both coefficients would remain at the higher levels throughout August. The widening gap between ρ and $\hat{\rho}$ during this period suggests an increase in the comovement of bond returns that is driven by developments in mature markets. The behavior of EM bond spreads confirms that the increase comovement, especially the "excessive" one captured by $\hat{\rho}$, reflects an increased perceptions of risk for EM bonds: spreads declined somewhat between early May and mid-June 2007 but rose markedly in July, when $\hat{\rho}$ rose to about 0.3 (Exhibit 20.4, right panel).

The events surrounding the collapse of Lehman Brothers in September 2008 represent a shift in the evolution of EMs relative to developments since the beginning of the subprime-related financial crisis. Both ρ and $\hat{\rho}$ remained at relatively low levels until mid-September 2008 ($\hat{\rho}$ actually rose moderately while ρ remained constant) despite a virulent financial crisis in advanced economies (Exhibit 20.5, left panel). But in the second half of September both correlations rose sharply, as did sovereign spreads (Figure 20.5, right panel). The rise in ρ preceded that in $\hat{\rho}$ but in late-October, $\hat{\rho}$ rose sharply suggesting, according to our framework, that investors' attitudes towards EM had become much less discriminating. This is consistent with the commonly held view that the collapse of Lehman Brothers marked a turning point in the propagation of the financial crisis to EM bonds—see, for example, Chapter 8 in IMF (2009).

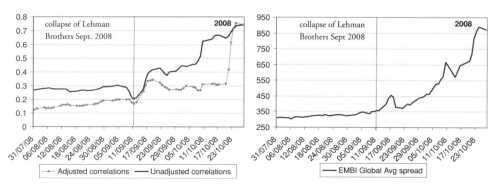

Exhibit 20.5   Collapse of Lehman Brothers: Evolution of Correlations and EM Spreads

CONCLUSION

The use of a simple measure of cross-country correlations, namely the partial correlation after controlling for global factors, together with the commonly used simple
correlation can be more informative during episodes of heightened market instability. To capture the impact of global factors, we estimated correlations corrected
for developments in U.S. markets for Treasury bonds, high-yield bonds, and equity. The correlation coefficients of residuals were interpreted as measures of *excess
comovement* or *true contagion* and were compared to simple correlations.

Our analysis of EM bond market comovement over the past decade shows that
contagion risk coming from country-specific factors declined over time until very
recently, with EMs bond returns being increasingly driven by global factors. While
excess comovement eventually rises, the joint behavior of adjusted and unadjusted
correlations since the onset of the subprime crisis shows that the initial increase
is driven by global factors and that, only after a while, the behavior of EM bond
returns that is unrelated to these global factors takes on a life of its own.

Our main result implies that in an aftermath of an adverse global shock, a
significant number of EMs are at risk of being affected simultaneously through
a rise in the cost and/or availability of external financing, given the strong link
between developments in secondary markets examined in this chapter, and primary market issuance conditions. Although concerns about global deleveraging
in the aftermath of the turmoil associated with the collapse of Lehman Brothers
have often focused on the issue of external financing by banks, the analysis in this
article suggests that common global shocks also have the potential of resulting
in disruption of external financing through the portfolio bond channel, and may
require a simultaneous policy response across a range of countries.

NOTES

1. Prominent examples include the Tequila crisis of 1994–1995, the Asian crisis of 1997, the
   Russian default and the collapse of LTCM in 1998, the market reaction after the September
   11 terrorist attacks, the run-up to the Argentine debt default in late 2001, the U.S. HY
   market sell-off of 2002, or most recently the U.S. subprime market-related volatility of
   the summer of 2007, and the collapse of Lehman Brothers in mid-September 2008.

2. Forbes and Rigobon (2002).

3. See, for example, IMF (2001) for an application.

4. The sample contains 18 of the 33 EM countries initially included in JPMorgan's EMBI
   Global (Argentina, Brazil, Bulgaria, Colombia, Croatia, Ecuador, Malaysia, Mexico,
   Morocco, Panama, Peru, Philippines, Poland, Russia, South Africa, South Korea, Turkey,
   and Venezuela) that accounted for about 90 percent of the index throughout the period. The daily closing prices were provided by Bloomberg; data for non-Asian countries
   were lagged by one day to adjust for the time difference between Asian and non-Asian
   markets.

5. We assume here that the shock in question is anticipated with less than full certainty.
   Typical examples of such shocks could be a liquidity shock in a financial system or the
   unexpected release of poor economic data.

6. Pure contagion could also imply decreasing values of ρ while $\hat{\rho}$ is increasing in the run-up
   to a crisis, if global factors are pushing returns in opposite directions.

7. Aggregate correlations were computed as the average of all 153 pair-wise canonical correlations of the 18 countries in the sample over a 60-day rolling window.

8. In Bunda, Hamann, and Lall (2010) the episodes of "pure contagion" are defined as a statistical significant rise in adjusted correlation to more than 50 percent.

REFERENCES

Bunda, Irina, A. Javier Hamann, and Subir Lall. 2005. "Comovements in Emerging Market Bond Returns: An Empirical Assessment," paper presented at the *Emerging Markets Finance–JIMF Conference*, Cass Business School, U.K.
———. 2010. "Correlations in Emerging Market Bonds: The Role of Local and Global Factors." *IMF Working Papers* 10/6, International Monetary Fund.
Forbes, Kristin, and Roberto Rigobon. 2002. "No Contagion, Only Interdependence: Measuring Stock Market Comovements." *Journal of Finance* LVII (October), 2223–2261.
International Monetary Fund. 2001. *Emerging Market Financing*. Washington, DC.
———. 2009. *Global Financial Stability Report* April 2009. Washington DC.
Pindyck, Robert S., and Julio J. Rotemberg. 1990. "The Excess Comovement of Commodity Prices." *Economic Journal* 100:1173–1189.

ABOUT THE AUTHORS

Irina Bunda is an international consultant economist at the IMF-Singapore Training Institute, which provides training in the formulation and implementation of macroeconomic and financial policies to government officials from the Asia-Pacific region. Before joining the IMF's regional training center in Singapore, Irina worked for two years at the European Central Bank in Frankfurt, Germany, in the economics, monetary policy and International relations directorates. She has also visited the Bank of England's International Finance and the IMF's Policy Development and Review and Research departments. Her areas of expertise are in the fields of international macroeconomics, banking, and finance. She conducts applied research on international financial crises, monetary policy and exchange rates, financial contagion, asset price dynamics, and has published in a number of journals. She received a master's of science and technology in market finance, an MSci in economics and finance, and a PhD in economics from University of Orléans, France.

A. Javier Hamann is the deputy chief of the Advanced Countries and Multilateral Surveillance Division at the International Monetary Fund. He received his PhD and MA in economics from Boston University and his BA in economics from Universidad del Pacifico in Lima, Peru. Dr. Hamann has written about disinflation and contagion in emerging markets and on the impact of aid to low-income countries.

Subir Lall is division chief in the Asia and Pacific Department of the International Monetary Fund. His research interests and publications are in the areas of financial crises, market microstructure, and globalization. He holds a BA (first class with honors) in economics from the University of Delhi and a PhD in economics from Brown University, where he was the recipient of the Susan B. Kamins Fellowship.

CHAPTER 21

Risk Appetite and Emerging Market Spreads[*]

MARTÍN GONZÁLEZ-ROZADA
EDUARDO LEVY YEYATI
UTDT

G lobal credit conditions have often been key determinants of the borrowing costs of emerging economies, for good reasons. In principle, the pricing of debt issued by financially integrated emerging economies should be no different from the pricing of noninvestment grade securities in general, and low-grade bonds in developed economies in particular. Both should reflect the level of risk of the security, and a risk premium (the price of risk) that is, in turn, a reflection of the risk appetite of the international investor. In addition, global liquidity influences the international cost of capital and, to the extent that this cost affects debt sustainability, emerging market spreads. Then, an important part of the variability of emerging spreads could be seen as a reflection of exogenous factors (such as the international business cycle, or global liquidity crunches and asset sell-offs) that simultaneously determine both risk appetite and the interest rate.

The aftermath of the 2008 global financial crisis is a case in point: The combination of fiscal stimulus packages across the board in 2009 with a disappointing growth performance, sovereign spreads in 2010 has started to reflect growing concerns about the ability of developed economies to service their debt obligations. In this context, improving fundamentals in most emerging economies have been offset by a deteriorating risk appetite, and fears of a debt restructuring in the Eurozone have been detrimental to risk assets in general, and noninvestment grade credits in particular. At any rate, global factors continue to be a critical input in debt sustainability analysis in the developing world.

In this chapter, we document in a rigorous and systematic way the degree to which the evolution of emerging market spreads has been determined by exogenous global factors. Specifically, we show how changes in international interest rates and corporate bond spreads in advanced countries explain the dynamic (within) country variability of emerging market spreads in recent years. Indeed,

[*]The authors would like to thank Cristian Alonso for excellent research assistance. This chapter is based on our research paper "Global Factors and Emerging Market Spreads" published by the *Economic Journal* 118: 533, 1917–1936, November 2008.

global factors such as risk appetite, global liquidity, and contagion from systemic events like the Russian and Mexican debt crises in the 1990s account for the major part of emerging market spread movements. On the other hand, we do not find a significant effect on the pricing of emerging market debt from changes in credit ratings, which appear to lag large spread corrections. The evidence reported here highlights the recent shift in the policy debate from debt sustainability to debt vulnerability, including through the emphasis of liquidity as much as solvency issues, as spread widening episodes are often triggered by external, exogenous factors rather than by country-specific fundamental changes.

MODEL AND DATA

We consider a model where spreads depend on the price of credit risk, which depends on the international risk-free rate and the risk appetite of international investors, the incidence of the default risk of the issuer as a function of its fundamentals, and global factors such as global liquidity or episodes of financial distress that affect corporate and emerging markets differently. We explain the evolution of the spreads using a panel error correction model that describes a basic long-run equilibrium relationship between markets spreads, the price of credit risk, and the international rate but at the same time allow us to have a complete characterization of the impact of global factors in the short-run (see González-Rozada and Levy Yeyati 2008 for a detailed description of the model, the statistical properties of the individual variables, and the econometric estimation).

We use Credit Suisse First Boston's High Yield Index (HY), which measures the spread over the U.S. Treasury yield curve at the redemption date with the worst yield as a proxy for the price of risk and the 10-year U.S. Treasury rate (10YT) as a proxy for international liquidity. We also construct a credit rating variable based on Standard & Poor's rating for long-term debt in foreign currency to use mainly as a control for country-specific fundamentals.

Emerging market sovereign spreads are measured as the spread over Treasuries of JPMorgan's EMBI Global Index (EMBI) for each of the 33 emerging economies in the Global portfolio. We work alternatively with monthly, weekly, and (occasionally) daily data for the period 1993–2005.

GLOBAL FACTORS AND SPREADS

At first sight, data appear to support the view that global factors exert a strong influence on emerging market spreads. In Exhibit 21.1, we present the median of individual EMBI spreads at each point of time, and the distribution around its cross-section mean. We include as well the evolution of our two main proxies of global factors. As can be seen, HY and EMBI have indeed moved together over the past 10 years. Even in the previous period there is a comovement, but somewhat lower because of the strong impact of contagion from the Mexican and Russian crisis. Moreover, there seems to be also a direct relationship between the emerging market spreads and international liquidity.

A more rigorous analysis confirms this first impression. We estimate the spread as a long-run function of the high yield index, the international interest rate, contagion from crisis abroad (Mexican and Russian ones) and the credit rating. Using monthly data, the correlation is large and highly significant for all the variables. In

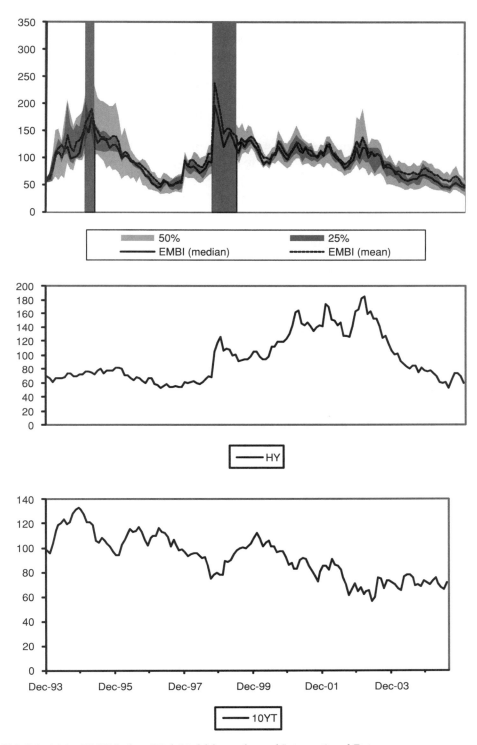

Exhibit 21.1 EMBI Index, High Yield Spreads, and International Rates

particular, two exogenous global factors, HY and 10YT, explain about 30 percent of the dynamic within variability of spreads, 37 percent if we add contagion and close to 60 percent if we include credit ratings, too. Short-run estimates are also consistent. All variables have strong contemporaneous impact on spreads but not delayed effect, and only 7 percent of deviations from the long-run level are eliminated per month, so the average lag length is about 14 months. Same story is told when weekly data is considered: high correlation, strong explanatory power, and slow convergence.

It is interesting to highlight that sovereign spreads adjust close to one-to-one to changes in the international interest rate in this baseline specification. This would suggest that the influence of the risk-free rate goes beyond the standard arbitrage view (Calvo et al. 1993) and that borrowing costs in emerging economies respond more than proportionally to the interest rate cycle in the developed world.

GLOBAL FACTORS THEN AND NOW

Capital markets have experienced significant changes over the past two decades, especially for emerging economies. Due to the increasing integration of capital markets and to the growing familiarity with the emerging market asset, it would be natural to think that the impact of global factors over spreads has changed. In particular, we would expect this connection to have strengthened over the years.

To check this hypothesis, we split the sample into two subsamples, 1993–1999 and 2000–2005, and we re-estimate our model. We find that the HY coefficients are larger for the earlier period both in the short- and long-run equation, while their explanatory power is comparable and even increases for the long-run equation in the later years. However, from an economic perspective, the estimates for the second part of the sample indicate that a 10 percent increase in the risk-free rate brings a 7.6 percent increase in spreads, whereras the same change in the high-yield spread is reflected almost one-to-one on emerging market spreads. On the other hand, a one-notch upgrade in ratings is associated with a reduction in spreads of 35 bps. These results would indicate that, based on the values of global factors and the emerging market average rating by end-2005 (BB+, roughly equal to the mean for the whole sample), an upgrade to BBB– could be undone by an increase in the risk-free rate of 70 bps, or by a rise in the high-yield corporate spread of 50 bps.

RATINGS

Credit ratings seldom anticipate changes in the macroeconomic context. On the contrary, there is a growing belief, especially after the experience of the 2007 U.S. mortgage crisis, that rating agencies reflect credit risk only imperfectly. In particular, they tend to respond to markets as much as they do to fundamentals and often lag spreads in their reaction to significant news. If so, ratings will be just a partial proxy for country-specific factors, which would call for a robustness check of our results using a more parsimonious specification.

Our baseline results indicate that ratings exhibit a significant explanatory power for both the long-run level and the short-run variation of emerging spreads. But could ratings be considered as an additional exogenous factor that influences the borrowing cost of emerging economies, independently of whether they reveal valuable information? These considerations presume that actual fundamentals may influence both the level of spreads and the way they comove with risk appetite beyond what is summarized by the credit rating.

In order to check this hypothesis, we add to our baseline specification dummies per country-year (when using monthly data) and country-month (when using weekly data) to capture the influence of fundamentals identified in the literature as determinants of sovereign risk, such as the country's leverage ratio, the degree of financial and institutional development, or cyclical output fluctuations, which are typically sampled at those frequencies. We include interactions between global factors and the country dummy variables in order to allow elasticities to vary across countries. The coefficients and explanatory power of the original baseline equation remain notably strong, indicating that the influence of global factors is largely independent of country's fundamentals. The explanatory power of both global factors combined jumps to close 80 percent, at the expense of the country-time dummies. Irrespective of whether the latter truly captures the incidence of domestic factors, the evidence on the explanatory power of global factors appears to be remarkably strong.

Although the robustness of the results is reassuring for the two exogenous global factors, it is somewhat intriguing for the case of ratings that, in principle, are conceived as summary indicators of the relevant country-specific factors now included. As noted, this may be due to the fact that, although investors generally recognize the limitations that ratings display in practice, the norms that inform their decisions force them to take credit ratings as a source of variability that is partially exogenous to the policy maker.

The strong empirical association between ratings and spreads has typically been interpreted as evidence that ratings have an impact on the cost of borrowing. In this line, Kaminsky and Schmukler (2002) show that changes in ratings and outlooks are positively correlated with emerging market spreads, particularly so during crisis periods. Then they conclude that ratings are a cause of instability during crises time as they act as a signal that coordinates investors toward a bad equilibrium. Similarly Reinsen and von Maltzan (1998) find evidence of a two-way Granger causality and conclude that negative rating news elicit a significant impact on spreads.

However, over the last fifteen years, rating agencies have been criticized for overreacting after lagging behind the facts in the context of the Asian and Uruguayan crises. This is the point of Reinsen and von Maltzan (1998), Huhne (1998), IMF (1999), among others. It has also been argued that they have been excessively inertial (stabilizing the markets in the run up to a crisis; Mora 2004) as well as excessively procyclical (contributing to the collapse by downgrading a country by several notches once the crisis is inevitable, Ferri et al. 1999).

We could summarize these ideas suggesting a simpler hypothesis to explain the robustness of the spreads-rating link to the inclusion of country-time dummies: Ratings are endogenous to spreads in most cases. To check it, we compare spreads evolution with the date of changes in ratings. We find that downgrades are preceded by increases in spreads and, apart from a mild contemporaneous adjustment (of about 50 bps), exert no substantial impact. However, this does not necessarily prove that ratings are endogenous to market reaction (as reflected by spreads) because the market may be simply reacting in anticipation of change in ratings. Nevertheless, refining our analysis by considering changes in the credit outlook given by the rating agency does not modify our conclusions.

In sum, the presumption that ratings are a reasonable proxy for fundamental risk is questioned by the data. While their inclusion as control may still be justified, attributing the strong link between ratings and spreads to the incidence of country-specific factors may be misleading, overstating the role of the latter and understating the influence of global factors.

PREDICTIONS

In order to gauge how much of the variation in emerging market spread can be explained by the few exogenous variables identified in our baseline model we simulate individual spread paths. First, we re-estimate the long-run equation using data through the end of 2001, and then we simulate the behavior of spreads that results from variations in the global variables, keeping ratings fixed at their end-2001 levels, for the remainder of the period.

Exhibit 21.2 compares the actual EMBI spread with the predictions from the long-run equation for four emerging countries.[1] As can be seen, predictions are generally quite good, even for the Latin American countries that underwent severe episodes of capital account reversals during the period. These predictions highlight the explanatory power of the two exogenous variables: despite short-term, transitory swings due to country-specific episodes, spread movements closely reflect these three variables, and eventually converge to levels that are largely explained

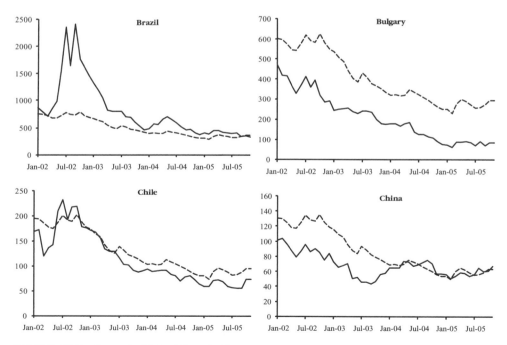

Exhibit 21.2   Spreads: Out-of-Sample Forecast

by them. Brazil is a case in point: The financial turmoil of late 2002 associated with the uncertainty surrounding the election and the transition to a new government, which was clearly independent of the evolution of global factors; once over, spreads rapidly converged to their long-run levels.

FINAL REMARKS

This chapter presented empirical evidence showing that global exogenous factors explain a large part of the substantial volatility exhibited by emerging market spreads since the inception of the asset class in the mid-1990s. We found that emerging market spreads depend negatively on international risk appetite, and positively on international liquidity. These two exogenous factors explain just more than 50 percent of the long-run time variability of emerging market spreads (14 percent of the short-run variability) for the period following the Russian default (2000–2005) and close to 80 percent when the elasticities with respect to global factors are allowed to differ across countries. By contrast, ratings appear to be largely endogenous, reflecting changes in spreads rather than anticipating them. Indeed, a closer look reveals that credit ratings or outlook changes lag spread movements, and elicit little if any additional effect on spreads.

These findings contribute to the debate about the nature of emerging market stability, specifically on the degree of exogeneity in the determination of the highly volatile borrowing costs faced by emerging economies—a major source of financial distress in the recent past. In particular, this chapter suggests that the policy focus should be placed on debt vulnerability to global swings, and on ways to cope with an exogenus deterioration of market access, motivating the ongoing debate on precautionary reserve accumulation and global liquidity safety nets.

NOTE

1. See González-Rozada and Levy Yeyati (2008) for the full results.

REFERENCES

Calvo, G., L. Leiderman, and C. Reinhart. 1993. "Capital Inflows and Real Exchange Rate Appreciation in Latin America." *IMF Staff Papers* 40:1 (March), 108–151.

Ferri, G., L.-G. Liu, and J. E. Stiglitz. 1999. "The Pro-Cyclical Role of Rating Agencies: Evidence from the East Asian Crisis." *Economic Notes* 28:3, 335–355.

González-Rozada, M., and E. Levy Yeyati. 2008. "Global Factors and Emerging Market Spreads." *Economic Journal* 118:533, 1917–1936.

Huhne, C. 1998. "How the Rating Agencies Blew It on Korea." *International Economy* 12 (May–June):46–63.

International Monetary Fund. 1999. "Emerging Markets in the New International Financial System: Implications of the Asian Crisis." In *World Economic and Financial Surveys, International Capital Markets*, IMF, Chapter 3.

Kaminsky, G., and S. Schmukler. 2002. "Emerging Market Instability: Do Sovereign Credit Ratings Affect Country Risk and Stock Returns?" *World Bank Economic Review* 16:2, 171–195.

Mora, N. 2004. "Sovereign Credit Ratings: Guilty beyond Reasonable Doubt?" *Mimeo*. Beirut: American University of Beirut.

Reinsen, H., and J. von Maltzan. 1998. "Sovereign Credit Ratings, Emerging Market Risk and Financial Market Risk." HWWA-Institut fur Wirtschaftsforschung, *Discussion Paper* No. 55.

ABOUT THE AUTHORS

Martín González-Rozada is a professor of econometrics at the Department of Economics at the Universidad Torcuato Di Tella, where he is the program chair of the master in econometrics. He received a PhD from Boston University. Dr. González-Rozada has done extensive work in the areas of emerging markets and labor economics. His work has been published in several international journals such as the *Economic Journal, Economica, Economic Development and Cultural Change, Economics of Education Review, CVD Prevention and Control,* and in a number of specialized books.

Eduardo Levy Yeyati is professor at the School of Business of Universidad Torcuato Di Tella (where he also directed the Center for Financial Research from 1999 to 2007) and guest professor at Barcelona Graduate School of Economics. He is also director of economics at CIPPEC (Argentina's top think tank) and senior fellow at Brookings Institution. Previously, he was head of Latam Research and Emerging Markets Strategy at Barclays Capital, senior financial adviser for Latin American at the World Bank, senior research associate at the Inter-American Development Bank, and chief economist of the Central Bank of Argentina. He works regularly as an international consultant for emerging market governments, multilateral organizations, and other public and private institutions. His research on banking, exchange rate policy, and emerging markets finance has been published extensively in top international academic journals. He holds a PhD in economics from the University of Pennsylvania.

CHAPTER 22

Emerging Countries' Sovereign Risk

Balance Sheet Effects, Global Risk Aversion, and Contagion

ALICIA GARCÍA HERRERO
Banco Bilbao Vizcaya Argentaria (BBVA)

W e have reviewed three important external determinants of the sovereign spreads in emerging countries: balance sheet effects, global risk aversion, and contagion. Although there are ways to reduce the detrimental impact of balance sheet effects, these are either hard to implement or costly. Insurance against these might need to be considered either in the form of self-insurance (accumulation of reserves) or market insurance (instruments that are inversely related to a country's real exchange rate). The chapter also reviews the importance of global risk aversion in determining emerging countries' sovereign spreads. The same is true for contagion, even "pure contagion," which is the fact that events in one country may affect sovereign spreads in another totally independent from fundamentals or from any economic relation between the two countries.

REAL EXCHANGE RATE AND BALANCE SHEET EFFECTS

A growing strand of literature has explored the link between real exchange fluctuations and economic performance, which serve as a basis to analyze the relation between the real exchange rate and the risk premium. This is particularly relevant for emerging countries as their real exchange rate is much more volatile than that of industrial countries.

Conventional open economy models—from Mundell-Fleming onward, have argued that real depreciations are expansionary by switching global demand toward domestic production. Already in 1986, Edwards (1986) challenged this view on several grounds: the possible contractionary effect of a higher price level after a devaluation, as well as a potential negative impact on income distribution. More recently, theories based on what has started to be known as the open economy Bernanke-Gertler-Gilchrist financial accelerator, have challenged the Mundell-Fleming view. If a country's debt is denominated in foreign currency, a real depreciation will reduce the country's net worth through a balance sheet effect and, in the presence of financial imperfections, they may increase the cost of capital. This is particularly relevant for emerging economies given their relatively large share of foreign currency denominated debt, the frequency of large real depreciations and the presence of financial imperfections.

Recent theoretical studies (Aghion, Bacchetta, and Banerjee 2001; Berganza, Chang, and García-Herrero 2004; Céspedes, Chang, and Velasco 2004) have developed the above argument in some detail. The empirical evidence is scarce, particularly at the aggregate level,[1] although sorely needed since the theory by itself cannot determine whether the balance sheet effect of a real depreciation is strong enough to reverse conventional wisdom.

Berganza, Chang, and García-Herrero (2004) and Berganza and García-Herrero (2004) try to give an answer to that question by testing what is the aggregate impact of balance sheets on emerging countries and, in particular, on the sovereign risk premium. Both investigations conclude that the balance sheet effects of a real depreciation increase the sovereign risk premium, even when controlling for its positive impact on trade competitiveness.

The next relevant question is which factors make balance sheets more detrimental. This should help identify the countries that are bound to suffer most in case of a real exchange rate depreciation, quite an interesting question for policy makers. The two papers point to the importance of financial imperfections but also to the occurrence of a financial crisis with episodes of large devaluations. In addition, Berganza and García-Herrero (2004) find evidence that the exchange rate regime also matters; in fact, a fixed exchange regime makes balance sheets more detrimental. For the sake of brevity, this section does not show the detailed results of this chapter, but only some of those in Berganza, Chang, and García-Herrero (2004).

The objective is to estimate the aggregate impact of balance sheet effects on the country risk premium, so macroeconomic data are used. This substantially limits the number of observations available. In addition, the difficulties in proxying sovereign country risk reduces the sample even further. We therefore end up with 27 emerging economies and a period from 1993 to 2002 for most countries.

The most widely used proxy for the country risk premium are the returns implicit in the Emerging Markets Bond Indices (EMBI) provided by JPMorgan, after having subtracted total returns of U.S. Treasury bonds[2] (from now on this variable shall be named COSTBORROWING).

Apart from the dependent variable, the focus of this study area's balance sheet effects (BALANCESHEET), which amount to the change in the value of financial wealth due to an unexpected change in the real exchange rate. In emerging countries, we can safely assume that financial wealth is negative and corresponds with the increase in the foreign currency-denominated debt burden. Berganza, Chang, and García-Herrero (2004) proxy it with the external debt service (DEBT).[3] They also extend the concept of balance sheets to those stemming from domestic foreign-currency denominated debt and find that these are also detrimental for the sovereign risk premium.

The change in the real exchange rate is calculated as the yearly change in the bilateral nominal exchange rate against the U.S. dollar adjusted by the domestic inflation (EXSURPRISE). We use the bilateral exchange rate because we assume that all foreign currency debt is denominated in U.S. dollars. This is a relatively safe assumption for the countries in our sample.

Competitiveness, the other relevant channel of influence of real exchange rate depreciations, is measured by the increase in the dollar value of exports (ΔEXPORT). Finally, a number of control variables are included in all specifications. The first is the lag of the sovereign risk (COSTBORROWING_1), which accounts for its persistence. The second is the sovereign spread for all emerging countries for which the EMBI is available (EMBIWORLD). This should capture a possible similar comovement stemming from the market integration of this asset class and potential contagion effects. We also include past economic growth (RGDP_1) and the level of international reserves (RRES), which obviously constitutes financial wealth.

The results show that the balance sheet effect increase the cost of capital; that is, the coefficient of BALANCESHEET is positive and significant at the one percent level (Exhibit 22.1). Its magnitude is also reasonable in economic terms: It implies that if a real depreciation increases a country's debt service by 1 percent of its 1995 GDP, the sovereign risk premium will rise by about 61 basis points, *ceteris paribus*. Furthermore, Berganza and García-Herrero (2004) find that the effect of real exchange rate changes is asymmetric: Real depreciations are clearly detrimental while real appreciations are not found significant in lowering the risk premium, at least in the short term.[4] In a second regression (whose results are shown in the rightmost column in Exhibit 22.1), we included the year-to-year change in exports as an explanatory variable. As stressed earlier, our aim is to test whether the significance of BALANCESHEET in the regression hinges on an omitted variable problem, namely the competitiveness effect. While the inclusion of ΔEXPORT results in a lower estimate for the BALANCESHEET coefficient, the fall is relatively small. The next question we address is whether the significance of the BALANCESHEET

Exhibit 22.1 Baseline Regression

Number of Obs.	177	177
R-squared	0.5733	0.5909
Dependent variable: COSTBORROWING		
COSTBORROWING_1	0.7480*** (0.0618)	0.7713*** (0.0613)
EMBIWORLD	0.4373** (0.2142)	0.5259** (0.2129)
RGDP_1	330.4769 (250.1205)	219.9893 (248.9829)
BALANCESHEET	60.9356*** (13.7547)	49.4570*** (14.1568)
RRES	−48.4515** (23.3747)	−47.1219** (22.9589)
ΔEXPORT	—	−5.6623*** (2.0914)
CONS	−484.3599 (328.3529)	−387.5060 (324.4174)
Wald test[a]	—	0.03
(*p*-value)	—	0.8689

OLS estimation.
Standard errors in parenthesis.
*Significant at 10%; ** significant at 5%; *** significant at 1%.
[a]The Wald test assesses the equality of the coefficient of the variable BALANCESHEET in both regressions. It is distributed as chi-square.

variable is really due to the impact of debt accumulation on the cost of credit and not to the presence of balance sheet effects.

Finally, Berganza and García-Herrero (2004) also show that it is not only external debt that matters to suffer from balance sheets but also domestic foreign-currency denominated debt.[5] The evidence just reviewed is, on the whole, supportive of the view that balance sheet effects (i.e., the increase in the debt burden after a real depreciation) significantly raise the sovereign risk premium, other things given.

If one accepts the view that balance sheet effects are significant for the cost of credit in an emerging country, the policy implications are severe. There is an argument to avoid sharp changes in the real exchange rate unless financial imperfections are small. The other policy venue is obviously to reduce financial imperfections. If none of the two were possible, countries should think of obtaining insurance against potential balance sheet effects. This is discussed further in the conclusions.

GLOBAL RISK AVERSION

The risk appetite of global investors has become a key variable to understand trends in financial markets in the past few years. When measured by the most common proxy, namely the U.S. Baa corporate spread, global risk aversion (GRA) seems to have been closely related to the evolution of Latin American sovereign spreads for quite some time. In the traditional literature, the main external factor affecting sovereign spreads was the risk-free interest rate in the United States. Although this is clearly relevant, investors' sentiment toward risk should also have a bearing on high-risk markets, to which emerging countries' sovereign bonds belong. This is probably even more the case today in which risk issues play an increasing role due to the sophistication of financial markets.

Against this background, García-Herrero and Ortiz (2007) analyze how investors' attitude toward risks affects Latin American sovereign spreads and whether the impact is different across countries. Exhibit 22.2 shows the results under two different estimation techniques: OLS (Ordinary Least Squares) adjusted

Exhibit 22.2 Semi-Elasticities of the Spread to GAR[*]

Country	OLS	TSLS[**]
Argentina[***]	0,13	0,06
Brazil	0,21	0,21
Chile	0,40	0,29
Colombia	0,20	0,20
Mexico	0,20	0,19
Panama	0,15	0,15
Peru	0,24	0,23
Venezuela	0,16	0,17

[*] Coefficients significant to 95% level.
[**] Estimated with two lags of GRA.
[***] The observations when the country was in default have been excluded.

for autocorrelation of the error term and TSLS (Two Stage Least Squares). The parameters are always significant and have relatively high values. This confirms the relevance of investor's risk aversion for the evolution of spreads.

Chile—the country with the lowest average sovereign spread—has the largest estimated parameter for GRA in both cases. Instead, those parameters are lowest for Argentina and Venezuela (the two countries with the highest average sovereign spread). This highlights the idea that countries with worse fundamentals, and, thus, with a higher probability of default, should be relatively less affected by GRA, at least in the short run. In fact, their weak fundamentals basically explain most of the variability of their sovereign spreads:[6] Instead, well-performing countries, like Chile, tend to be relatively more affected by external factors. The much smaller impact of GRA on Mexico does not necessarily contradict this finding since Mexico has good fundamentals fairly recently in our sample.

The authors also show the impact of GRA to be persistent and even increases over time in most countries. This might be explained by the growing integration of Latin American sovereign bonds in global investors' portfolios (Wooldridge, Domanski, and Cobau 2003). In fact, the range of investors purchasing emerging market securities has broadened. In the early 1990s, only specialized investors, such as hedge funds and mutual funds, invest in these securities, but today large institutional investors are also exposed to this kind of paper. This cannot but strengthen the interrelation between U.S. corporate paper and emerging countries' sovereign bonds.

CONTAGION

Some of the episodes of high sovereign spreads (as shown in Exhibit 22.1) have been associated with contagion. In the last few years, the economic literature has devoted substantial efforts to explain the phenomenon of contagion between countries. The possibility of separating pure contagion from fundamental-related changes in financial variables is key in the design of the international financial architecture. In fact, the understanding is that countries with crises originated by pure contagion should be bailed out since such crises are not related to the country's situation.

The phenomenon of contagion is also of particular interest for investors because they can profit from events where there is no perfect arbitrage or where herd behavior exists. In particular, if an investor were to know beforehand that a country's financial variables suffer contagion from another country's financial variables when a shock occurs, he or she could profit from this information.

For both interests (the international community and investors), the concept of contagion needs to be defined accurately because decisions need to be taken on the basis of its existence or absence. The lack of consensus in the literature is related to the difficulty in measuring such a high-frequency event. Distinguishing contagion events from other market movements is, thus, an empirical question, which is crucial in view of the role that contagion plays in the provision of international financial assistance. Díez de los Rios and García-Herrero (2004) aim at improving the measurability and comparability of events of potential contagion, by narrowing down the concept and testing it empirically. To that end, they concentrate on pure contagion, that is, on those interrelations that cannot be explained by other factors, such as general market movements.

They also concentrate on one market, emerging countries' sovereign bonds, and in one type of shock, a downgrade in a country's sovereign rating different than the one that may potentially suffer from contagion.

The reasons for these two choices are the following. First, emerging countries are those more dependent on international financial assistance and their sovereign bonds are particularly relevant financial assets, being closely associated with country risk. In addition, emerging countries' sovereign bonds constitute an asset class in which investors are interested. Second, sovereign ratings are an aggregate measure of a country's fundamentals. Downgrades in sovereign ratings should be a relatively good proxy for a shock because they generally reflect a sharp deterioration in fundamentals. Notwithstanding the caveats—the downgrade does not coincide with the shock and not all shocks are reflected by a downgrade—a rating downgrade is still an important piece of information that agents incorporate in their investment decisions.

To narrow down the definition of pure contagion to a more operational one, it seems important to identify which are the main factors that determine the returns of emerging countries' sovereign bonds. In fact, only what cannot be explained by such factors should be called *contagion*. Interest rate, exchange rate, and credit (or sovereign) risks are the most widely accepted determinants of sovereign bond excess returns (Kamin and Von Kleist 1999). The interest rate risk hinges on the interest rate structure (and maturity) of sovereign bonds as compared to other bond portfolios.

Exchange rate risk is particularly relevant for local currency denominated sovereign bonds. Credit risk depends on the country's economic fundamentals (Min 1998). The ability to clean sovereign bonds from these factors' influence before testing for contagion is another important objective of our paper. The measure of credit risk is particularly problematic, because it is related to a large number of variables reflecting a country's fundamentals. We shall use credit ratings to that end.

After cleaning up by interest rate currency and credit factors, through a three-market asset pricing model, the residuals obtained will be the pricing errors. We, then, test for a dynamic causal relation between such pricing errors, after a shock occurs (i.e., a downgrade in a third country's sovereign rating).

Such a test should allow us to say something about the direction of the transmission of pricing errors and, thereby, to identify the country causing contagion (or a portfolio shift) and the country being affected. This is important when designing insurance tools for contagion. Granger causality tests will be used to test for such a dynamic causal relation.

In the case of contagion, the comovement will necessarily be positive while it will be negative in the event of a portfolio shift. In addition, we carry out a Wald test to assess whether such causal comovement can actually be attributed to a third country's downgrade. The results (in Exhibit 22.3) show a number of cases of pure contagion as well as pure portfolio shifts. In particular, portfolio shifts seem to have occurred from Mexico to Venezuela, from Poland to Russia, and from Venezuela to Poland in the period of analysis. Contagion events seem to have occurred from Brazil to Mexico, and from Poland to Argentina.

Exhibit 22.3 Granger Causality Tests: Three-Factor Model with Ratings Wald Tests

Countries	Argentina	Brazil	Ecuador	Mexico	Morocco	Nigeria	Panama	Peru	Poland	Russia	Venezuela
Argentina	11.570***	3.140	0.380	0.110	16.821***	1.213	2.044	10.909***	9.675***	6.957**	0.402
	(0.003)	(0.208)	(0.827)	(0.946)	(0.000)	(0.545)	(0.360)	(0.004)	(0.008)	(0.031)	(0.818)
Brazil	4.107	6.157**	0.731	1.995	0.459	2.797	4.068	0.468	2.201	9.569***	1.957
	(0.128)	(0.046)	(0.694)	(0.369)	(0.795)	(0.247)	(0.131)	(0.791)	(0.333)	(0.008)	(0.376)
Ecuador	6.632**	11.272***	3.100	2.630	6.063**	1.674	7.471**	0.885	1.948	5.305	0.250
	(0.036)	(0.004)	(0.212)	(0.268)	(0.048)	(0.433)	(0.024)	(0.642)	(0.378)	(0.070)	(0.882)
Mexico	10.031***	9.139**	2.129	0.931	0.998	1.116	0.283	2.094	0.899	1.085	19.923***
	(0.007)	(0.010)	(0.345)	(0.628)	(0.607)	(0.572)	(0.868)	(0.351)	(0.638)	(0.581)	(0.000)
Morocco	1.326	1.513	2.578	0.698	0.843	0.221	2.997	2.858	4.071	1.487	1.546
	(0.515)	(0.469)	(0.276)	(0.705)	(0.656)	(0.895)	(0.223)	(0.240)	(0.131)	(0.475)	(0.462)
Nigeria	2.914	8.304**	10.928***	0.275	2.025	12.701***	1.715	1.422	3.010	0.996	4.232
	(0.233)	(0.016)	(0.004)	(0.872)	(0.363)	(0.002)	(0.424)	(0.491)	(0.222)	(0.951)	(0.121)
Panama	2.231	3.875	1.094	1.937	1.593	2.310	2.595	1.228	2.934	1.839	1.861
	(0.328)	(0.144)	(0.579)	(0.380)	(0.451)	(0.315)	(0.273)	(0.541)	(0.231)	(0.399)	(0.394)
Peru	3.134	5.470*	7.046**	2.073	0.280	1.203	2.395	12.361***	1.259	0.759	0.152
	(0.209)	(0.065)	(0.030)	(0.355)	(0.869)	(0.548)	(0.302)	(0.002)	(0.533)	(0.684)	(0.927)
Poland	0.701	4.033	0.250	3.252	2.702	1.094	0.296	1.045	2.672	1.289	8.957**
	(0.704)	(0.133)	(0.988)	(0.197)	(0.259)	(0.579)	(0.862)	(0.593)	(0.263)	(0.525)	(0.011)
Russia	4.771*	5.128*	2.280	1.682	3.148	3.915	2.820	11.867***	6.754**	0.749	4.267
	(0.092)	(0.077)	(0.320)	(0.431)	(0.207)	(0.141)	(0.244)	(0.003)	(0.034)	(0.688)	(0.118)
Venezuela	0.706	1.744	0.850	9.403***	1.879	2.938	0.687	0.055	0.837	0.669	0.227
	(0.703)	(0.418)	(0.654)	(0.009)	(0.391)	(0.230)	(0.709)	(0.973)	(0.658)	(0.716)	(0.893)

Wald Test of the joint hypothesis that: $\gamma_\xi = 0$, $\xi_\xi = 0$.

In estimated equation: $v_{it} = \gamma_{ij} v_{if-1} + \xi_{ij} v_{jt-1} DownOwn_{jt-1} + \xi_{ij} v_{jt-1} DownOther_{it-1} + \varepsilon_{jt}$

Where $v_{kt} = r_{kt} - \beta_{\varepsilon j} f_{\varepsilon t}{}^R - \beta_{vi} f_{vt}{}^R \beta_{vf} f_{\varepsilon i}{}^R$.

(***), (**), (*) indicates coefficient significantly different from zero at the 1%, 5%, and 10% level, respectively. p-value in parenthesis.

To sum up, we narrow down the definition of contagion/portfolio shift by concentrating on one single-asset class, cleaning up general market movements, and assessing the response to a third country's shock. We do find a few cases of both contagion and portfolio shifts but these are probably at odds with the existing literature. This is probably because our definition focuses on short-term causal comovements (one week after the shock), which does not need to coincide with longer-term causal relations. This makes our definition more useful for investors in search of arbitrage opportunities than for policy decisions by international organizations related to the international financial architecture. Furthermore, rating downgrades are a variable that investors focus on more than the international community. For the latter, a longer-term definition of contagion and a broader definition of a shock would be warranted because the granting of financial assistance to a country subject to contagion needs to be based on a problem that is not to disappear quickly. However, the broadening of the definition should not be such as to make it impossible to compare across events in an objective way.

CONCLUSIONS

We have reviewed three important external determinants of the sovereign spreads in emerging countries: balance sheet effects, global risk aversion, and contagion. Although there are ways to reduce the detrimental impact of balance sheet effects, these are either hard to implement (for example, reducing financial frictions) or costly (such as maintaining a stable real exchange rate). This is why insurance against such a shock might need to be considered. This could be in the form of self-insurance (accumulation of reserves) or market insurance (instruments that are inversely related to a country's real exchange rate). In addition, the cost of self-insurance might be too high and private insurance might not be easily available because of shallow markets. This is where regional insurance may have a role to play. This could be achieved through some kind of reserve pooling. Its effectiveness will obviously depend on the degree of correlation of real exchange rate movements within a region.

The same case can be made for negative shocks stemming from a sudden increase in global risk aversion or for contagion effects, particularly if this is pure contagion. Obviously, developing adequate measures of global risk aversion and contagion is key so as to design the insurance device and when a country is allowed to draw from its insurance.

NOTES

1. As for firm-level data, Forbes (2002) analyzes the impact of 12 major depreciations on a sample of emerging countries' large firms and finds no significant balance sheet effects on performance, although firms with higher debt ratios tend to show lower net income growth. It should be noted, though, that Forbes does not take into account the currency composition of debt. In the same vein, Bleakley and Cowan (2002) show evidence that the competitiveness effect associated with exchange rate depreciations offsets the potential contractive balance sheet effect on investment for a panel of Latin American firms.

2. It should be noted that EMBI spreads reflect sovereign risk while our objective is broader: country risk in general because we do not concentrate on public debt only, but in all debt denominated in foreign currency, be it public or private. In any event, the EMBI spread

continues to be the best available proxy as sovereign spreads are generally a floor for private sector country risk.

3. Berganza and García-Herrero (2004) show that the results do not change using flows (debt service) or stocks. They also conduct robustness tests with a measure of net wealth, subtracting international reserves to the stock of debt. The results are maintained as well.

4. Results only reported in the original paper.

5. For details on the results, consult the paper.

6. It is also the result of the model developed by Blanchard (2004).

REFERENCES

Aghion, P., P. Bacchetta, and A. Banerjee. 2001. "A Corporate Balance-Sheet Approach to Currency Crises." *Study Center Gerzensee Working Paper* 01–5.

Berganza, J., R. Chang, and A. García-Herrero. 2004. "Balance Sheet Effects and the Country Risk Premium: An Empirical Investigation." *Working Paper* 0316, Banco de España.

Berganza, J., and A. García-Herrero. 2004. "What Makes Balance Sheet Effects Detrimental for the Country Risk Premium?" *Documentos de Trabajo* N0423, Banco de España.

Bernanke, B., and M. Gertler. 1989. "Agency Costs, Net Worth, and Business Fluctuations." *American Economic Review* 79:1, 14–31.

Blanchard, Olivier J. 2004. "Fiscal Dominance and Inflation Targeting: Lessons from Brazil." *MIT Department of Economics Working Paper* No. 04-13.

Bleakley, H., and T. Cowan. 2002. "Corporate dollar debt and depreciations: Much Ado about Nothing?" *Federal Reserve Bank of Boston Working Paper* 02–5.

Céspedes, L., R. Chang, and A. Velasco. 2004. "Balance Sheet Effects and Exchange Rate Policy." *American Economic Review* 94:4, 1183–93.

Díez de los Rios, A., and A. García-Herrero. 2004. "Contagion and portfolio shift in emerging countries' sovereign bonds" in *Monetary integration, markets and regulation*, Elsevier, also *Banco de España Working Paper* No. 0317.

Edwards, S. 1986. "Are Devaluations Contractionary?" *Review of Economics and Statistics*, 68:501–8.

Forbes K. 2002. "How Do Large Depreciations Affect Firm Performance?" *NBER Working Paper* 9095.

García-Herrero, A., and A. Ortiz. 2007. "The role of global risk aversion in explaining Latin American sovereign spreads," *Economia* 7, No. 1 (also Banco de España Working Paper No. 0505).

Gertler, M., S. Gilchrist, and F. Natalucci. 2003. "External Constraints on Monetary Policy and the Financial Accelerator." *NBER Working Paper* 10128.

Kamin, S. and K. von Kleist. 1999. "The Evolution and Determinants of Emerging Market Credit Spreads in the 1990s." *Bank for International Settlements Working Paper* 68.

Min, H.G. 1998. "Determinants of Emerging Market Bond Spreads. Do Economic Fundamentals Matter?" *World Bank Policy Research Working Paper*, 1899.

Neumeyer, A., and F. Perri. 2004. "Business Cycles in Emerging Economies: The Role of Interest Rates." Federal Reserve Bank of Minneapolis Staff Report 335.

Wooldridge, P. D., D. Domanski, and A. Cobau. 2003. "Changing links between mature and emerging financial markets," *BIS Quarterly Review*, September, 45–54.

ABOUT THE AUTHOR

Alicia García-Herrero has been chief economist for emerging markets at Banco Bilbao Vizcaya Argentaria (BBVA) since December 2007. She is also a member of the advisory board of the Hong Kong Institute of Monetary Research, an adjunct professor at the Lingnan University (Hong Kong), and a research fellow at the University of Hong Kong and at IESE center for emerging markets in Spain.

Prior to BBVA, Alicia was part of the Asian Research Program of the Bank for International Settlements in Hong Kong. From 2001 until 2006, she was head of the international economy division of Bank of Spain. She was also visiting professor at Johns Hopkins University and at Universidad Carlos III. From 1998 to 2001, she was a member of the Counsel to the Executive Board of the European Central Bank. From 1997 to 1998, she was head of emerging economies at the research department at Banco Santander, as well as associate professor at Universidad Autónoma. From 1994 to 1997, she worked as an economist at the International Monetary Fund.

García-Herrero holds a PhD in economics from George Washington. Many of her papers have been published in reference journals and books. She has also been a research fellow at the Bank of Japan and the Bank of Finland. She can be reached at alicia.garcia-herrero@bbva.com.hk.

CHAPTER 23

Responses of Emerging Countries to the Global Financial Crisis

TATIANA DIDIER
Research Economist in the World Bank's Office

CONSTANTINO HEVIA
Economist in the Macroeconomics and Growth Unit of the World Bank's Development Economics Research Group (DECRG)

SERGIO L. SCHMUKLER
Lead Economist in the Development Research Group of the World Bank

I n contrast to previous crisis episodes, the 2008–2009 crisis found many emerging countries with the required credibility and space to conduct countercyclical policies, more solid financial positions, and, therefore, better prepared to cope with the global crisis. This chapter discusses and documents the policy and institutional developments that allowed these countries to partially absorb the negative external shock. In particular, it considers developments in (1) fiscal policy, (2) monetary policy, (3) exchange rate policy, (4) external financial factors, and (5) domestic financial factors.

INTRODUCTION

Many financial crises have had large effects, generating contagion that was transmitted around the world. To make things worse, previous worldwide turmoil episodes found most emerging countries unable or unwilling to perform countercyclical policies. Moreover, in many cases, their own vulnerabilities and poor institutional framework amplified the initial external shock, leading to sharper and more painful recessions. For instance, the lack of access to world capital markets during turbulent times may have hampered the ability of governments to conduct counter-cyclical fiscal policies (C. Reinhart and V. Reinhart 2008). Moreover, Kaminsky, Reinhart, and Vegh (2004) document in their famous paper, "When It Rains, It Pours," that emerging economies have typically followed pro-cyclical policies, in both good and bad times.

In contrast, the 2008–2009 global financial crisis found many emerging economies with the required credibility and space to conduct countercyclical fiscal and monetary policies and a more consolidated financial stance, which allowed them to partially offset the global shock. This chapter discusses and documents these developments in emerging market economies. To shed light on the discussion on how different countries performed under such large shocks, the chapter distinguishes between two broad factors: (1) the transmission of external shocks and (2) the resilience of countries to those shocks.

The transmission of external shocks depends both on the size and nature of the shocks, as well as on the links between each country and the rest of the world. External shocks get transmitted across countries through two main channels: trade and finance.

Trade involves not only the direct exposure to other countries' demands, but also the overall effects on each country's trade balance. Conceptually, the trade channel could be decomposed into a direct (quantity) component, and an indirect (price) component. As high-income countries were hit by the 2008–2009 crisis, they became poorer and demanded fewer goods from the rest of the world—the direct or quantity component. As global demand declined, the price of these goods and other commodities declined as well—the indirect or price component. Both effects implied that exporter countries received fewer dollars for the fewer goods they sold. For example, when the U.S. economy began its recession in late 2007 and as its economic slowdown deepened, it not only demanded fewer exports from China, but it also depressed commodity prices, hitting all net commodity exporters regardless of the final destination of the exports. Naturally, countries open to trade and dependent on exports were hit severely, for example, as witnessed by the sudden sharp contractions in East Asia. As the United States and other economies recovered, both international trade and East Asia rebounded fast.

The financial channel is more complex and operates through the financial account that connects economies to the international financial system. When a crisis of global dimensions affects the world economy, like the post–Lehman Brothers meltdown, the negative wealth effects suffered in high-income countries led to a decrease in foreign investments and, therefore, to less available capital, especially for emerging countries. This direct financial effect can be amplified by mechanisms that affect how financial intermediaries typically operate. For example, international investors (banks, mutual funds, hedge funds, and so forth) might have to reduce their exposure to emerging economies in response to shocks affecting the size, liquidity, and quality of their assets. Likewise, leveraged investors, such as banks and hedge funds, might face regulatory requirements, internal provisioning practices, or margin calls that prompt them to rebalance their portfolios by selling their asset holdings in other economies. In addition, international banks and other agents in different countries might generate capital outflows during crises, for example, if a parent bank in another country finds itself in need to boost its capital. Therefore, losses in a crisis-hit economy might lead international investors to sell off assets or curtail lending in other economies as well. The financial channel might also become active beyond some of these mechanical factors. The negative income shock might lead to higher risk aversion. For example, investors became very risk averse after Lehman Brothers collapsed because they did not know which other banks were exposed to the subprime sector or Lehman Brothers' contracts.

The higher risk aversion, in turn, led many investors to pull out of risky assets, dumping their investment in emerging countries in exchange for assets perceived to be safer (mostly U.S. T-bills).[1]

Once a country is hit by an external shock, how it performs, how resilient it is depends, at least in part, on its fundamentals. Because of the many crises suffered in the 1990s and early 2000s, many emerging countries became better prepared to withstand external shocks and were consequently in relatively stronger positions when the crisis in the U.S. subprime sector erupted. In particular, several factors proved to be useful during late 2008 and early 2009, creating buffers between the external conditions and the local economy. The rest of this chapter discusses these factors.

RESILIENCE AND POLICY RESPONSES TO THE GLOBAL CRISIS

This section describes the policy responses and institutional developments that allowed emerging countries to cope better with the global crisis. We consider developments in (1) fiscal policy, (2) monetary policy, (3) exchange rate policy, (4) external financial factors, and (5) domestic financial factors.

Fiscal Policy

Previous to the 2008–2009 crisis, many countries had improved their fiscal stance and had acquired enough fiscal space to design and implement packages to counteract the contraction in the world economy (Exhibit 23.1). The most noticeable case is China, which had great ability to rapidly deploy its fiscal resources. Countries that did not have this fiscal space ended up becoming more vulnerable, as the crisis in peripheral Europe has shown in 2010. The recent fiscal expansion in emerging countries is in stark contrast with past experience: historically, fiscal policy in emerging countries was highly pro-cyclical, particularly so during crisis episodes.

Monetary Policy

Perhaps one of the most surprising features of the emerging country responses to the recent global financial crisis was the drastic reduction in interest rates. In previous crises in emerging economies, countries were forced to increase interest rates to contain capital outflows and the drainage in reserves as their currencies came under attack. This time, however, countries were able to use countercyclical monetary policy.

The recently acquired credibility and institutional capacity of emerging country central banks was an essential asset to conduct an active monetary policy when the world economy came to a halt. For example, countries in Latin America, which historically had to increase interest rates to protect their currencies during financial crises, were able to implement drastic reductions in their policy interest rates during the current crisis (Exhibit 23.2).

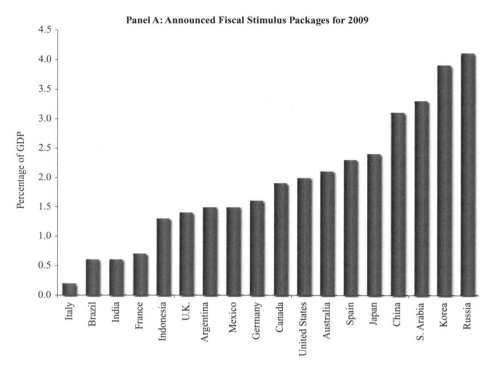

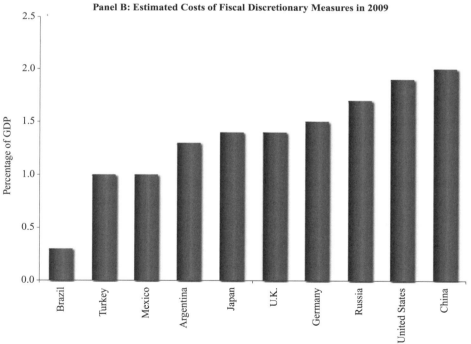

Exhibit 23.1   Fiscal Policy

Data sources: IMF (2009). This figure shows the announced fiscal packages in 2009 as well as the estimated costs of discretionary fiscal measures adopted during the 2008–2009 crisis.

Panel A: Monetary Policy Rates in Inflation-Targeting Latin American Countries

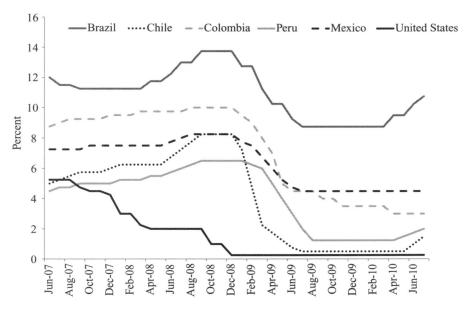

Panel B: Changes in Monetary Policy Rates in Inflation-Targeting Latin American Countries

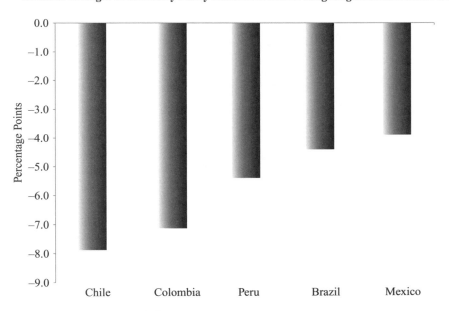

Exhibit 23.2 Monetary Policy

Data source: Bloomberg. This figure shows monetary policy rates in inflation-targeting Latin American countries in Panel A. Panel B shows the changes in these rates, in percentage points, around the 2008–2009 crisis. We consider December 2008 as the starting month to calculate changes in policy rates for all countries. Declines in policy rates ended in May 2010 for Brazil and Chile, July 2010 for Colombia and Mexico, and April 2010 for Peru.

Exchange Rate Policy

Another key factor that contributed to the ability to lower interest rates was the exchange rate regime. With the notable exception of Europe, most emerging countries have moved toward more flexible exchange rate regimes, especially after witnessing the negative consequences of the emerging market crises that began in the mid-1990s and culminated with the Argentine crisis of 2001–2002. This movement toward greater flexibility was possible due to the improved monetary policy credibility and institutional capacity of emerging country central banks. This flexible monetary regime allowed exchange rates to depreciate in late 2008, cushioning the global shock and, at the same time, improving the external balance (Exhibit 23.3).

External Financial Factors

Two key developments in the management of their financial accounts helped emerging countries decrease their vulnerabilities to external shocks. First, many countries improved their current account positions by becoming less dependent on foreign financing sources. Second, and perhaps more importantly, many emerging

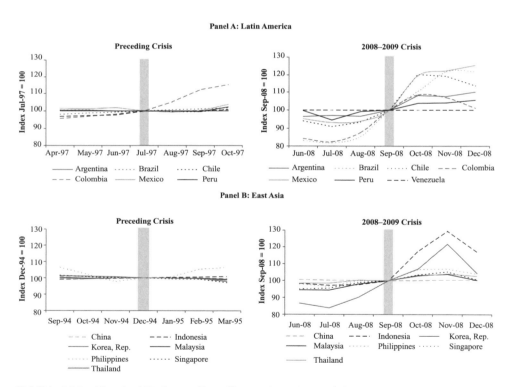

Exhibit 23.3   Nominal Exchange Rate Fluctuations Around Crises

Data sources: IMF's International Financial Statistics. This figure shows fluctuations in nominal exchange rates (against the U.S. dollar) around the 2008–2009 and preceding crises for selected countries in Latin America (Panel A) and East Asia (Panel B). We normalized exchange rates at 100 at the beginning of each crisis: December 1994 (East Asia) and July 1997 (Latin America) for the preceding crisis, and September 2008 for the 2008–2009 crisis.

countries have wisely changed the nature of their external assets and liabilities, making the balance sheet effects work in their favor this time. On average, these countries switched their foreign liabilities from debt to equity while accumulating debt assets in foreign currency. As their domestic currency depreciated, the local currency value of their external assets increased, while their liabilities remained constant, or even shrank due to the collapse in equity markets. Of course, emerging economies were able and willing to let their currencies depreciate—thus partially offsetting the external shock—precisely because the change in foreign assets and liabilities did not create concerns of negative balance sheet effects. In contrast, developed countries increased their debt liabilities vis-à-vis emerging countries, in part reflecting the large debt flows used to finance the U.S. current account deficit. Simultaneously, however, developed countries became net claimants on emerging countries on the equity side (Exhibit 23.4) (Gourinchas and Rey 2007; Lane and Milesi-Ferretti 2007).

Another consequence of the better external balance was the accumulation of foreign reserves, especially since the Asian currency crises of the late 1990s (Exhibit 23.5). Apart from the effect of the reserve accumulation to slow down the appreciation of the domestic currency during the pre-crisis expansionary period, sizeable international reserves not only gave central banks room to contain the depreciation of their currencies during the crisis period but also served as a self-insurance mechanism to deter the possibility of currency and banking panics. In effect, many countries held international reserves in excess of their total levels of short-term foreign liabilities. In practice, it eliminated concerns about difficulties in rolling-over their short-term debt, giving investors less incentives to attack domestic currencies.[2]

Domestic Financial Factors

An important factor in allowing exchange rates to depreciate was the shift in emerging country borrowing (except in Eastern Europe) from foreign currency to domestic currency (Exhibit 23.6). This change in the denomination of debt has avoided the negative balance sheet effects common in previous crises, when devaluations led to debt overhang problems. In fact, the discussions on the European crises partially miss this point. For instance, even if Greece were allowed to devalue its currency (or other countries like Portugal and Spain managed to reduce local wages and prices) to become more competitive and boost growth through the trade channel, the fact that the debt is denominated in euros would increase the real financial burden. Consequently, this would make the necessary price adjustment even larger and possibly trigger the beginning of a vicious cycle (de la Torre, Levy Yeyati, and Schmukler 2003 and 2010).

The domestic financial positions had also improved in several emerging countries due to better regulation, more prudent practices by financial intermediaries, and abundant local liquidity. For example, in many countries banks now depend heavily on domestic deposits to fund their operations (Exhibit 23.7). When the international wholesale interbank market dried up in the last quarter of 2008, banks that relied on the short-term wholesale market were hit harder and suffered serious rollover problems (Raddatz 2010). To the extent that the external environment deteriorated and that the local financial system proved to be in sound footing,

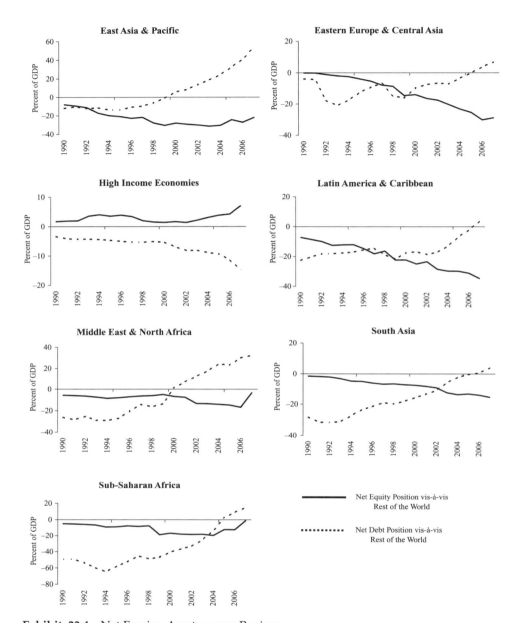

Exhibit 23.4 Net Foreign Assets across Regions

Data sources: Lane and Milesi-Ferretti (2007). This figure shows the evolution of net foreign assets as a percentage of GDP across the different geographical regions of the world. These figures report regional aggregates taking into account each country's positions vis-à-vis the rest of the world. Net debt positions (vis-à-vis the rest of the world) are calculated as the sum of foreign portfolio debt assets and international reserves minus foreign portfolio debt liabilities. Analogously, net equity positions (vis-à-vis the rest of the world) are calculated as the sum of FDI assets and portfolio equity assets. Economies are classified into regions according to the World Bank's July 2010 Country Classification.

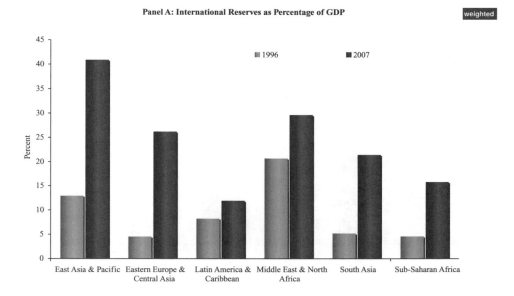

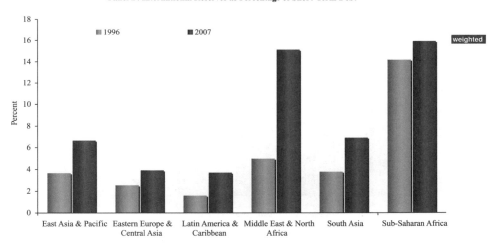

Exhibit 23.5   International Reserves

Data sources: World Bank's World Development Indicators and IMF's World Economic Outlook. This figure shows the level of international reserves (excluding gold) in the years before the 1997 and 2008–2009 crises, as a percentage of GDP in Panel A and as a percentage of short-term debt in Panel B. Regional averages in both periods are constructed by weighting each observation by its relative level of GDP in 2007 measured in current U.S. dollars.

Panel A: Corporate Sector Foreign Currency Debt Issues

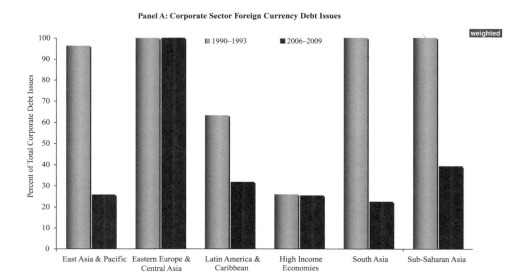

Panel B: Banks Foreign Liabilities

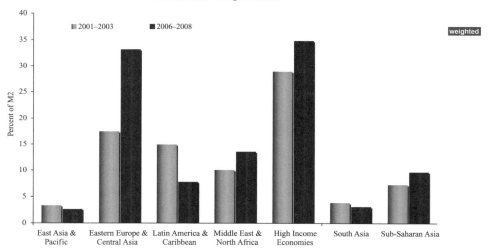

Exhibit 23.6 Foreign Currency Borrowing

Data sources: Thomson-Reuters' Securities Data Company, IMF's International Financial Statistics, and IMF's World Economic Outlook. This figure shows corporate debt issues in foreign currency as percentage of total corporate debt issues in Panel A. Panel B shows total foreign liabilities of deposit money banks as percentage of money and quasi-money (M2). Regional averages in both periods are constructed by weighting each observation by its relative level of GDP in 2007 measured in current U.S. dollars.

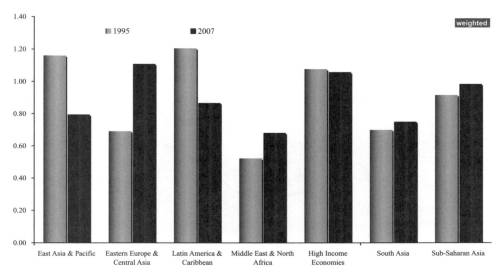

Exhibit 23.7 Loan to Deposit Ratios in Emerging Economies
Data sources: Beck and Demirgüç-Kunt (2009) and IMF's World Economic Outlook. This figure shows loan to deposit ratios for deposit money banks in 1995 and in 2007. Regional averages in both periods are constructed by weighting each observation by its relative level of GDP in 2007 measured in current U.S. dollars.

depositors did not flee local banks (unlike previous crises). Perhaps for the first time, the domestic financial systems at least did not amplify the shock emanating from the international financial system.

Although total bank credit declined during the crisis, evidence from Latin American countries suggests that foreign banks present in these countries did not act as a particular destabilizing force during the crisis, behaving similarly to local private banks.[3] In addition, in some countries the use of credit policies through public banks proved to be useful to mitigate the contraction in private sector credit (Exhibit 23.8).

CONCLUSIONS

Historically, emerging countries did not have the ability or the institutions to cope effectively with negative external shocks. Not only did these countries lack the required space to conduct countercyclical policies, but their faulty institutions and weak macroeconomic fundamentals also typically amplified the initial shock.

Fortunately, many countries learned from the experience of previous crises, and started to adopt more sustainable and credible policies since the late 1990s. This investment in institutions and credibility seems to have paid off during the 2008–2009 global crisis, as many emerging countries were able to perform counter-cyclical policies. Moreover, this time their macroeconomic fundamentals helped to cushion the external shock instead of amplifying it. The following developments in many emerging countries served that purpose: (1) better fiscal positions and more reliable central banks, giving countries space in both fronts; (2) the change in the composition of their foreign liabilities from debt to equity, making the balance

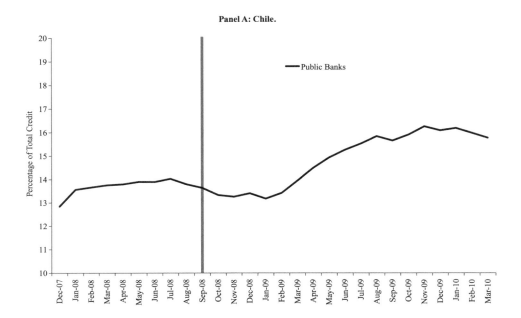

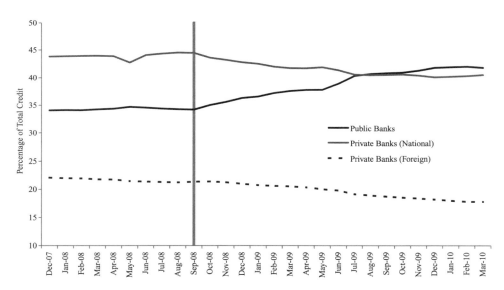

Exhibit 23.8   Credit by Public and Private Banks

Data sources: Superintendencia de Bancos e Instituciones Financieras and Banco Central do Brasil. This figure shows total credit to the private sector from public banks as a percentage of total credit for Chile (Panel A) and Brazil (Panel B). Panel B also shows the participation of domestic and foreign private banks on total credit for Brazil. The decline in the participation of foreign private banks on total credit during the 2008–2009 crisis was not larger than that of domestic private banks.

sheet effect work in their favor during the current crisis; (3) the accumulation of foreign reserves in excess of their short-term foreign liabilities, discouraging currency attacks; (4) the shift in their borrowing from foreign currency to domestic currency, avoiding the balance sheet effects common of previous crises; and (5) the improvement in the regulation of their domestic financial system and the greater reliance on domestic deposits to fund the banks' operations, reducing their dependence on the international short-term wholesale interbank market.

NOTES

1. Many observers have argued that the financial channel has been the main channel of transmission of shocks across countries during the 1990s (Baig and Goldfajn 1999; Kaminsky and Reinhart 2000; Van Rijckeghem and Weder 2001; Caramazza, Ricci, and Salgado 2004). See also Kaminsky and Reinhart (2000) and Martinez Peria, Powell, and Vladkova-Hollar (2005) on the role of banks; Borensztein and Gelos (2003), Kaminsky, Lyons, and Schmukler (2004), and Broner, Gelos, and Reinhart (2006) on the role of mutual funds, among many others. Similar channels also operated during the global crisis.

2. Obstfeld, Shambaugh, and Taylor (2009) and Frankel and Saravelos (2010) argue that countries with higher levels of reserves suffered less severe crises. For a different view, see Blanchard, Faruqee, and Klyuev (2009).

3. This claim, however, does not imply that foreign banks did not play a role in the transmission of the crisis (Cetorelli and Goldberg 2010).

REFERENCES

Baig, Taimur, and Ilan Goldfajn. 1999. "Financial Market Contagion in the Asian Crisis." *IMF Staff Papers* 46:2, 167–195.

Beck, Thorsten, and Asli Demirgüç-Kunt. 2009. "Financial Institutions and Markets Across Countries and over Time: Data and Analysis." *World Bank Policy Research Working Paper* 4943.

Blanchard, Olivier, Hamid Faruqee, and Vladimir Klyuev. 2009. "Did Foreign Reserves Help Weather the Crisis?" *IMF Survey Magazine* October.

Borensztein, Eduardo R., and R. Gaston Gelos. 2003. "A Panic-Prone Pack? The Behavior of Emerging Market Mutual Funds." *IMF Staff Papers* 50:1, 43–63.

Broner, Fernando, R. Gaston Gelos, and Carmen M. Reinhart. 2006. "When in Peril, Retrench: Testing the Portfolio Channel of Contagion." *Journal of International Economics* 69:1, 203–230.

Caramazza, Francesco, Luca Ricci, and Ranil Salgado. 2004. "International Financial Contagion in Currency Crises." *Journal of International Money and Finance* 23:1, 51–70.

Cetorelli, Nicola, and Linda S. Goldberg. 2010. "Global Banks and International Shock Transmission: Evidence from the Crisis." *NBER Working Paper* 15974.

de la Torre, Augusto, E. Levy Yeyati, and Sergio L. Schmukler. 2003. "Living and Dying with Hard Pegs." *Economia*, 43–107.

de la Torre, Augusto, Eduardo Levy Yeyati, and Sergio L. Schmukler. 2010. "Varieties of Internal Devaluation: Peripheral Europe in the Argentine Mirror." VoxEU.org, March 6 www.voxeu.org/index.php?q=node/4724.

Frankel, Jeffrey A., and George Saravelos. 2010. "Are Leading Indicators of Financial Crises Useful for Assessing Country Vulnerability? Evidence from the 2008–2009 Global Crisis." *NBER Working Paper* 16047.

Gourinchas, Pierre-Olivier, and Helene Rey. 2007. "From World Banker to World Venture Capitalist: U.S. External Adjustment and the Exorbitant Privilege." In R. Clarida, ed. *G-7 Current Account Imbalances: Sustainability and Adjustment* 11–55. Chicago, IL: University of Chicago Press.

International Monetary Fund. 2009. "The State of Public Finances: Outlook and Medium-Term Policies after the 2008 Crisis." *Fiscal Affairs Department Report*. Washington, DC.

Kaminsky, Graciela L., Richard K. Lyons, and Sergio L. Schmukler. 2004. "Managers, Investors, and Crises: Mutual Fund Strategies in Emerging Markets." *Journal of International Economics* 64:1, 113–134.

Kaminsky, Graciela L., and Carmen M. Reinhart. 2000. "On Crises, Contagion, and Confusion." *Journal of International Economics* 51:1, 145–168.

Kaminsky, Graciela L., Carmen M. Reinhart, and Carlos A. Vegh. 2004. "When It Rains, It Pours: Pro-Cyclical Capital Flows and Macroeconomic Policies." *NBER Macroeconomics Annual* 19:11–53.

Lane, Philip R., and Gian Maria Milesi-Ferretti. 2007. "The External Wealth of Nations Mark II." *Journal of International Economics* 73:2, 223–250.

Martinez Peria, Maria Soledad, Andrew A. Powell, and Ivanna Vladkova-Hollar. 2005. "Banking on Foreigners: The Behavior of International Bank Claims on Latin America, 1985–2000." *IMF Staff Papers* 53:3, 430–461.

Obstfeld, Maurice, Jay C. Shambaugh, and Alan M. Taylor. 2009. "Financial Instability, Reserves, and Central Bank Swap Lines in the Panic of 2008." *NBER Working Paper* 14826.

Raddatz, Claudio. 2010. "When the Rivers Run Dry: Liquidity and the Use of Wholesale Funds in the Transmission of the U.S. Subprime Crisis." *World Bank Policy Research Working Paper* Series No. 5203.

Reinhart, Carmen M., and Vincent M. Reinhart. 2008. "Capital Flow Bonanzas: An Encompassing View of the Past and Present." In Jeffrey A. Frankel and Christopher Pissarides, eds. *NBER International Seminar on Macroeconomics: 2008*. Chicago, IL: University of Chicago Press.

Van Rijckeghem, Caroline, and Beatrice Weder. 2001. "Sources of Contagion: Is It Finance or Trade?" *Journal of International Economics* 54:2, 293–308.

ABOUT THE AUTHORS

Tatiana Didier is a research economist in the World Bank's Office of the Chief Economist for Latin America and the Caribbean. She obtained a PhD in economics from the Massachusetts Institute of Technology in 2008. She also holds a BA in economics from PUC-Rio, Brazil. She is currently doing research on international finance, with a focus on international capital flows, the role of institutional investors, and financial crises.

Constantino Hevia is an economist in the Macroeconomics and Growth Unit of the World Bank's Development Economics Research Group (DECRG). He joined the World Bank after earning a PhD in economics from the University of Chicago. He also holds an MA and a degree in economics from the Universidad Torcuato di Tella, Buenos Aires. Hevia has done work in the areas of international finance, macroeconomics, and development.

Sergio L. Schmukler is lead economist in the Development Research Group of the World Bank. He obtained his PhD from the University of California at Berkeley in 1997, when he started working as a Young Professional at the World Bank. Since joining the bank, he has been based at the research department. He has also worked continuously for the Office of the Chief Economist for Latin America and for the East Asia and South Asia regions. Besides his work for the bank, he has been treasurer of LACEA (Latin America and Caribbean Economic Association) since 2004, was associate editor of the Journal of Development Economics (2001–2004), visited and taught at Department of Economics, University of Maryland (1999–2003), and visited and worked at the International Monetary Fund Research Department (2004–2005). Before joining the World Bank, he worked at the U.S. Federal Reserve (Board of Governors), the Inter-American Development Bank Research Department, and the Argentine Central Bank. His research area is international finance and international financial markets and institutions. He has published several articles in academic journals and edited volumes on emerging markets finance, financial globalization, financial crises and contagion, and financial development. He also co-authored the book *Emerging Capital Markets and Globalization*, published by Stanford University Press and the World Bank. He has served as editor and referee for many academic journals and institutions.

PART FOUR

Contagion in the Financial Crisis of 2007–2009

The raw economic wounds resulting from the financial crisis are still very much with us. For those who followed the crisis as it developed, the appearance of contagion was omnipresent. Each day seemed to bring a tale of economic woe migrating from one firm to another. Thus, the events of 2007–2009 provide a laboratory for exploring financial contagion. If this financial crisis was not a prime example of contagion, then contagion probably does not exist.

Contagion in the crisis had many dimensions, with woe spreading from the financial sector to the real economy, from one financial firm to another, from one financial asset type to another, from one country to another, and from financial institutions to financial markets. A key question concerns contagion from the financial sector to the real economy. Clearly, the financial crisis was quickly followed by a severe recession. Is this transition to be understood as a matter of contagion? If so, what was the method by which the financial difficulties resulted in reduced output and higher unemployment?

As we have seen in Part Two, "Contagion and the Asian Financial Crisis," the events of 1997–1998 unpleasantly emphasized the degree of interconnectedness that characterized a globalizing world. Thus, in the financial crisis of 2007–2009 it was not surprising to see severe problems in major economies affect other economies around the world. However, the problems that originated in sophisticated financial markets had markedly different consequences on countries that seem to be equally distant from the scene of the accident. Chapters in this section also try to explain the channels of contagion that led some countries to suffer more than others that seemed to be at an equal remove from the epicenter of financial difficulties.

CHAPTER 24

Contagion and the Real Economy during the Global Financial Crisis

DIRK G. BAUR
Senior Lecturer in Finance at the School of Finance and Economics,
University of Technology, Sydney

T he Global Financial Crisis of 2007–2009 has been linked to the Great Depression of 1929 due to its strong adverse effects on the real economy. Changes in key economic variables such as GDP and unemployment during the crisis are similar to those during the Great Depression (see Eichengreen and O'Rourke 2009). The Global Financial Crisis (GFC) is not only special in this respect but also due to the breadth and the depth of the crisis compared to other financial crises: The crisis affected a larger number of countries for a longer period of time with more extreme negative stock returns than previous crises.

The number of studies that analyze the spread of a financial crisis increased dramatically with the East Asian crisis in 1997 and 1998. The academic literature introduced the term *contagion* that analyzes changes in the transmission of shocks during crisis periods. If the comovement of stocks across countries increases in a crisis period compared to a tranquil period, there is contagion. If the comovement does not increase the joint deterioration of stock markets is due to the interdependence of these markets in normal times and not crisis-specific. This relatively narrow definition of contagion entails some issues that are potentially more problematic for an application to the GFC. Tests for contagion depend on the location of the crisis period in time and the identification of the source of the crisis among other issues. The difficulty in specifying the crisis period is recognized in the literature but not finally resolved. The fact that the GFC clearly exceeds commonly used crisis lengths in empirical studies warrants additional care in the determination of the adequate crisis period location. The second issue mentioned above focuses on the source of the crisis. The name suggests that the GFC was a financial crisis with the source in the financial sector. However, the name does not imply that the GFC was also an economic crisis despite its broad impact on financial and economic variables. The objective of the article underlying this chapter is to study the comovement of the financial sector and the nonfinancial sector (the real economy) and to determine whether the GFC was mainly a financial crisis confined to the

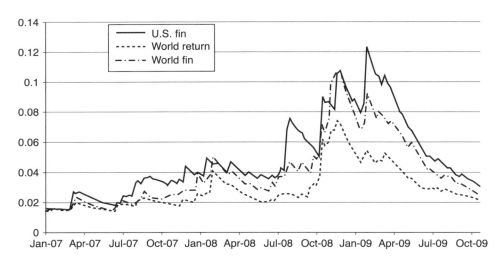

Exhibit 24.1 Conditional Volatility during Global Financial Crisis 2007–2009

financial sector or whether it also spread to the nonfinancial, real economy sector affecting the stock market valuations of firms in this sector. The first issue of an adequate crisis period definition is addressed by using a new approach based on the estimation of regimes of high volatility. The high-volatility regimes are used as an indicator for a crisis or turmoil regime. A subsequently employed systematic robustness analysis demonstrates that the peak of the GFC in terms of extreme negative stock returns and the incidences of contagion cluster in the last quarter of 2008 despite other financial and economic events in 2007, the first half of 2008, and 2009. The second issue, namely the identification of the source of the crisis, is avoided by using systematic shocks in the global financial sector as opposed to country-specific shocks.

Exhibit 24.1 presents the conditional volatility estimates of the aggregate return of a global stock index (world), a global financial sector index, and the U.S. financial sector index for the years 2007–2009. The graph shows that volatility increased significantly in the second half of 2008 for all three series with the greatest change for the U.S. financial index followed by the global financial sector index and the aggregate stock index. The period in which weekly stock return volatility is in the 90, 95, or 99 percent quantile between 2007 and 2009 varies between 2 years and 15 weeks for a sample period of 30 years (from 1979 until 2009). These volatility regimes identify the crisis period used to test for contagion. In many crises, key financial or economic events can be associated with the outbreak of a crisis (e.g., the stock market crash in October 1987, the collapse of LTCM in 1998, or the bankruptcy of Lehman Brothers in 2008). In contrast, the end of a crisis period is generally not marked by a specific event. Hence, while regimes of volatility estimates can identify both the outbreak of a crisis and the end of a crisis, the estimates are particularly useful to determine the end of a crisis.

Exhibit 24.2 shows the index levels of global (world) and U.S. aggregate and financial sector stocks. The time-series plot for the entire sample period illustrates that the comovement of the four indices increased in the period from 2007 to 2009

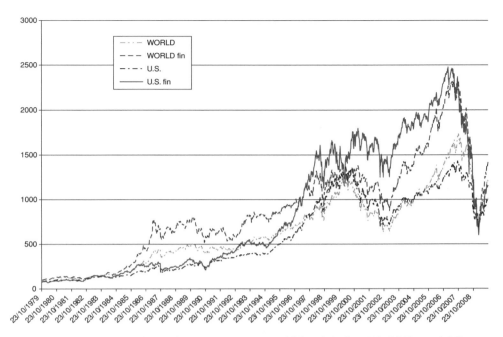

Exhibit 24.2 Stock Market Indices 1979–2009: World Stock Index, World Financial Sector Index, U.S. Stock Index, U.S. Financial Sector Index

compared to pre-crisis levels. This is preliminary evidence that the crisis affected both the financial sector and the nonfinancial sector due to the increased and strong comovement of the financial and the aggregate sector.

Exhibit 24.3 is additional descriptive evidence that there is increased comovement of global stocks for specific sectors (Basic Materials, Industrials, Consumer Goods, and Financials) from 2007 to 2009 compared to prior and relatively tranquil periods.

A formal test of increased comovement is based on a regression of the return of a specific sector index on the return of a global financial sector index in normal times and in crisis times. The returns of a local financial sector index are also included in the regression to distinguish between global and local contagion effects. The crisis period is defined from July 2007 until March 2009 based on a mixture approach where both key financial and economic events in 2007–2009 and estimates of high-volatility regimes are used. The mixture yields a longer crisis period than implied by the volatility estimates, which is due to the inclusion of a liquidity shock in the money markets in August 2007 (see Taylor and Williams 2008). This relatively long crisis period is used as a benchmark and is systematically changed to assess the sensitivity of contagion effects with respect to different crisis periods and to examine the evolution of the GFC through time.

The structure of the regression model can be used to test three hypotheses.

1. Financial sector contagion: Increased comovement of a country's financial sector stocks and world portfolio of financial stocks in a crisis period compared to a tranquil period.

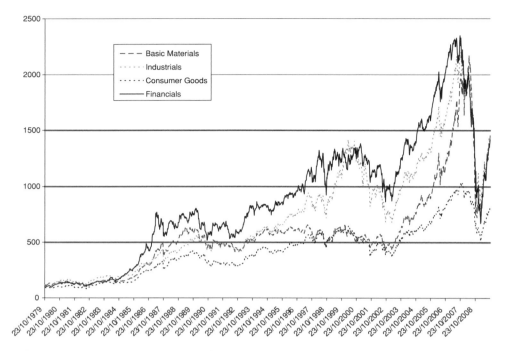

Exhibit 24.3   World Sector Stock Indices: Basic Materials, Industrials, Consumer Goods, Financials

2. Nonfinancial sector contagion (global): Increased comovement of a country's nonfinancial sector stocks and world portfolio of financial stocks in a crisis period compared to a tranquil period.
3. Nonfinancial sector contagion (local): Increased comovement of a country's nonfinancial sector stocks and financial sector stocks in a crisis period compared to a tranquil period.

Exhibit 24.4 presents the results of the tests for contagion based on a sample of 10 sectors for 25 major developed and emerging countries. The tests are based on regressions of weekly stock index returns of a specific sector and country (e.g., financial sector in the United Kingdom) on the weekly return of a global financial sector stock index.[1] Changes in the comovement during the crisis period are modelled via an interaction term comprising the global financial sector stock index return and a dummy, which is equal to one if the weekly return is in the crisis period and zero otherwise.

The table summarizes the estimation results of the regression models and focuses on incidences of contagion. The Cs in Column 2 of the table indicate financial sector contagion, that is, increased comovement of a country's financial sector stocks with the global financial sector. The figures in Columns 3 and 4 show the number of contagion incidences in the sectors representing the real economy for each country based on increased comovements with a global financial sector index and a local financial sector index, respectively.

Exhibit 24.4   Contagion—Summary of Estimation Results

	Financial Sector Contagion	Contagion from Financial System (global)	Contagion from Financial System (domestic)
Australia	C	4	1
Brazil	C	0	4
Canada	C	1	1
Chile	C	0	8
China	C	0	7
France	C	7	0
Germany	C	3	0
Hong Kong	C	0	5
Indonesia	C	0	8
India	C	0	4
Italy	C	6	0
Japan		0	4
Mexico		2	0
New Zealand		1	6
Norway	C	3	3
Russia	C	1	6
South Africa		5	1
South Korea		5	1
Spain	C	3	1
Sweden	C	1	3
Switzerland	C	6	1
Taiwan	C	0	3
Thailand		1	6
U.K.	C	6	0
United States	C	8	0

Note: Columns three and four display contagion incidences in different sectors.

Column 2 shows that 19 out of 25 countries exhibit an increased comovement of the local financial sector with the global financial sector. The countries for which the null hypothesis of "no contagion" cannot be rejected (no C in Column 2) are Japan, Mexico, New Zealand, South Africa, South Korea, and Thailand. However, most of these countries display a high level of interdependence with the systematic component in general. India stands out as an example of a country whose financial market is only moderately linked to the global financial sector in normal times (0.3650) but highly linked in the crisis period (1.1593). In addition, there is a considerable homogeneity in the coefficient estimates across the entire sample and a strong similarity in the contagion effect for a group of 11 countries, which exhibit a contagion coefficient around 0.2.

Column 3 demonstrates that there are 63 cases of real economy contagion stemming from an increased comovement with the global financial sector. Ten sectors (except the local financial sector, which is not examined in this test) in 25 countries can be infected, so this represents an infection rate of 28 percent. The lowest number of contagion incidences is presented by emerging markets (many countries show no incidence of contagion). In contrast, most developed markets display relatively high incidences of contagion across sectors. The United States has the highest number with eight (out of nine) sectors infected followed by France with seven sectors infected. The sectors most affected are Basic Materials (12) and Utilities (11) while the least affected sectors are Telecommunications (3), Consumer Services (4), and Health Care (4). The results demonstrate that developed countries' firms are more directly exposed to the global financial system than emerging market firms.

Column 4 shows the results of a test that implicitly assumes that the domestic financial sector is infected by the crisis and subsequently spreads to other domestic, nonfinancial, sectors. There are 73 cases of contagion, most of them in emerging markets. Many developed markets exhibit no case of contagion including Germany, the United Kingdom, and the United States. The countries with the highest number of contagion incidences are Chile (8), Indonesia (8), and China (7). The sectors most affected are Oil and Gas (12), Basic Materials (11) and Consumer Services (11), and the sectors least affected are Technology (5), Telecommunications (5), and Utilities (6).

The results illustrate that there is contagion of real economy sectors in developed markets due to increased comovements with stocks representing the global financial sector and real economy contagion in emerging markets due to comovements with stocks representing the local financial sector. In other words, if the local financial sector is infected through interdependence or contagion with the global financial sector, the crisis spreads to the nonfinancial sector. The findings imply that the GFC is not only a financial crisis with falling stock prices in the financial sector but also an economic crisis with falling stock prices in the nonfinancial sector.

Systematic variations of the crisis period, that is, variations of the crisis period location in time and the length of the crisis, demonstrate that the second half of 2008 exhibits the strongest contagion effects in the years 2007–2009. The incidences of contagion in the financial sector increase from 19 to 21 cases out of 25 for this shortened period relative to the benchmark period. A similar effect is found for contagion in the real economy sector. This sensitivity analysis shows that volatility regime estimates are a good crisis identifier due to the temporal commonality of the strength of contagion and regimes of high volatility. In addition, the findings also demonstrate that the benchmark crisis period for which results are reported yield rather conservative estimates despite the longer crisis period.

The empirical analysis of financial contagion and the effects on the real economy shows that the GFC is truly global in the sense that no country escaped the crisis. Contagion is most prevalent in the financial sector; evidence for real economy contagion exists but to a lesser extent than in the financial sector. Some sectors representing the real economy are relatively immune to the effects of the crisis, which is in stark contrast to the incidence of contagion in the financial sector. The heterogeneity of contagion incidences in the real economy sectors provides important information for regulators and policy makers. Regulators need to know which sectors are most affected and which sectors are least affected by the crisis to adequately react to a crisis. Government funding schemes can possibly be allocated in a more effective way if information about how a financial crisis spreads to the sectors representing the real economy is provided. The link between stock market volatility in certain regimes and the incidences of contagion can also add to the information set used by regulators and policy makers. Finally, it is likely that a sector-specific analysis of contagion provides a more detailed picture than a study based on aggregate data.[2]

NOTE

1. The weekly returns are based on total market and sector indices obtained from Data-stream.
2. This article is based upon Baur (2010).

REFERENCES

Baur, Dirk G. 2010. "Financial Contagion and the Real Economy." *University of Technology, Sydney Working Paper* School of Finance and Economics.

Eichengreen, Barry, and Kevin H. O'Rourke. 2009. "A Tale of Two Depressions." VoxEU.org, mimeo www.voxeu.org/index.php?q=node/4724.

Forbes, K., and R. Rigobon. 2002. "No Contagion, Only Interdependence." *Journal of Finance* 57:5, 2223–2261.

Taylor, J. B., and J. C. Williams. 2008. "A Black Swan in the Money Market." *Federal Reserve Bank of San Francisco Working Paper* 2008–04.

ABOUT THE AUTHOR

Dirk G. Baur is a senior lecturer in finance at the School of Finance and Economics, University of Technology, Sydney. Dirk obtained a M.Sc. in economics and a PhD in financial econometrics from the University of Tuebingen, Germany. Dirk worked for the Joint Research Centre of the European Commission from 2002 to 2005 where his main tasks were the execution of economic impact assessments of changes in the regulatory framework of the financial system within the European Union. In 2005, Dirk assumed a post-doc position at Trinity College Dublin and became a lecturer in finance at Dublin City University in 2007. Dirk joined the School of Finance and Economics in November 2009. His main research interests are the modeling and estimation of dependence, financial crises, financial contagion, and the role of gold in the global financial system. His papers have been published in the *Journal of Money and Finance*, *Japan and the World Economy*, *Journal of Multinational Financial Management*, *Journal of Financial Stability*, *Journal of International Financial Markets, Institutions and Money* and the *Journal of Banking and Finance*.

CHAPTER 25

The Financial Crisis of 2008 and Subprime Securities

GERALD P. DWYER[*]
Federal Reserve Bank of Atlanta
University of Carlos III, Madrid

PAULA A. TKAC
Federal Reserve Bank of Atlanta

S ubprime mortgages are commonly defined as loans issued at high rates to borrowers with lower credit quality. So, it is perhaps not so surprising that subprime mortgages suffered large losses in the financial crisis of 2008. It is more surprising that these losses in the United States created financial difficulties around much of the world.

However, securities based on subprime mortgage loans are indeed the key to understanding how financial problems spread both geographically, as well as across and within many different types of asset markets and institutions in 2007 to 2009. A worldwide demand for exposure to the United States real estate market spurred the creation of such securities, called collateralized debt obligations (CDO). These securities were purchased by international financial institutions, firms, and even municipalities.[1] This chapter outlines the complexities of CDOs and their pivotal role in the transmission of financial distress.

HOUSING PRICES AND SUBPRIME MORTGAGES

The beginning of the story is in the U.S. housing market. Housing prices in much of the United States rose substantially (depending on the index used between 60 and 100 percent) until 2006 or 2007 and then began falling substantially until at least 2010. During a period of low inflation, these changes represented large capital gains, and subsequent losses, for people owning houses.

[*]Dwyer thanks the Spanish Ministry of Education and Culture for support of project SEJ2007–67448/ECON. Any errors are our responsibility. The views expressed here are ours and not necessarily those of the Federal Reserve Bank of Atlanta or the Federal Reserve System.

This run-up in housing prices was accompanied by substantial increases in the number of subprime mortgages originated. Subprime mortgages grew from $160 billion in 2001 to $625 billion in 2005. Over the same period, conventional (or prime) mortgage origination actually fell, from $1,265 billion to $990 billion.

Prime mortgages are well defined as mortgages accepted by two government-sponsored enterprises—Fannie Mae and Freddie Mac—but there is no formal definition of the term *subprime*. Probably the most common characteristic mentioned is a lower credit rating, although other characteristics such as a mortgage payment that is too large relative to income also can make a mortgage subprime.

This decrease in housing prices has been associated with a dramatic increase in delinquencies on mortgages and in foreclosures. Although concentrated in California, Las Vegas, Phoenix, and Florida, delinquencies and foreclosures have risen in other parts of the United States as well.

It is not an accident that foreclosures are concentrated in geographic areas that experienced large housing price increases and subsequent decreases. People were more inclined to stretch to buy a house where prices were increasing substantially. In part, the higher foreclosures reflect the greater risk borne by mortgage lenders when borrowers stretch to buy a house and things do not work out. In addition, borrowers in areas with larger price increases were more likely to take out exotic mortgages such as interest-only loans and optional adjustable-rate loans.

In part, higher foreclosures reflect what can be called strategic or opportunistic default. A person with a mortgage on a house that has fallen substantially in value not only loses the hoped-for gain but can be facing a known loss. The mortgage can be for substantially more than the value of the house and it may be many years before the house is worth more than the loan. In these circumstances, a question naturally occurs: Should I keep paying on this house? It might be better to bail out of the house and "give the house back to the bank." Indeed, the borrower may well be able to rent a similar house down the street for far less than the monthly mortgage payment.

Confronted with such stark choices, some borrowers choose to go into foreclosure. These circumstances help to explain why falling housing prices are associated with more foreclosures and why foreclosures of subprime loans are higher than in earlier years.

Still, how does this loss get spread around the financial system and create substantial global problems? We (Dwyer and Tkac 2009) estimate that subprime loans outstanding were about $1 trillion in 2007. Although this is a big number, this is not large when compared to an estimated world financial market on the order of $100 trillion (and this is likely an underestimate). Subprime mortgages were thus likely less than 1 percent of all financial assets. To put the problem in perspective, the U.S. stock market (valued at approximately $15 trillion in 2007) often goes up or down 1 percent in a day without dire consequences. It is hard to imagine that a 1-percent loss of the value of financial instruments created a financial crisis.

And it didn't.

COLLATERALIZED DEBT OBLIGATIONS

The key to how problems in subprime loans became widespread problems in financial markets is a financial instrument called a *collateralized debt obligation* (CDO).

It is a bit of a path from a home mortgage loan to a CDO, but it is worth grasping the essentials.

Contrary to practice 50 years ago, mortgages today typically are sold rather than held to maturity by the lender. Indeed, many lenders do not have the financial resources to hold the mortgages that they make; instead they specialize in making mortgage loans and selling them to another firm, which turns around and securitizes the mortgage.

Mortgages are securitized by pooling many mortgages together to form a Residential Mortgage Backed Security (RMBS), shares of which are sold to investors wishing to include real estate in their portfolio. Although the actual financial and legal arrangements can be complicated, a basic feature of RBMS is that payments on mortgages by households flow through to the investors who own the securitized pools.

There is one wrinkle that is important for the subsequent story. In a typical security—say AT&T corporate bonds—if AT&T fails to pay, all holders of the bonds suffer the same proportionate loss. All the holders of the bonds have the same risk. This is not so for many RMBSs. Some holders of RMBS bear more risk than others and some bear less. This is accomplished by *tranching* the RMBS security and constructing what is called a *waterfall* of payments.

Exhibit 25.1 shows the waterfall of payments on a simple RMBS. There are three tranches in the figure, an AAA tranche, a BBB– tranche, and an equity tranche. An actual security would have more tranches but three are enough to illustrate how tranching works.

You can view the mortgage payments coming in at the top of the waterfall. First, the mortgage payments go to the highest-rated tranche, the AAA tranche in the figure. If there are remaining funds—water in the figure—the remaining payments go to the next tranche, the BBB– tranche. Last, any remaining payments go to the equity tranche. In economics, equity holders are often called *residual claimants* and that holds here. The equity tranche gets whatever is left over.

Another way of seeing the effect of tranching is from the bottom up. The equity tranche also is said to be the first-loss position. The equity tranche suffers initial losses if any of the mortgages defaults and the higher-rated tranches suffer no

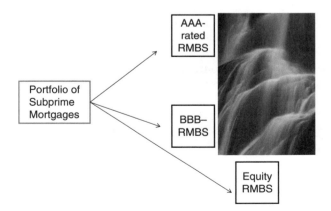

Exhibit 25.1   Three Securities Instead of One

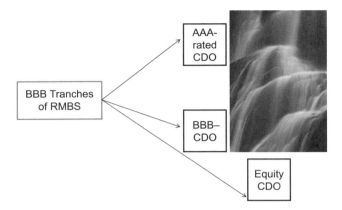

Exhibit 25.2   CDOs from Tranches

losses until enough defaults occur so that the equity tranche receives nothing. If the equity tranche is wiped out, the BBB– tranche suffers losses. If the BBB– tranche is wiped out, then the AAA tranche suffers losses.

Although actual RBMS have more tranches than this example, the general principle that higher-rated tranches experience less risk of loss still holds. Actual tranches generally cover the entire range from the AAA to the equity tranche with each intermediate grade included (AAA, AA, A, BBB, BBB–, equity) and often there is more than one AAA tranche.

The collateralized debt obligations (CDOs) at the center of the financial crisis are created from tranches of RMBSs. Exhibit 25.2 illustrates how this is done. The figure is similar to Exhibit 25.1 except that the underlying portfolio is not a portfolio of subprime mortgages. The underlying portfolio of a CDO is a portfolio of BBB tranches of different RMBSs. The allocation of risk is similar, with the waterfall of payments being similar. The AAA tranche often was roughly 85 percent of the value of these CDOs. The lower-rated tranches account for the remaining 15 percent and represent the degree of subordination in the CDO. The higher the subordination, the less risk that a AAA tranche will experience a loss.

Exhibit 25.3 shows the path of cash flows from the underlying subprime mortgages to the tranches of the CDO. This path is quite complicated. People pay on their mortgages and payments are allocated to tranches of the RMBS. Some of the tranches are used to create CDOs and the payments to these tranches of the RMBSs start the waterfall of payments to the tranches of the CDO. As long as everyone is paying on the mortgages, the complex nature of this path is not necessarily evident or problematic.

Once some people are not paying on their mortgages though, how much are the tranches of the CDO worth?[2] This is not so easy to determine.

An immediate answer might be to look at market prices to determine the value of the CDO. Unfortunately, the value of any particular CDO depends on the specific mortgages underlying that CDO. CDOs are idiosyncratic securities. Trying to value one CDO by looking at another would be like trying to value AT&T bonds by looking at Sprint bonds. It is possible to get some indication of the value of a

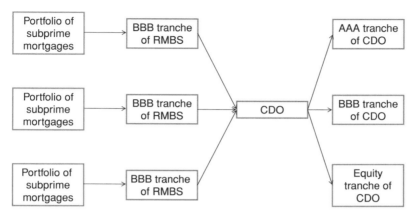

Exhibit 25.3   Mortgages to CDOs

CDO by looking at the prices of similar deals, but it will not get one all the way to what this particular CDO is worth.

Moreover, CDOs are not standardized contracts. Each CDO has its own contractual terms and these terms can differ materially. CDOs are noticeably more complicated than the simple example provided here, with payments across tranches often depending on delinquencies. CDOs also can have reserve accounts that act to limit losses to higher rated tranches. These differences make it even harder to compare CDOs.

As a result of their idiosyncracy, CDOs are traded over the counter, not on an organized exchange. There is no CDO analog to the NYSE, no organized market with readily available prices, and thus there is no "market price" that reveals all.

For the overall financial system, the problem with CDOs is the complexity of valuing them once some borrowers begin to default. Two problems arise. First, buying CDOs when delinquencies and defaults are common requires time-consuming and expensive research into the underlying mortgages to determine what payments are likely. Second, because the values are problematic even for the owners of CDOs, the value of CDOs held by another institution can be practically impossible to determine. This, in turn, makes it difficult for institutions to assess whether their trading partners are solvent.

VALUES OF COLLATERALIZED DEBT OBLIGATIONS

Exhibit 25.4 shows the evolution of indices that track the values of subprime mortgage CDOs formed at the start of 2006 and 2007.[3] When initiated, the indices generally traded at 100. The index beginning in January 2006 (2007) is based on CDOs created in the last half of 2005 (2006) using mortgages originated at about the same time.

These indices show that the values of CDOs fell substantially. There are similarities in the price falls across these two vintages. The lowest rated tranches fall more, which is consistent with the waterfall of payments into these tranches and

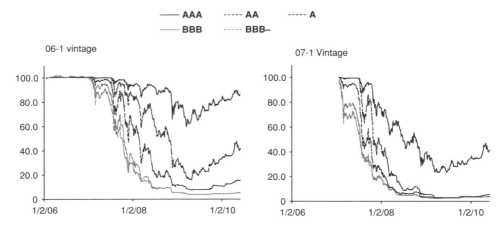

Exhibit 25.4   ABX Indices by Vintage January 19, 2006, to May 31, 2010
Sources: Markit Group Limited/Haver Analytics.

the cash flows in periods of opportunistic default. The lowest rated tranches, the BBB– and BBB tranches, are essentially worthless by the end of 2008.

The AAA tranches of both vintages fall by amounts that are hard to square with a low-risk security. The AAA tranche of the 2006 vintage falls close to 40 percent, from 100 to about 60 by early 2009. The AAA tranche of the 2007 falls quite a bit more, from 100 to about 25 by early 2009, a 75 percent decline in value.

There are two possible, though not mutually exclusive, explanations for the greater losses in the 2007 vintage. It is possible that the loans made in the last half of 2006 (at the end of the period of housing price increases) were riskier, less well documented, and included more fraud. In addition, though, the people who obtained mortgages in the last half of 2006 were doing so at the end of the increases in house prices. Since prices have subsequently fallen dramatically, these people are more likely to owe more than the house is worth. Consequently, they are more likely to default.

Either way, it is not surprising that the value of the 2006 vintage of the CDOs has held up better than the 2007 vintage.

RELATIONSHIP TO THE FINANCIAL CRISIS

The problems with these securities contributed to the financial crisis in two ways.

First, CDOs were purchased by entities all over the world, spreading the risk far outside the borders of the United States. For example, four townlets in northern Norway took substantial positions in AAA tranches of subprime CDOs. The AAA rating made these tranches seem like a fine, and safe, purchase and it is certain that some entities purchasing highly rated tranches CDOs bought them because of the rating and understood little else about them. Furthermore, high-rated tranches were used in a variety of other financial transactions and arrangements. Some commercial banks created special purpose vehicles (SPVs) that held subprime CDOs and some investment banks funded themselves by using AAA tranches of CDOs as collateral. As things turned out, these were not low-risk choices. The decline in housing prices and the rise in defaults ate away at the cash flows expected of the AAA tranches.

When faced with difficult to value securities, potential buyers demand a risk premium. As defaults began to climb beyond the expected levels, the value of all CDO tranches began to decline and the declines were reinforced by demands for higher risk premiums prompted by the growing level of uncertainty surrounding the still declining housing market.

Second, the difficulty valuing these securities created concerns across the financial system about the solvency, or potential insolvency, of many financial institutions. These problems were heightened with the failures of Bear Sterns and Lehman Brothers. Such concerns about counterparty risk led to higher interest and funding costs for institutions known or suspected to be holding subprime CDOs, exacerbating any direct subprime losses. In such extreme cases, this lack of liquidity and concerns about counterparties can lead institutions to pull back from risky credit markets and pursue a flight to safety (i.e., invest in U.S. Treasury securities that were immune to these credit risk concerns).

CONCLUSION

Collateralized debt obligations based on subprime mortgages are themselves subprime securities. Although they are simple to value when all cash flows arrive as expected, they are hard to value when mortgage payments are delinquent. They inevitably are illiquid because any purchaser must spend significant resources to determine their value. A purchaser will thus demand a lower price—a higher risk premium—than if the security was simple to value. This is both because of the lack of full information on the security's cash flows but also because they know that if they wish to sell in the future, a similar premium is likely to be demanded. This illiquidity was not evident before the financial crisis but it is evident to all now.

Focusing on these securities should not be interpreted as implying that CDOs caused the financial crisis. This would be a misreading of our research. CDOs were the mechanism by which problems were transmitted. A more fundamental examination of the causes of the financial crisis would examine why the quantity of subprime mortgages originated increased. An increase in the quantity of loans desired by borrowers is one answer. It is also quite possible that the creation of CDOs increased the demand for subprime mortgages by transforming risk in ways that holders preferred or thought they preferred. A consequential explanation is that increased holdings by Fannie Mae and Freddie Mac contributed substantially to the increase in demand.

NOTES

1. This information is discussed in detail in Dwyer and Tkac (2009).

2. Smithson (2009) provides a summary of the valuation issues.

3. There are indices that begin in the middle of 2006 and 2007 that provide information consistent with these two indices.

REFERENCES

Dwyer, Gerald P., and Paula Tkac. 2009. "The Financial Crisis of 2008 in Fixed-income Markets." *Journal of International Money and Finance* 28 (December), 1293–1316.

Smithson, Charles. 2009. "Valuing 'Hard-to-Value' Assets and Liabilities: Notes on Valuing Structured Credit Products." *Journal of Applied Finance* 19 (Spring/Summer):1–12.

ABOUT THE AUTHORS

Gerald P. Dwyer is the director of the Center for Financial Innovation and Stability at the Federal Reserve Bank of Atlanta. He also teaches at the University of Carlos III in Madrid and Trinity College in Dublin. Dr. Dwyer has been a faculty member at Texas A&M University, Emory University, the University of Houston, and Clemson University. He also has been a visiting scholar at the Federal Reserve Banks of Atlanta, St. Louis, and Minneapolis.

Dr. Dwyer's research focuses on financial markets, banking, and economic growth. This research has appeared in leading economics and finance journals as well as in Federal Reserve Bank Reviews, books, and conference volumes. Dr. Dwyer is on the editorial boards of the *Journal of Financial Stability* and *Economic Inquiry*. He has served as president and a member of the Executive Committees of the Society for Nonlinear Dynamics and Econometrics and the Association of Private Enterprise Education.

Paula A. Tkac is a senior financial economist and assistant vice president in the research department of the Federal Reserve Bank of Atlanta. Dr. Tkac coordinates financial markets policy briefings for Atlanta Fed president Dennis Lockhart and conducts research on various financial market topics including investor decision making, the mutual fund industry, and financial regulation. Her research has been published in several academic journals and recognized by two William F. Sharpe Awards at the *Journal of Financial and Quantitative Analysis*. Before joining the Federal Reserve Bank of Atlanta in 2000, Dr. Tkac was on the faculty of the finance department at the University of Notre Dame. Dr. Tkac earned her bachelor's, master's, and doctorate in economics from the University of Chicago.

CHAPTER 26

The Transmission of Liquidity Shocks during the Financial Crisis of 2007–2009*

NATHANIEL FRANK
Researcher at Nuffield College and the Oxford-Man Institute of Quantitative Finance

BRENDA GONZÁLEZ-HERMOSILLO
Deputy Division Chief of Global Financial Stability at the IMF

HEIKO HESSE
Economist in the Middle East and Central Asia Department at the IMF

T he rapid transmission of the subprime mortgage crisis in the United States to other domestic and foreign financial markets raises several questions of great importance to central banks and financial regulators. Through which mechanisms were the liquidity shocks transmitted across financial markets during this period? Why did the episode of funding illiquidity in structured investment vehicles (SIVs) and conduits turn into an issue of bank insolvency?

Conceptually, a number of new transmission mechanisms are likely to have been established (or become more important than usual) during periods of turbulence, either through increased market liquidity, funding liquidity, or even default risks. The relative strength of the interaction between these factors during the subprime crisis of 2007 is an empirical question, which we analyze in our research.

GOOD VERSUS BAD TIMES

The mechanisms through which liquidity shocks influence various markets during normal times may operate through different channels to those that appear during times of financial stress. During tranquil periods, market illiquidity shocks are typically short-lived as they create opportunities for traders to profit and, in doing so, provide liquidity and contribute to the price discovery process.

---

*The views expressed here are those of the authors and do not necessarily represent those of the IMF or IMF policy.

During periods of crisis, however, several mechanisms may amplify liquidity shocks across financial markets, creating systemic risks. These mechanisms can operate through direct linkages between the balance sheets of financial institutions, but also indirectly through asset prices. As the current crisis has demonstrated, price movements are set in motion when financial institutions face mark-to-market losses. As a consequence, positions are deleveraged, and if the value of the corresponding assets is significantly affected, the creditworthiness of the respective institutions will deteriorate because of increasing default risk. Clearly, then, leverage is pro-cyclical and amplifies the financial cycle.

A STYLIZED ANATOMY OF THE CRISIS

In investigating how the various segments of financial markets in the United States were affected during the subprime crisis, we distinguish between *market liquidity* and *funding liquidity*. Market liquidity is an asset-specific characteristic measuring the ease with which positions can be traded, without significantly affecting their corresponding asset price. In contrast, funding liquidity refers to the availability of funds such that a solvent agent is able to borrow in the market so it can service outstanding obligations.

It is useful to briefly review the chronology of the recent turbulence, starting in the summer of 2007. As is well known, the initial shock came in the form of deteriorating quality of subprime mortgages in the United States. This was essentially a credit, rather than a liquidity event. This shock spread across different asset classes and financial markets because of a high degree of asymmetric information associated with the complexity of the structured mortgage products. This process was subsequently strengthened by a widespread repricing of risk and a general decrease in investors' risk appetite.

The next step in the crisis saw an increase in delinquencies on subprime mortgages leading to greater uncertainty surrounding the value of a number of other structured credit products that had these assets in their underlying portfolios. Consequently, rating agencies downgraded many of these securities and announced changes in their methodologies, first in mid-July but then again in mid-August and in mid-October. Meanwhile, structured credit mortgage–backed instruments measured by the ABS indexes (ABX) saw rapid declines, and the liquidity for initially tradable securities in their respective secondary markets evaporated. The losses, downgrades, and changes in methodologies shattered investor confidence in the rating agencies' abilities to evaluate risks of complex securities. As a result, investors pulled back from structured products en masse.

Spotlight on SIVs

It soon became apparent that a wide range of financial institutions had exposures to many of these mortgage-backed securities, often off-balance-sheet entities such as conduits and structured investment vehicles (SIVs). The SIVs or conduits were funded through the issuance of short-term asset-backed commercial paper (ABCP) for it to take advantage of a yield differential resulting in a maturity mismatch.

This created an inherent maturity mismatch. Because of the increasing uncertainty associated with exposures to the underlying mortgage-backed securities (and their values), investors became unwilling to roll over the corresponding ABCP.

As the problems with SIVs and conduits deepened, banks came under increasing pressure to rescue those that they had sponsored by providing liquidity or by taking their respective assets onto their own balance sheets. As a result, the balance sheets of these banks were particularly strained. A further strain on banks' balance sheets came from warehousing a higher than expected amount of mortgages and leveraged loans, the latter usually passed on to investors so they could fund the highly leveraged debt deals of private equity firms. Both the market for mortgages and leveraged loans dried up because of the collapse of transactions in the mortgage-related securitization market and collaterized loan obligations. Banks also felt obliged to honor liquidity commitments to alternative market participants such as hedge funds and other financial institutions, which were also suffering from the drain of liquidity. Consequently, the level of interbank lending declined for both reasons of liquidity and credit risk. Money markets were affected, as was evident from a widening of the Libor and overnight index swap spreads, which in turn led to increased funding costs.

Flight to Transparency

As turbulence related to subprime mortgages heightened, financial markets more generally showed signs of stress, and investor preference moved away from complex structured products in a flight to liquidity. Subsequently, positions were shifted in order to invest in only the safest and most liquid of assets, such as U.S. Treasury bonds.

Hedge funds also felt the sting of reduced liquidity. Those that held asset-backed securities and other structured products were burdened by increased margin requirements, driven in turn by greater market volatility. As a consequence, they attempted to offload the more liquid parts of their portfolios in order to meet these margin calls and also limited possible redemptions by investors.

The Specter of Insolvency

The evident deterioration of market and funding liquidity conditions had implications for the solvency position of banks for several reasons. First, financial institutions saw a decline in the values of the securitized mortgages and structured securities on their balance sheets, resulting in extensive writedowns. Second, funding liquidity pressures forced rapid deleveraging during this period, further depressing asset prices. Third, funding costs increased because of rising money market spreads, which was amplified by an increasing reliance on funding from wholesale money markets. These pressures resulted in declining capital ratios throughout the banking sector and significant increases in credit default swap spreads across the banking sector.

DATA AND METHODOLOGY

The transmission mechanisms of liquidity shocks across differing U.S. financial markets outlined so far have been described as being unidirectional and

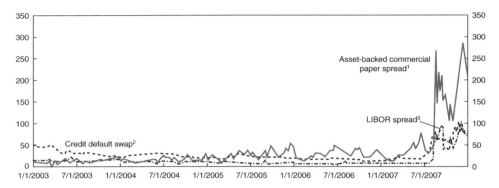

Exhibit 26.1   Aggregate Bank Credit Default Swap Rate and Selected Spreads (in Basis Points)
[1]Spread between yields on 90-day U.S. asset-backed commercial paper and on three-month U.S. Treasury bills.
[2]The unweighted daily average of the five-year credit default swaps for the following institutions: Morgan Stanley, Merrill Lynch, Goldman Sachs, Lehman Brothers, JPMorgan, Deutsche Bank, Bank of America, Citigroup, Barclays, Credit Suisse, UBS, and Bear Stearns.
[3]Spread between yields on three-month U.S. LIBOR and on three-month U.S. overnight index swap.
Sources: Bloomberg L.P.; and IMF staff estimates.

sequential. But in periods of financial stress, reinforcing *liquidity spirals* are likely to be set in motion. The likely multidirectionality with which shocks are transmitted during a crisis motivates the use of a Dynamic Conditional Correlation GARCH specification to test these effects.[1] This specification allows us to model the correlation dynamics between asset classes in order to evaluate whether the comovement between different markets increased during the crisis.

The model uses a system of five corresponding variables to capture key linkages, which act as proxies for overall market liquidity, funding liquidity, default risk, and volatility. First, *funding liquidity* conditions in the *asset-backed commercial paper market* are modeled by the spread between the yield of three-month ABCP and that of three-month U.S. Treasury bills. The second variable examined in the system is the spread between the three-month U.S. interbank Libor rate and the overnight index swap, which measures *bank funding liquidity* pressures.

Third, S&P 500 stock market returns are included into the reduced form model, whereby in its second moment, it serves as a proxy for *market volatility*. The spread between the yield on two-year on-the-run (the most recently issued) and off-the-run (previously issued) U.S. Treasuries captures *overall market liquidity* conditions. Finally, the *default risk* of banks is modeled by the credit default swap spreads of 12 large complex financial institutions. Exhibit 26.1 provides a visual representation of the movement in three of the key variables before and during the crisis.

RESULTS

The results from our model indicate a sharply increased interaction between the various proxies for market and funding liquidity. The implied correlations between the ABCP and Libor spreads rise from a pre-crisis average of approximately 0.3 to above 0.5, a level at which they remain. Furthermore, the linkages between these two funding liquidity measures and the two-year on-the-run–off-the-run spread jump from around zero to 0.2 (see Exhibit 26.2, for example). Stronger interactions between the market liquidity in the bond market and the stock market return volatility are evident with S&P 500 returns and the two-year on-the-run spread becoming more highly correlated with each other and with all other variables.

Implications of the Crisis for Our Economic Systems

Finally, the comovement between liquidity and solvency also increases sharply, as again illustrated in Exhibit 26.2. Before the hypothesized structural break at the end of July 2007, changes in the credit default swap spreads remain approximately uncorrelated with all other measures.

In summary, the various proxies for funding and market liquidity, stock market volatility, and bank default risk exhibited extraordinary comovement during the subprime crisis. As the correlations on these variables were fairly small in the pre-crisis period, the results suggest that new channels for transmission of liquidity shocks were established during the second half of 2007. The results of a pronounced interaction between market and funding liquidity are consistent with the emergence of reinforcing liquidity spirals during the crisis. On the one side of this liquidity spiral, financial institutions were exposed to refinancing needs in the form of issuing ABCP, a situation in which market illiquidity in complex structured products led to funding illiquidity. In this regard, the results also show that increased correlations between the ABCP and Libor spreads reduced the possibilities of funding from the interbank money market, thus highlighting systemic risks. Though not shown explicitly in the paper, on the other side of this spiral, many European banks with large exposures to U.S. asset-backed securities had difficulties accessing wholesale funding, leading to subsequent market illiquidity in different market segments.

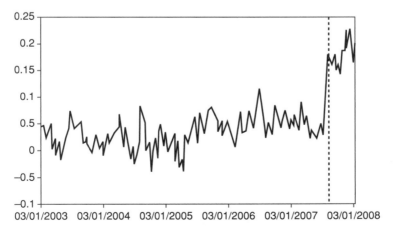

Exhibit 26.2   Correlation (Libor, Two)

From Liquidity to Solvency Concerns

In addition to the described period of illiquidity, the subprime crisis increasingly became one of insolvency, as banks such as Northern Rock, IKB, and Bear Stearns had to be rescued. This is captured by the implied correlations between the credit default swaps and other variables in the model, which show clear signs of a structural break during the crisis period. Furthermore, these correlations have remained at elevated levels since then, suggesting that solvency concerns remain an issue.

Finally, it is also shown that seemingly unrelated stock and bond markets were affected during these times of severe stress. These transmission mechanisms were not restricted to the U.S. financial markets, but were also observed across other advanced and key emerging market economies.

NOTE

1. See Frank, González-Hermosillo, and Hesse (2008) and Chapter 3 in the latest Global Financial Stability Report (IMF 2008). We employ the specification developed by Capiello, Engle, and Sheppard (2006). This allows for an evaluation of the time variation in the conditional correlations between variables, in addition to accounting for structural breaks in their respective data generating processes. The multivariate GARCH framework also takes the heteroskedasticity exhibited by the data into account, which is particularly useful for the analysis of crisis periods.

REFERENCES

Cappiello, L., R. Engle, and K. Sheppard. 2006. "Asymmetric Dynamics in the Correlations of Global Equity and Bond Returns." *Journal of Econometrics* 4:537–572.
Frank, N., B. González-Hermosillo, and H. Hesse. 2008. *Transmission of Liquidity Shocks: Evidence from the 2007 Subprime Crisis*. Washington, DC: International Monetary Fund.
International Monetary Fund. 2008. *Global financial stability report*. Washington, DC: World Economic and Financial Surveys.

ABOUT THE AUTHORS

Nathaniel Frank holds a PhD from Oxford University and is currently a researcher at Nuffield College and the Oxford-Man Institute of Quantitative Finance. He was previously a visiting scholar at New York University and has also worked for the IMF and the World Bank. Recent research and publications mainly lie in the field of financial econometrics and include modeling the current financial crisis using high frequency data.

Brenda González-Hermosillo is a deputy division chief of global financial stability at the IMF. She has led several analytical chapters of the IMF *Global Financial Stability Report*, including "Market and Funding Illiquidity: When Private Risk becomes Public"; "Stress in Bank Funding Markets and Implications for Monetary Policy"; and "Detecting Systemic Risk." She has a number of publications on global financial stability, financial crises and early warning indicators, global spillovers and contagion, and international investors' risk appetite, several of which have been published in *Quantitative Finance, Journal of Financial Stability*, and the *North American Journal of Finance and Economics*. She also co-authored a book *Transmission of Financial Crises and Contagion* (Cambridge University). Before joining the IMF, she held positions at the Bank of Canada, Canada's Department of Finance, several investment banks (Bank of Montreal, Bank of Nova Scotia, Banco Nacional de Mexico), Mexico's Ministry of Finance, and Banco de Mexico. She has taught in the economics department at the University of Western Ontario and obtained her PhD in economics at the University of Tilburg in the Netherlands.

Heiko Hesse is an economist in the Middle East and Central Asia department at the IMF after having worked two years on the IMF's *Global Financial Stability Report*. Before that, he was an economist at the World Bank from 2006 to 2007, working on the Commission on Growth and Development, which brings together 21 leading practitioners from government, business, and the policymaking arenas and is chaired by Nobel laureate Michael Spence. Before that, in 2005 and 2006, he was a visiting scholar at Yale University and a consultant at the World Bank. He also worked at McKinsey, NERA Economic Consulting, and PriceWaterhouse-Coopers. Some of his current research involves systemic risk, sovereign wealth funds, Islamic finance, and spillovers to EM countries. He has published in refereed academic journals such as the *Journal of Development Economics*, frequently speaks at conferences and central banks, and is a regular contributor to the economics blogs VOX and RGE Monitor. Heiko obtained his PhD in economics from Nuffield College, University of Oxford.

CHAPTER 27

Credit Contagion from Counterparty Risk

PHILIPPE JORION
Professor of Finance at the Paul Merage School of Business,
University of California at Irvine

GAIYAN ZHANG
Assistant Professor of Finance, the University of Missouri, St. Louis

F inancial institutions have recently developed portfolio credit risk models that focus on potential credit losses at the top level of the institution. These new portfolio credit models are now in widespread use. Notably, they are used to assess economic capital, which is the amount of equity capital the institution should carry to absorb a large loss over a specified horizon with a high level of confidence. These models are also the basis for the recently established Basel II regulatory capital charges for commercial banks. In addition, these models are employed to structure collateralized debt obligations (CDOs), where the junior tranches are sized to absorb most of the losses.

These models are difficult to calibrate, however. Unlike market risk models, correlations between defaults cannot be observed directly for the borrowers in the portfolio. Instead, default correlations are modeled indirectly, typically using a reduced-form model of default intensity or a structural model of the value of the firm based on a Gaussian copula. Standard models, including the new Basel II capital charges, assume a factor structure in which correlations are induced by a common factor that can be interpreted as the state of the economy. This common feature largely explains why recent comparative studies of industry portfolio models show remarkable similarities in their outputs, or measures of economic capital.[1]

These first-generation models, unfortunately, do not fully capture the clustering in default correlations, sometimes called *credit contagion*. Das et al. (2007) observe some excess clustering in corporate debt default from 1979 to 2004. Unexplained default clustering is a major problem for traditional credit risk models because it generates greater dispersion in the distribution of credit losses.

Fatter tails imply a greater likelihood of large losses and an understatement of economic capital. This could lead to a greater number of bank failures in periods of stress, or losses on CDOs that exceed worst estimates. Indeed, unexpectedly large losses on CDOs have been at the heart of the financial crisis that started in 2007. The recent credit crisis demonstrates that credit contagion is a more severe problem than anybody had expected and that traditional credit risk models need reexamination.

CREDIT CONTAGION FROM COMMON FACTORS

Second-generation models attempt to account for this default clustering. They can be classified into two approaches. The first relies on a richer description of the common factor structure. The second relies on counterparty risk and will be described in the next section. The common factor approach could be made more complex. For instance, Duffie et al. (2009) estimate a frailty model whereby defaults are driven by an unobserved time-varying latent variable, which partially explains the observed default clustering. This could be explained by multiple factor effects, or industry factors. Alternatively, the factor exposures or relationships within common factors need not be linear, as implied by the Gaussian copula model. If so, some common effects would only manifest themselves for large enough shocks.

Exhibit 27.1 describes channels of credit contagion. When Firm A files for bankruptcy, we generally expect negative effects for other firms in the same industry. Contagion effects reflect negative common shocks to the prospects of the industry, and may lead to further failures in Industry A. On the other hand, the failure of a firm could help its competitors gain market share, which is a competitive effect. Generally, the net of these two effects is intra-industry contagion.

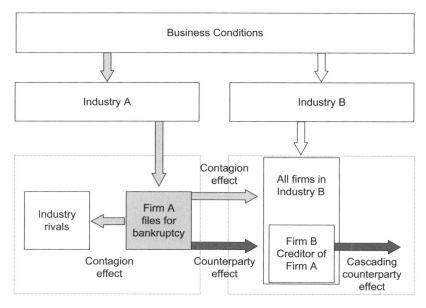

Exhibit 27.1 Channels of Credit Contagion

Common factor-based contagion effects can also arise across industries. Suppose that Industry A is a major client of Industry B. The default of Firm A could reveal negative information about sales prospects for firms in Industry B.

CREDIT CONTAGION FROM COUNTERPARTY RISK

The second approach to credit contagion is through counterparty risk. This effect arises when the default of one firm causes financial distress for its creditors. In Exhibit 27.1, say that Firm B has made a trade credit, or loan, to Firm A. Default by Firm A would cause a direct loss to Firm B, possibly leading to financial distress, even if it is in a different industry. For example, financial distress in the U.S. automobile industry had negative effects on the parts supplier industry. This could cause cascading effects to creditors of Firm B. Generally, cascading or looping effects are too complex to model analytically because firms may hold each other's debt and also because of the sheer number of networked firms. Jarrow and Yu (2001), for example, provide closed-form solutions but only for a simple case with two firms and no cascading effects. Their model is of limited use, however, because of its simplistic assumptions. The practice instead is to analyze counterparty contagion effects through simulations, called counterfactual because they focus on what might have happened. Researchers start from the topology of the financial system and examine the cascading effects of one bank defaulting at a time. Upper (2007) summarizes the literature, which suggests that pure counterparty contagion, due to lending in the interbank market, is likely to be rare. However, when it happens, the costs could be high. In addition, when the default of the first bank is due to common factors that affect other banks, the probability of a systemic crisis increases greatly.

Counterparty risk thus motivates regulatory actions to minimize systemic risk. Chairman Bernanke (2008), for example, justified the rescue of Bear Stearns by explaining that, "The company's failure could also have cast doubt on the financial positions of some of Bear Stearns' thousands of counterparties and, perhaps, of companies with similar businesses."

EVIDENCE ON COUNTERPARTY RISK EXPOSURES

This section examines the creditors' exposures to counterparty default.

Components of Exposures

The total economic effect from a counterparty default can be decomposed into two parts. The first part is the amount of direct exposure, a fraction of which can be lost through the bankruptcy proceedings. This represents assets either on the balance sheet or off the balance sheet, such as credit default swaps (CDS) positions. The second part is the value of the lost business if the counterparty cannot be easily replaced. This is an income effect.

Define *EXP* as the relative exposure, measured as the dollar amount of unsecured credit exposure scaled by the market value of the equity *MVE*; *REC* as the fractional recovery rate; and *NPV* as the dollar amount of lost future business, also scaled by *MVE*. The stock price effect for the creditor can be decomposed into a direct expected credit loss (*ECL*) and *NPV*:Rate of Return = $-ECL - NPV = -EXP(1 - REC) - NPV$.

For industrial firms, most exposures take the form of trade credit, defined as direct lending in a supplier-customer relationship. In the case of default, the trade creditor will lose part of the unsecured exposure. Also, the ongoing business of the trade creditor can be impaired by the bankruptcy of its borrower because this is often a major customer.

Empirical Evidence

In this bankruptcy sample, the mean exposures are $3 million, $12 million, and $164 million for trade credits, bonds, and loans, respectively. Industrials are exposed to trade credits and bonds only. Financials are exposed to all three categories.

When scaled by the market value of the creditor's equity, exposures are generally small. For industrials, the mean is 0.32 percent. Some industrial firms have large and undiversified exposures, however, reaching 37 percent of equity. For financials, the mean exposure is 0.16 percent. Thus, exposures are generally larger in dollar amounts for financial than industrial creditors, but less so in relative terms, when considering the larger balance sheets of financial creditors.

EFFECTS OF COUNTERPARTY RISK

This section now examines the effect of counterparty risk on the creditor's stock prices.

Price Effects of Borrower's Bankruptcy

To investigate the market effects of counterparty risk, Jorion and Zhang (2009a) analyze the reaction of the creditor's stock price and credit spread around the announcement of the borrower's bankruptcy. To abstract from common factor-based contagion risk, stock returns are adjusted for general movements in the creditor's industry; credit spreads are adjusted for general movements in spreads with the same credit rating. Hence, these results should reveal pure counterparty risk effects. Results are summarized in Exhibit 27.2. Creditors experience negative abnormal equity returns and increases in their credit spreads around the announcement of the bankruptcy of the borrower. On average, the creditor's equity falls by 1.9 percent. The size of this effect is greater than the average exposure of around 0.3 percent, which suggests a lost future business effect. As the bottom panel shows, the counterparty effect is indeed more important for industrials than for financials.

The creditor's CDS spread increases by 5.2 basis points, on average. In comparison, the median spread was 59bp for BBB-rated debt. Overall, these effects are relatively small.

Exhibit 27.2 Contagion Effects of Chapter 11 Bankruptcy on Creditors' Stock Prices and CDS Spreads

Sample	Observations	Exposure (Percent of MVE)	Stock Return (Percent)	Change in Spreads (Basis Points)
Total	694	0.32	1.9	5.2
Industrials	583	0.32	2.3	5.5
Financials	111	0.16	0.3	2.6

Shown is the average of cumulative abnormal stock returns and credit default swap spread changes for unsecured creditors of the 521 firms filing for Chapter 11 bankruptcy over the period 1999 to 2005. Returns are adjusted for the industry and spread changes for the credit rating. The period covered is 11 days around the announcement date.

FINANCIAL DISTRESS EFFECTS

As usual with events studies, this approach can only reveal unanticipated effects in market prices. In practice, bankruptcy is often preceded by other major public announcements about the debtor, such as financial distress, or even some kind of default. If so, the results are biased toward finding no effect. Also, focusing on actual price movements cannot identify the full cascading effects of counterparty risk for large financial institutions, given that regulators regularly bail out important banks.

To investigate this question directly, Jorion and Zhang (2009a) track creditor firms over the following years. Among the 461 industrials that experience a counterparty loss, 12 firms are delisted, and 149 firms are downgraded within two years. These numbers are compared to a control sample of firms in the same industry, with the same credit rating and size. The control sample experienced 3 delisted firms and 60 downgraded firms. These numbers are significantly lower than the sample that suffered credit losses. As a result, we can conclude that counterparty losses have a direct effect on the health of industrial creditors. For financials, differential effects are more tenuous, in line with weaker price effects.

IMPLICATIONS OF THE CRISIS FOR OUR ECONOMIC SYSTEMS

Jorion and Zhang (2009a) also perform simulations of counterparty defaults in a credit portfolio. They find an increase in correlation that fits the value reported by Das et al. (2007). Thus, counterparty risk provides a potential explanation for the observed excess clustering of defaults.

Price Effects from Lehman's Bankruptcy

Thus, in normal times, counterparty risk seems minor for financial firms. The recent upheaval in financial markets, however, provides a relevant environment to evaluate counterparty risk that originates from financial firms. Jorion and Zhang (2009b) examine the stock price reactions of firms that announced the extent of their exposure to Lehman Brothers Holdings after the investment bank declared bankruptcy on September 15, 2008. Out of 81 firms in the sample, 44 had positive exposure, which averaged 7.4 percent of their equity; the other 37 firms reported no exposure.

For firms with exposure, the average abnormal return over the three days surrounding the announcement was –6.4 percent. Firms with no exposure experienced a price increase of 0.1 percent instead. Because these results are adjusted for industry effects, they abstract from common factors and can be solely attributed to counterparty risk. The magnitude of these effects demonstrates that counterparty risk is indeed a channel of credit contagion, which is more severe when the originator is a financial firm and during stress periods.

CONCLUSIONS

By now, it is clear that traditional portfolio credit models have failed badly during the recent credit crisis. The question is how to identify the roots of these failures.

One approach is to extend common factor models. Another is to focus on counterparty risk. This debate has important policy implications. On the one hand, Helwege (2009) argues that if financial defaults are due to common factors, for example, bad investments in mortgage-backed assets, regulators should not prop up the failing institutions. If assistance is required, the best course of action calls for broad intervention, supporting the mortgage market in this example. On the other hand, if counterparty risk is a major channel of credit contagion, there is a rationale for bailing out institutions that could cause a domino effect in the financial system.

In practice, regulatory intervention is predicated on the belief that counterparty risk is a major source of systemic risk. U.S. regulators have responded to fears of cascading defaults by bailing out large troubled financial institutions, including Bear Stearns and American International Group (AIG), and (probably) regret their decision not to bail out Lehman Brothers. In addition, the fear of counterparty risk largely explains movements toward greater disclosure requirements and centralized clearing counterparties (CCPs). A CCP has a better picture of each member's overall risk position than any dealer in a bilateral market, which improves overall transparency in the financial system.

Finding direct empirical evidence of counterparty risk is no easy task, however. Jorion and Zhang (2009a) provide evidence that industrial firms that suffer a counterparty credit loss suffer negative stock price effects and are more likely to experience financial distress later. The effect on financials is harder to trace. Their sample, however, covers a limited period without major disruptions for financial institutions.

The more recent experience of the Lehman bankruptcy, unfortunately, allows us to evaluate counterparty effects directly. Holding common factors constant, financial institutions that had greater exposure to Lehman suffered much larger losses in equity valuations. This confirms the importance of counterparty risk as a direct channel of credit contagion.

NOTE

1. The IACPM and ISDA (2006) study reports similar measures of economic capital across models when adjusted for other parameters.

REFERENCES

Bernanke, B. 2008. "Developments in the Financial Markets." Testimony before the Senate Banking Committee, April 3, Washington, DC: Board of Governors of the Federal Reserve System.

Das, S., D. Duffie, N. Kapadia, and L. Saita. 2007. "Common Failings: How Corporate Defaults Are Correlated." *Journal of Finance* 62:93–117.

Duffie, D., A. Eckner, G. Horel, and L. Saita. 2009. "Frailty Correlated Default." *Journal of Finance* 64:5, 2089–2123.

Haldane, A. 2009. *Why Banks Failed the Stress Test*. London: Bank of England.

Helwege, J. 2009. "Financial Firm Bankruptcy and Systemic Risk." *Regulation*, Summer 2009, 24–29.

IACPM and ISDA. 2006. *Convergence of Credit Capital Models*. New York: International Swaps and Derivatives Association.

Jarrow, R., and F. Yu. 2001. "Counterparty Risk and the Pricing of Defaultable Securities." *Journal of Finance* 56:1765–1799.

Jorion, P., and G. Zhang. 2009a. "Credit Contagion from Counterparty Risk." *Journal of Finance* 64:5, 2053–2087.

———. 2009b. "Counterparty Contagion from the Lehman Bankruptcy." *Working Paper*. Irvine: University of California.

Upper, C. 2007. "Using Counterfactual Simulations to Assess the Danger of Contagion in Interbank Markets." *Working Paper*. Basel, Switzerland: Bank for International Settlements.

ABOUT THE AUTHORS

Philippe Jorion is a professor of finance at the School of Business at the University of California at Irvine, where he holds the Chancellor's Professor Chair. He received an MBA and a PhD from the University of Chicago, and a degree in engineering from the Université Libre de Bruxelles. Dr. Jorion has done extensive work in the area of international finance and financial risk management, and has received numerous prizes and awards for his research. He has written a number of books, including *Value at Risk: The New Benchmark for Managing Financial Risk* and the *Financial Risk Manager Handbook*.

Gaiyan Zhang holds a PhD from the University of California at Irvine (finance 2005) and an MS degree in finance from Fudan University, China. She is an assistant professor of finance at the University of Missouri at St. Louis. Her research interests include credit risk and credit derivatives, empirical corporate finance, and international finance. Her research has appeared in a number of journals, including *Journal of Finance, Journal of Financial Economics, Journal of Empirical Finance, Journal of Fixed Income, Journal of Alternative Investment, Journal of Management Studies,* and *Chinese Economy*. She wrote book chapters for the book *International Investments: Traditional and Alternative,* and *China's Capital Markets: Challenges from WTO Membership*. Zhang received research awards from the FDIC Center for Financial Research, University of Missouri at St. Louis, University of California at Irvine, and Fudan University. Her papers were presented at conferences including NBER, AFA, WFA, FMA, FDIC, and Bank of Canada.

CHAPTER 28

Contagion and Spillover Effects of the U.S. Subprime Crisis

Evidence from International Stock Markets

INCHANG HWANG
PhD student in Management Engineering with an emphasis in Finance,
Korea Advanced Institute of Science and Technology

FRANCIS IN
Monash University, Australia

TONG SUK KIM
Graduate School of Finance, Korea Advanced Institute of Science and Technology

INTRODUCTION

During the past years, financial markets have been stricken by the U.S. financial crisis triggered by the bursting of the U.S. mortgage bubble. In the early stages of the crisis, the securities backed with subprime mortgages held by many financial institutions rapidly lost most of their market value because of a dramatic rise in these mortgages' delinquencies and foreclosures in the United States. This led to the reorganizations, liquidations, and government bailouts of major U.S. financial institutions (e.g., Bear Stearns, Lehman Brothers, and the American International Group) because their capital largely vanished.

A prominent feature of the U.S. subprime crisis is that the U.S. subprime crisis started in the U.S. financial sector and rapidly spread, spilling over into not only other sectors of the economy but also other countries. These events resulted in a collapse of the banking industry, stock market crashes, a large decrease in liquidity on the credit market, economic recession, and furthermore they have engulfed sovereign insolvency in almost all countries. Moreover, this crisis affected real economies as well as financial markets, resulting, for example, in drops in productivity growth, increases in unemployment rate, and a decrease in international trade.

The contagious effect of financial crises has been of great concern to practitioners as well as academics because of its important consequences for the global economy in relation to monetary policy, optimal asset allocation, risk measurement, capital adequacy, and asset pricing. This attention has reached its peak after the advent of the U.S. subprime crisis because it has been unprecedented since the Great Depression in terms of range, depth, and speed of its impact.

In this chapter, we explain some findings on contagion and spillover effects of the U.S. subprime crisis on international stock markets. These findings provide some insights into the nature of the U.S. subprime crisis and a broader understanding of the U.S. subprime crisis in terms of financial contagion.

INTERNATIONAL STOCK MARKET MOVEMENT DURING 2005–2009

Exhibit 28.1 shows cumulative returns across regions during 2005–2009. In what follows, we refer to the period January 2005 to July 2007 as a *tranquil period* and August 2007 to August 2009 as a *turmoil period*. We assume that the bursting of the U.S. mortgage bubble occurred in August 2007. The solid vertical line marks the beginning of turmoil period and the dotted vertical line denotes the collapse of Lehman Brothers.

This figure gives some visual insights on the advent of the U.S. subprime crisis. During the tranquil period, all international stock markets had a steep growth with the stock price in Latin America being almost doubled and that in the other region having risen at least by 50 percent. At the beginning of turmoil period, there was a substantial drop that lasted for a short period, but the stock prices recovered soon. After the collapse of Lehman Brothers, the fall of the international stock market has been dramatic with the cumulative return of Latin America turning negative and that of the other regions becoming almost –50 percent.

CONTAGION EFFECTS

This section reviews previous studies of financial contagion. The discussion then extends the analysis to the effects of contagion emanating from the U.S. to international equity markets during the financial crisis of 2007–2009.

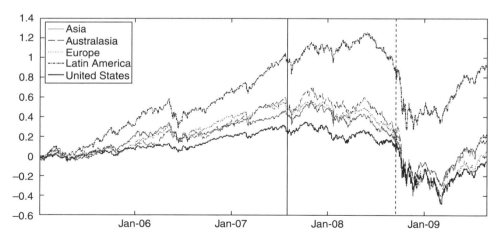

Exhibit 28.1 Cumulative Returns Across Regions during 2005–2009

Previous Studies on Financial Contagion

Even though financial market participants seem to obviously perceive financial contagion during periods of financial crises and there exist extensive theoretical analyses of financial contagion, it is difficult to investigate empirically. Even nowadays there is little consensus on empirically defining financial contagion, let alone its existence.

The issue of the existence of financial contagion in relation to financial crisis is related to the statistical definition of financial contagion and how to measure the spread of market disturbances. With recent empirical studies having colligated its definition, financial contagion, in general, refers to the comovement of exchange rates, stock prices, sovereign spreads, and capital flows in one market as a result of a financial crisis in another market. Hence, financial contagion is used to refer to the spread of market shocks (mostly, on the downside) from one country to another.[1]

Many researchers have focused on simple historical correlation as a measurement of comovement or dependence structure. To verify the existence of financial contagion between countries, many studies have attempted to test whether the correlations significantly change between tranquil and turmoil periods. The results from previous studies on the existence of financial contagion are not compatible. Some studies report that there is contagion effect during periods of financial crises such as the East Asian crisis, Mexican crisis, or 1987 U.S. market crash. It means that there is a significant increase in the cross-country correlation during the crises. However, the others show that there is no evidence of contagion effect during the same periods of financial crises and conclude that these crises are not the result of contagion but rather of interdependence.

As pointed out by many previous literatures like Bae et al. (2003), the most important limitation of these studies on financial contagion is that contagion effects are mostly measured using correlation coefficients. The concerns expressed about contagion seem to be founded not on linear measures of association for macroeconomic or financial market events but some presumption that there is something different about extremely bad events that might lead to irrational outcomes, excess volatility, and panic. In the context of stock returns, this means that if panic grips investors as stock returns fall and leads them to ignore economic fundamentals, one would expect large negative returns to be contagious in a way that small negative returns are not. The problem with correlations is that they give equal consideration to small and large price changes, which precludes an evaluation of the special impact of large changes. Moreover, as pointed out by Forbes and Rigobon (2002), estimation of cross-country correlation coefficients can be biased because of heteroskedasticity. In other words, even though there is no contagion effect on some financial markets in practice, the test based on correlation tends to show evidence of contagion effect because during crises when markets are more volatile, estimates of correlation coefficients tend to increase and be biased upward.

In this article, to overcome this limitation,[2] we build a dynamic conditional correlation generalized autoregressive conditionally heteroskedastic (DCC-GARCH) model.[3] The following findings are based on the empirical results of this model.

Contagion Effects of the U.S. Subprime Crisis on International Stock Markets

Exhibit 28.2 shows dependence structures[4] between U.S.- and region-level stock returns, and developed/emerging market stock returns during the U.S. subprime crisis. The vertical line indicates the start date of the turmoil period. Although the dependence increases in the short period close to the start of the turmoil period, it significantly decreases during the early stage of the turmoil period. However, the dependence rises quickly and reaches its peak during the second half of 2008. Although the dependence declines and is steady after the peak, the average level of dependence is higher than that before the sudden surge in dependence.

The results indicate evidence of financial contagion in the early stages of the U.S. subprime crisis and then a transition to herding behavior in latter stages. In the early stages, investors did not recognize the financial crisis or view its source as a local country problem. For this reason, dependence decreased during the early stages of the turmoil period, because investors rebalanced their portfolio from risky assets directly related to the source of the crisis to other risky assets, instead of from risky assets to risk-free assets. As the crisis evolved and most risky asset prices declined due to the contagion effect spreading through various channels, investors panicked and rebalanced their portfolios from risky assets to risk-free assets. This investor behavior can result in sudden increases in dependences between international stock market returns.

As the crisis was recognized by most market participants, investor decisions converged because the cost of collecting credible information was relatively high during the crisis. Investors tended to follow major investors in making decisions about investments and overreacted to information, interpreting news about one country as news about a whole region. This investor behavior leads to the persistence of high dependences after their sudden increase.

Compared with the results of previous literatures about the East Asian crisis, during the U.S. subprime crisis, the period of decreasing dependences during the early stages of the turmoil period is relatively longer, the sudden period of rising

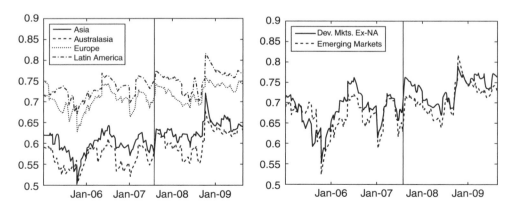

Exhibit 28.2 Dependences between U.S. and Other International Stock Returns during the U.S. Subprime Crisis

dependences is quite short, and the pace of increasing dependences is extremely fast. The U.S. subprime crisis became apparent in 2007 when U.S. housing prices began to decline steeply and mortgage delinquencies in the United States soared. Since securities backed with subprime mortgages lost their value, the financial institutions that held these securities suffered heavy losses. However, the important thing is that no investor could estimate the loss of these financial institutions due to a lack of information and regulatory control about such securities. It was not until several major financial institutions began going bankrupt and announced the reduced value of their securities that investors recognized the seriousness of the U.S. subprime crisis. For example, the five largest U.S. investment banks failed during 2008. (Lehman Brothers went bankrupt, Bear Stearns and Merrill Lynch were taken over by other companies, and Goldman Sachs and Morgan Stanley were bailed out by the U.S. government.) In addition, government-sponsored enterprises (GSE) Fannie Mae and Freddie Mac either directly owed or guaranteed nearly $5 trillion in mortgage obligations in September 2008. Compared with the East Asian crisis, investors were relatively late in recognizing the U.S. subprime crisis. Therefore, the shock during the U.S. subprime crisis had a larger surprise component than that during the East Asian crisis.

SPILLOVER EFFECTS

Changes in sovereign credit ratings have spillover effects, and the information generating these spillovers can give rise to both common and differential effects, as this section explains. The analysis also examines the spillover effects of the U.S. subprime crisis to international stock markets.

Spillover Effects of News about Sovereign Credit Ratings

Another issue of the empirical study of financial contagion is related to the spillover effects of news about sovereign credit ratings across markets during specific crisis periods. A sovereign credit rating is a rating agency's evaluation of the potential ability of a sovereign obligor to assure timely and accurate payments of debt service. News concerning sovereign credit ratings has far-reaching implications for investors because the sovereign bond market is regarded as a benchmark for all other bond markets in the local economy, as well as the fact that sovereign credit ratings basically indicate the risk level of a country's investing environment.

As classified by Gande and Parsley (2005), the spillover effects of the sovereign credit rating or credit outlook changes of one country (labeled the event country) to the financial markets of all other countries (labeled the nonevent countries) can be divided into two conceptual categories: common information effects and differential effects. Although common information spillovers mean that the financial markets of event and nonevent countries move in tandem, differential spillovers imply that the effects of rating events lead to opposing results across countries. For example, a positive rating event, such as an explicit upgrade of a credit rating or a favorable revision in a country's credit outlook, could signal a widespread common trend, thus providing a positive signal to all other countries. In this case, the financial markets across countries would be more correlated. This case is referred to as common information spillover. Alternatively, such positive events can reveal that the event country's financial market has been more attractive to investors than those of all the other countries, providing a negative signal to these other countries. In this case, the correlation between event and nonevent countries would decrease. This case is referred to as differential spillover (Gande and Parsley 2005).

Spillover Effects of the U.S. Subprime Crisis on International Stock Markets

We find evidence of spillover effects on dependences for both upgrades and downgrades of sovereign credit ratings during the U.S. subprime crisis. However, the characteristics of the spillover effects for positive rating changes differ from those for negative rating changes. Although the spillovers for positive rating changes indicate differential effects, those for negative rating changes indicate common information effects. If the sovereign credit rating of one country is upgraded, other countries' stock returns are less correlated with U.S. stock returns. On the other hand, if a sovereign credit rating of one country is downgraded, other countries' stock returns are more correlated with U.S. stock returns.

We also find that recent ratings activities can affect the spillover effect of news about sovereign credit ratings across countries. In addition, our finding shows that, during the U.S. subprime crisis, the positive news events of developed markets have a greater impact on cross-country dependences and developed markets are easily influenced by the positive news events of other countries. This finding is compatible with some reports, which describe that developed markets were more seriously affected than emerging markets during the U.S. subprime crisis comparing with other financial crises.

These findings suggest that not only negative rating news but also positive rating news was informative during the U.S. subprime crisis. This means that positive news events as well as negative news events were not anticipated by the market participants. These findings also imply that the market participants tended to consider upgrades as local country information and downgrades as common trend information, such as a wake-up call, during the U.S. subprime crisis.

These findings are quite different from previous literatures about other financial crises, which reports asymmetric spillover effects: Negative rating events abroad have a significant common information effect while positive ratings events have no discernible impact. These inconsistent results reveal the severity of the U.S. subprime crisis. Previous literature explains the asymmetric spillover effect as being an incentive for the event country's government to leak information about positive ratings news and a reason for rating agencies to be reluctant to lower sovereign credit ratings. However, there is a severe level of uncertainty about the future economy induced by the high cost of gathering credible information during the U.S. subprime crisis. Thus, any news about sovereign credit ratings, both positive and negative rating events, could have a greater impact on the financial market in terms of the resolution of uncertainty.

CONCLUSION

Our findings provide some insights into the nature of the U.S. subprime crisis. These findings imply that the U.S. subprime crisis has a larger surprise component than any previous crisis, such as the East Asian crisis. Also, the U.S. subprime crisis seems to support the wake-up call hypothesis as a transmission channel of financial contagion. To explore these issues further, one should study which factors explain the degree of contagion effect and news spillover effect on international stock markets in financial crises using microeconomic data related to each market as well as macroeconomic data. These studies will help us to understand not only the channel or mechanism of financial contagion but also the vulnerability of a financial system to financial contagion.

NOTES

1. This definition is from Dornbusch et al. (2001). Other conceptual contributions are due to Masson (1999), Kodres and Pritsker (2002), and Forbes and Rigobon (2002).
2. A number of recent studies have tried to overcome this limitation using various methods to measure financial contagion. Some studies developed models based on extreme value theory, while others extended multivariate generalized autoregressive conditionally heteroskedastic (GARCH) models with asymmetry, Markov regime-switching and time-varying conditional correlations. Instead of building new models of asset return, some studies measure the dependence between asset returns using a copula approach.
3. For further details about econometric methodology such as model specification and estimation method, see Hwang et al. (2010).
4. This is measured by conditional correlations obtained from the DCC-GARCH model.

REFERENCES

Bae, K., G. Karolyi, and R. Stulz. 2003. "A New Approach to Measuring Financial Contagion." *Review of Financial Studies* 16:717–763.

Dornbusch, R., Y. Park, and S. Claessens. 2001. "Contagion: How It Spreads and How It Can Be Stopped?" In S. Claessens and K. Forbes, eds. *International Financial Contagion*, 19–42. New York: Kluwer Academic.

Forbes, K., and R. Rigobon. 2002. "No Contagion, Only Interdependence: Measuring Stock Markets Comovements." *The Journal of Finance* 57:2223–2261.

Gande, A., and D. Parsley. 2005. "News Spillovers in the Sovereign Debt Market." *Journal of Financial Economics* 75:691–734.

Hwang, I., I. Francis, and T. Kim. 2010. "Contagion Effects of the U.S. Subprime Crisis on International Stock Markets." *Working Paper*, KAIST and Monash University.

Kodres, L. E., and M. Pritsker. 2002. "A Rational Expectations Model of Financial Contagion." *The Journal of Finance* 57:769–799.

Masson, P. 1999. "Contagion: Macroeconomic Models with Multiple Equilibria." *Journal of International Money and Finance* 18:587–602.

ABOUT THE AUTHORS

Inchang Hwang is a PhD student in management engineering with an emphasis in finance at Korea Advanced Institute of Science and Technology (KAIST), Republic of Korea. He is currently a visiting scholar at Monash University, Australia. He received his B.S. in physics and mathematics (double major) from KAIST. He worked on several projects that assessed pricing models and analyzed hedge performance of exotic derivatives. He was a managing fellow of KAIST Student Investment Fund (KSIF). He provided advice about the strategies worked out by fellows of KSIF and services to facilitate fellows' trade. His main research interests are in investment, asset pricing, risk management, and advanced econometrics, in particular in the study of financial contagion, hedge funds, systemic risk, credit risk modeling, dynamic conditional correlation model, and copulas.

Francis In is a professor of finance in the Department of Accounting and Finance at Monash University, Australia. He received a PhD from Cornell University. He held a visiting research fellow position at the University of Melbourne, University of Rochester, University of Montreal, and Harvard University. Professor In has a strong research background in the areas of financial econometrics and asset price modeling. Professor In is regarded as one of the leading researchers in wavelet time series analysis and its application to mainstream finance research in Australia. He is the author of more than 50 refereed articles. Francis In's recent articles include *Journal of Financial and Quantitative Analysis, Journal of Economic Dynamics and Control, Studies in Nonlinear Dynamics and Econometrics, Journal of Empirical Finance, Journal of Business, Journal of International Money and Finance, Quantitative Finance,* and *Journal of Portfolio Management.*

Tong Suk Kim is an associate professor of finance at the Graduate School of Finance, Korea Advanced Institute of Science and Technology (KAIST) in Seoul, Republic of Korea. Before joining KAIST, he was a finance faculty at San Diego State University. He received a PhD from the Ohio State University. Dr. Kim has done numerous works in the area of portfolio theory and investments. He served as president of Korean Association of Futures and Options and as an editor of the Korean Journal of Futures and Options. He is also one of the founders of the Asia-Pacific Association of Derivatives. He has been on the advisory board of numerous Korean financial institutions including Korea Exchange and Korea Securities Depository.

CHAPTER 29

Market or Bank Contagion

Evidence from the Market Crisis of 2007–2009

WILLIAM F. JOHNSON
Florida Atlantic University

The market crisis of 2007–2009 was one of the most dramatic and vicious events in modern financial history. Bankruptcy and nationalization for some of the largest banks was used as a short-term solution by many governments to prevent further bank index declines during the crisis. In response to this situation, many pundits and government officials have supported the idea that a lack of regulation was the major cause of the market crisis, and an increase in controls will serve to protect the integrity of the economy and financial institutions in the future. Although numerous measures have been proposed to curb speculation, reduce leverage, and manage derivative trading, academic evidence that banks caused the market crisis has yet to be found.

This crisis may also be considered a significant test of financial integration in the globalization era. Since the cause of this market crisis was largely blamed on the banking sector, contagion would most likely have spread through banking indexes around the world. If this was a banking centered crisis, Bank Index Return Correlations (BIRC) would have experienced a much higher degree of contagion compared to Market Index Return Correlations (MIRC). However, if market indexes actually experienced higher levels of contagion during the crisis, this would be evidence that banks may not be the primary cause of the crisis and any increase in regulation would not address the true culprit of the market turmoil.

Using Datastream weekly returns from 46 country market and bank indexes from October 1, 2007, to May 2, 2009, MIRC were greater than BIRC in both local currency (LC) and U.S. dollar (USD). This suggests that the worldwide market crisis can't be blamed on the banking sector, as market indexes experienced a greater degree of contagion, measured by correlations, during the crisis. The results are contrary to the current popular belief that banks were the primary cause of the market crisis.

There has been much academic literature detecting and testing for market integration and contagion during extreme market movements. Karolyi (2003) provides numerous examples and counterexamples to measure integration and contagion. Bunda et al. (2009) examine comovements of bonds in emerging markets during extreme market volatility. Chandar et al. (2009) investigate how currency crisis affects returns of cross-listed securities. Didier et al. (2008) find evidence that contagions have been less likely in the recent past, but conditions for future contagions remain and Brusco and Castiglionesi (2007) provide a theoretical framework for contagion to spread through open markets. Edwards (2009) investigates the factors that increase the likelihood of contagion and Johnson (2010) investigates how regulation affected the recent market contagion. Flavin et al. (2008) find a link between high volatility and presence of contagion and Haile and Pozo (2008) identify macroeconomic factors that contribute to contagion. This chapter examines the existence of contagion among the banking indexes around the world during the crisis period. Since the crisis has largely been blamed on the banking sector, conventional wisdom would expect to see higher levels of contagion among the banking index returns compared to the overall index returns during the crisis period.

BIRC did increase during the crisis period, but in a lower magnitude compared to overall MIRC. The ultimate source and cause of the market crisis was more complicated than a banking-centered crisis and changes to regulatory regimes may not serve to buffer or prevent a future worldwide market crisis. This evidence refutes the belief that increasing regulations on the banking industry will reduce future market crises. It was more likely the causes of the crisis were centered outside the banking sector and the banks simply reflected the weaknesses in the overall economy. This analysis concludes that the cause of the market crisis remains elusive and was outside the banking sector.

HYPOTHESIS AND METHODOLOGY

To test the level of contagion experienced by the banking sector in each country compared to the market indexes, four simple correlation comparisons were conducted. More elaborate measures of contagion are available, but complexity may not be the most efficient means to measure this simple relationship. BIRC were subtracted from MIRC during the crisis and the prior 16 months. Crisis BIRC (MIRC) were also subtracted from the prior bank (index) return correlations. Having higher correlations during extreme trading periods is one definition of market contagion. These comparisons provide evidence to confirm or contradict the belief that banks were the primary cause of the market crisis. The following formula was used for all correlation calculations for all 46 countries in the study for both the bank index and market index simple weekly returns.

$$\rho \text{Index}_1 \text{Index}_2 = \text{correlation}\,(\text{Index}_1 \text{Index}_2) = \text{Covariance}\,(1, 2)/(\sigma 1 \sigma 2)$$

Hypothesis one: BIRC will be higher than MIRC during the crisis period.

Hypothesis two: BIRC will increase at a greater magnitude than MIRC from prior period to crisis period.

Hypothesis one analyzes whether the weekly banking index return correlations experienced during the crisis period were greater than the weekly MIRC. If the crisis was centered in the banking sector, BIRC would be higher relative to MIRC. A similar analysis could be conducted based on the Internet bubble where technology-based firms would most likely have experienced a greater degree of return correlation compared to the overall market indexes. However, if MIRC experienced a greater degree of return correlation, this would suggest the cause of the crisis lay outside of the bank sector.

Hypothesis two analyzes the relationship between bank indexes and market indexes prior to and during the crisis. If the cause for the market crisis was centered on the banking sector, then BIRC should exhibit a much greater increase in magnitude of correlation during the crisis compared to the MIRC. However, if MIRC increased at a greater magnitude compared to BIRC, this would suggest the cause of the crisis lay outside the banking sector.

Reinhart and Rogoff (2008) investigate the financial crisis from a global perspective, analyzing developed and developing nations, but during different time periods. This study examined 46 countries over one time period. The sample was selected from the top 60 countries with the highest GDP in USD where all data were available. Datastream was used to collect weekly bank index returns and weekly market index returns from October 1, 2007, to March 2, 2009, denominated in USD and LC.

RESULTS

It was clear that the market and bank indexes experienced a traumatic sell-off during the crisis period. From Exhibits 29.1 and 29.2, nearly all indexes, both banks and markets, experienced returns below negative 30 percent denominated in both USD and LC. Given the scope of the countries studied, this was a unique episode in modern financial history and creates additional puzzles for both academics and practitioners. One question pondered is if investing in international equities will still provide diversification benefits, given that all bank and market index returns were negative during the crisis period?

Ireland's bank index experienced the worst return with a negative 98.31 percent in USD and 98.09 percent in LC. The worst performing market index was in Romania with a negative 87.13 percent return in USD and negative 81.39 percent return in LC. Although the losses and chaos experienced by investors in U.S. bank and market indexes during the crisis were significant, it is noteworthy that U.S. indexes experienced a relatively mild sell-off compared to many indexes around the world. The U.S. bank index experienced the 12th (11th) worst return in USD (LC). The U.S. market experienced the 35th (20th) worst return in USD (LC).

A surprising relationship was also uncovered in the descriptive statistics exhibits. Nearly all banking indexes that experienced lower returns during the crisis period were in European countries. It was peculiar because many have proposed the U.S. needs to emulate European bank regulations, which did not protect many European banking indexes from major sell-offs. This begs the question: Why is the U.S. looking to align regulatory regimes with Europe? Emulating European banking regulation may exacerbate future market crisis within the U.S. banking sector.

Exhibit 29.3 is a summation of the four correlation tests run between the bank and market index during the crisis and the prior 16 months to the crisis denominated in USD and Exhibit 29.4 denominated in LC. All correlation tests were run using weekly return correlations from Datastream bank indexes and market indexes from 46 countries during the crisis period. Correlation test one in Exhibit 29.3 Panel A is comparing MIRC and BIRC during the crisis period. Only 8.21 percent of the BIRC were higher than MIRC during the crisis period. This compares to

Exhibit 29.1   Datastream banking index return for crash period and standard deviation of weekly returns during crash period denominated in U.S. Dollars

Bank			Market		
Country	Return %	Std Dev	Country	Return %	Std Dev
Ireland	−98.31	0.1812	Romania	−87.13	0.0829
Netherlands	−93.74	0.1333	Ireland	−77.43	0.0643
Belgium	−93.60	0.1095	Hungary	−74.97	0.0766
Romania	−89.62	0.0827	Poland	−72.86	0.0685
Hungary	−88.00	0.0973	Russia	−71.64	0.0826
Russia	−87.00	0.087	Pakistan	−71.32	0.0505
U.K.	−84.75	0.0909	Greece	−70.99	0.0582
Denmark	−83.28	0.0718	Austria	−70.78	0.0587
Germany	−82.83	0.0806	Finland	−70.38	0.0576
Greece	−82.05	0.0733	Netherlands	−68.12	0.0565
Austria	−81.89	0.0786	Norway	−67.65	0.0764
United States	−79.46	0.0975	Turkey	−67.43	0.0786
Norway	−79.06	0.1024	Belgium	−67.29	0.0603
France	−78.89	0.0741	Switzerland	−66.80	0.0682
Poland	−78.77	0.0824	Italy	−66.64	0.0512
Pakistan	−78.35	0.071	Australia	−64.38	0.064
Sweden	−78.21	0.0837	U.K.	−62.70	0.0532
Portugal	−76.80	0.0589	New Zealand	−62.34	0.0461
Italy	−75.46	0.0621	Denmark	−61.69	0.0615
Switzerland	−71.27	0.0733	India	−61.59	0.0737
Turkey	−70.32	0.0927	Singapore	−60.47	0.0491
Czech Republic	−69.58	0.0928	France	−60.26	0.0511
Argentina	−68.76	0.043	Germany	−58.85	0.0496
Spain	−68.40	0.0672	Mexico	−58.62	0.0575
Finland	−67.46	0.0711	Portugal	−58.50	0.0492
Australia	−66.01	0.0682	Brazil	−58.03	0.079
South Korea	−65.91	0.0653	Spain	−57.77	0.0519
Israel	−65.32	0.063	Canada	−57.42	0.0631
India	−63.01	0.0876	China	−56.63	0.0882
Canada	−62.43	0.0666	South Africa	−56.30	0.0664
South Africa	−60.38	0.0777	Taiwan	−56.26	0.052
Brazil	−60.30	0.0905	Hong Kong	−56.11	0.0628
New Zealand	−59.92	0.0411	Argentina	−55.37	0.0395
Singapore	−59.70	0.0568	Thailand	−55.16	0.0544
Hong Kong	−56.91	0.0606	United States	−53.93	0.0438
Philippines	−54.14	0.0499	Czech Republic	−53.72	0.0738
Thailand	−52.31	0.0575	Philippines	−50.76	0.0512
Mexico	−51.07	0.0508	Sweden	−49.85	0.0397
Taiwan	−48.96	0.0632	Indonesia	−48.25	0.0616
China	−47.95	0.0881	South Korea	−47.47	0.0519
Japan	−45.08	0.0611	Japan	−45.07	0.0414
Indonesia	−44.12	0.0712	Israel	−43.90	0.0418
Malaysia	−38.63	0.035	Malaysia	−41.04	0.0326
Chile	−33.33	0.0504	Chile	−36.19	0.0495
Venezuela	−26.79	0.0226	Venezuela	−12.54	0.0174
Columbia	−26.55	0.0384	Columbia	−7.34	0.0377

Exhibit 29.2 Datastream banking index return for crash period and standard deviation of weekly returns during crash period denominated in local currency

Bank			Market		
Country	Return %	Std Dev	Country	Return %	Std Dev
Ireland	−98.09	0.183601	Romania	−81.39	0.071417
Netherlands	−92.92	0.132334	Ireland	−74.47	0.06243
Belgium	−92.76	0.105518	Greece	−67.19	0.048674
Romania	−84.89	0.069689	Australia	−66.94	0.049624
Hungary	−83.39	0.082421	Finland	−66.49	0.048953
Denmark	−81.09	0.066768	Hungary	−65.32	0.058169
Russia	−80.78	0.087437	Netherlands	−63.95	0.047454
Germany	−80.58	0.073906	Belgium	−62.99	0.052887
Greece	−79.69	0.06671	Italy	−62.25	0.040483
Australia	−79.51	0.071549	Pakistan	−62.17	0.049928
United States	−79.46	0.097484	Poland	−61.07	0.044463
U.K.	−77.75	0.08264	Singapore	−58.34	0.044012
France	−76.12	0.071648	Russia	−57.46	0.079612
Portugal	−73.75	0.052095	Canada	−57.43	0.063124
Italy	−72.23	0.053916	Norway	−56.90	0.057963
Norway	−72.11	0.088183	Denmark	−56.69	0.052274
Pakistan	−71.51	0.071005	China	−56.63	0.088166
Switzerland	−71.10	0.076479	Hong Kong	−56.18	0.06278
Poland	−69.55	0.05956	France	−55.04	0.041312
Sweden	−68.94	0.069262	United States	−53.94	0.043836
South Korea	−65.75	0.065214	Japan	−53.65	0.05227
Czech Republic	−64.68	0.077801	Germany	−53.45	0.03849
Argentina	−64.25	0.040969	Turkey	−53.21	0.054342
Spain	−64.25	0.059831	Portugal	−53.08	0.039568
Israel	−63.43	0.059718	Taiwan	−52.82	0.047086
Finland	−63.19	0.065873	Sweden	−52.67	0.051787
Singapore	−57.54	0.052541	Thailand	−52.51	0.052598
Turkey	−57.37	0.069984	Spain	−52.23	0.04171
Hong Kong	−56.98	0.060566	India	−49.97	0.064676
Japan	−53.89	0.071413	Austria	−49.81	0.03749
Austria	−52.13	0.049836	Switzerland	−49.56	0.038294
India	−51.81	0.078994	Argentina	−49.55	0.03818
Canada	−51.30	0.058854	Indonesia	−48.25	0.061639
Philippines	−49.85	0.044011	South Korea	−47.45	0.051877
Thailand	−49.56	0.055405	Czech Republic	−46.34	0.057398
China	−47.95	0.08813	Philippines	−46.15	0.045305
Brazil	−47.21	0.073285	U.K.	−45.58	0.042046
Taiwan	−44.81	0.058006	Brazil	−44.20	0.05889
Indonesia	−44.12	0.071241	Mexico	−41.84	0.045871
South Africa	−39.65	0.053598	New Zealand	−41.48	0.023238
New Zealand	−37.73	0.020505	Israel	−40.84	0.038515
Malaysia	−32.61	0.031676	Chile	−36.18	0.049455
Mexico	−31.23	0.038043	Malaysia	−35.26	0.028499
Venezuela	−26.79	0.022605	South Africa	−33.43	0.042623
Columbia	−26.55	0.038394	Venezuela	−12.54	0.017361
Chile	−20.88	0.03527	Columbia	−7.34	0.037723

Exhibit 29.3 Correlation between market and bank weekly returns during crisis period and 16 month prior period denominated in U.S. Dollars

Panel A	Time	Index	Total	Market Higher	Bank Higher	Market %	Bank %
1	Crisis	Market – Bank	1,035	950	85	91.79	8.21
2	Prior	Market – Bank	1,035	977	58	94.40	5.60
Panel B	Index	Time	Total	Prior Higher	Crisis Higher	Prior %	Crisis %
3	Bank	Prior – Crisis	1,035	371	664	35.85	64.15
4	Market	Prior – Crisis	1,035	227	808	21.93	78.07

correlation test two in Exhibit 29.3 Panel A, which evaluates the correlations in the 16 month prior period; 5.6 percent of the BIRC were higher than MIRC during the prior period. The difference between the two periods does represent a significant increase in correlations for banking index returns, but was mainly due to the low correlations in the prior period. MIRC were higher in 91.79 percent of the total return correlations. Correlation test one and two in Exhibit 29.4 Panel A were the same correlation tests, but run with returns denominated in LC. The results for LC correlations were consistent with correlation tests in USD, where correlations increased from 4.83 percent during the prior period to 9.86 percent during the crisis period. This again was a significant increase in correlation, but was largely due to low banking index return correlations in the prior period. T-tests showed (not reported) the differences between the BIRC and MIRC were significant at the 1 percent level during the crisis, denominated both in USD and LC.

This analysis only uncovers the fact that banking indexes experienced significantly higher levels of correlations during the crisis period when compared to the prior period. This can be attributed to a low starting point from the prior period. Although banks did experience higher levels of return correlations during the crisis period, MIRC still outnumbered the BIRC 9 to 1. Further investigation is needed before banks can be blamed as the primary reason and culprit for the market crisis.

Exhibit 29.4 Correlation between market and bank weekly returns during crisis period and 16 month prior period denominated in local currency

Panel A	Time	Index	Total	Market Higher	Bank Higher	Market %	Bank %
1	Crisis	Market – Bank	1,035	933	102	90.14	9.86
2	Prior	Market – Bank	1,035	985	50	95.17	4.83
Panel B	Index	Time	Total	Prior Higher	Crisis Higher	Prior %	Crisis %
3	Bank	Prior – Crisis	1,035	302	733	29.18	70.82
4	Market	Prior – Crisis	1,035	247	788	23.86	76.14

Panel B in both Exhibit 29.3 and Exhibit 29.4 compare BIRC and MIRC during the crisis and prior period to determine whether banks or market indexes experienced a greater increase in magnitude of return correlations. Exhibit 29.3 Panel B test three shows BIRC denominated in USD were higher in 64.15 percent of the correlations during the crisis and test four reveals MIRC were higher in 78.07 percent of the correlation tests during the crisis. The results in Exhibit 29.4 Panel B test three denominated in LC were consistent with the above results where 70.82 percent of the BIRC were higher and 76.14 percent of MIRC were higher during the crisis period in test four. This was evidence that the bank indices did not experience contagion at the same or greater magnitude than the overall market indexes in each country during the crisis. This was a surprising result and stands in contrast to the belief that weakness in the banking sector was responsible for the poor overall market performance.

DISCUSSION

This evidence suggests the sell-off spread throughout the world and the contagion was magnified beyond the banking sector in each country. The banking sector was not the sole contributor to the crisis and other ideas outside of increasing regulation in banks should be considered in order to prevent future market crisis. Banks, which were highly leveraged for a positive and growing economic environment, would be expected to crash if the prospects for future growth and prosperity were suddenly dashed. Based on the above analysis, the sell-off among banking indexes reflected a sudden change in growth prospects or market valuations. With FINREG currently being debated among politicians, it is still unclear what part banks played in the market crisis and if changing regulation will do anything to prevent future crisis. The findings should serve to dampen what Statman (2009) warns when investors become fearful and urge an overreaction from legislators.

The first and easiest target to blame for the crisis were the large banks, which had been aggressive in their assessment of future growth prospects and real estate valuations. The use of investment derivatives and other exotic financial products were simply mechanism for investment. The products' failure does not constitute causation, but according to this analysis, a symptom of an economic slowdown or change in perceptions of value. Had these tests found that banks experienced greater magnitudes of correlations during the crisis, then this chapter would serve as evidence that banks across the world caused the market crisis. This evidence would justify calls for new and expansive banking regulations, but the findings in this analysis contradicted the belief that banks caused the market crisis.

CONCLUSION

This chapter analyzes Market Index Return Correlations and Bank Index Return Correlations to test the magnitude of contagion during the market crisis of 2007–2009. It was clear that something dramatic caused the market sell-off experienced during the crisis period. The banking sector indexes experienced a lower magnitude of return correlations compared to the market index correlations during the crisis, suggesting the banking sector was not the primary cause of the market crisis.

Based on this evidence, the crisis may have been triggered by other complex factors in the overall economy. Therefore, the financial crisis of 2007–2009 cannot be blamed on the banking sector and the crisis should not serve as the justification for additional regulations. According to this analysis, the true cause of the crisis lay outside the banking sectors around the world. It appears that the banking sector was simply reacting to changes in economic activity, a rapid change in growth opportunities, perceptions of valuation, or other unobserved variables in the economy. Focusing efforts on banking regulation will not truly address the causes of the market crisis and won't serve to protect the markets and economies of the world from future market crisis.

REFERENCES

Brusco, Sandra, and Fabio Castiglionesi. 2007. "Liquidity Coinsurance, Moral Hazard, and Financial Contagion." *The Journal of Finance* 62:5 (Oct.), 2276–2302.

Bunda, Irina, A. Javier Hamann, and Subir Lall. 2009. "Correlations in Emerging Markets Bonds: The Role of Local and Global Factors." *Emerging Markets Review* 10:67–96.

Chandar, Nandini, Dilip K. Patro, and Ari Yezegel. 2009. "Crises, Contagion and Cross-Listing." *Journal of Banking and Finance* 33:1709–1729.

Didier, Tatiana, Paolo Mauro, and Sergio L. Schmukler. 2008. "Vanishing Financial Contagion?" *Journal of Policy Modeling* 30:775–791.

Edwards, Sebastian. 2009. "Sequencing of Reforms, Financial Globalization, and Macroeconomic Vulnerability." *Journal of Japanese International Economies* 23:131–148.

Flavin, Thomas, Ekaterini Panopoulou, and Deren Unalmis. 2008. "On the Stability of Domestic Financial Market Linkages in the Presence of Time-Varying Volatility." *Emerging Markets Review* 9:280–301.

Haile, Fasika, and Susan Pozo. 2008. "Currency Crisis Contagion and the Identification of Transmission Channels." *International Review of Economics and Finance* 17:572–588.

International Monetary Fund, www.imf.org/external/index.htm.

Johnson, William F. 2010 "International Economic Freedom, Regulation, Banks and the Market Crisis of 2007–2009." *Working Paper.*

Karolyi, G. Andrew. 2003. "Does International Finance Contagion Really Exist?" *International Finance* 6:179–199.

Reinhart, Carmen, and Kenneth Rogoff. 2008. "Banking Crisis: An Equal Opportunity Menace." *Working Paper* (December).

Statman, Meir. 2009. "Regulating Financial Markets: Protecting Us from Ourselves and Others." *Financial Analysts Journal* 65:3 (May), 22–31.

ABOUT THE AUTHOR

William F. Johnson is a PhD student in finance at Florida Atlantic University, holds an M.B.A. from California State University Long Beach (2004) and a BS from University of Arizona (1995). He has worked as a NASD registered representative for Charles Schwab, TD Ameritrade, and AXA Equitable. He has also worked as a visiting professor at Hanoi School of Business and La Trobe University in Vietnam. His research focus is in financial institutions and international investing and he has published numerous articles on these subjects in various academic journals.

CHAPTER 30

China, India, and the Global Financial Crisis of 2007–2009

SHALENDRA D. SHARMA
Professor, Department of Politics, University of San Francisco

As the United States and the G7 were battered by the subprime-induced financial crisis, it was widely assumed that China and India, with little exposure to the subprime loans, would remain relatively immune from the crisis. In fact, the popular "decoupling" hypothesis claimed that since economic growth in emerging markets like China and India was becoming more independent of the United States and Europe, they were no longer as vulnerable to an economic slowdown in these advanced economies. However, China and India hardly were immune from the financial crisis of 2007–2009—their experiences unambiguously underscoring that in an interconnected world, no country is an island.

Why did a crisis in the U.S. subprime mortgage markets (a relatively small part of the U.S. financial system) soon affect the global economy? The typical explanations that the sheer size of the U.S. economy means that "when it sneezes everyone else gets a cold," or that in an increasingly globalized economy no country is really immune from the contagions spillover effects are only partly true (Shiller 2008). This chapter, drawing on the experiences of China and India, provides a more nuanced explanation as to why and how these two economies were impacted. In particular, it highlights the complex trade and financial linkages or the contagion's transmission channels. Moreover, the chapter provides some guidelines as how both China and India can better insulate their economies from the future vagaries of global market turmoil.

The volume of international capital flows surged from just under US$2 trillion in 2000 to US$6.4 trillion in 2006 (World Bank 2009). These funds cross national borders, often at will, despite attempts by governments to control and regulate their movement. Increasingly integrated financial markets also mean that there is more rapid and powerful spillover across economies through both traditional and new types of channels. For example, although spillover through the traditional trade channel remains a central transmission mechanism (even though global trade patterns have become more diversified), financial spillovers have become more pronounced as the rising correlation of global equity prices and the potential for sudden capital flow reversals mean that shocks at the core can be transmitted rapidly throughout the entire global financial system (IMF 2008).

However, each financial crisis is also different. Financial–macro linkages are at the core of the current crisis as two key sectors of the financial system, traditional banking activities and the securities market unraveled simultaneously (Shiller 2008). With several major banks suffering massive losses, and the securities markets virtually paralyzed, the resultant loss of confidence has taken a huge toll and made earlier policy responses somewhat redundant. Although past monetary policy support has been effective (as reductions in policy rates have facilitated the normalization of credit conditions), in the crisis of 2008, the effective intermediation of funds has proven to be difficult given the ever-tightening credit market.

China and India's embrace of openness has meant that their economies are now deeply interwoven into the global economy. Consequently, both are subject to the vagaries of economic globalization (Naughton 2007; Panagariya 2008). However, globalization is not a linear or seamless process. Unlike many banks and financial institutions around the world that invested heavily in assets and derivatives backed by U.S. subprime mortgages, banks and financial institutions in India and China generally chose to exclude themselves from such investments. As a result, the Indian financial sector has remained relatively insulated and none of the major Indian banks have had much exposure to U.S. subprime debt. The State Bank of India, the ICICI Bank (the country's largest private bank), the Bank of Baroda, and the Bank of India have been exposed to international securitized debt in the form of collateralized debt obligations, with this debt amounting to approximately US$3 billion. This is tiny in comparison to ICICI's US$100 billion balance sheet. According to the Reserve Bank of India (RBI), the country's central bank, only US$1 billion out of India's total banking assets of more than US$500 billion was invested in toxic assets or related investments.

By the end of 2008, the Bank of China confirmed that it was holding approximately US$9.7 billion in securities backed by U.S. subprime loans, while the Industrial and Commercial Bank of China and China Construction Bank have reported exposure of approximately US$1 billion each. Of course, in the larger scheme of things, these are extremely small debts. Even if the three Chinese banks have a total US$12 billion exposure to subprime debt, this equates to just 6 percent of the US$199 billion in private foreign securities they held in 2008.

More importantly, the Chinese authorities have made public that none of its massive US$1.5 trillion foreign reserves (the largest in the world) was invested in the subprime debt. The same is true for India's reserves. Although India's total reserve assets declined by approximately 7 percent from August 2008 to US$274 billion in the second week of October 2008, its foreign currency reserves were more than adequate to cover India's debt obligations.

What explains this paradox? China and India both integrated into the global economy, and yet are seemingly not fully integrated? This is because both countries are still minor players in the global financial system. For example, Chinese and Indian banks, some of which are large by global standards based on market capitalization and the size of their balance sheets, have only modest international presence. The rupee is not fully convertible (and hardly used outside India), and the RMB is hardly used outside China. The Chinese capital markets are not a major source of financing for foreign borrowers. In fact, capital markets in both countries are small relative to the size of their domestic economy and both rely heavily on foreign direct investment (FDI) rather than securities investment and other forms of capital flows to access international capital markets (Calomiris 2007; Chow 2007). Moreover, although there has been gradual liberalization, both China and India subject portfolio capital flows to various restrictions.

So what explains China and India's vulnerabilities to the subprime-induced meltdown? The answer: Economic globalization not only creates deep and entwining linkages between economies, but also "convergence" among them. As such, fallout in one part, especially the largest part (the United States), inevitably creates contagion that spreads across the globe. In the case of China and India, what were ripples when the subprime crisis broke in mid-2007 became heavy waves by 2008. There are two major reasons for this. First, the stock markets in each country are particularly vulnerable to swings in investor sentiment. Foreign institutional investors sold billions of dollars of shares in Chinese and Indian companies to cover losses accrued in their home markets. As a result, not only the stock exchanges took a beating, there was also an intense liquidity crisis, particularly in the Indian economy due to the tightening of global credit markets and the withdrawal of foreign institutional investors. Second, in both countries, as external trade in merchandise and services accounts for a significant portion of their economies, a global slowdown in demand, especially the sharp declines in consumer spending in the rich economies, only exacerbated the negative impact of the crisis.

In the case of India, its outsourcing industry and export-dependent information technology sector suffered from declining revenues, not only due to the slowdown in global demand, but also due to the rise in the value of the rupee against the U.S. dollar. In fact, tightening credit and the declining value of the U.S. dollar hit India's information technology companies hard as the industry derives more than 60 percent of its revenues from the United States. In addition, as some 30 percent of business coming to Indian outsourcers includes projects from U.S. banking, insurance, and the financial services sector, a sharp slowdown in these sectors negatively impacted Indian businesses. For example, Infosys and Satyam, two major outsourcing companies were severely impacted. India also saw a sharp decline in remittances some 6 million Indians working abroad send home each year. In 2008, migrant remittances totaled more than US$30 billion, making India the top receiver of such income. Finally, the drying up of liquidity within the United States has forced U.S.-based investors to withdraw their investments from the Indian economy, and from elsewhere around the globe.

In the case of China, the financial crisis has shown that its investment-driven and export-oriented development model, with exports accounting for 40 percent of GDP, is increasingly difficult to sustain (Lardy 2008; Wu 2007). Second, the exponential growth of China's massive foreign exchange reserves has been the result of trying to sustain a stable exchange rate between the RMB and the U.S. dollar even in the face of strong economic pressure for appreciation. To prevent this appreciation and to avoid loss of export competitiveness, the People's Bank of China has been aggressively buying dollars and selling RMB. However, this strategy has not been without cost. Besides making domestic macroeconomic management difficult (China's controls on private exchanges of RMB for other currencies are not always effective), concentration on exchange rate stabilization has meant that Beijing has largely ceded the ability to use monetary policy to target domestic objectives like controlling inflation. Consequently, the continuous depreciation of the U.S. dollar has not only increased uncertainties associated with capital movement, but by driving up commodities prices in dollar terms, the weakening dollar is exerting the pressure of imported inflation on China.

In both countries, the subprime lending-induced general tightening of the global credit markets and the resultant "credit crunch" have reduced capital flows. Over the short term, this might not be a serious problem as both countries have a fair amount of liquidity within their domestic economies. However, if the problem persists over time, the credit crunch could have a negative impact on both economies. For example, an impact on the business sector's ability to raise funds from international sources could impede investment growth as these businesses would have to rely more on costlier domestic sources of financing, including bank credit. This could, in turn, put upward pressure on domestic interest rates. This is already happening in India. The tightening of liquidity has meant that companies that could previously borrow at attractive rates from the United States and from other markets do not have that luxury now and are forced to borrow at higher rates within the domestic market.

To better insulate their economies against future crises, both China and India need to further reform their banking and financial sectors. In both countries, the mainly state-owned banks are saddled with inefficiencies, and in the case of China, dangerously large volumes of nonperforming loans (Lardy 2008). Equally important, it would be prudent for China to adopt a more flexible exchange rate. After all, China's emphasis on exchange rate stability in the face of a rising current account surplus has not only generated intense protectionist pressures in the United States and elsewhere, it has also forced the central bank to accumulate massive foreign exchange reserves with negative domestic consequences. Keeping the RMB from rising against the U.S. dollar not only means that China's central bank has to print more money to keep interest rates low, but such a strategy can also exacerbate the problem of inflation if more money ends up chasing too few goods. It also means that China is exposed to large capital losses on its foreign reserve holdings (which are largely held in U.S. dollars) as the RMB appreciates. Moreover, an appreciation of the exchange rate would also boost domestic consumption: something China needs. The adoption of a flexible exchange rate would give China greater leverage to limit deviations of inflation and growth from chosen targets by means of a monetary policy focused on domestic objectives. Of course, such a policy does not imply totally ignoring the exchange rate as it might require the authorities to intervene in the exchange market to limit short-run currency fluctuations. In addition, it does not mean that a move toward a more flexible rate is an argument for capital account liberalization. Suffice it to note, there are numerous cases of countries operating managed floats while maintaining capital controls. In contrast, the adoption of a monetary policy aimed at domestic objectives would help China develop a more balanced and resilient financial system.

India's exchange rate policy has been more flexible and variable than China's (in both nominal and real terms). Although this variability might not be huge (and the RBI does indeed intervene), India's exchange rate policy and outcomes have greater flexibility than China's. As a result, India does not face the challenges China does. In addition, the RBI has infused 3 trillion rupees ($60.2 billion) into the financial system. Although these measures have helped to unfreeze liquidity, there is not much more the authorities can do. India's problem is that it already has a large fiscal deficit on top of a debt-to-GDP ratio of more than 80 percent.

More government spending will only make matters worse. Clearly, making its financial system efficient at intermediating resources and directing them to the most productive investments is essential to India's long-term growth (Panagariya 2008; Rozhkov 2006). Although India has performed better than China on this front, much more work needs to be done. Over the past decade, India's overregulated financial and banking sector has undergone substantial restructuring and is now better prepared to meet the needs of the country's growing economy. Although financial sector reforms have included deregulation of interest rates and elimination of credit controls, strengthening regulation and supervision of the domestic banking sector along the lines of Basle Core Principles, policy makers have been cautious with one particular aspect of external liberalization: the liberalization of capital flows.

Specifically, although the rationale for capital account liberalization is that it provides increased opportunity for risk diversification and greater efficiency in resource allocation, the problem of market failure and financial crisis associated with free capital mobility has not been lost on India's policy makers. As a result, India has adopted a gradualist approach to capital account liberalization. For example, unlike Chinese authorities, Indian authorities have put in place a set of prudential regulations, such as limits on assets in real estate, currencies, and stocks that has served to prevent banks from putting their balance sheets at risk. Moreover, cognizant of the fact that there could be links between current and capital accounts, procedures have been put in place to avoid capital flows in the guise of current account transactions. Equally important, the extent and timing of capital account liberalization is sequenced with other reforms, such as strengthening of banking systems, fiscal consolidation, and trade liberalization. Policy makers have also maintained controls regarding who can borrow in foreign currency, and in what form (debt versus equity), including the volume of borrowing and length of maturity. Prudently, corporations, banks, nonbank financial institutions, residents and nonresidents are treated differentially with regard to such regulations. The high fiscal deficit and a weak banking system underscore that India's macroeconomic fundamentals are not yet ready for full capital account convertibility.

Similarly, reforms in corporate governance have made India better equipped to deal with global competition. The Securities and Exchange Board of India, by creating an environment of improved transparency and better regulation, has allowed the Bombay Stock Exchange (BSE) to become a more efficient institution. To its credit, the RBI has maintained tight regulation of banks and external capital transactions, and has successfully resisted government pressure to deregulate banks and open India to external capital account transactions. This is no small achievement as the RBI is subservient to the Finance Ministry and lacks the kind of independence from the government that occurs in developed world central banks, including the U.S. Federal Reserve. The RBI has moved from a regulatory model of direct interference to governance by "prudential norms." This means that banks now have stronger disclosure norms and are under greater surveillance. The upgrade in transparency through better regulatory and supervisory systems has led to a marked improvement in banks' capital base and asset quality: with a growing number of banks actually showing profitability. This has helped the Indian banking system to reduce the volume of nonperforming loans to a much more manageable 4 to 5 percent. However, despite these achievements, India's banking sector still remains vulnerable. At the heart of the problem (as in China), is that state ownership in the banking sector is high, with a few government-owned banks (particularly the State Bank of India, the country's largest commercial bank) accounting for roughly 80 percent of the banking sector. However, many of these state-run banks are chronically undercapitalized and burdened with substantial volumes of nonperforming loans, high personnel costs, excessive dependence on interest income, and inadequate skills to manage the variety of risks associated with free capital mobility. Finally, although India's financial system is more effective than China's in allocating capital, and private sector companies in India have better access to funds than those in China do, there is room for improvement. In particular, the RBI's insistence that priority sectors (agriculture and small business) receive at least 40 percent of all loans and advances and that 25 percent of all bank branches serve rural and semi-urban areas tends to distort lending decisions. Finally, China and India need to strengthen their bilateral trade relations. Clearly, expanding these trade and economic linkages has the potential to provide both nations with buffers against global market turmoil.

REFERENCES

Calomiris, Charles, ed. 2007. *China's Financial Transition at a Crossroads*. New York: Columbia University Press.

Chow, Gregory C. 2007. *China's Economic Transformation* (2nd ed.). Malden, MA: Blackwell.

International Monetary Fund. 2008. *World Economic Outlook Update*. Washington, DC: International Monetary Fund.

Lardy, Nicholas. 2008. "Financial repression in China." Policy Brief No. PB08–8, September. Washington, DC: Peterson Institute for International Economics.

Naughton, Barry. 2007. *The Chinese Economy: Transitions and Growth*. Cambridge, MA: MIT Press.

Panagariya, Arvind. 2008. *India: The Emerging Giant*. New York: Oxford University Press.

Rozhkov, Dmitriy. 2006. "On the Way to a World-Class Banking Sector." In Catriona Purfield and Jerald Schiff, eds. *India Goes Global: Its Expanding Role in the World Economy*, 88–108. Washington, DC: International Monetary Fund.

Shiller, Robert J. 2008. *The Subprime Solution*. Princeton, NJ: Princeton University Press.

World Bank. 2009. *Global Economic Prospects 2009*. Washington, DC: World Bank.

Wu, Harry. 2007. "The Chinese GDP Growth Rate Puzzle: How Fast Has the Chinese Economy Grown?" *Asian Economic Papers* 6:1, 1–23.

ABOUT THE AUTHOR

Shalendra D. Sharma, PhD, is professor in the Department of Politics at the University of San Francisco. He also teaches in the MA program in the Department of Economics. Sharma is the author of *Democracy and Development in India* (Lynne Rienner Publishers, 1999), which won the Choice Outstanding Academic Title for 1999; *The Asian Financial Crisis: Meltdown, Reform and Recovery* (Manchester University Press, 2003); *Achieving Economic Development in the Era of Globalization* (Routledge, 2007); and editor of *Asia in the New Millennium: Geopolitics, Security and Foreign Policy* (Institute of East Asian Studies, UC Berkeley, 2000). His latest book is *China and India in the Age of Globalization* (Cambridge University Press, 2009). Sharma has also published more than four dozen single-authored articles (mostly in the field of international political-economy and international relations) in leading peer-reviewed journals. Sharma was the recipient of USF's universitywide Distinguished Teaching Award for 1996–1997 and universitywide Distinguished Research Award for 2002–2003. During 2006–2007 he was a visiting professor in the Departement Politieke Wetenschap, Faculteit der Sociale Wetenschappen, Universiteit Leiden, the Netherlands.

CHAPTER 31

Financial Contagion from the U.S. to Asian Markets in Global Financial Turmoil

MATTHEW S. YIU
Research Department, Hong Kong Monetary Authority*

WAI-YIP ALEX HO
Research Department, Hong Kong Monetary Authority and Department of Economics, Boston University, Boston, MA, USA

DANIEL F. S. CHOI
Department of Finance, the University of Waikato, Hamilton, New Zealand

INTRODUCTION

The financial crisis that originated in the United States in 2007 has become a global financial turmoil and affected many economies around the globe. A large number of emerging market economies, such as Hungary, Ukraine, Latvia, and Iceland, have suffered severe financial crises and have sought emergency assistance from the International Monetary Fund to restore stability and confidence in their banking systems and financial markets. Many Asian financial markets have suffered sharper losses than the major developed markets, even if the banks in the region were relatively less affected by the subprime problem compared to those in North America and Europe.

Asian equity markets started falling from their previous peaks at the end of 2007. They stabilized somewhat after the announcement of the rescue plan of Bear Stearns in March 2008. However, when the U.S. government let Lehman Brothers go bankrupt in September of that same year, a worldwide sell-off of financial assets began and the asset prices fell throughout the world. The Asian equity markets plunged again.

Significant correlations between movements in Asian financial markets vis-à-vis the U.S. stock market can be observed during these months. When the

---

*The views and analysis expressed in this chapter are those of the authors, and do not necessarily reflect the views of the Hong Kong Monetary Authority.

correlations of asset returns in cross-border markets increase excessively relative to the correlations during "tranquil" periods, we term this jump of cross-markets correlation as *contagion*. Contagion effects between financial markets can transmit through different channels. There was some preliminary evidence of financial shock spillover and contagion among financial markets across different regions in 2007. The wave of shocks to the Asian financial markets seems to emanate from one source, the U.S. economy.

Spillover and contagion can change the correlations between cross-border financial markets rapidly. As these correlations are crucial inputs for international portfolio management and risk assessment, monitoring the changes of the correlations is important in international investment. Furthermore, at the time of financial crises, like this episode, cross-border contagion may have significant consequences for financial stability. Thus, it is essential to provide policy makers with timely and appropriate measures of correlation changes and contagion. This would certainly help them to design appropriate policy responses and to prepare for contingency plans.

This chapter focuses on examining the existence of contagion effect from the U.S. equity market to the equity markets in the EMEAP group in the Asia region (Executives' Meeting of East Asia-Pacific Central Banks, which consists of Australia, China, Hong Kong SAR [of China], Indonesia, Japan, Korea, Malaysia, New Zealand, the Philippines, Singapore, and Thailand) during the current crisis episode. The significance of the U.S. equity market to the equity markets in the region has been studied in Cheung, Cheung, and Ng (2007). They found that the U.S. market led the four Asian emerging markets (Hong Kong SAR, Korea, Singapore, and Taiwan) before, during, and after the Asian financial crisis in 1997–1998 while the four markets Granger-caused the U.S. market during the crisis period. Thus, understanding and monitoring the dynamics of correlation between the U.S. market and Asian equity markets, especially during the crisis era, is important for portfolio decisions and asset allocations for international investors as well as for policy makers in the region.

In this chapter, we examine the correlation between the U.S. equity market and the Asian equity markets within the Dynamic Conditional Correlation (DCC) framework. Moreover, instead of estimating the DCC of the 11 markets vis-à-vis the U.S. equity market at the same time and then looking at the pair-wise dynamic conditional correlation between EMEAP markets and United States, we first use principal component analysis to extract the major driving force behind the 11 equity markets and then estimate the DCC between this driving force and the U.S. equity market. By doing so, we can eliminate the market-specific component existing in each individual market within the group and focus only on the interplay between the U.S. equity market and the EMEAP equity markets as a whole.

DATA AND METHODOLOGY

Similar to Cappiello, Engle, and Sheppard (2006), the data used in this study are Wednesday-on-Wednesday returns of the benchmark equity indices of the 11 EMEAP markets as well as the U.S. equity market. All indices are denominated in the local currency, dividend-unadjusted, and collected as the daily closing prices in each market.

We examine the dynamic correlation of volatility between the weekly returns of Asia stock markets and weekly returns of U.S. stock market from February 1993 to March 2009 by adopting a two-step approach. In the first step, we assume that the returns of the 11 EMEAP stock markets are driven by a dominant unobservable component, which we interpret as the "Asian factor." Principal Component Analysis was used to extract this component. In the second step, we first pre-whiten the Asian factor and the return series of the U.S. market by a vector-autoregressive filter. Under the assumption of multivariate normality, the asymmetric DCC model (Cappiello et al. 2006; Engle 2002) and the residuals from the pre-whitening are employed to estimate the DCC $\hat{\rho}_{F,US,t}$ between the returns of the Asian factor, F, and the U.S. stock market. Like Engle's DCC model, the asymmetric DCC model can also alleviate the dimensionality problem presented in the general MGARCH model.

We model $\hat{\rho}_{F,US,t}$ as an autoregressive process with intercept breaks to test the hypothesis that the Asian financial crisis and the 2008 global financial crisis have significant impacts on the dynamics of $\hat{\rho}_{F,US,t}$, which is considered as evidence of "contagion." Specifically, we estimate the following model for $\hat{\rho}_{F,US,t}$:

$$\hat{\rho}_{F,US,t} = \gamma_0 + \sum_{j=1}^{p} \gamma_j \hat{\rho}_{F,US,t-j} + \xi_1 Crisis1_t + \xi_2 Crisis2_t + v_t$$

where $Crisis1$ is a dummy variable of the Asian financial crisis period (from October 1997 to December 1998) and $Crisis2$ is a dummy variable of the 2008 global financial turmoil period (from September 2007 to March 2009).

One of our interests is comparing the impact of the Asian financial crisis and the current financial crisis on the dynamics of the correlation between the Asian markets and the U.S. market. To this end, we adopt a typical regression with dummy variables for the two crises. It is commonly agreed that the effects of the 2008 global financial turmoil on the Asian region as well as on other regions began in September 2007 because of the occurrence of the subprime problem. Thus, we define the second crisis dummy variable ($Crisis2$) as taking value of 1 from September 2007 on and zero otherwise. On the other hand, it is difficult to come out with a unanimous agreement on the periods of the Asian financial crisis for different markets in the group for defining the first crisis dummy variable. Although the Thai government gave up defending the value of baht in July 1997, the large-scale attacks on the Asian currencies only occurred after Taiwan decided in October 1997 to depreciate its currency value to increase the competitiveness of its exports. So, we used October 1997 as the beginning of the Asian financial crisis and the last day of 1998 as the ending date to define the first crisis dummy variable ($Crisis1$).

EMPIRICAL RESULTS

In comparing the characteristics of the two crises, we first examine some descriptive statistics of the returns of the EMEAP equity markets before and during the crises. When the first two moments for the tranquil and crisis periods are compared, we find that the weekly returns are generally higher in the two tranquil periods whereas the standard deviations are larger in the crises periods. It is also interesting to compare the first two moments for the 2008 global crisis and the Asian financial crisis. The EMEAP markets and the U.S. market suffered much greater losses in the 2008 episode. On the other hand, in the Asian crisis, Australia, China, Korea, and the Philippines were having positive weekly returns. Regarding the volatility, the markets of Hong Kong SAR, Indonesia, Korea, Malaysia, the Philippines, Singapore, and Thailand were more volatile in the Asian financial crisis.

In the estimation of the Asian factor, the largest principal component explains 46 percent of the total variation of the 11 EMEAP markets, with the five largest principal components together explaining 78 percent. The explanatory power of these principal components drops dramatically after the first component, indicating that a substantial amount of the weekly returns of these markets is driven by one common factor. Thus, in the subsequent analysis, this largest principal component is taken as the overall movement of all these markets and is named the *Asian factor*.

In terms of the estimated dynamic conditional correlations between the U.S. equity market and the Asian factor, as well as individually with four selected markets (namely: Hong Kong SAR, Japan, New Zealand, and Singapore), our results indicate that the Asian equity markets were not shocked asymmetrically more by bad news than good news from the United States. There are some variations and some possible structural breaks in the dynamic correlations. Nevertheless, the effects of the U.S. stock market on the Asian factor and the four selected markets in the sample period seem to be relatively stable, albeit with some clustering effects. We find that the shocks in the U.S. market are positively correlated with those in the Asian factor and the selected markets. Moreover, the correlation between the U.S. and the Asian factor is the highest with a value of 0.51, indicating the dominant effect of the U.S. market on the Asian region.

The crisis dummies of the 2008 global turmoil, *Crisis2*, are all positive and significant at least at the 5-percent level except for Hong Kong SAR, which is only significant at the 10-percent level. However, the crisis dummies of the Asian financial crisis, *Crisis1*, are not significant except the one in the Asian factor equation, though only at the 10-percent level. So, the contagion effect of the U.S. equity market on the region is apparent in the 2008 crisis episode but there is no strong evidence of this in the Asian financial crisis period. Our finding can be justified by the fact that the two crises originated from different sources: the Asian financial crisis originated locally and the current one emanated from the United States.

CONCLUDING REMARKS

In this chapter, a factor framework was employed to investigate the volatility contagion effect from the U.S. equity market to the equity markets of the 11 EMEAP markets. The common Asian equity market factor extracted using principal component analysis explains a substantial proportion of variation in the returns of the EMEAP equity markets. We can see that the common factor, which we call the Asian factor, has the heteroskedasticity property like many other financial returns series.

The asymmetric dynamic conditional correlation (DCC) models were used to model the time-varying nature of the volatility correlations between the U.S. market versus the Asian factor as well as the four selected markets. From the estimates of the asymmetric DCC models, there is no strong evidence of asymmetry. Thus, the impacts of bad news and good news on the correlation between markets are not very different.

The autoregressive equation of the estimated dynamic conditional correlation series was used to test the existence of contagion by including the two crisis dummy variables. The estimated parameters of the 2008 global financial turmoil dummy variable are significant in the cases of the Asian factor, Japan, New Zealand, and Singapore at the 5-percent level, whereas the estimated parameter in the Hong Kong case is only significant at the 10-percent level. One possible explanation is that the Hong Kong equity market was extremely buoyant in the last quarter of 2007 speculation that the Chinese government would allow Chinese citizens to invest directly in the Hong Kong equity market. This speculation masked the contagion effect of the U.S. market.

The insignificance of the crisis dummy variable of the Asian financial crisis reveals that the crisis originated locally in the region. Thus, there was no contagion effect between the U.S. market and the individual markets in the region. On the other hand, the crisis dummy variable is significant at the 10 percent level in the case of the Asian factor. We suspect that this may be due to the feedback channel between the United States and the region as a whole, though the effect was mild.

Predicting the volatility in different markets and correlation between them is essential to international investors. Our factor framework is expected to be useful because it can greatly reduce the dimensionality problem of studying the dynamics of correlation between the U.S. market vis-à-vis with 11 Asian equity markets. Predictions of the dynamic correlation between the whole region and the United States are also relevant to policy makers, and could be useful inputs for predicting financial contagion in crisis episodes. Again the factor framework will simplify the task.

REFERENCES

Cappiello L., R. Engle, and K. Sheppard. 2006. "Asymmetric Dynamics in the Correlations of Global Equity and Bond Returns." *Journal of Financial Econometrics* 4:4, 557–572.
Cheung, Y.-L., Y-W. Cheung, and C. Ng. 2007. "East Asian Equity Markets, Financial Crises, and the Japanese Currency." *Journal of Japanese and International Economies* 21:138–152.
Engle, R. 2002. "Dynamic Conditional Correlation: A Simple Class of Multivariate Generalized Autoregressive Conditional Heteroskedasticity Models" *Journal of Business and Economic Statistics* 20:339–350.

ABOUT THE AUTHORS

Matthew S. Yiu, senior manager of the research department of the Hong Kong Monetary Authority (HKMA), is responsible for research on financial economics and policies related to financial and monetary stability. In the mid-1990s, he was seconded from the HKMA to work as technical assistant to the U.K. executive director at the International Monetary Fund in Washington, DC, for two years. Mr. Yiu earned his doctoral degree from Lancaster University, United Kingdom. Since 2006, he has been appointed as honorary associate professor in the Department of Statistics and Actuarial Science of the Hong Kong University. His recent research papers have appeared in the *International Journal of Finance and Economics, Applied*

Financial Economics, Pacific Economic Review, and *Journal of Japanese and International Economies.*

Wai-Yip Alex Ho is an economist (official title is manager) in the market research division in the Hong Kong Monetary Authority since January 2009. He is currently a PhD candidate in economics in the Department of Economics of Boston University and expected to graduate in June 2011. His research interests are macroeconomics and empirical finance. He has published three refereed articles on state-dependent-pricing and inflation dynamics.

Daniel F. S. Choi is a senior lecturer at Waikato Management School, the University of Waikato, Hamilton, New Zealand. He received an MASc from the University of Waterloo, Canada, an MA from the University of Lancaster, England, and a PhD from the University of Stirling, Scotland. Dr. Choi started his career at Hong Kong Baptist University in 1977 and continued to 1998 before he emigrated to New Zealand. His current research interests are information transmission in the futures markets and the relationship between post-earnings announcement drift and uncertainty in the stock markets. His major teaching responsibility is in derivative securities and capital markets.

CHAPTER 32

Signals of Global Financial Problems

JOHN L. SIMPSON
Associate Professor in the School of Economics and Finance at Curtin University

Growing pains of global financial integration were identified in a period prior to the 2008–2009 global financial crisis. The problems are revealed in the analysis of daily country banking index data from December 1999 to September 2008 (Simpson 2010). Econometric and statistical analysis of daily bank price index data show that only the major Western banking systems had achieved a high level of integration participation. Though not specifically tested in this study, this interdependence was exemplified in the extensive United Kingdom and Western European investment banking involvement in the U.S. subprime mortgage market. It is also proposed that the major Western commercial and investment banks, predominantly those in the United States and the United Kingdom, had engaged in significant interbank borrowing and lending; they had mutual client and customer lists and there was substantial cross-bank shareholdings. Integration implies interdependence, which, if undiversified, implies the existence of systemic risk or the threat of contagion through the "domino" or "chain reaction" effect. The short-term solution to the crisis has been the injection of many billions of dollars, by predominantly Western governments and central banks, in order to recapitalize their banking systems (including, in the case of the United States, the recapitalization of a dominant mortgage insurance organization).

This chapter provides the results of an analysis of commercial banking system market models, which indicate the extent of the pre-crisis problem. The chapter does not deal in depth with the lessons to be learned, nor does it deal with an analysis of investment banking data. However, it seems obvious that regulatory authorities must redefine, redifferentiate and redelineate commercial and investment banking roles and activities. Banking authorities must re-enforce the need for sound practices in credit risk assessment, credit risk management, and corporate governance and continue to improve prudential supervision. A return of commercial banking to traditional core activities of diversified on-balance-sheet lending seems desirable. Western countries must also assist developing and transitional economies to step up the pace of reform, particularly in their banking sectors, to enable these countries to enter the fold of financial integration and to dilute the power and interdependence of Western banking. Refocusing by all banks on a culture of portfolio diversification of investments and borrowings is necessary.

Greater involvement by a global banking regulatory authority such as the Bank for International Settlements (BIS) to monitor undiversified systemic interdependence may be inevitable (for example, the administration of insurance schemes for interbank lines of credit).

THE MODEL AND DATA

Daily time series banking price index data were collected for each country–region, as well as a world banking price index, covering the period December 31, 1999, to September 20, 2008. The study commenced with the specification of a basic linear market model[1] to initially analyze unlagged banking stock price index return data as follows:

$$Br_{i_t} = \alpha_t + \beta_t Br_{w_t} + e_t \qquad (32.1)$$

Where:
  Br_{i_t} is the banking price index return for country i at time t.
  Br_{w_t} is the world banking price index return at time t.
  α_t, β_t, and e_t are the regression intercept, coefficient, and error terms at time t, respectively.

Based on Granger (1988) findings that financial and economic time series may contain unit roots and in the development of the theory of nonstationary time series analysis, the unlagged regression model is respecified into a vector autoregressive (VAR) model to implement VAR based tests for both cointegration and causality in optimally lagged data.[2]

The respecified model in level series price index values is as follows:

$$B_{i_t} = c + a_1 B_{i_{t-1}} + a_n B_{i_{t-n}} + b_1 B_{w_t} + b_n B_{w_{t-n}} + e \qquad (32.2)$$

Where:
  B_i is a vector of endogenous variables being bank price index values for country i (at times t to $t-n$).
  B_{w_t} is the vector of exogenous world banking price index values at time t.
  a and b are matrices of coefficients to be estimated.
  e is the error term and specifically it represents a vector of innovations that may be contemporaneously correlated but are uncorrelated with their own lagged values and uncorrelated with all of the right hand side variables. Note: In the model specified in Equation 32.2, both variables for the banking system in a country and the global banking system are optimally lagged at $t-n$.

FINDINGS

The initial indication of the strength and direction of the strong interrelationship between Western banking systems is indicated in correlation coefficients, when regional banking systems interact with the Americas region (see Exhibit 32.1).

Exhibit 32.1   Correlation Analysis: Banking Systems with the Americas Banking System

Ranking According to Correlation	Banking System	Correlation Coefficient
1	U.S.	0.9974
2	Canada	0.5955
3	Europe (excluding emerging economies)	0.4300
4	EMU	0.4148
5	Europe (excluding the U.K.)	0.4124
6	U.K.	0.3707
7	Latin America	0.3604
8	Europe (excluding the EU)	0.3323
9	Singapore	0.1213
10	Asia (excluding Japan)	0.0979
11	Pacific Basin (excluding Japan)	0.0975
12	Pacific Basin	0.0964
13	Asia	0.0961
14	Japan	0.0939
15	Far East	0.0911
16	Taiwan	0.0834
17	Hong Kong	0.0829
18	South East Asia	0.0695
19	Korea	0.0585
20	Australasia	0.0442
21	Australia	0.0284
22	Thailand	0.0225
23	Philippines	0.0212

Source: Simpson (2010).

Higher levels of interdependence are seen with the larger and more developed banking systems such as those in the United States, Western Europe, and the United Kingdom. Subsequently, the ranking of regression adjusted R square values and Betas from Equation 32.1, with country banking systems regressed on the world banking system, are considered (see Exhibit 32.2). The major Western country banking systems in the United States, United Kingdom, and Western Europe are strongly interrelated with the world banking system.

The analysis in a VAR model (Equation 32.2)[3] indicates the existence of cointegration in most of the country banking models, but these relationships are shown to be stronger with the major Western banking systems. No significant cointegrating (long-term equilibrium relationship) was found in the Chinese, Thailand, and Australian systems interacting with the world banking system. In consideration of these latter findings, Australia is a developed economy with a sophisticated and well-managed banking system. However, Australia has a smaller banking system than other Western systems. China is a major trading partner of Australia and, though in transition, is a major global economy. China, too, is not cointegrated with the world banking system. China has built up strong current account surpluses, which it is now using to maintain growth by expending substantial funds

Exhibit 32.2 Regression Analysis

Country and Regional Banking Price Index. First differences regressed on the world banking price index first differences	Rank (Adjusted R^2 Value and t Statistic Value)	Regression-Adjusted R^2 Value	Regression Coefficient (Beta)	t Statistic
Europe without emerging European systems	1	0.6881	0.8284	52.0867
Americas	2	0.6572	1.0544	48.577
Europe without U.K.	3	0.6378	0.7559	46.5411
U.S.	4	0.6340	1.4740	46.1639
EMU	5	0.6150	0.7003	44.3240
Europe without countries in the EMU	6	0.6103	1.2249	43.8934
Europe without the EU	7	0.4689	1.1482	32.8939
U.K.	8	0.4546	7.3415	32.0174
Canada	9	0.2796	0.7140	21.9207
Pacific Basin Countries without Japan	10	0.1879	0.2701	16.8739
Latin American Countries	11	0.1833	0.0339	16.6136
Asian countries including Japan	12	0.1720	0.4024	15.9998
Asia excluding Japan	13	0.1652	0.2821	15.6026
East Asia	14	0.1576	0.4279	15.1825
Hong Kong	15	0.1314	1.7724	13.6528
Japan	16	0.0938	0.1423	11.3225
Singapore	17	0.0887	0.1874	10.9430
Australasia	18	0.0796	0.1949	10.3611
South East Asia	19	0.0789	0.1110	10.3035
South Korea	20	0.0557	0.0305	8.5310
Australia	21	0.0354	0.2116	6.7778
Taiwan	22	0.0289	0.0370	6.0462
Thailand	23	0.0235	0.0617	5.4680
Malaysia	24	0.0061	0.0926	2.8017**
Philippines	25	0.0014	0.0248	2.0180**
Indonesia	26	0.0017	0.0059	1.900**

Note: All t statistics are significant at the 1% level except those marked ** where significance is at the 5% level. The ranking is according to explanatory power in the adjusted R square value and the t statistic value. These are unlagged data. The results for China are not significant and not reported.
Source: Simpson (2010).

on domestic infrastructure projects. To an extent, continued Chinese imports of Australian mineral and energy resources for such projects have assisted to immunize Australia from the global financial crisis.

All other interrelationships were confirmed in causality analysis. It would be expected that the world banking system would be the driving influence in all cases of the various country and regional systems and the evidence shows in most cases that the world system was the exogenous force. These relationships are greater in the major Western banking systems. It is noted that the U.S. banking system was the major exogenous influence on the world banking system leading up to the financial crisis.

It is maintained that integration and systemic risk can be studied by the use of banking stock market price indices. The study is in concurrence with researchers such as Ratanapakorn and Sharma (2002) and Sell (2001). Moreover, it is felt that the issue of systemic risk is primarily a financial issue (as suggested by Sell 2001) because large international banks, as key economic agents with their substantial interbank borrowing and lending (predominantly in floating U.S. dollar commitments) and investment activities have been at the heart of the globalization process. Important studies of financial contagion arising from integration and interdependence of banking systems and foreign exchange systems have examined the change in correlations between returns in different systems between periods of "crisis" and periods of "noncrisis." Studies such as those by Baig and Goldfajn (1998), Forbes and Rigobon (1999), Ellis and Lewis (2000), Dungey and Zhumabekova (2001), Caporale, Cipollini and Spagnolo (2005), and Rigobon (2004) have encountered problems relating to "crisis" sample size, heteroskedasticity, and issues relating to endogeneity.

In this chapter, a full pre-crisis period only is examined for the purpose of identifying undiversified interdependence of major Western banking systems in the decade leading up to the crisis. Sample size is not an issue. The evidence reported supports other evidence that the undiversified integration of major Western country and regional banking systems continued in the period prior to the current global financial crisis (for example, studies of Europe by Gual 2003; Kleimeier and Sander 2003; Simpson 2005). Because of the growing integration of the U.S. banking industry since the 1980s, other researchers have examined the associated issues of increasing systemic risk and prudential supervision (for example, Aharony and Swary 1983; Goodhart 1987; Goodhart and Schoenmaker 1995; Kaufman 1994; Swary, 1986). However, it is probably not coincidental that many of the above studies were undertaken at the time of the Latin American debt crisis when issues of international systemic risk first became apparent, spawning the first Basel Accord. The literature review has also revealed that the channel of contagion arising out of interbank borrowing and lending is evident (Simpson et al. 2005) and requires particular examination in future research as to how the risk may be mitigated. Perhaps this could be achieved, not withstanding increased moral hazard problems, through interbank deposit insurance (for example, Allen and Gale 2000; Calomiris 1999; Rochet and Tirole 1996).

CONCLUSION

Western banking systems in the United States, Western Europe, and the United Kingdom were highly interdependent and were the major drivers of the world banking sector in the period leading up to the global financial crisis. It was possible (in the absence of central bank intervention) that the collapse of one major Western bank could lead to a "domino" effect collapse of others both domestically and internationally. The evidence is demonstrated in analysis of both unlagged data and optimally lagged banking market data. Causality analysis initially indicates that the U.S. banking system has been a significant driver of the world banking system. Banking reform is also needed in Western systems. Economic reforms need to drive more developing countries into the financial services globalization fold. The dominance of Western banking interdependence needs to be diluted.

In the world's largest developed economy, the U.S. subprime mortgage market problems, overheated stock markets, and property markets as well as high energy prices up to early 2008 have conspired with Western banking sector interdependence to induce the 2008–2009 global financial crisis. This was evident prior to the onset of the rapid decline of share markets across the world, which defined the commencement of the crisis. At the time of this writing, a new global crisis is emerging, sourced in the financial mismanagement by several governments in the European Monetary Union. It is apparent that global financial system recovery and true global financial integration may have to wait a little longer.

NOTES

1. The market model used is a simplified version of Sharpe's capital asset pricing model (Sharpe 1964) as discussed and reported in Reilly and Brown (2003) who also feel that the analysis of indexed data is feasible in the study of risk/return relationships in stock markets, assuming the indices studied are representative. The indices used in this study are taken from Datastream database.
2. Unit root tests showed level series to be nonstationary and first differences (returns) to be stationary.
3. Proven in a VAR stability condition check test to be stable.

REFERENCES

Aharony, J., and I. Swary. 1983. "Contagion Effects of Bank Failures: Evidence from Capital Markets." *Journal of Business* 56:305–302.
Allen, F., and D. Gale. 2000. "Financial Contagion." *Journal of Political Economy* 108:1, 1–33.
Baig, T., and I. Goldfajn. 1998. "Financial Market Contagion and the Asian Crisis." *IMF Working Paper* WP98/155.
Calomiris, C. W. 1999. "Building and Incentive Compatible Safety Net", *Journal of Banking and Finance, Elsevier* 23:10 (October), 1499–1519.
Caporale, G. M., A. Cipollini, and N. Spagnolo. 2005. "Testing for Contagion: A Conditional Correlational Analysis." *Journal of Empirical Finance* 12:3, 476–489.
Dungey, M., and D. Zhumabekova. 2001. "Testing for Contagion Using Correlations: Some Words of Caution." *Working Paper* PB01–09, Centre for Pacific Basin Monetary and Economic Studies, Economic Research Department, Federal Reserve Bank of San Francisco.
Ellis, L., and E. Lewis. 2000. "The Response of Financial Markets in Australia and New Zealand to News About the Asian Crisis." *BIS Conference on International Financial Markets and the Implications for Monetary and Financial Stability* 8. Basle, October 1999, 25–26.
Forbes, K. J., and R. Rigobon. 1999. "No Contagion, Only Interdependence: Measuring Stock Market Co-Movements." *NBER Working Paper* 7267.
Goodhart, C. 1987. "Why do Banks Need a Central Bank." *Oxford Economic Papers* 39:75–89.
Goodhart, C., and Schoenmaker, D. 1995. "Should the Function of Monetary Policy and Banking Supervision be Separated?" *Oxford Economic Papers* 47:539–560.
Granger, C. W. J. 1988. "Some Recent Developments in a Concept of Causality." *Journal of Econometrics* 39:199–211.
Gual, J. 2003. "The Integration of EU Banking Markets." *IESE Business School Working Paper* D/504.

Kaufman, G. 1994. "Bank Contagion: A Review of Theory and Evidence." *Journal of Financial Services Research* 8:123–150.

Kleimeier, S., and H. Sander. 2003. "Convergence in Eurozone Retail Banking? What Interest Rate Pass-Through Tells Us About Monetary Policy Transmission, Competition and Integration." *Maastricht University LIFE Working Paper* 03–009.

Ratanapakorn, O., and S. C. Sharma. 2002. "Interrelationships Among Regional Stock Indices." *Review of Financial Economics* 11:91–108.

Reilly, F. K., and K. C. Brown. 2003. *Investment Analysis: Portfolio Management* Mason, OH: Thomson South-Western, 247–250.

Rigobon, R. 2004. "Identification Through Heteroskedasticity." *Review of Economics and Statistics* 85/4, forthcoming.

Rochet, J. C., and J. Tirole. 1996. "Interbank Lending and Systemic Risk", *Journal of Money Credit and Banking* 28:4 (November), 733–762.

Sell, F. L. 2001. *Contagion in Financial Markets* Cheltenham, UK: Edward Elgar Publishing Ltd.

Sharpe, W. F. 1964. "Capital Asset Prices: A Theory of Market Equilibrium under Conditions of Risk." *Journal of Finance* 19:3 (September), 425–442.

Simpson, J. L. 2005. "Financial Integration in Europe: Should the UK Banking System Formally Integrate." *University of Wollongong in Dubai Working Paper Series* 30.

Simpson, J. L. 2010. "Were There Warning Signals for the 2008/2009 Global Financial Crisis?" *Applied Financial Economics* Routledge (Taylor and Francis Group), 20:1 and 2 (January), 45–61.

Simpson, J. L., J. Evans, and L. De Mello. 2005. "Systemic Risk in the Major Euro Banking Markets; Evidence from Interbank Offered Rates." *Journal of Global Finance* forthcoming.

Swary, I. 1986. "Stock Market Reaction to Regulatory Action in the Continental Illinois Crisis." *Journal of Business* 59:451–473.

ABOUT THE AUTHOR

John L. Simpson is an associate professor in the School of Economics and Finance at Curtin University, in Western Australia. His PhD in the field of financial economics was obtained from the University of Western Australia. John is a fellow of the Finance and Securities Institute of Australasia and a professional member of the Economist's Society of Australia. His academic experience spans 20 years in the areas of teaching and learning and in research and development. A three-year secondment as an associate professor at the University of Wollongong in Dubai Business School was undertaken from 2003 to 2006. He also served as vice president of Australian Business in the Gulf Association, at the time the largest Australian business association of its type in the Middle East. John has traveled extensively during his career. He worked with the United Nations Development Program in Mongolia, in partnership with Curtin University, for academic development of Mongolian University lecturers. He is a board member of the Centre for Energy and Value and the editor of the Energy and Value Newsletter. He has around 40 articles in internationally refereed journals and around five book chapters on research in financial economics. His areas of research interest broadly relate to international banking, international finance, international business risk and risk management, and the financial economics of energy and value. He can be reached at simpsonj@cbs.curtin.edu.au.

PART FIVE

Regional Contagion

Perhaps the most palpable example of contagion occurs between two countries through trade or financial linkages. For this reason, links among geographical neighbors provide an interesting laboratory for the study of contagion. The chapters in this section focus on contagious episodes within regions such as East Asia and Europe.

One study examines linkages among China, Japan, and South Korea. These near-neighbors represent radically different types of economies. China is a manufacturing giant, yet has a nascent financial sector. Japan has the largest equity market in Asia and a fully developed and sophisticated economy. South Korea lies between Japan and China in terms of having a fully developed financial sector, and it possesses an equity market of long standing, but one that is not as large as its history and the size of the South Korean economy might suggest. Europe has its own emerging financial markets, particularly in the countries of Central, Eastern, and Southeastern Europe (CESE). These countries are characterized by a heavy reliance on bank financing, particularly from banks whose ownership lies outside the region.

This common reliance on external funding sources suggests a potential avenue of contagion. For example, the home country of a major foreign bank lending to these emerging European nations could provide a shock that would affect several countries in the CESE region simultaneously. Alternatively, a financial shock originating in one of the CESE countries could serve as notice of more widespread problems in that region, thereby causing a reduction in the extension of credit to other nations in the region. The result would be reduced economic activity across the region. This theme is amplified by a more concentrated focus on the multinational banking system as a means by which contagious episodes could arise.

CHAPTER 33

Efficiency, Cointegration, and Contagion in East Asian Stock Markets

Implications for Investors and Policy Makers

A.S.M. SOHEL AZAD
SAAD AZMAT
Accounting and Finance, Faculty of Business and Economics, Monash University

INTRODUCTION

Market efficiency is one of the fundamental concepts in finance. It implies that when markets are completely efficient all information is fully captured in prices. Any informational advantage that an investor has would be quickly acted on and eventually be incorporated in the prices. Any profit from trading would quickly dissipate with no gains to be made from further trading of the asset. With increasing technological sophistication, the change would be instantaneous making information-based trading risky. In efficient markets, any price change is completely random and unpredictable. Moreover, in efficient markets, asset returns fully capture their underlying risks, making excessive returns highly unlikely. The study of individual market efficiency helps us to understand the behavior of specific markets while enabling investors to exploit potential arbitrage opportunities. However, in a world with increasing globalization, high trade interaction, and the easing of regulations governing the movement of capital, investors are able to benefit from international portfolio diversification and arbitrage opportunities traversing several markets. Therefore, studies of joint efficiencies, cointegration, and contagion have assumed paramount importance.

This chapter is based on the work of Azad (2009) published in *Asian Economic Journal* and discusses the efficiencies, both individual and joint, cointegration and contagion among three East Asian stock markets of China, Japan, and South Korea. The need to study the behavior of several stock markets has encouraged academicians, policy makers, and the international fund managers to know whether these markets are truly cointegrated and contagious. Cointegration reflects the long-term equilibrium contemporaneous relationship between stock prices in each market while contagion reflects the causal transmission of shocks from one market to the other.[1] The general notion is that if there exists strong contagion between two markets, it makes each susceptible to shocks in the other. It also implies that volatility in one market will spill over to other.[2]

There does not exist any conclusive evidence that might explain the link between cointegration and market efficiency. The existing empirical literature uses several assumptions to clarify this relationship. One of these assumptions is that if asset prices in two different markets are efficient, then these prices cannot be cointegrated (see also Granger 1986). The second assumption relates to statistical cointegration and market integration. The premise is that if asset prices in two different markets are integrated of the same order, that is, $I(1)$, then these prices must be cointegrated. However, combining the two assumption results in an incorrect conclusion that integrated financial markets cannot be efficient. These issues have been discussed in the literature leading to the assertion that cointegration is unrelated to market integration and efficiency (see Lence and Falk 2005 for details).

East Asian equity markets, namely, China, Japan, and South Korea, are a good sample to examine efficiency, cointegration, and contagion for they are geographically and economically close to each other and, hence, are expected to exert strong influence on individual as well as joint market efficiency. Before looking at the empirical results and implications, we provide an overview of the three markets in the following section.

BACKGROUND OF THE MARKETS

China: China's equity market came into existence in 1990, when both Shanghai Stock Exchange (SSE) and Shenzhen Stock Exchange (SHSE) were created. China's equity market is less developed than Japan and South Korean equity markets. It facilitates the trading of two types of shares, one for domestic investors (Share A) and other foreign investors (Share B). In the early 1990s, the market experienced its first peak led by intense speculation and rent-seeking activities. The trade returned to moderate levels in the mid-1990s (see Wong 2006). Throughout the 1990s, the market remained volatile; between the late 1990s and 2000 the trend remained upward. Market capitalization, liquidity, and trading volume doubled in 2000.

Japan: In terms of market capitalization, Japan's equity market is the largest in Asia Pacific region and the second largest in the world. It started equity trading in the late 1800s when the Tokyo and Osaka stock exchanges were set up. In late 1989, Japan's equity market experienced both bubble and burst while the market capitalization exceeded that of the United States sometime between 1989 and 1990.

South Korea: South Korea's equity market has been in existence since 1956 with the set up of the country's first exchange, the Daehan Stock Exchange (DSE). The DSE was reorganized in 1962 as a joint-stock company while it became the Korea Stock Exchange in 1963. It is highly regulated. However, unlike other Asia Pacific stock markets it has maintained a sustained growth in listings, trading volume, and market capitalization.

The price trend shows that the Chinese stock market, as compared to the Japanese and Korean stock markets, is extremely volatile. Apart from the high speculation, the high volatility is attributed to three main factors (see Wong 2006). First, the stock market is used by the government as a vehicle for raising funds for state-owned enterprises. Second, the flow of capital and competition among financial assets was significantly curbed by the financial regime. Third, the legal framework was not strong enough to offer sufficient protection to the share holders.

EFFICIENCY, COINTEGRATION, AND CONTAGION

Using the results from Azad (2009) this section reviews: (1) individual efficiency; (2) cointegration (or joint market efficiency); and (3) the contagion in China, Japan, and South Korean stock markets. Each of these hypotheses is tested using different methodologies. Azad (2009) uses the random walk and variance ratio tests to examine the individual market efficiency. The joint efficiency is examined through two cointegration tests. The contagion hypothesis is examined through modified Wald tests of Granger causality. The tests were applied to the daily closing prices of all the three stock exchanges: Shanghai Stock Exchange (SSE, China), Tokyo Stock Exchange (TSE, Japan), and Korea Stock Exchange (KSE, South Korea).

The test statistics indicate that the Chinese stock market is characterized by intertemporal inefficiency under the hypothesis of individual as well as joint market efficiency. Japanese and South Korean markets, however, exhibit market efficiency under the hypothesis of individual market efficiency while these two markets along with the Chinese markets are found to be jointly inefficient. This is expected as the individual inefficiency of the Chinese market is strong enough to make them jointly inefficient. The joint inefficiency also implies that the three markets are cointegrated and have a long-term relationship. Tests for causality are also carried out by Azad (2009) to detect if there exists any contagion among the markets. Causality is examined from Tokyo (TSE) and Seoul (KSE) to Shanghai (SSE) because of time difference, which entails that the closing stock prices are observed at different hours. SSE is the last to close of the three markets, which implies that investors have access to closing prices in Tokyo and Seoul on the same day. The results indicate that even though the markets are cointegrated, there is not much evidence of contagion between three markets. However, when testing for pairwise contagion, there exists evidence of bidirectional causality/contagion between Japan and South Korea. Let us review in the following subsection the implications of these results.

Implications for the Investors

First, the Chinese market is found to be inefficient while Japan and South Korea are found to be efficient, implying that there might exist more opportunities for arbitrage in the Chinese market while these gains would be minimal in Japanese and South Korean markets. If there does not exist a causal relationship between two markets then it implies that there are gains to be made from pairwise portfolio diversification between the two markets. The (long-term) causal relationship between Japan and South Korea indicates that there would be no long-range benefits from pairwise portfolio diversification between these two markets. However, the noncausal relationship between China–Japan and China–Korea implies that there are some gains to be made from pair-wise portfolio diversification between these markets. Related to the above findings on individual and joint market efficiency, the investors in these markets may try to exploit the cases of market inefficiency to generate market returns. But they are advised to be more cautious in forecasting the returns. Other investors may also try to exploit the opportunity of informational inefficiency as observed in these markets and these gains might dissipate quickly. The investors also need to be cautious about the information flows, the noise, and the overall understanding of the markets they are interested in.

Implications for Policy Makers

The market inefficiencies, both in the individual and cointegration sense, give the speculators the chance to manipulate the prices. Any short-term price movements may persuade the weak market players to wrongfully estimate the returns from their stocks. Therefore, we suggest that the regulators control unrealistic price movements in order to protect the interests of the weak market players and to facilitate the potential development of the capital markets. The regulators and policy makers also have to constantly monitor the financial markets to avoid potential contagion effects. For instance, the causal relationship between Japan and South Korea implies that a potential financial crisis can easily dissipate from one market to the other. Therefore, effective regulations and capital controls should be put in place to avert potential losses. The policy makers should also look at the possible reasons for the presence of this contagion effect. Geographic closeness and economic integration could be possible causes of this contagion effect between Japan and South Korea. Hence, better and more coordinated policy measures would be important to ensure the smooth progression of the two economies.

CONCLUDING REMARKS

Ignorance of joint market efficiencies and contagion effects during the Asian financial crisis and the recent subprime crisis has badly hurt interlinked and interdependent economies. The analysis of market efficiency, interdependences, and contagion of the three East Asian stock markets offers important insight into both opportunities for portfolio diversification and crisis prevention. The study indicates that the Chinese stock market is (informationally) inefficient while Japanese and South Korean stock markets are efficient. Yet, the three markets are jointly inefficient in the cointegrating sense. Further, although these three markets are cointegrated, the contagion effect exists only between Japanese and South Korean stock markets. The results in this study are not against the general wisdom that the developed and emerging markets are by and large efficient while underdeveloped markets are not. Although the causal relationship between Japan and South Korea suggests market inefficiencies and possible short-term arbitrage opportunities, the evidence of noncausality (no contagion) for other pairs, namely, China–Korea and China–Japan, indicates that knowledge of past return behavior in one market is unlikely to improve forecasts of returns in another. There is a need for future researchers to use more high-frequency data to explore the reasons for the presence of contagion effect between different East Asian economies. To deepen the understanding, the future studies can explore the fundamental links including real and potential, and the impact of the fundamental links on the market efficiency and contagion. This will allow the policy makers and market participants to gauge the potential driving forces of efficiency and contagion.

NOTES

1. Some define *contagion* more restrictively as the excess comovement usually observed during a financial crisis. See World Bank classification/definition of contagion.
2. The literature on market contagion typically looks at volatility spillovers using the ARCH/GARCH approach. Because we focus more on the interrelationships, we do it here investigating the long-run equilibrium relationship and the causal relationship.

REFERENCES

Azad, A. S. M. Sohel. 2009. "Efficiency, Cointegration and Contagion in Equity Markets: Evidence from China, Japan and South Korea." *Asian Economic Journal* 23:93–118.

Granger, C. W. J. 1986. "Developments in the Study of Cointegrated Economic Variables." *Oxford Bulletin of Economics and Statistics* 48:213–218.

Lence, S., and B. Falk. 2005. "Cointegration, Market Integration and Market Efficiency." *Journal of International Money and Finance* 24:873–890.

Wong, S. M. L. 2006. "China's Stock Market: A Marriage of Capitalism and Socialism." *Cato Journal* 26:389–424.

ABOUT THE AUTHORS

A. S. M. Sohel Azad is an associate professor of finance and banking at University of Chittagong, Bangladesh. He received an MBA from the University of Chittagong, Bangladesh, an MSc from the Ritsumeikan Asia Pacific University, Japan, and is currently at the final stage of his PhD in finance at Monash University, Australia. Mr. Sohel has extensively published in the area of market efficiency and derivative markets, and has received numerous prizes and awards for his academic achievements. He was a visiting research fellow (2004–2005) at Kobe Gakuin University, Japan, and received the Academic Excellence Award (2006) from the United Nations University (UNU). He has written a book on Japanese banking efficiency and contributed chapters in different edited books.

Saad Azmat holds a master's degree in economics from the University of British Columbia. Currently, he is pursuing his PhD in accounting and finance at Monash University. He is the director of Barakah Group, Australia, which offers Shariah-compliant financial solutions. He is also a faculty member in the business school at the Lahore University of Management Sciences.

CHAPTER 34

Regional Financial Interlinkages and Financial Contagion within Europe

ZSÓFIA ÁRVAI*
KARL DRIESSEN
İNCI ÖTKER-ROBE
International Monetary Fund

W ith foreign ownership levels of the banking systems in Central, Eastern, and Southeastern Europe (CESE) among the highest in the world, the degree of financial interlinkages among Western European and CESE countries has grown markedly in the past decade. Foreign ownership of CESE banking systems has brought important benefits to the host countries, including advanced technology and risk management techniques and increased access to cross-border funding, and contributed to rapid financial deepening in CESE countries. At the same time, the rapid growth of financial links has also raised susceptibility to contagion for the host countries, as well as the home countries of the foreign banks active in many CESE countries. The ongoing global crisis has increased the importance of capturing the potential spillover effects brought about by these financial interlinkages.

Bank credit to the private sector in CESE countries has expanded rapidly, by about 23 percent a year on average in real terms between 2000 and 2007 across the region. Although this phenomenon partly reflected the process of catching up from low levels of financial intermediation, the fast convergence in credit ratios was mainly driven by similar business strategies of (mostly) Western European banking groups that dominate the banking sectors of most CESE countries. These banks have been taking advantage of the opportunity to expand their presence in CESE banking systems, with such operations accounting for a substantial share of their profits.

With the brisk pace of private sector credit growth, dependence on nondeposit funding has increased in many countries in emerging Europe. Loan-to-deposit ratios (LTD) rose in most countries, particularly in the Baltics where LTDs roughly

---

*Based on Árvai, Driessen, and Ötker-Robe. 2009. "Regional Financial Interlinkages and Financial Contagion within Europe." *Czech Journal of Economics and Finance* 59. The views expressed here are those of the authors and should not be attributed to the IMF, its executive board, or its management.

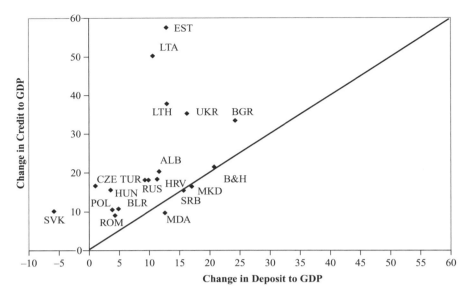

Exhibit 34.1 Regional Financial Interlinkages and Financial Contagion within Europe
Source: International Financial Statistics and authors' calculations.

doubled from the early 2000s, and in Ukraine, Hungary, and Russia where they ranged from 120 to 150 percent in 2007. Except in a few cases, the changes in bank credit-to-GDP ratios significantly exceeded those in the ratio of bank deposits-to-GDP, suggesting that deposit growth has not been able to keep up with the rapid credit growth in recent years (Exhibit 34.1). High and rising LTDs therefore required increasing reliance on foreign funding channeled through the banking sector in several countries. This reflects the relatively undeveloped state of domestic capital markets as a funding source in most of these countries, and easy access by the mostly foreign-owned banks to cheap funding from their parents before the global financial and economic crisis.[1]

The differences in funding structures suggest that some countries have been more exposed than others to financial market disturbances originating from advanced markets or to spillovers from problems in other countries in the region. Indeed, following the intensification of the global financial crisis in the wake of Lehman's bankruptcy, CESE banking systems heavily dependent on foreign funding to support credit growth faced a sudden shortfall of, or costly access to funds. Although reputational risks and long-term business links give incentives to parent banks to support their subsidiaries in general, the degree of support depends on market conditions; as funding conditions in home countries became more difficult during the crisis, banks have been pressured to slow lending and liquidity provision abroad and at home.

POSSIBLE PROPAGATION CHANNELS OF REGIONAL SHOCKS

In general, there are a number of channels through which a financial shock can be transmitted between home and host countries' banking systems (Exhibit 34.2).

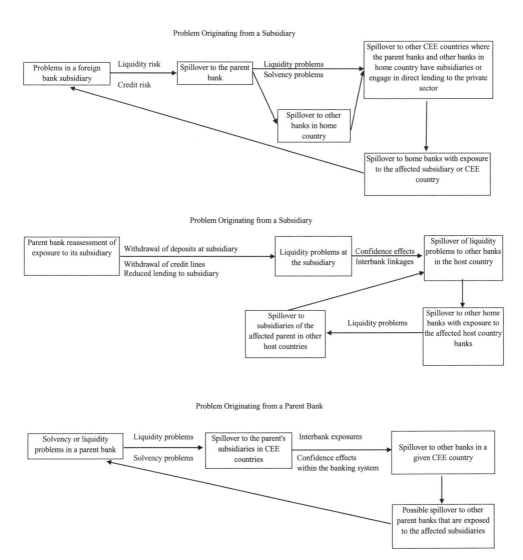

Exhibit 34.2   Possible Channels of Regional Financial Contagion

One channel is the presence of a "common lender" that may be the main funding source for several countries. The private sectors of two countries in the region, A and B, for instance, may borrow mainly from the banking system of a third country, C (the common lender). A shock affecting A may result in liquidity or solvency pressures in the banks of C, provided that the latter is highly exposed to A. The problems in A could then spill over to B, even when B's economy is not directly linked to A's, simply because of the presence of the third country, C, in both A and B. The parent bank's presence in the region could therefore transfer a shock in one country to other countries in the region in which the parent bank has significant operations. Other parent banks exposed to each of the affected host countries (directly or indirectly through their subsidiaries) could be affected, creating second-round effects.

Similarly, a sudden reassessment of a parent bank's exposure to a host country could expose its subsidiary to sudden liquidity problems. Contagion could also go in the other direction, with host countries affected by problems in a parent bank. Liquidity or solvency problems experienced by a parent bank could spread to its subsidiaries or branches in other countries. Host country banking systems could be affected through a deterioration of confidence in the subsidiaries or branches and/or through direct funding exposure to the parent bank. A spillover to a host banking system could also be propagated through a change in the market's risk assessment of a parent bank that belongs to a banking group with a deteriorated financial standing.

The magnitude of potential contagion effects through these channels depends in general on: (1) the size of the exposures of home banks (common lender) to the host country with a problem; and (2) the dependence of the host country on funds from the home country. As pointed out in Sbracia and Zaghini (2001), three conditions must be satisfied for such channels of transmission to operate: (1) the common lender's exposure to the country initially affected by a problem must be large, implying substantial losses, and in turn a need to restore capital; (2) the lender must be an important source of funds for other countries; and (3) the potentially affected countries must not have other sources of funding readily available.

CROSS-BORDER EXPOSURES AND REGIONAL CONTAGION RISK IN CESE COUNTRIES

To get a sense of the magnitudes of cross-border linkages between CESE and Western European countries, we used consolidated claims data of BIS reporting banks on individual CESE countries.[2] From the lenders' perspectives, the statistics provide the exposures of Western European countries to a given CESE economy. From the borrowers' perspectives, they give an idea of the magnitude and distribution of the dependence of CESE economies on Western European banking systems, and illustrate the magnitude of control over a country's assets and liabilities by foreign banks. They do not necessarily give an indication of exposure to potential funding risks through the banking sector.

The analysis of foreign claims shows that most CESE economies are indeed heavily exposed to Western European banks, either directly by their nonfinancial private sector or through their local banking systems. Austria, Germany, and Italy account for the largest share of foreign claims for CESE countries as a whole, while non-European reporting banks hold less than 10 percent of the total claims on CESE (Exhibit 34.3). The exposures are significant for many CESE countries, both in relation to the recipient countries' GDP and the size of their banking system assets. These exposures could contribute to the potential vulnerabilities if their composition reflects heavy reliance on foreign funding and if the exposures are heavily concentrated. Most CESE countries have concentrated exposures measured by foreign claims, particularly to banks in Austria and Italy, as well as to France and Germany, and the Baltic countries have large exposures to Sweden.

On the contrary, the magnitude of Western European bank exposures to CESE is far smaller, with a few exceptions. For Austria, the foreign claims of the reporting banks on emerging Europe amounted to more than 70 percent of Austria's GDP

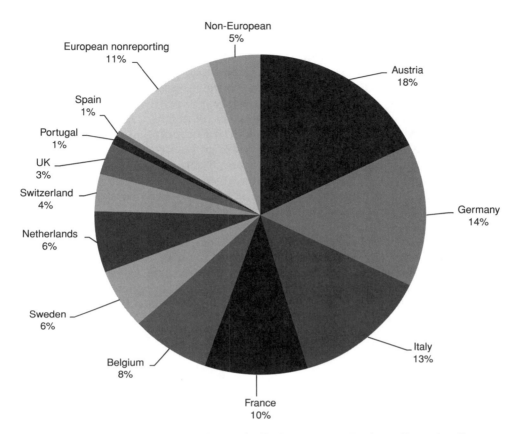

Exhibit 34.3   Shares in Foreign Claims of All BIS Reporting Banks on Emerging Europe, December 2007

Sources: BIS Quarterly Review, June 2008, Table 9A (immediate borrower basis) and authors' calculations.

and 26 percent of its banking system assets at end-2007. The exposures of banks in Belgium and Sweden are also relatively high in terms of their GDP (25 percent and 20 percent, respectively at end-2007), but much less so in terms of banking system assets (at most 10 percent). For the remaining countries, the exposures to CESE countries are negligible, including for France, Germany, and Italy with active presence in the region.

What do the stylized facts on the exposures of Western and CESE countries say in terms of exposure to contagion risks? We explore two main forms of contagion affecting a CESE country: (1) exposure to a shock originating from the foreign bank's home country, and (2) exposure to regional contagion triggered by a problem in another CESE country to which a Western European country has significant exposures.

The first contagion channel involves a shock transmitted from a home to a host country, taking as trigger a country in Western Europe with active banks in the CESE region. In general, the larger a CESE country's exposure to the trigger home country, the stronger would be the adverse effects from problems in the home country banks. The measure of absolute dependence, defined as the amount of claims owed to a home country as a share of the CESE country's GDP provides an indication of the extent to which a given CESE country will be affected. Exhibit 34.4 provides an illustration of the impact of a shock from home to host country under the assumptions of Austria, Italy, and Sweden being the home countries.

The second contagion channel analyzes how problems in one CESE country might spread to others in the region. One such mechanism is provided by the "common lender channel," in which a Western European banking sector has a large exposure to a trigger CESE country and is an important source of credit for other countries in the region. A shock affecting the trigger country may result in pressures in the banks of the common lender, given its high exposure to the trigger country, and could spill over to another CESE country, simply because of the large presence of the common lender in both countries.

We now focus on this second propagation channel, and adopt, with some variations, an approach suggested in Sbracia and Zaghini (2001), to the CESE countries to compute two indices of exposure to regional contagion. The indices attempt to evaluate contagion exposure in terms of dependence of each country on a common lender that is exposed to another country experiencing a problem. Since the calculation of such indices requires the knowledge of the trigger country, which can only be known ex-post, an ex-ante indicator is computed instead, using as trigger the country to which the common lender has the highest exposure. See Árvai, Driessen, and Ötker-Robe (2009) for more details of the methodology on the contagion indices.

The following two indices have been computed:

1. $I_i^1 = ad_{CL}^i AE_j^{CL}$
2. $I_i^2 = ad_{CL}^i AE_j^{CL} REB_i^{CL}$; where $REB_i^{CL} = \dfrac{A_i^{CL}}{\sum\limits_{h \in DC} A_h^{CL} - \max\limits_{j \neq i} A_j^{CL}}$

For Index 1 in (1), ad_{CL}^i is the "absolute dependence" of country i on the common lender, defined as foreign claims owed by country i to the common lender (CL)'s banks in country i's GDP. AE_j^{CL} is the ex-ante "absolute exposure" of the common lender to the trigger country (the country with which it has the highest exposure). The absolute exposure of the common lender to country j is defined as the ratio (in percentage terms) of the common lender's claims vis-à-vis country j to its own funds (proxied by the common lender's banking system assets).

For Index 2 in (2), REB_i^{CL} indicates some measure of rebalancing, that is, the amount of funds that may be cut from a borrower country i, following a problem in a trigger country the common lender has exposure to. It is defined as the amount of claims of the common lender on country i, A_i^{CL} in ratio to the total amount of funds lent to all other developing countries, excluding the amount of claims on the trigger country. This ratio is an increasing function of the amount of funds that the common lender provides to country i and to the trigger country j.

The indices have been computed under several assumptions for the common lender and associated trigger countries. In particular, Austria, Italy, Sweden, and Germany have been chosen as the common lenders, since most countries in

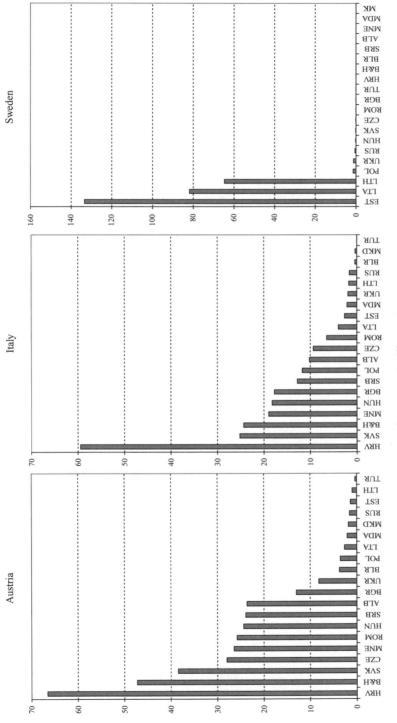

Exhibit 34.4 The Impact of a Shock from Home to Host Country—An Illustration
Sources: Authors' computations based on BIS December 2007 data.

the region are highly dependent on Austria, but many also depend on Italy and Germany; the Baltic countries are dependent predominantly on Sweden. The three countries to which each common lender has the largest exposure among the other CESE countries have been chosen as the triggers. Exhibit 34.5 illustrates the indices for the foreign claims concept for a selected group of common lenders: Austria, Italy, Sweden, and Germany.[3]

The indices provide some interesting results for the degree of exposure of the CESE countries to regional contagion and their sensitivity to the source of contagion:

In general, the larger the dependence of a country on funds from home country banks (directly or indirectly through the domestic banking systems), and the larger the exposure of home country banks to the trigger country, the higher the values of the contagion indices. Taking into consideration the possibility of rebalancing in the common lender's funding through a potential cutback in credit lines reduces the value of the index significantly (Index 2 versus Index 1). The countries for which absolute dependence on foreign banks is lower drop out of the group of most exposed countries under the second index.

Contagion indices are the highest when the common lender has activities substantially concentrated in the region. In turn, the indices are smaller when the common lender has large presence in, but smaller exposure to CESE in terms of its economic size, because in the latter case, the exposures to any country in the region are economically too small to affect the funds available to others when problems emerge in a trigger country. Austria as the common lender would hence have the highest effect in propagating shocks across a wide range of CESE countries.

The indices also suggest that potential contagion between Sweden and the Baltic countries is highly concentrated. Although the Baltic countries exhibit the highest exposure indices for a hypothetical problem triggered in Estonia, Latvia, or Lithuania, a potential spillover to the other CESE countries through the common lender channel seems to be contained within the Baltic region. This is because the dependence of non-Baltic CESE countries on Sweden is immaterial, making the likelihood of any rebalancing effect rather small.

Although differences in magnitude of the exposure indices across scenarios signal varying degrees of spillover effects among countries, the group of countries most exposed to regional contagion remains broadly similar.

It is important to note that the contagion exposure indices computed here do not represent an assessment of the financial or macroeconomic vulnerability and stability of individual countries studied. Although the group of countries most exposed to regional contagion remains broadly similar regardless of which financial claims concept is used, these indices only measure the degree to which shocks from foreign markets can affect a given country, and help identify the likely pressure points associated with a regional shock originating from a given country.

CONCLUSION

The high degree of financial interlinkages in the region and the risk of regional contagion argue strongly for a more regional approach to managing potential vulnerabilities. Our findings highlight a number of policy implications.

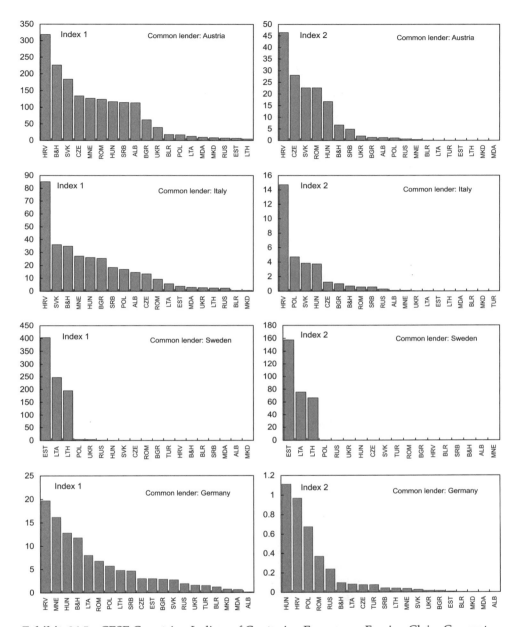

Exhibit 34.5   CESE Countries: Indices of Contagion Exposure—Foreign Claim Concept

Sources: Authors' computations based on BIS December 2007 data. The figures illustrate the regional impact of a hypothetical shock to a country, to which each common lender has the largest absolute exposure.

First, in addition to strengthening bank supervision and prudential regulation where warranted, close cooperation between home and host supervisory authorities is needed. At a minimum, this calls for conducting coordinated inspections of internationally active banks and undertaking joint risk assessments. Initiatives are needed to develop cooperative arrangements for crisis management, some of which are already taking place.

Second, given the extent of susceptibility to regional contagion that can spread very quickly, better contingency planning is essential. There is a need to develop contingency plans to deal with more systemic disturbances associated with regional spillovers of financial troubles and contagion, including those triggered by individual institutions highly active with concentrated exposures. Crisis simulations for regional spillovers could be conducted by monetary and financial supervisory authorities to help develop coordinating procedures in crisis management and to test the adequacy of internal and international processes, potential weaknesses in communication channels and procedures, and the understanding of the responsibilities within and between countries, and the nature of information and data needs.

Third, the rapid growth and cross-border integration of the CESE financial sectors require that stress tests conducted to assess the stability of financial systems take greater account of regional spillovers.

The analysis of cross-border financial linkages and contagion channels discussed in this paper could provide a useful surveillance tool. The magnitude of cross-border exposures could help in assessing the extent of susceptibility to regional contagion arising from the reliance on foreign banks. Contagion indices can be used to identify the likely pressure points, to capture potential spillover effects and propagation channels of a regional shock originating from a given country. The analysis could in particular help in evaluating the risks a home or a host country might face in light of the vulnerabilities that may be building up elsewhere in the region.

NOTES

1. In many cases, the business model of the banks (e.g., granting long-term foreign exchange denominated loans to unhedged borrowers) made the increasing reliance on foreign funding particularly risky.

2. The BIS statistics differentiate between (a) cross-border claims, (b) local claims of foreign affiliates in foreign currency in a host country, (c) local claims of foreign affiliates in local currency, and (d) domestic claims in the reporting country. In BIS terminology, (a) + (b) refers to "international claims," while (a) + (b) + (c) refers to "foreign claims." That is, foreign claims include local claims of foreign-owned subsidiaries in local currency, which, to a large extent are financed by local deposits in local currency. Foreign claims correspond to the direct gross on-balance sheet exposure of foreign banks to individual countries, while international claims represent the level of foreign bank claims that could result in foreign exchange outflows.

3. The same exercise can be repeated with the concept of international claims data and with international claims data only on CESE banking sectors.

REFERENCES

Árvai, Zs., K. Driessen, and Ötker-Robe, İ. 2009. "Regional Financial Interlinkages and Financial Contagion within Europe." *Czech Journal of Economics and Finance* 59.

Sbracia, M., and A. Zaghini. 2001. "The Role of the Banking System in the International Transmission of Shocks." *Banca D'Italia, Temi di Discussione del Servizio Studi* No. 409.

ABOUT THE AUTHORS

Zsófia Árvai is an economist in the monetary and capital markets department at the International Monetary Fund. She previously held various positions in economics and research, as well as the financial stability departments of the National Bank of Hungary. Her research has been mostly in the areas of the monetary transmission mechanism in emerging economies, financial sector development, and financial stability.

Karl Driessen is a deputy division chief in the monetary and capital markets department at the International Monetary Fund.

İnci Ötker-Robe is a division chief at the monetary and capital markets department of the International Monetary Fund, where she heads the financial sector analysis division. She received a PhD in economics from Carnegie Mellon University in Pittsburgh. She has written extensively and published articles on financial stability, capital controls and their liberalization, exchange rate regimes and speculative attacks, monetary policy and inflation targeting, financial interlinkages and contagion, and more recently has been working on systemically important large complex financial institutions and financial regulation. She co-authored and co-edited the book *Rapid Credit Growth in Central and Eastern Europe: Endless Boom or Early Warning* (2007).

Domino Effects from Cross-Border Exposures[*]

HANS DEGRYSE
CentER—Tilburg University, European Banking Center, TILEC, and CESifo

MUHAMMAD ATHER ELAHI
CentER—Tilburg University

MARÍA FABIANA PENAS
CentER—Tilburg University, European Banking Center, and TILEC

INTRODUCTION

The instability of the banking sector in a country may have severe effects on other sectors of the economy. However, a shock can also be easily transmitted across borders due to an unsustainable loss on bank lending to foreign counterparties. In this chapter, we focus on cross-border financial contagion, defined as the situation when an idiosyncratic shock that hits the foreign counterparty of a banking system results in nonpayment of its foreign claims. If the banking system's aggregate equity is not enough to absorb this shock, the affected banking system will not fulfill its foreign obligations in the next round. This starts a domino effect that impacts other banking systems worldwide. Our focus is then on contagion through the banking system due to nonrepayment of cross-border credit exposures.

This chapter studies cross-border contagion for the first time using data on foreign claims from the BIS. Second, although most papers focus on domestic interbank contagion at one point in time, this chapter provides an extension by looking at the evolution of cross-border contagion over the period 1999 to 2006. Third, we attempt to identify the size of a systemically important shock for cross-border contagion.

---

[*]We thank Robert W. Kolb for his suggestions on a previous draft. This chapter is mainly based on Degryse, H., M. Elahi, and M. Penas. 2010. "Cross-Border Exposures and Financial Contagion." *International Review of Finance* 10, 209–240. Hans Degryse holds the TILEC-AFM Chair on Financial Market Regulation.

DATA AND METHODOLOGY

We use *bank credit* to borrowers in foreign countries as the source of cross-border exposures. These foreign claims include the exposure of a country's banking system to all sectors (i.e., bank, nonbank, and public). BIS provides information on such foreign claims of reporting countries to the rest of the world in the *Consolidated Banking Statistics*.[1] It covers data on (national) contractual lending by the headquartered banks and all of their branches and subsidiaries worldwide to borrowers residing outside the country of origin (where the bank's headquarters is stationed) on a consolidated basis (i.e., net of interoffice account). Further, we use foreign claims on immediate borrower basis, that is, the allocation of foreign claims of reporting banks to the country of operations of the contractual counterparty. It means that, for example, we employ the foreign claims of British banks on *all* financial institutions operating in the United States (irrespective of their nationality).

The reporting institutions in each country include all institutions that are allowed to *receive deposits and/or close substitutes for deposits and grant credits or invest in securities on their account*. Our sample includes foreign claims outstanding at the end of each year for the banking systems of 14 European countries, Canada, Japan, and the United States, for a long time period (1999–2006).[2]

Data on bank equity for the financial institutions of each reporting country are taken from BankScope. We sum up ordinary equity of all financial institutions except the Central banks to get the aggregate bank equity at country level for each year.

We use the methodology of Upper and Worms (2004) for our contagion exercises. We first explain the intuition behind this methodology in plain English. In a second step, which may be skipped by the less technically oriented reader, we introduce matrix notation. Consider as initial shock the default of an individual country (i.e., the default of its bank, nonbank, and public sector). We call this the triggering country. Another country's banking system (i.e., a recipient country) that has claims on this triggering country may go into default. This happens when the capital of this recipient banking system, which serves as a cushion against shocks, is insufficient to absorb the shock resulting from the default of the triggering country. We have domino effects or contagion when there is at least one recipient country's banking system that has insufficient capital available. After the initial domino effects, further domino effects may arise. This happens when the joint default of the triggering country and the failing recipient countries in previous rounds leads to too large losses for some remaining banking systems. That is, the capital of these banking systems is too low to absorb the shock caused by the failure of the triggering country and the previously failing countries. The contagion ends when the banking capital of all remaining recipient countries is sufficient to absorb the shock, or when all recipient countries have already failed.

We now present the methodology in a more formal way. As mentioned before, the less technically oriented reader can immediately move to the results section. The methodology of Upper and Worms (2004) simulates a mechanical chain of domino effects caused by an exogenous initial shock. Our exogenous shock is the default of a triggering country (i.e., its bank, nonbank, and public sector) on its foreign liabilities. As a result, the banking system of the recipient countries suffers from nonpayment of its foreign claims on the triggering country. The banking system of a recipient country defaults in the first round when its foreign claims against the bank, nonbank, and public sector of the triggering country exceed its aggregate bank equity. The failing recipient countries in each round may affect other countries in successive rounds due to their combined effects. The contagion process stops when there is no new country that defaults in that round (i.e., combined foreign liabilities of both the trigger and failed recipients of previous rounds are less than the bank equity of each nonfailed recipient country). We employ this methodology over our entire sample period 1999–2006 to evaluate the impact of contagion over time.

We can represent the countries' foreign claims and liabilities as follows:

$$X = \begin{bmatrix} \overbrace{x_{1,1} \cdots x_{1,j} \cdots x_{1,N}}^{\text{Reporting Countries}} & \overbrace{x_{1,N+1} \cdots x_{1,N+M}}^{\text{Non–Reporting Countries}} \\ \vdots \ddots \vdots \ddots \vdots & \vdots \ddots \vdots \\ x_{i,1} \cdots x_{i,j} \cdots x_{i,N} & x_{i,N+1} \cdots x_{i,N+M} \\ \vdots \ddots \vdots \ddots \vdots & \vdots \ddots \vdots \\ x_{N,1} \cdots x_{N,j} \cdots x_{N,N} & x_{N,N+1} \cdots x_{N,N+M} \end{bmatrix} \text{ with } \sum_{j=1}^{N+M} x_{ij} = a_i \text{ and } \sum_{i=1}^{N} x_{ij} = l_j$$

where x_{ij} are the consolidated foreign claims of the banking system of country i on the bank, nonbank, and public sector of country j, N is the number of reporting countries ($N = 17$ in our case) and M is the number of nonreporting countries. The summation $\sum_{j=1}^{N+M} x_{ij} = a_i$ represents the total foreign claims of country i on the rest of the world. Similarly, $\sum_{i=1}^{N} x_{ij} = l_j$ represents the total foreign liabilities of country j toward the rest of the reporting countries. This matrix also shows the foreign claims on the M nonreporting countries.

The aggregate bank equity has an initial value C_i equal to the ordinary equity directly observed from the balance sheets of financial institutions in country i. It is reduced by the amount of the foreign claims of country i against the triggering country in the first round, and then by the cumulative amount of the foreign claims of country i against all failing recipient countries in each round of contagion. Therefore, the country i defaults when:

$$C_i - \sum_{j=1}^{N+M} \lambda_j \theta x_{ij} < 0$$

where C_i represents aggregate bank equity of country i, λ_j is a dummy variable whose value is 1 if the country j defaults, and 0 otherwise, θ shows the percentage of loss given default (LGD), whereas x_{ij} is obtained from the previous matrix representing the consolidated foreign claims of country i on country j.

RESULTS

We present simulation results for two different cases: (1) *all* banks are internationally exposed; (2) only *large* banks are internationally exposed. We report results for 60 percent LGD.

In Case 1, we investigate cross-border contagion of a default of the triggering country on all its foreign liabilities, under the assumption that foreign claims towards a recipient country are distributed among all banks in that country. Cross-border contagion occurs when the banking system in at least one of the recipient countries is not able to absorb the shock triggered by the nonpayment of its foreign claims for LGD of 60 percent (i.e., the banking system's aggregate equity is less than the foreign claims on the triggering country). In this exercise, the national banking system acts as one unit, that is, we assume that all banks hypothetically pool their equity to compensate the losses incurred on foreign claims to defaulting countries. We have 17 reporting countries that may be a trigger. We label these as *reporting triggers*. We also have the claims of the banking systems of the different reporting countries on 20 nonreporting countries, which we label as *nonreporting triggers*. These nonreporting countries include countries from Eastern Europe (plus Russia and Turkey), Latin America, and Asia.

Exhibit 35.1 displays the results of our simulation exercise for 60 percent LGD. It shows that contagion risk has increased over time particularly in terms of an increasing number of triggering countries that may lead to contagion. The number of reporting triggers increased to five in 2006 (i.e., the United States, United Kingdom, Germany, Denmark, and Finland), as compared to only two countries in 1999 (i.e., the United States and the United Kingdom). The United States and the United Kingdom would have triggered cross-border contagion over the entire sample period. The contagion triggered by the United States is the most severe, and spreads to almost all reporting countries in many years. The default of the United Kingdom also affects a majority of other reporting countries (6 to 12 countries).

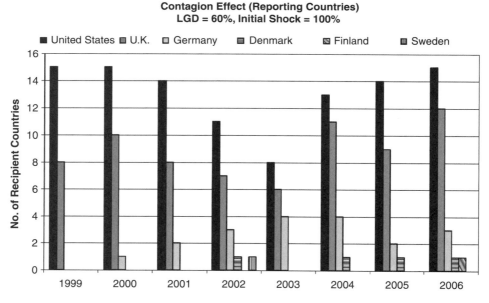

Exhibit 35.1 Contagion Triggered by Reporting Countries—All Banks Are Internationally Exposed

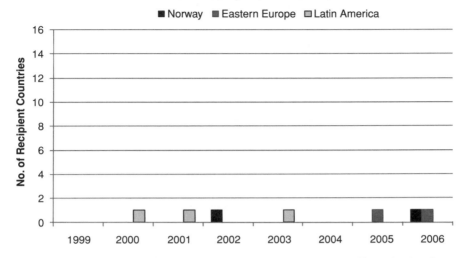

Contagion Effect (Nonreporting Countries)
LGD = 60%, Initial Shock = 100%

■ Norway ■ Eastern Europe □ Latin America

Exhibit 35.2 Contagion Triggered by Nonreporting Countries—All Banks Are Internationally Exposed

The United States and the United Kingdom have triggering potential even at low percentages of LGD, while default of any Scandinavian country often affects at least one country in the region.

Exhibit 35.2 illustrates the number of countries (on y-axis) that default due to cross-border contagion from nonreporting countries. Each column represents a trigger during 1999–2006. The contagion effect is based on assumptions that the loss given default is 60 percent and the triggering country defaults on all foreign obligations (i.e., initial shock is 100 percent).

Similarly, Exhibit 35.2 reports contagion triggered by nonreporting countries— regions at 60 percent LGD. It shows a low-contagion potential from nonreporting countries. When Norway causes cross-border contagion, it is always to one of its neighboring countries in the Scandinavian region. Moreover, the default of Latin American countries has cross-border implications only for Spain. The default of Eastern Europe (plus Russia and Turkey) only affects Austria.

Another interesting question is which banking systems are more vulnerable to contagion, and thus often appear as failing recipient countries. Exhibit 35.3 (gray cells) provides the direct and total cross-border contagion risk in 2006. The rows indicate the triggering countries that initiate contagion whereas the columns represent the recipient countries. Sweden is the most directly exposed banking system as it would default three times already in the first round.

Our results also show that the U.S. banking system is always resilient to cross-border contagion risk. Also, in recent years, the Italian banking system has become resilient to contagion risk from any of the triggering countries. This may stem from the large number of small banks in Italy that are not exposed heavily. Therefore, the result here may be driven by our strong assumption that all banks, including small

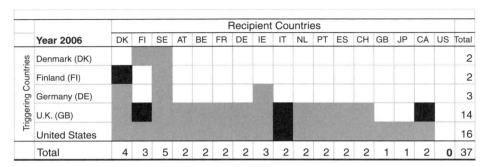

	Year 2006	Recipient Countries																	
		DK	FI	SE	AT	BE	FR	DE	IE	IT	NL	PT	ES	CH	GB	JP	CA	US	Total
Triggering Countries	Denmark (DK)																		2
	Finland (FI)																		2
	Germany (DE)																		3
	U.K. (GB)																		14
	United States																		16
	Total	4	3	5	2	2	2	2	3	2	2	2	2	2	1	1	2	0	37

Exhibit 35.3   Total Contagion Effect—(All Rounds, LGD = 60%)

This table shows the extent of contagion in 2006 taking into account all round effects. For each triggering country (left column), the defaulting recipient countries are marked with a gray or black box. The gray cells indicate the recipient countries when all banks are internationally exposed, while the gray cells together with the black cells indicate the recipient countries when only large banks (assets of more than $10 billion) are internationally exposed. The number on the right column gives the total of recipient countries for each triggering country when only large banks are internationally exposed. The total number of times a country defaults when only large banks are internationally exposed is mentioned at the bottom.

banks, are internationally exposed. We relax this assumption in the next exercise. Other recipient countries include Austria, Denmark, Finland, Japan, and Portugal that are not completely resilient to contagion risk but they default occasionally only in the last rounds. Therefore, we classify them as less vulnerable recipient countries. Last, Ireland, Netherlands, Sweden, and Switzerland have moderate levels of contagion risk as they often default in initial rounds.

We also find that the number of banking systems that default in the first two rounds has increased for major triggering countries in recent years. The increase is more profound when the triggers are the United States and United Kingdom. Specifically, the United States affects 11 or more countries in just two rounds. Similarly, the default of the United Kingdom leads to a cross-border contagion affecting seven or more countries in first two rounds in recent years.

In Case 2, we assume the same initial shock as in Case 1; however, foreign claims are assumed to be distributed among large banks only. Large banks are defined as banks with more than $10 billion in assets. There are 947 banks of the total 6,392 banks that report to BankScope that have $10 billion or more total assets. Large banks are more likely to interact with international players and may therefore be more prone to contagion risk via cross-border exposures. This is in line with findings in Gropp and Vesala (2006) showing that small banks neither cause nor suffer from cross-border contagion, even though all banks are equally likely to experience domestic contagion. Here we investigate whether the aggregate bank equity of the large banks only is sufficient to absorb the shock. In this case, our assumption about domestic spillovers is more stringent (i.e., the failure of large banks leads to the default of all sectors of the recipient country). In general, we expect more contagion to take place compared to Case 1, as we only include banks' equity of large banks as a cushion for default on foreign claims.

As expected, we find more intense contagion. The United States remains the crucial triggering country leading to default of all other countries over the entire sample period. Similarly, the United Kingdom also affects major countries except the United States and Japan. These two countries are gaining contagion momentum in recent years, especially in 2006. Germany triggers contagion, but only on a limited scale. Last, Scandinavian countries only trigger regional contagion.

In Exhibit 35.3, Italy is not immune anymore. The United States is the only country that is not affected by cross-border contagion.

The recent financial crisis also raises questions whether a single large bank or a group of banks can trigger a chain of dominos that potentially leads to cross-border contagion. Therefore, we next investigate this possibility by considering a shock to a fraction of a country's cross-border exposure only. We simulate initial shocks ranging from 5 percent to 100 percent, in steps of 5 percent each. This allows us to check the critical magnitude of the initial shock that would potentially cause a significant loss of banking assets of recipient countries through cross-border contagion, and compare it with the concentration of the triggering country's banking system. There is no clear definition of a systemically important shock. For our analysis, we consider a systemically important shock to be one affecting 20 percent of other banking systems assets.

In 2006, an initial shock of as low as 25 percent of the United States' foreign exposure would have triggered cross-border contagion, eroding 95 percent of the banking assets at 100 percent LGD, of which 80 percent of banking assets are lost in the first round. At 60 percent LGD, an initial shock of 60 percent shock could lead to a massive erosion of 72 percent of the banking assets.

A similar analysis for the United Kingdom assuming a LGD of 100 percent reveals that an initial shock of 35 percent of its cross-border exposures leads to an erosion of 45 percent of the banking assets of all recipient countries. On the other hand, assuming 60 percent LGD, a 75 percent initial shock would have resulted in cross-border contagion eroding 45 percent of the banking system. For Germany, an initial shock wiping out 60 percent of Germany's cross-border liabilities affects 50 percent of the banking assets assuming 100 percent LGD. However, Germany would not trigger any significant contagion assuming 60 percent LGD during our sample period.

In sum, based on an LGD of 100 percent and for 2006, we find that a 25 percent, 35 percent, and 60 percent shock to the United States, United Kingdom, and Germany, respectively, can be classified as a systemically important shock. This compares to three-bank concentration ratios of 20 percent, 44 percent, and 25 percent for the United States, United Kingdom, and Germany, respectively. This shows that a shock that would affect the liabilities of the three largest banks (and an equal fraction of the nonbank and public sector) in the United States and the United Kingdom has the potential to lead to a systemically important shock. In unreported exercises, we also find that over time a smaller shock might become a systemically important one. For example, the size of a systemically important bank/shock dropped for the United States from 45 percent in 1999 to 25 percent in 2006, and for the United Kingdom from 50 percent to 35 percent.

In Case 1 and Case 2, we assumed that the idiosyncratic shock affects all exposures equally whether short-term or long-term. We understand that this may be a strong assumption, given that it is likely that recovery rates will be higher for long-term exposures. Therefore we next assume that countries default only on their short-term liabilities. This exercise can be seen as a scenario in which a country faces a shortage of liquidity and therefore the shock is mainly due to a refinancing problem.

We refer to short-term liabilities as foreign claims of less than one-year maturity. This presents an extreme scenario when short-term claims have no collateral whereas long-term loans are completely secured. Results reveal that, for 60 percent LGD, there is no global contagion. The United Kingdom affects only Ireland from 2004 to 2006; the United States has no impact at all.

CONCLUDING REMARKS

We find that contagion risk and the speed of contagion through cross-border exposures have increased during 1999–2006. We find that a shock that affects partially the liabilities of one country may undermine the stability of the entire financial system. Particularly, a shock wiping out 25 percent (35 percent) of the United States (United Kingdom) cross-border liabilities against non-U.S. (non-U.K.) banks could lead to bank contagion eroding at least 94 percent (45 percent) of the recipient countries' banking assets, assuming 100 percent loss given default (LGD). Our simulations also reveal that contagion is often more confined to geographical proximities (i.e., regional, if not global), and that the United States is the only country immune to cross-border shocks and contagion stemming from other countries.

NOTES

1. Reporting countries include all participating countries in the BIS consolidated banking statistics. These countries report foreign claims vis-à-vis each other as well as against all nonparticipating countries. These nonparticipating countries are hereby called the nonreporting countries.
2. Included European countries are Austria, Belgium, Denmark, Finland, France, Germany, Ireland, Italy, Netherlands, Portugal, Spain, Sweden, Switzerland, and United Kingdom.

REFERENCES

Gropp, R., M. L. Duca, and J. Vesala. 2009. "Cross-Border Bank Contagion in Europe." *International Journal of Central Banking* 5:97–139.
Upper, C. and A. Worms. 2004. "Estimating Bilateral Exposures in the German Interbank Market: Is There a Danger of Contagion?" *European Economic Review* 48:4, 827–849.

ABOUT THE AUTHORS

Hans Degryse is professor of financial intermediation and markets at CentER-Tilburg University and a CESIfo fellow. He also holds the TILEC-AFM chair on financial market regulation and is a board member of the European Banking CentER in Tilburg. He received a PhD in economics from the University of Leuven in 1995. He has published in many journals including the *American Economic Review*, *Journal of Finance*, *Journal of Financial Economics*, *Review of Financial Studies*, *Journal of Financial Intermediation*, *Economic Journal*, *Review of Finance*, *European Economic Review*, *Journal of Industrial Economics*, and other journals.

Muhammad Ather Elahi is a doctorate student at the Tilburg School of Economics and Management at the Tilburg University. He is also affiliated with State Bank of Pakistan in the research department. His research interests are macroeconomics, banking, financial stability, and financial contagion.

María Fabiana Penas is an assistant professor of finance at Tilburg University, and a member of the European Banking Center and TILEC. She received a B.A. in economics from the University of Buenos Aires, and a PhD from the University of Maryland. She held positions as economist at the Central Bank of Argentina and at the field office of the World Bank in Buenos Aires. She has published in the *Journal of Financial Economics*, and the *Journal of Financial Intermediation*, among other finance journals. Her current research interests include the banking industry, banking regulation, relationship banking, and small business finance.

CHAPTER 36

Interbank Markets as a Source of Contagion

RAJKAMAL IYER
MIT

JOSÉ-LUIS PEYDRÓ
ECB

How important are financial linkages among banks in transmitting shocks across the financial system? What are the factors that dampen the extent of contagion? How does interbank contagion interact with the weakness of the banking system in generating systemic risk? Understanding these questions are central to the design of micro- and macroprudential regulation and supervision, in particular policies related to crisis management and ex-ante policies, including safety nets.[1]

The current global financial crisis has once again highlighted the risks posed by interbank markets. One of the main motivations for regulators in bailing out large banks and other large financial institutions was the fear of propagation of the crisis due to the high financial connections. However, the question that remains unanswered is how significant are these risks and how these risks vary depending on the fundamentals of the banking system.[2]

Despite the importance of these questions, understanding the magnitude of risk posed by the failure of large financial institutions has been difficult to measure. One of the main problems is that the fear of the unknown has led regulators to bail out large institutions at the first sign of trouble. Thus, the question that remains unanswered is what if there had been no bailout. Note that bailing out a large financial system has its own costs. First, there are the tax dollars that are utilized for the bailout. More importantly, bailouts could lead to reckless risk-taking behavior by banks in the future—that is, the moral hazard cost. Thus, from a regulatory point of view, one needs to weigh the risk of contagion that might arise due to the failure of a large institution against the costs incurred due to bailouts.

The major challenges in *studying* financial contagion due to interbank linkages are (1) the lack of detailed data on interbank linkages during a crisis time, (2) the dearth of large-bank failures as most often regulators resort to bailouts,[3] and (3) very often—as in the current crisis—it is difficult to examine whether the subsequent trouble in other banks is due to the failure of a large financial institution or is due the fact that the general economic conditions were bad to begin with. In effect, it is difficult to clearly examine and measure the risks posed by contagion arising out of financial linkages.

Given these challenges, in a forthcoming paper we overcome these hurdles by exploiting: (1) an event of sudden failure of a large bank in India—the bank failed due to fraud and was not bailed out (there was no other fraud in other banks and the economy was performing well); and (2) a unique dataset that allows us to identify interbank exposures at the time of the bank failure.[4] This provides us with an ideal platform to examine how contagion spreads across the financial system.

FINDINGS

To measure the risk of contagion, we first construct the extent of exposure of each bank in the system with the failed bank. We examine whether banks that had a higher fraction of assets with the failed bank (henceforth referred to as exposure) experienced large deposit withdrawals. We find robust evidence that higher interbank exposure to the failed bank generates large deposit withdrawals. We find that the probability of facing large deposit withdrawals increases by 34 percentage points if a bank has a high level of exposure. Moreover, we find that the impact of exposure on deposit withdrawals is greater for higher levels of exposure, thus suggesting a nonlinear effect of bank exposure on deposit withdrawals—that is, nonlinearities associated to financial contagion.

The finding that banks with higher exposure to the failed bank experience more withdrawals highlights that there is propagation of the initial shock to the rest of the financial system through linkages among institutions. However, what is interesting is that the withdrawals are primarily related to exposures with the failed bank. That is, we do not find random panic across all institutions. Thus, the fear that if a large institution fails, investors will panic across all institutions does not find empirical support. From a policy perspective, this is important as this suggests that regulators do not need to worry about a breakdown of the whole system due a large failure if the failing institution's exposures are not too widespread.

Another important question that arises is the role of bank fundamentals. We first explore whether stronger bank fundamentals play a role in reducing the magnitude of contagion. Specifically, we find that the impact of exposure on deposit withdrawals is higher for banks (1) with lower level of capital, (2) smaller in size, and (3) classified as weak by the regulator. These results suggest that weaker fundamentals of the banking system amplify the magnitude of interbank contagion. This suggests that contagion is stronger when the financial system is weak. Thus, from a policy perspective, a bailout of a bank may be necessary especially when the banking system is weak.

We also find that once there is a failure, other banks move away from the line of contagion by withdrawing deposits away from banks with a higher exposure to the failed bank. Thus, banks unwind their claims in other banks with higher exposure to protect themselves from further propagation of the shock, in turn making the banking system more fragile, at least for the banks with high exposure.

Although we find interbank contagion, it is important to study the real effects it could have on firms that borrow from these banks. We find that banks with higher exposure levels experience reductions in loan growth and profitability. However, to understand the effects on firms, it is important to investigate whether other banks that are unaffected increase their lending to compensate for this decline. Interestingly, we find that banks with lower exposure competitively gain deposits. However, this competitive gain in deposits does not translate into a corresponding increase in loans or profitability, which suggests that these banks hoard on the excess liquidity given the difficult banking environment they face. Given the borrowers' small size and bank dependence, the previous results suggest that there are real economic effects in terms of reduction in lending associated with interbank contagion.[5]

MAIN POLICY IMPLICATIONS

Our results have important implications for regulatory policy for banks. Since interbank linkages transmit shocks, regulators and banks can devise ex-ante risk management systems to curtail excessive exposure to a single institution in order to limit the destabilizing effects stemming from the risk of idiosyncratic shocks.

Our findings suggest that the risk of purely random transmission of panic may be low. Bailouts of banks are generally motivated by the fear of systemic risk due random transmission of a shock. If random transmission of panic is not a serious threat, then regulators could exercise forbearance in use of bailouts and thereby reduce the moral hazard problems that arise. Furthermore, our results suggest that regulators should provide liquidity for solvent but illiquid banks instead of using bailouts.

The other policy implication stemming from our paper is that systemic risk implications of a failure of a financial institution are very important, especially when *both* the rest of the financial system has (1) a high interbank (financial) exposure to the failed institution, and (2) weak fundamentals. This suggests that if a highly connected bank fails at a time when the banking system fundamentals are weak, a bailout may be compulsory to prevent a systemic crisis.

NOTES

1. For a recent survey on systemic risk in banking, see Bandt, Hartmann, and Peydró (2009).

2. See also the recent CEPR Vox article: "Contagion through Interbank Markets." www.voxeu.org/index.php?q=node/4929.

3. After studying more than 100 bank failures before the current crisis, Goodhart and Schoenmaker (1995) conclude: "It has been revealed preference of the monetary authorities in all developed countries to rescue those large banks whose failure might lead to a contagious, systemic failure." This view also comes forth in a speech by the Chairman of the Federal Reserve, Ben Bernanke, in October 2008 in the context of the current financial crisis. He asserted, "The Federal Reserve will work closely and actively with the Treasury and other authorities to minimize systemic risk." In consequence, due to the bailouts, there is a dearth of large bank failures and, hence, it is difficult to find events to test contagion.

4. See Iyer and Peydró (2010).

5. For evidence on the current crisis, see Iyer, Lopes, Peydró, and Schoar (2010).

REFERENCES

Bandt, Olivier de, Philipp Hartmann, and José-Luis Peydró. 2009. "Systemic Risk in Banking: An Update." *Oxford Handbook of Banking*. New York: Oxford University Press.

Goodhart, Charles, and Dirk Schoenmaker. 1995. "Institutional Separation between Supervisory and Monetary Agencies." In Charles Goodhart, ed. *The Central Bank and the Financial System*. New York: Macmillan.

Iyer, Rajkamal, and José-Luis Peydró. 2010. "Interbank Contagion at Work: Evidence from a Natural Experiment." *Review of Financial Studies* forthcoming.

Iyer Rajkamal, Samuel Lopes, José-Luis Peydró, and Antoinette Schoar. 2010. "The Interbank Liquidity Crunch and the Firm Credit Crunch: Evidence from the 2007–09 Crisis." *MIT* mimeo.

ABOUT THE AUTHORS

Rajkamal Iyer is an assistant professor of finance at MIT, Sloan. His research interests are in banking and contract theory. Recent research projects include examining the factors that mitigate depositor incentive to run on banks and examining how market participants overcome frictions in contracting. He holds a PhD in finance from INSEAD and a master's in finance and economics from London School of Economics.

José-Luis Peydró works at the European Central Bank. His research interests are in banking, systemic risk, monetary policy, and macro-finance, and he has published and presented in top academic journals and conferences. His main policy areas have been stress-testing, interbank markets, bank capital requirements, lending behavior, the credit channel of monetary policy, and macroprudential regulation, and he has presented in top policy seminars. His recent research in systemic risk has been published in the *Review of Financial Studies* and in the *Handbook of Banking from the Oxford University Press*. José-Luis holds a PhD in finance from INSEAD, a master's in economics from CEMFI, and a B.A. in economics from the University of Barcelona. He was awarded by the Government of Spain with the First National Award in Economics to the student with the highest overall GPA in finishing a B.A. in economics in Spain in 1998.

PART SIX

Contagion within an Economy

T o date, the intellectual life of the idea of contagion has been fairly brief, and the main focus has been on contagion from one country to another. This country-to-country focus was particularly well-suited to the Asian financial crisis of 1997–1998, as economic difficulties originating in Thailand swept around the world. The financial crisis of 2007–2009 certainly had dramatic elements of international contagion, but one of its most dominant features was contagion within a single country, the United States, and even within a single industry, the financial sector.

Chapters in this section focus on contagion within a single economy. Nonetheless, the possibilities of different kinds of contagion are quite numerous. For example, one study considers contagion between the stock prices of firms in different industrial sectors as characterized by the S&P 500 sector indexes. Contagion can also be a problem in corporate governance. Large firms often have boards of directors with overlapping membership. This common membership of some directors provides an easily understood avenue of contagion from firm to firm, as a common director carries a good or bad idea from one board to another. For example, overlapping board membership has been advanced as an explanation for the widespread rash of stock option backdating schemes among top executives of technology firms.

Further examples of contagion come from other economic sectors within a single economy. For example, there may be price contagion from one property to another as a result of a foreclosure in a neighborhood. Still other potential instances of contagion arise for accounting restatements. Does a restatement by one firm lead in some way to restatements by other firms? Similarly, if a bank announces a quarterly earnings result that surprises the market, does that lead other banks to announce earnings that are also surprising?

CHAPTER 37

Cross-Border Lending Contagion in Multinational Banks*

ALEXIS DERVIZ
Senior Economist, Czech National Bank

JIŘÍ PODPIERA
Economist, the International Monetary Fund

We investigate the parent influence on lending by affiliates of a multinational bank (lending spillover) and its implications for cross-border shock propagation. The spillover, which is modeled as an international portfolio optimization influenced by shareholder-affiliate manager delegation and precautionary motives, takes the form of either contagion (the loan volume in the affiliate follows the direction of the parent bank country shock) or performance-based reallocation of funds (substitution). Empirical investigation shows that multinational banks that are likely to delegate lending decisions or be more liquidity-sensitive are more inclined toward contagionist behavior. Such banks constitute a majority in the sample and the time period considered in the study.

MOTIVATION

Many open economies exhibit high levels of multinational bank (MNB) penetration, so shock transmission by an MNB can be an important channel of cross-border financial contagion. As the last global financial crisis has demonstrated, the involvement of prominent international bank groups in toxic investment products can create a credit crunch in completely unrelated economies. However, the link between loan-quality changes in one country and credit creation in another is not limited to times of crisis. Given that MNBs are usually among the leading, systemically important banks in the country of incorporation (hereinafter the home country), bank regulators are preoccupied with destabilizing spillovers on it

---

*This is a short nontechnical version of a working paper with the same title published by the authors as ECB WP No. 807 (September 2007).

from foreign country units. For similar reasons, some MNBs suffered rating downgrades when considered "overstretched" by foreign bank acquisitions. In other
cases, policymakers in countries where MNBs operate (hereinafter host countries)
are concerned that a shock affecting the parent bank, although it has nothing to do
with the domestic economic fundamentals, may distort lending decisions within
their jurisdiction.

In this chapter, we do not either discuss the reasons for foreign bank penetration
or explore the causality between foreign bank presence and the real economy. What
we look for are the probable causes and empirical relevance of shock transmission
from a parent bank's loan returns and economic conditions in its home country to
lending by its foreign affiliate (cross-border lending spillover).

Interdependence of investment decisions can be studied for any multinational
financial institution, but the case of banks is specific. Namely, units in different
countries predominantly lend to local customers and are also managed locally.
But then, why should the performance of one country unit be relevant for fund
allocation in another? As commercial bank assets are for the most part nontrad-
able, the rationale for lending spillover in an MNB is not as readily available as
for cross-border contagion in securities markets. At first glance, there should be less
cross-border spillover in a bank than in a secondary security market. Nevertheless,
lending by many foreign-owned banks cannot be fully explained by local driving
factors. Multinational banks often cross-subsidize between different country units
in reaction to changes in loan quality in one country. In the data, the effect looks like
cross-border lending *contagion*, meaning that loan volumes in the affiliates move
in the same direction as the condition of the parent.[1]

We start by looking for a general economic rationale behind lending contagion.
In the standard frictionless portfolio-optimization theory, cross-border spillovers
happen because a shock to the asset-return pattern in one country induces wealth
reallocation across divisions in different countries (*substitution*). If instead of substitution one observes contagion, it is reasonable to suspect the presence of frictions that influence the optimal home-host country fund split. We focus on two
frictions in particular: management delegation in the affiliate and sensitivity to
the threshold value of liquid wealth that triggers termination (a bank run, regulatory intervention, a takeover with reorganization, etc.) in the parent. We propose
a model in which the two frictions are able to shift the rational reaction to shocks
from substitution to contagion.

This theoretical finding feeds into an empirical model in which parent bank
performance joins the list of more traditional explanatory variables of affiliate
lending growth. We then test for the presence of intra-MNB agency determinants
of cross-border spillovers. Our hypothesis, supported by the estimation results,
is that for the period and set of host countries studied, the direction of parent
bank influence corresponds to the lending contagion in MNBs under termination
sensitivity or affiliate management delegation.

Literature on MNBs' behavior is not particularly rich, so tangency points with
our research are scattered across several other areas of finance. We draw heavily on
the theory of banks developed by Diamond and Rajan (2001), whose agency effects
are easily extended to the MNB case, and the internal capital market literature
(Scharfstein and Stein 2000), which demonstrates how the workings of an internal
capital market can lead to "socialist" redistribution of an investment budget from

a stronger to a weaker division. This result could be reinterpreted as contagion in our setting (the MNB CEO, instead of increasing the funds of a well-performing affiliate, supports weak ones consolidated with the parent bank).

There also exist empirical investigations of lending volume determinants in MNB affiliates, such as de Haas and van Lelyveld (2006a, 2006b). However, these studies do not offer an explicit decision-theoretic foundation for either substitution or contagion. This is what we propose and discuss next.

THEORY

Decisions about allocating funds in different countries by an MNB, as by any other international investor, would be mutually dependent in any model containing optimization of an international portfolio. Under our approach, an MNB differs in two aspects.

First, because it is a bank, that is, an investment firm funded by deposits along with shareholder capital, there exists a termination trigger. If earnings are insufficient to compensate for the withdrawal of deposits, the disposable funds fall below a given threshold and the bank fails. A decrease of the distance to termination starts influencing the bank's choices long before the termination level itself is reached, so that even banks without any actual solvency or liquidity problems may behave differently from frictionless portfolio optimizers.

Second, an MNB can delegate the operation of a foreign affiliate to a local manager in possession of nontransferable skills. The affiliate manager acts in a relationship-banking environment and is more successful in collecting on debt because of his "soft" knowledge about local borrowers. Without the local manager, the shareholder would have the outside option to run the affiliate at arm's length (without recourse to any soft knowledge). Arm's-length management by the shareholder would save on the manager fee, but result in losing a part of the potential returns.

The agency effect of delegation is embedded in an otherwise conventional optimal portfolio selection problem of the bank. This allows one to extend the standard no-friction investment paradigm in order to account for the termination risk sensitivity of banks.

In this setting, cross-border spillovers arise because the manager, while investing locally, is forced to think globally. To develop the intuition, consider an example in which the shareholder extracts higher–lower returns under an arm's-length operation abroad at the same time as at home, whereas the hired manager's performance in the foreign unit is completely independent of the parent bank performance. Then, in the "low return state of nature" the shareholder earns less abroad in net terms due to the high fee paid to the manager. The foreign affiliate may then obtain a low budget, there is a loan volume reduction both at home and abroad and lending contagion materializes. The full version of our model shows that the phenomenon of lending contagion is much more general than that.

The measure of parent-affiliate lending spillover is defined as the dependence of the lending volumes in the affiliate, on the mean return on loans in the parent. The partial derivative of the former with respect to the latter is generically non-zero; that is, some dependence of the affiliate credit creation on the home country loan performance is always present and MNB transmit shocks across the border. Depending on the sign of this transmission, one obtains either substitution (negative sign, shock inversion) or contagion (positive sign, shock propagation).

Our main theoretical result is a formula relating the said partial derivative to risk factor parameters and the bank characteristics, among them termination risk and delegation effects. This stylized comparative statics result with many unobservable variables is not immediately testable, so that one has to interpret individual terms in a wider context of existing knowledge about financial institution operations in open economies. There are three main empirical priors that we derive in this way. First, the model confirms that lending spillover is driven by both aggregate and bank-specific factors. Second, gains from delegation support substitution *ceteris paribus*; however, the effect is likely to dwindle with increasing termination sensitivity of the parent. Third, substitution will typically give way to a contagionist outcome as internal capital market frictions in an MNB related to termination sensitivity and, in the absence of that, manager delegation gain importance.

EMPIRICAL ANALYSIS

We proceed by incorporating the empirical priors of the theoretical part into an econometric model of MNB affiliate lending dynamics.

Our sample consists of 34 multinational banks with foreign affiliates of some significance for either the host country or the bank holding company. We consider both standard organizational forms of foreign-bank presence: branches and subsidiaries, operating in mature industrial and advanced emerging countries, thereby excluding bank branching into emerging markets with elevated risk: Emerging market participations constitute a separate segment of eligible investment opportunities, for which credit risk management and asset valuation are formally different from the ones applied in legally stable developed economies.

The time span cannot be too wide, as structural changes such as mergers and acquisitions between both parents and affiliates would grow quickly with the length of the period considered. To minimize their incidence, we concentrate on the most recent period of stable MNB landscape in industrialized countries. The result is a sample covering the years 1999–2004, when most of the considered affiliates were in operation and belonged to a fixed international banking group in the set of parents.

The dependent variable is the annual growth of loans of the affiliate. The explanatory variables comprise aggregate and bank-specific ones. The former include home and the host country macro fundamentals (GDP growth, inflation, and long-term interest rates) and a measure of home/host country bilateral exchange rate volatility.[2] The latter include two controls of the affiliate's specific credit creation drivers: return on assets (ROA) and the ratio of loan loss reserves to total loans. Next, the parent bank's loan loss reserves–total loans-ratio is used to measure the parent bank cost of managing home credit risk.[3] Finally, in accordance with our empirical priors, one needs an operational measure of shareholder-manager frictions, that is, the degree of presumed manager delegation and/or termination sensitivity. To this end, we construct a zero-one dummy taking the value of unity if one or both of the two conditions is satisfied: (1) at least one of the affiliates has a significant local loan market share; (2) capital ratio of the parent is not too much in excess of the regulatory limit. Both indicators are quite stable across the covered years, so that an average number well characterizing the whole analyzed period is available.

The local loan market share criterion was used because it seems rational to assume that an MNB cannot manage a significant share of the commercial lending business on a purely arm's-length basis.[4] As for the role of the capital ratio, tight prudential capital figures should indicate that the bank grants loans without spare risk-cushions, closer to the hypothetical exogenous intervention boundary than banks with slack constraints.

We ran a panel regression on data structured according to the affiliate and clustered residuals at the parent bank level, with fixed effects representing autonomous credit creation factors at the affiliate level. To assess the influence of parent-affiliate frictions on cross-border lending spillovers, we used the parent loan loss reserves ratio and that same variable multiplied by our friction dummy as the interaction variable.

Among the aggregate economic fundamentals, the home country factors turn out to be relatively unimportant for local credit growth. On the contrary, the host country current and expected economic conditions (GDP growth and alternatively the real long-term interest rate) appear to be important. The home-host exchange rate is significant at least in some variants of the estimated model: Apparently, the fundamental risk factor underlying exchange rate volatility is present in some other financial variables picked up by alternative regressors.

Of the affiliate side regressors, only loan loss reserves turned out to be significant. On the parent side, its loan loss reserves proved significant for affiliate lending volume in all specifications.

Our main topic of interest is the direction given to cross-border lending spillover by the frictions inherent in the MNB-internal capital markets, visible in the performance of MNB-specific regressors.[5] Our theoretical investigation suggests that, for the period we look at, arguably characterized by increasing financial integration, yield search, and overpricing of local assets, lending contagion should be typical. And indeed, we obtain significant coefficients by the regressors responsible for bank-specific lending spillovers. Confirming the view that parent-affiliate frictions should contribute to contagionist shock transmission, we find that contagionist behavior is typical for banks with tight capital ratios and/or delegated management of affiliates. In other words, affiliates with high/low presumed frictions experience a decrease/increase in credit growth when the parent bank faces increased credit risk.

IMPLICATIONS

The consequence of cross-border parent-affiliate lending spillovers can be either shock suppression, when funds go to the MNB division with superior returns (substitution), or shock amplification, when the affiliate lending follows the sign of the parent's performance (contagion). In light of our results, materialization of one of these shock propagation modes depends on the extent to which the MNB is subject to solvency/liquidity constraints and the influence of local managers on lending in affiliates. The two MNB-internal capital market frictions, associated with termination sensitivity and affiliate management delegation, are likely to support the contagionist type of cross-border lending spillover, especially under inflated asset prices in the host countries where MNB affiliates operate.

Among the banks prone to lending contagion, we mostly find European banks with affiliates in other European countries. This should come as no surprise, as termination sensitivity is likely to be more pronounced in a more interventionist regulatory environment, even though a regulatory action is often more of a rescue than a penalty for the shareholders. Thus, we should frequently observe precautionary rebudgeting in response to credit risk cost shocks. If this result carries over to the near future, we are bound to see more lending contagion in multinational banks worldwide exactly because a more interventioninst approach to financial regulation has become a clear trend in the course of the latest financial crisis.

NOTES

1. The term *contagion* here refers to both positive and negative developments, meaning better–worse performance in the parent inducing more–less lending in the affiliate. So, some foreign bank affiliates forego business opportunities for years in markets with a lot of potential, while others undertake ambitious expansion programs despite downturns and crises in the host country.

2. There are several variants of the estimated equation depending on the measure of economic activity, but they all produce quantitatively similar results.

3. These data, in annual frequency, are taken from BankScope. One of the factors restricting the choice of variables in a study like this is the availability of an indicator for all the financial institutions considered. ROA and loan loss reserves are among the few that exist in BankScope for all the banks in our sample.

4. This criterion happens to nearly coincide with the one based on the origin, that is, a green-filed affiliate versus takeover of a preexisting bank. The latter, without exception, were prominent local players at the time of acquisition. Other considered criteria, such as the balance sheet size of the affiliate relative to the parent, did not change anything in the classification obtained.

5. Although our model predicts these frictions to interact with aggregate risks as well, it assigns the resulting synergies a lower weight and allows the sign of their impact to vary.

REFERENCES

Diamond, D., and R. Rajan. 2001. "Liquidity Risk, Liquidity Creation, and Financial Fragility: A Theory of Banking." *Journal of Political Economy* 109:2, 287–327.

de Haas, R., and I. van Lelyveld. 2006a. "Foreign Banks and Credit Stability in Central and Eastern Europe. A Panel Data Analysis." *Journal of Banking and Finance* 30:1927–1952.

de Haas, R., and I. van Lelyveld. 2006b. "Internal Capital Markets and Lending by Multinational Bank Subsidiaries." *Working Paper* 101, Amsterdam: De Nederlandsche Bank (June).

Scharfstein, D., and J. Stein. 2000. "The Dark Side of Internal Capital Markets: Divisional Rent-seeking and Inefficient Investment." *Journal of Finance* 50:2537–2564.

ABOUT THE AUTHORS

Alexis Derviz is a senior economist and heads a team of international economy analysts at the Czech National Bank. He received a PhD in mathematical physics from the Leningrad (now St. Petersburg) State University in Russia. He later studied economics at Charles University in Prague, Czech Republic, and taught industrial organization and international finance at a graduate school of that university. He then joined the Czech National Bank to lead a research team on international monetary issues. He contributed to several books on economies in transition, later authored and co-authored a number of refereed journal articles on asset pricing, exchange rates, and international banking. He can be reached at Alexis.Derviz@seznam.cz.

Jiří Podpiera has been an economist at the International Monetary Fund since 2009. He worked as division chief at the Czech National Bank and represented the Czech National Bank in the Monetary Policy Committee of the European Central Bank. During autumn 2006, he joined the research department at the European Central Bank as principal economist. He received his PhD in economics (accredited by the New York State Board of Regents) from Centre for Economic Research and Graduate Education at the Charles University, Prague. He was a visiting lecturer in international trade and finance at the New York University in Prague (2000–2002). His prime research interests are economic convergence and banking and finance. He has recently published in a wide range of journals including *Economics of Transition*, *Economics Letters*, *Economic Modelling*, and *Journal of Financial Stability*. He can be reached at JPodpiera@imf.org.

CHAPTER 38

The Transmission of Speculative Bubbles between Sectors of the S&P 500 during the Tech Bubble[*]

KEITH ANDERSON
University of York, U.K.

CHRIS BROOKS
ICMA Centre, University of Reading, U.K.

APOSTOLOS KATSARIS
Caliburn Partners LLP, U.K.

Equity markets have historically enjoyed periods of spectacular growth in prices followed by rapid reversals. Such phenomenal price movements have motivated the development of asset-pricing models that try to explain the evolution of prices as well as to produce profitable forecasts for investment decisions. The behavior of stock prices prior to the 1929 and 1987 stock market crashes are frequently cited examples of periods of fundamental value irrelevance, where factors such as dividends or earnings play limited roles in explaining changes in market prices (see, for example, Shiller 2000). Similarly, variation in the prices of certain S&P 500 stocks during the 1990s is particularly difficult to explain. The evolution of prices in these periods has inspired the search for other variables beyond fundamentals that might affect market prices and thus cause their *apparent* deviations from fundamental values. One possible explanation for these deviations is the presence of speculative bubbles.

Bubbles have been defined in various ways, but one useful definition for our purposes is that they represent systematic, persistent, and increasing deviations of actual market prices from their fundamental values. Market practitioners and

---

[*]This chapter is a shortened version of Anderson, K., Brooks, C., and Katsaris, A. 2010. "Speculative Bubbles in the S&P 500: Was the Tech Bubble Confined to the Tech Sector?" *Journal of Empirical Finance* 17, 345–361. © Elsevier B.V. All rights reserved.

academic researchers have suggested that the Information Technology and Re-sources sectors were significantly affected by speculative bubbles in the past 25 years, but by implication, that other sectors remained bubble-free. The study by Anderson et al. (2010) that is summarized here was the first to consider the possible presence of speculative bubbles at the stock market sector level, and to consider possible bubble spillovers between industries.

DEFINITIONS AND DISCUSSION OF THE GICS SECTORS

Anderson et al. (2010) employ data on the 10 S&P 500 Global Industry Classifica-tion Standard (GICS) sector indices over the period January 1973–June 2004. The GICS is an industry classification system created by Standard & Poor's in collabo-ration with Morgan Stanley Capital International that is used to classify firms into sectors, and the ones they examine are: Cyclical Services, Financials, Basic Indus-tries, General Industrials, Cyclical Consumer Goods, IT, Non-Cyclical Consumer Goods, Non-Cyclical Services, Resources, and Utilities. The appropriate series are then transformed into real series using the monthly CPI, and the implied cash dividends are obtained from the dividend yield, using the methodology described in Brooks and Katsaris (2005a); they obtain all data from Datastream.

It is noteworthy that the IT Sector had only grown by around 40 percent until January 1996, yielding most of its extraordinary growth of 650 percent to the peak in the following five years of the sample before the equally spectacular collapse in value from April 2000. By contrast, the S&P 500 Composite Index had grown by just over 200 percent in the same period. Interestingly, the General Industrials sector shows a remarkably similar pattern to the IT sector, although the price growth of the former is somewhat less spectacular than the latter. Thus, many "old economy" sectors also appeared to show bubble-like growth in the 1990s. The only sector that does not exhibit such behavior in the slightest is Resources. Hence the GICS sector indices display behavior that could be considered consistent with the existence of speculative bubbles. That is, an apparent undervaluation relative to dividends in the 1970s, an increasing overvaluation up until 1987, and an ever increasing overvaluation after that. However, some sector indices display significantly more variation around dividends than others.

MODELS FOR PERIODICALLY PARTIALLY COLLAPSING SPECULATIVE BUBBLES IN ASSET PRICES

Blanchard (1979) was the first to formulate a speculative bubble model in which the bubble component continues to grow with explosive expectations in the next time period or crashes to zero. If the bubble collapses, the actual price will be equal to the asset's fundamental value. In this model, the explosive behavior of bubble returns compensates the investor for the increased risk of a bubble crash as the bubble grows in size.

Van Norden and Schaller (hereafter vNS, 1993) formulate a periodically par-tially collapsing, positive and negative speculative bubble model that has a time-varying probability of collapse. This switching model has two regimes: one where the bubble survives and continues to grow, and another where the bubble collapses. Their study is among the first to recognize that bubble collapses are a result of a change in investors' beliefs concerning the future of the bubble rather than arising from exogenous factors. Brooks and Katsaris (2005b) propose an extension of their model to incorporate a measure of abnormal volume in the equations for returns in the surviving regime and in the probability of bubble collapse. In these models, the expected size of the bubble is a function of the probability of a crash, the size of the bubble at that time, and of the size of the bubble in the collapsing state. The probability of the bubble continuing to exist is a negative function of the size of the bubble, and the measure of abnormal volume. The returns in the surviving regime are a function of the size of the bubble and of the measure of abnormal volume. In effect, this implies that as the bubble grows, investors demand higher returns in order to compensate them for the probability of a bubble collapse and since abnormal volume signals a possible change in the long run trend in equity prices, investors want to be compensated for this risk as well.

All speculative bubble models require an approach for the determination of fundamental values. A number of methods for achieving this can be found in the literature, including approaches based on dividend multiple measures, or based on an augmented Gordon growth model. Anderson et al. adopt the dividend multiple measure of fundamentals employed by Van Norden and Schaller (1999), while recognizing the limitations of using dividend-based fundamentals to value high growth sectors such as Information Technology; other authors argue and empirically show that the fundamentals of equity valuation still apply to high technology firms and that classic accounting variables are still relevant in the pricing of such stocks. Anderson et al. (2010) first apply this vNS model augmented with volume separately to each of the sectors before developing a multivariate model that allows for bubble contagion between sectors.

EMPIRICAL EVIDENCE

Overall, the results are indicative of the presence of bubbles in several of the sectors, namely Financials, General Industrials, Information Technology, and Non-Cyclical Services. There is also some evidence in favor of periodic, partially collapsing speculative bubbles in the Cyclical Services, Basic Industries, and Utilities sectors. This leaves only three sectors for which there is virtually no evidence for bubble-like behavior. It is thus concluded that the bubble-induced separation of the S&P 500 from its dividend-based fundamental values are a result of the deviation of not only the Information Technology sector but of the deviations of other, more traditional sectors from their fundamental values. If we now turn our attention to the 1990s, several sectors—namely the Cyclical Services, Non-Cyclical Services, Resources, General Industrials, Cyclical Consumer Goods, Non-Cyclical Consumer Goods, and Information Technology indices—were overvalued by at least 30 percent in January 1996. These sectors represented more than 60 percent of the S&P 500 Composite index, which was overvalued in the same period by almost 40 percent. More importantly, in January 2000, the estimated bubble deviation of the Composite index was 60 percent. One point worth noting is that after March 2000, when the bubble deviations in the aforementioned sectors began to deflate, sectors that were overvalued by less than 40 percent relative to the dividend multiple fundamental values in January 2000 (namely the Utilities, Financials, and Basic Industries in- dices) experienced a relatively significant increase in their bubble deviations until the end of the sample period. These sectors accounted for around a quarter of the total capitalization of the Composite index in January 2000, and by January 2001 their share had grown to over 30 percent. This could be taken as evidence that once investors realized that the bubble was bursting, they shifted funds to relatively "safe" sectors with a smaller risk of observing a bubble collapse.

MODELING BUBBLE CONTAGION

Even a casual examination of actual prices and fundamentals at the sector level reveals some divergence between the sectors in terms of when the fast growth phase of the bubble started and when the price index hit its peak. For example, the Basic Industries sector arguably started its strongest expansion phase in March 1995; it began its collapse in May 1999 and then started to recover by October 2000 although it remained volatile. While General Industrials started its ascent at around the same time, the reversal in this case did not take place until September 2000. Similarly, the Information Technology sector, widely attributed as being the root of the tech bubble, showed no signs of slowdown until September 2000, more than a year after Basic Industries but a month before Utilities. The Resources sector grew fairly rapidly from February 1995 and became volatile from May 1998 although it largely avoided a full-scale collapse. The downfall in Financials did not start until February 2001 although it had fully recovered by April 2004. These anecdotal observations suggest that, contrary to popular opinion, even if the formation of the tech bubble can be attributed to Technology, Telecommunications, and the Media, the subsequent collapse started with faltering prices in more conventional sectors that one might expect to be affected at the early stages of an impending economic slowdown (Basic Industries and Resources). This motivates Anderson et al. (2010) to examine whether a bubble that is present in one sector may subsequently spread to other sectors.

They build an empirical model that can allow for spillovers in both the levels of returns in the sectors and in the generating equations. Although there is poten- tially a large number of ways that this could be achieved, they focus on a natural extension of the augmented vNS model, ruling out contemporaneous spillovers between sectors, allowing only for lagged effects. Several approaches are adopted, the most general of which allows the returns in the surviving regime to depend on the lagged size of the bubble in all sectors and on the lagged abnormal volume in all sectors; likewise, the return in the collapsing regime also depends on the one period lagged value of the size of the bubble in all sectors. This model is tricky to estimate given that it contains a total of 55 parameters and thus a number of simplified versions are also considered, including a specification where the model is dependent on the bubble in the sector under consideration and in the market as a whole rather than all the other sectors.

It is clear from the results that both the sector returns and the probabilities of bubble collapse in a number of individual sectors respond to the size of the bubble in the market as a whole as well as that in their own sector, and most of the additional parameters are statistically significant for the Cyclical Services, Information Technology, Non-Cyclical Services, Resources, and Utilities sectors. For example, in the case of the Resources sector, the return in the surviving regime is a positive and significant function of the marketwide bubble deviation, while for the return in the collapsing regime, it is negative as expected, albeit not significantly so. The probability of being in the surviving regime is, as expected, a negative and highly significant function of the size of the market bubble. Not only sector-specific changes in the size of the bubble and of abnormal volume, but also marketwide influences, are important determinants of subsequent bubble behavior at the sector level.

In order to determine more specifically whether the bubble-like behavior in the sectors and the market as a whole emanate from a small number of specific industries, Anderson et al. (2010) report the analysis for the unrestricted model where the next period returns are a function of the current size of the bubble and of abnormal volume not only in that sector but also in all of the other sectors.

The results demonstrate that the expected returns in the surviving and collapsing regimes and the probability of the bubble surviving respond to a much greater extent to the lagged bubble sizes and lagged volumes in some sectors than others. Notably, Cyclical Services, Financials, Basic Industries, and General Industries seem to be highly responsive while Non-Cyclical Consumer Goods and Utilities appear to be relatively isolated. Perhaps more importantly, in terms of the statistical significance of the parameter estimates, it appears that the bubbles in the Basic Industries, Cyclical Consumer Goods, Information Technology, and Resources sectors are particularly contagious from the perspective that the bubbles in these sectors influence the levels and probability of collapse of a considerable number of other sectors. For example, the size of the bubble in the IT sector affects either the size of the return in the surviving or collapsing regime or the probability of the bubble surviving for the Cyclical Services, Financials, Basic Industries, General Industrials, Cyclical Consumer Goods, Non-Cyclical Services, and Resources sectors. On the other hand, bubbles specific to the Utilities and Non-Cyclical Services sectors, for instance, have limited spillovers to other industries. Although the large number of parameters involved in this model makes interpretation a difficult task, the most salient feature is that bubble transmission at the sector level is multidirectional and did not originate purely from Information Technology and related industries.

Although some practitioners claim that a bubble was formed in the early 1980s in the global basic materials sector, no evidence is found that the perceived bubble deviations displayed periodically collapsing speculative bubble behavior during our sample period since the size of the bubble is unable to reliably predict the level or the generating state of returns. One particularly interesting observation is that towards the end of Anderson et al.'s (2010) sample after the IT bubble had begun to deflate, there is an increase in the deviations of actual prices from fundamental values in the four sectors with the lowest bubble deviations in March 2000. These sectors were Non-Cyclical Consumer Goods, Financials, Resources, and Utilities. This could be taken as evidence that investors shifted their capital to sectors with a smaller probability of a bubble collapse, since very few investors would completely liquidate their holdings in the S&P 500. This could also be thought of as suggesting that market participants were aware that some sectors had a smaller bubble deviation than others, and were thus less at risk from the bubble bursting in 2000 and 2001.

In summary, the results show that bubble-transmission during the 1990s arose from several sectors including Cyclical Consumer Goods and Basic Industries and not just from IT as popular opinion might suggest. The central conclusion is that bubble-like behavior is not confined to a small segment of the stock market, but appears to be present in more than 70 percent of it. A key implication of this result is that if market participants believe dividend-based fundamental measures not to be appropriate for valuing the technology stocks during periods of rapid price appreciation, they are equally inappropriate for companies in other more conventional sectors and for the market as a whole.

REFERENCES

Anderson, K., C. Brooks, and A. Katsaris. 2010. "Speculative Bubbles in the S&P 500: Was the Tech Bubble Confined to the Tech Sector?" *Journal of Empirical Finance* 17:345–361.

Blanchard, O. J. 1979. "Speculative Bubbles, Crashes and Rational Expectations." *Economics Letters* 3:387–389.

Brooks, C., and A. Katsaris. 2005a. "A Three-Regime Model of Speculative Behavior: Modelling the Evolution of Bubbles in the S&P 500 Composite Index." *Economic Journal* 115:767–797.

Brooks, C., and A. Katsaris. 2005b. "Trading Rules from Forecasting the Collapse of Speculative Bubbles for the S&P 500 Composite Index." *Journal of Business* 78:2003–2036.

Shiller, R. J. 2000. *Irrational Exuberance*. Princeton, NJ: Princeton University Press.

van Norden, S., and H. Schaller. 1993. "The Predictability of Stock Market Regime: Evidence from the Toronto Stock Exchange." *Review of Economics and Statistics* 75:505–510.

van Norden, S., and H. Schaller. 1999. "Speculative Behavior, Regime-Switching, and Stock Market Crashes." In Philip Rothman, ed. *Nonlinear Time Series Analysis of Economic and Financial Data*. New York: Springer, 321–356.

ABOUT THE AUTHORS

Keith Anderson is a lecturer in finance at the York Management School, University of York, England. He worked as a systems developer at Deutsche Bank in Frankfurt before receiving his PhD from the ICMA Centre, Reading. His book *The Naked PE* looks at new formulations of the price-earnings ratio (PE) in order to predict company performance more efficiently, and will be published in 2011 by Harriman House. His research interests include inefficient markets, behavioral finance, and bubbles.

Chris Brooks is professor of finance and director of research at the ICMA Centre, University of Reading, United Kingdom. He was formerly professor of finance at the Cass Business School, London. He holds a PhD and a BA in economics and econometrics, both from the University of Reading. His areas of research interest include asset pricing, fund management, statistical issues in risk management, and econometric analysis and modeling in finance and real estate. He has published widely in these areas, and has more than 80 articles in leading academic and practitioner journals including the *Journal of Business, Economic Journal, Financial Analysts*

Journal, Journal of Banking and Finance, and *Journal of Empirical Finance*. Chris is associate editor of several journals, including the *JBFA* and the *International Journal of Forecasting*. He acts as consultant for various banks and professional bodies in the fields of finance, real estate, and econometrics. Chris is also author of the first introductory econometrics textbook targeted at finance students, *Introductory Econometrics for Finance* (2002, Cambridge University Press), which is now in its second edition and has now sold more than 30,000 copies worldwide.

Apostolos Katsaris is a partner and the head of quantitative research at Caliburn Capital Partners, LLP. He has worked as a consultant in the area of risk management for Schroders Investment Management and as a lecturer at the ICMA Centre, University of Reading, and at Cass Business School, City University, in the United Kingdom. Apostolos graduated from Athens University of Economics and Business, Greece, with a BSc and an MSc in international and European economics. Following this, he undertook an MSc in international securities investment and banking at the ICMA Centre, University of Reading, United Kingdom, and graduated with distinction. He completed a PhD in finance at the ICMA Centre on the topic of "Periodically Collapsing Speculative Bubbles" and has co-authored several refereed finance articles on the subject.

CHAPTER 39

Overlapping Boards of Directors

Causes and Consequences for Corporate Governance

CHRISTA H. S. BOUWMAN
Assistant Professor of Banking and Finance at Case Western Reserve University and
Fellow at the Wharton Financial Institutions Center

*A practice such as adopting a poison pill, or changing a firm's portfolio of industries,
appears to spread through shared directors like a virus, cumulating in substantial changes
in the character of the largest corporations.*

—Davis, Yoo, and Baker (2003)

Board overlap occurs when two or more firms share the same directors. As I point out (Bouwman 2010), the average and median director of a Forbes 500 firm holds three directorships (see also Fich and Shivdasani 2006). Directors of larger firms tend to hold more directorships. Davis, Yoo, and Baker (2003) compare the cross-sections of several thousand directors serving on the boards of several hundred largest U.S. corporations in 1982, 1990, and 1999, and find that, "corporate America is overseen by a network of individuals who to a great extent know each other or have acquaintances in common." Thus, today's public corporations are connected through an informal network of directors.

What are the causes of these networks? And are they just an interesting social curiosity or do they have consequences for the governance of corporations? What is the nature of these consequences? These are the main questions I address in this chapter. My discussions will draw largely from my earlier work (Bouwman 2010), but I also bring in the findings of related papers to flesh out points of interest. I shy away from opining on whether board overlaps of this sort are "good" or "bad" because that depends on defining some kind of social welfare objective function, which is a difficult and somewhat peripheral task for the purposes of this chapter. Although there is some indication that board overlaps may have positive effects in some instances, the research findings on the effects of board overlap on firm performance are mostly ambiguous (e.g., Ferris, Jagannathan, and Pritchard 2003; Fich and Shivdasani 2006).

A survey of the literature shows that it is difficult to pin down a single dominant cause of director networks and board overlaps. Some of the reasons that have
been put forth are: desire to suppress product-market competition, interfirm dependence, and a desire for monitoring; signaling of legitimacy by signing directors
who are already on prominent boards; talent concentration among a few directors
that causes all firms to go to the same well; and social ties among board members.
I briefly review each of these explanations, and my conclusion is that it is difficult
to empirically determine which cause is the most important, although some can
be dismissed more easily than others.

On the issue of consequences, many aspects have been studied. Here I focus
primarily on what I find in my earlier paper (Bouwman 2010). The first goal
of that paper is to empirically test the hypothesis that director overlap leads to
cross-sectional governance similarity. Eight governance practices are examined.
The empirical tests provide strong evidence that firms that share directors have
governance practices that are more similar than those of firms that do not.

The second goal is to examine whether these results are driven by a "familiarity effect" or an "influence effect." According to the familiarity effect, the
relationship between director overlap and governance similarity arises because
firms are deliberately selecting directors who are serving at firms with similar
governance practices. The idea in this case is to bring in a director who will not
"rock the boat" but will provide support for what is already in place, a variant of
the reason why the proverbial drunk seeks a lamp post—for support rather than
illumination! The influence effect asserts that the relationship between director
overlap and governance similarity arises because a director—even one currently
serving at firms with *dissimilar* governance practices—exerts *influence* on the firm's
governance practices subsequent to joining the board. Empirically distinguishing
between the two causes is actually not easy. However, I am able to employ rigorous
techniques to delineate these effects, and find empirical support for *both* effects. In
other words, directors are often hired because they are serving on boards of firms
with similar governance practices, but when they do come from firms with dissimilar governance practices, they exert influence to change the firm's governance
practices in the direction of the practices they are already familiar with. It appears
that "support and illumination" go hand in hand.

The rest of the chapter is organized as follows. The next section reviews some
documented facts about board overlap. Section 3 examines the causes of this overlap. Section 4 discusses the empirical evidence related to the consequences of the
overlap. Section 5 concludes.

DIRECTOR NETWORKS AND BOARD OVERLAPS

All publicly traded corporations in the United States are required to have a board
of directors of at least three persons. Large corporations tend to have boards of
10 or more directors. The typical board of a large firm consists of both inside
and outside directors. Inside directors are (current or former) executives of the
firm or stockholding family members. A firm's inside directors often sit on the
boards of other firms. Mizruchi (1996) points out that a study of 456 Fortune 500
manufacturing firms in 1981 revealed that more than 70 percent of the firms had
at least one inside director who sat on the board of a financial institution. The

percentage is even higher when nonfinancial firms are included. However, most board overlaps are created by outside directors, many of whom sit on multiple boards. Ferris, Jagannathan, and Pritchard (2003) document that directors at firms with total assets of more than $100 million hold one to six directorships on average.

Director overlaps across firms have been a remarkably robust feature of American corporate capitalism since the turn of the twentieth century (Mizruchi 1982). The phenomenon has persisted despite the major upheavals in corporate governance that occurred in the 1980s and 1990s. The intertemporal consistency of connectivity among the several hundred largest U.S. corporations and the thousands of directors who sit on their boards is surprising because of the sweeping changes that have occurred in corporate America during the twentieth century. Because of mergers, growth, and the normal process of corporate attrition and birth, less than one-third of the largest firms in 1999 were among the largest in 1982, and less than 5 percent of the directorships were constant across this time (see Davis, Yoo, and Baker 2003). Yet, despite this sea change in terms of dramatic turnover among boards and directors, and changes in corporations themselves, board overlaps have remained a stable phenomenon.

In the research on board overlaps, various approaches have been used to determine the *extent* of overlap (see Mizruchi and Bunting 1981 for an overview), but the impact of board overlap on corporate governance practices was examined for the first time in Bouwman (2010). I briefly describe the novel approach I take in my earlier work (Bouwman 2010) in a subsequent section.

POSSIBLE CAUSES OF BOARD OVERLAP

What causes board overlap? A number of possible factors have been proposed. I discuss briefly each of the main ones, with no pretense at being exhaustive.

The first is *competition suppression*. If two firms competing in a product market end up with many common directors, collusion between these firms becomes easier, and competition can thus be more readily suppressed. Prior to 1914, there were no prohibitions in the United States on which firms could share directors. However, Section 8 of the Clayton Act of 1914 expressly prohibits overlapping boards among competitors. Not surprisingly, board overlaps dropped substantially after this (see Mizruchi 1982). Mizruchi (1996) also notes that there is little empirical evidence that board overlaps have actually been effective in restricting competition, or that it is even necessary to restrict competition.

The second possible factor is *interfirm dependence and the facilitating of monitoring* due to board overlaps. Think of a bank and a firm that has borrowed heavily from that bank. If the bank has directors on the board of the borrower, it becomes easier for the bank to monitor the borrower. Supporting this point of view, interviews with bankers suggest that they tend to join the boards of borrower firms when they are financially distressed (Richardson 1987), which is precisely when bank monitoring is the most valuable.

A third possible reason is *legitimacy signaling*. Having on your board a director from a prestigious company can signal to investors that your firm is a legitimate player. This signaling can have real consequences as it may convey to banks, for example, that the firm has competent management in place and may therefore make these banks more likely to lend to the firm (DiMaggio and Powell 1983).

A fourth reason is that there may be just a *limited set of highly qualified and talented individuals* that firms wish to draw from to appoint as directors. For example, Stokman, van der Knoop, and Wasseur (1988) show that for a 20-year period the vast majority of new director appointments at a sample of large Dutch firms were drawn from a relatively small number of persons with high levels of experience and expertise. Although it seems hard to believe that such people are in such short supply that board overlaps are inevitable, it should be remembered that CEOs are interested in board members who are not only qualified and talented but also noncontroversial individuals with views fairly aligned with those of the CEO. One way to ensure this is to select directors on the basis of recommendations by those currently on the board. This, in turn, limits the number of individuals under active consideration to those who belong to the social networks of existing directors.

THE CORPORATE GOVERNANCE CONSEQUENCES OF BOARD OVERLAP

Given the widely documented board overlap discussed in the previous sections, it is natural to conjecture that corporate governance practices will spread from one firm to another simply because these firms share directors. The result will be a great deal of convergence among firms in corporate governance practices. As discussed before, this can happen for two reasons. One is the "familiarity effect," whereby directors are being hired because they work at companies with similar governance practices. This increases the likelihood that the views of a director who is hired will be fairly aligned with those of the CEO, thereby minimizing the potential for conflict and controversy. If this effect is the only one at work, then board overlap is a *consequence* of corporate governance similarity across firms—Firm A is hiring a director from Firm B and thereby creating a board overlap because the governance practices of firms A and B are already similar.

There is, of course, another reason as well, and I call it the *influence effect*. This says that firms sometimes hire directors from firms with dissimilar governance practices—for some of the reasons discussed in the previous section—and these directors then exert influence to move the governance practices of the firm they join in the direction of the practices of the firms they were hired from. With this effect, corporate governance similarity is a *consequence* of board overlap, rather than the other way around as with the familiarity effect.

In my paper (Bouwman 2010), I have two main goals. One is to empirically test the hypothesis that director overlap leads to cross-sectional governance similarity. I examine eight governance practices. They are: (1) board size, measured as the number of directors; (2) the percentage of outside directors; (3) the number of board meetings; (4) director base pay; (5) CEO total pay; (6) the percentage of directors who are active CEOs; (7) the percentage of directors over the age of 70; and (8) CEO duality, that is, situations in which the CEO is also the chairman of the board. For the data, I use all firms included in the Corporate Library's Board Analyst database. This data set contains governance data on virtually every firm included in the S&P 500, the S&P midcap 400 index, the S&P smallcap 600 index, the Fortune 1000, and the Russell 3000 between 2001 and 2007. It also contains detailed information on each firm's directors. To examine whether the corporate governance practices at

Firm i can be explained by the governance practices at firms that have common directors with Firm i, each chosen corporate governance practice is regressed on the one-year-lagged weighted average governance practices of other firms at which its directors have board seats. A number of control variables are used to "filter out" the effects of other factors such as governance practices at peer firms and key firm and CEO characteristics previously found to be important in the literature. For all the governance practices I examine, I find strong support that board overlap shapes governance practices.

My second goal is to examine whether the results are driven by the familiarity effect or the influence effect. The familiarity effect says that the likelihood of a person being appointed as a director at a firm is greater if the person is already a director at other firms with more similar governance practices. To test this, I develop a "director selection" model. I perform statistical regression analysis and find empirical support for the familiarity effect for about two-thirds of the governance variables I study. The evidence also indicates that while the familiarity effect is important, it is not the sole driving force in the determination of director selection. For example, an individual is significantly more likely to be appointed as a director at a particular firm if in the previous year the person had a directorship at another firm in the same industry or at a geographically close firm. The person is also more likely to be picked as a director by say Firm k if in the previous year he served on the board of another company, say j, with someone who is currently a board member at Firm k. Director age has a slightly negative effect on the probability of being appointed.

I then examine the influence effect. Here the test is to examine whether a bigger gap in governance between the other firms at which a firm's directors serve and the firm leads to bigger subsequent governance changes. I find strong empirical support for the influence effect—for six out of the eight chosen governance measures, the influence effect is detected to be statistically significant. I also find evidence that the influence effect is asymmetric in the sense that positive governance gaps—such as the other firms having more board meetings in a year than the firm in question—have a stronger effect on the change in corporate governance at the firm in question than negative governance gaps. This makes intuitive economic sense.

To sum up, I find empirical support for both the familiarity and the influence effects in explaining corporate governance similarity at firms with overlapping boards.

CONCLUSION

In this chapter, I have discussed a long-standing and robust phenomenon in corporate governance—the tendency for boards of directors of major public corporations to overlap via informal networks of directors. This has been a remarkably consistent empirical regularity of the twentieth and twenty-first centuries. I have provided a discussion of the possible causes of such overlap and also of its consequences for corporate governance.

If indeed much of corporate governance is "learned" behavior, wherein companies observe and adopt what other companies are doing and the channel for such observation are the directors who sit on the boards of these companies, then we have to seriously reconsider the design of optimal corporate governance. It would appear that it may be more of a *social* phenomenon than something that is the outcome of well-articulated economic optimization.

REFERENCES

Bouwman, Christa H. S. 2010. "Corporate Governance Propagation through Overlapping Directors." *Working Paper.*

Davis, Gerald S., Mina Yoo, and Wayne E. Baker. 2003. "The Small World of the American Corporate Elite, 1982–2001." *Strategic Organization* I:301–326.

DiMaggio, Paul J., and Walter W. Powell. 1983. "The Iron Cage Revisited: Institutional Isomorphism and Collective Rationality in Organizational Fields." *American Sociological Review* 48:147–160.

Ferris, Stephen, Murali Jagannathan, and Adam Pritchard. 2003. "Too Busy to Mind the Business? Monitoring by Directors with Multiple Board Appointments." *Journal of Finance* 58:1087–1111.

Fich, Eliezer M., and Anil Shivdasani. 2006. "Are Busy Boards Effective Monitors?" *Journal of Finance* 61:689–724.

Mizruchi, Mark S. 1982. *The American Corporate Network: 1904–1974.* Beverly Hills, CA: Sage.

Mizruchi, Mark S. 1996. "What Do Interlocks Do? An Analysis, Critique, and Assessment of Research on Interlocking Directorates." *Annual Review of Sociology* 22:271–298.

Mizruchi, Mark S., and David Bunting. 1981. "Influence in Corporate Networks: An Examination of Four Measures." *Administrative Science Quarterly* 26:475–489.

Richardson, R. Jack. 1987. "Directorship Interlocks and Corporate Profitability." *Administrative Science Quarterly* 32:367–386.

Stokman, Frans N., Jelle van der Knoop, and Frans W. Wasseur. 1988. "Interlocks in the Netherlands: Stability and Careers in the Period 1960–1980." *Social Networks* 10:183–208.

ABOUT THE AUTHOR

Christa H. S. Bouwman holds a PhD in finance from the University of Michigan, a master's degree in economics and business (cum laude) from the University of Groningen, the Netherlands, and an MBA from Cornell University. She is an assistant professor of banking and finance at Case Western Reserve University where she held the Lewis-Progressive Chair from 2006 to 2009. She is also a fellow of the Wharton Financial Institutions Center at the University of Pennsylvania and a visiting scholar at the Boston Federal Reserve Bank. She was a visiting assistant professor of finance at MIT's Sloan School of Management in 2009–2010. Her professional experience includes five years in corporate finance at ABN AMRO Bank, in the areas of venture capital, project finance advisory, and capital structure advisory. She was a litigative consultant for the U.S. Department of Justice, assisting an expert witness in several cases related to the savings and loan crisis in the early 1980s. Her research papers have been published in the *Review of Financial Studies* and the *MIT/Sloan Management Review.*

CHAPTER 40

The Credit Default Swap Market in Turmoil

The Case of the GM and Ford Crisis of 2005

VIRGINIE COUDERT
Banque de France, Financial Stability Directorate; Economix, University of Paris Ouest-Nanterre; CEPII, Paris

MATHIEU GEX
Banque de France, Financial Stability Directorate; CERAG, University of Grenoble, France

A re credit derivatives markets particularly vulnerable to contagion effects? This question is important given that derivatives markets play a key role in asset pricing. The sharp increase in all credit default swap (CDS) premia during the subprime crisis tends to suggest a positive answer. The General Motors (GM) and Ford crisis in 2005 also triggered a surge in all CDS premia, which can be seen now as a premonitory event. Considering this precise crisis has the advantage of being well circumscribed in time, as its origin can be clearly tracked down by the announcement of losses by GM in March 2005, promptly followed by the downgrading of both firms by the major rating agencies. As some time has now elapsed, it is possible to look back on this episode as a case-in-point of contagion effects within the CDS market.

GM and Ford troubles in 2005 had important repercussions on the credit market due to the huge amount of debt issued by the two leading multinational firms. The spillovers were strengthened by the fact that their debt was also included in many collateral debt obligations (CDOs). At the start of the crisis, in March 2005, the cost of protection against default on the CDS market of both firms surged dramatically (by 260 bp for GM and 110 bp for Ford). This immediately rippled through the whole CDS market, the CDX high yield climbing from 300 bp to 530 bp. The bond market was also affected (rising by 150 bp in the U.S. high-yield segment) though to a lesser extent.

Most contagion phenomena studied in the economic literature consider either speculative attacks on currencies spreading over to different countries, or banking crises in dominos, stemming from the linkages between financial institutions, or simultaneous crashes in stocks markets (for a survey, see Allen and Gale 2000;

Pericoli and Sbracia 2003). A closer examination shows that channels of transmission considered in these studies can also apply to credit derivative markets. To be more precise, we see four broad categories of transmission channels that are able to spread a crisis in the CDS market: (1) liquidity problems, as investors confronted to losses need cash to restore their risk management ratios and to meet rising margin calls; (2) the updating of investors' beliefs and preferences, as all the risks are reassessed more severely across the board; (3) herding behavior, among others due to information costs and (4) counterparty risk.

These effects were certainly involved in the May 2005 episode. First, the GM and Ford crisis triggered liquidity effects as evidenced by Acharya et al. (2007). Second, as these two flagship firms were suddenly viewed as possible defaulters, agents may have updated their judgment on the probabilities of default of other firms, considered as safe assets until that time. Third, herd behavior could have taken place, just as in any other crises. Fourth, counterparty risk could have played a role, as suggested by Jorion and Zhang (2009) who have evidenced this kind of effect on the CDS market during bankruptcy episodes. Furthermore, contagion could also be due to the very nature of the CDS market, where bearish positions are easier to take than on the bond market (Coudert and Gex 2010b).

Whatever the underlying theoretical mechanisms, contagion on financial markets can be broadly defined by a simultaneous fall in asset prices, triggered by an initial drop in one specific market. Actually, the rise in correlations is often considered as the key symptom of contagion (Baig and Goldfajn 2002; De Gregorio and Valdes 2001). A number of empirical methods have been developed to measure comovements appropriately (Dungey et al. 2003). The most straightforward ones consist in comparing correlations during crises and tranquil periods.

More restrictive views confine contagion to falls in asset prices exceeding the usual comovements observed in tranquil periods. This phenomenon is called *shift-contagion* by Forbes and Rigobon (2002). In this framework, the contagion effects can also be measured by an increase in correlations, but correlation coefficients need to be adjusted of possible bias due to higher volatility during crises (Boyer et al. 1999).

Here, we set out to test contagion within the CDS market during the GM and Ford crisis (for more details, see Coudert and Gex 2010a). To do so, we calculate correlations, plain and adjusted, over a sample of 224 CDS of European and U.S. firms included in the major indices (CDX and iTraxx). We then test for an increase in the correlation coefficients during the crisis period.

THE GM AND FORD CRISIS AND THE CDS MARKET

The difficulties encountered by GM started to raise concerns in March 2005. On March 16, GM announced a profit warning for the first quarter, forecasting a loss of roughly US$850 million, compared to a previous target of breakeven. Later, on April 8, Ford also announced a profit warning, revising its annual earnings expectations down by 25 percent compared to forecasts.

As soon as March 2005, market participants reassessed both firms' default risk and were expecting a downgrading by rating agencies, before the latter took any decision. As a result, the CDS premium of GM climbed from 304 bp to 567 bp in March 2005, while that of Ford rose from 244 bp to 357 bp (Exhibit 40.1).

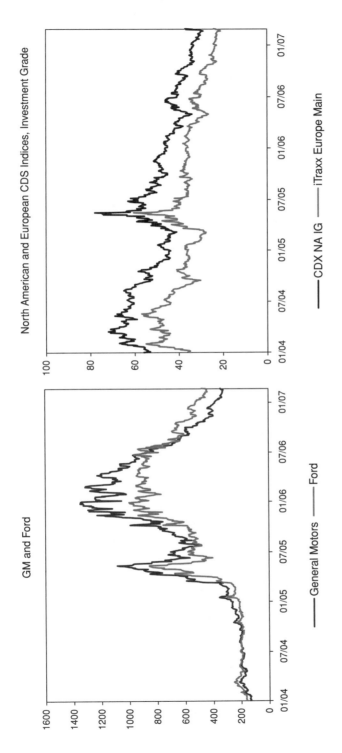

Exhibit 40.1 CDS Premia, in Basis Points

The ratings of both firms were successively downgraded by the three major rating agencies between May 5 and December 19, 2005. The downgrading was particularly harsh because the two firms were downshifted from investment grade to speculative grade.

Given the importance of these two firms, financial stress rippled over the whole CDS market. Contagion went through the usual channels but was also reinforced by specific phenomena: (1) as GM and Ford were no longer investment-grade, dedicated investment-grade investors started to sell both firms' bonds and bought protection to hedge their former positions, which contributed to the rise in CDS spreads. (2) There was an abnormal price movement between GM bonds and stocks. GM stock price surged by 18 percent on May 4 because of a tender offer made by Kirk Kerkorian; the day after, Standard & Poor's downgraded GM, causing its bond price to fall markedly. These odd price evolutions brutally hit a number of hedge funds that had arbitraged on GM capital structure, taking long positions in bonds combined with short equity positions. As both legs of their strategy were affected, those hedge funds suffered losses and tried to hedge themselves by bidding up the cost on GM protection (Packer and Woolridge 2005; Venizelos 2005). (3) The price of equity tranches in the CDS indexes increased relatively to the other tranches, which had adverse effects on other hedge funds, holding long equity and short mezzanine positions (Beinstein et al. 2005).

At any rate, all of the CDS market was immediately affected: index premia almost doubled in March 2005 (Exhibit 40.1). After having reached a peak on May 18, the CDS indices started to decline, which suggests that the market had then managed to absorb the shock.

THE SAMPLE OF CDS

We consider a sample of daily data on 224 CDS present in the North-American and European five-year CDS indices: (1) the CDX NA IG, for North-American investment grade (IG hereafter) firms; (2) the iTraxx Europe Main, for European investment grade firms; (3) the CDX NA HY, for U.S. speculative grade, or high yield, firms (HY hereafter); (4) the iTraxx Europe Crossover, for European speculative grade firms. We retain all entities present in these indices without missing data (for more details, see Coudert and Gex 2010a). Of course, we add to the sample the GM and Ford CDS.

We split the sample into three subperiods according to CDS spreads movements and volatility: (1) a reference period just before the crisis, when spreads and volatility were particularly low (from December 15, 2004, to March 15, 2005); (2) the crisis period, which is dated from March 16 to August 24, 2005; (3) the post-crisis period, running from August 2005 to February 2007, that is, prior to the renewal of turbulences in summer 2007.

During the reference period, CDS premia were low and stable: 33 bp on average for the CDS IG index and 73 bp for our global index. Then, during the crisis, CDS premia posted a sharp increase in all sectors, the global index reaching 94 bp. CDS volatility rose sharply during the crisis, jumping on average from 42 percent to 60 percent. The European and U.S. high-yield segments were also impacted.

Exhibit 40.2   Average Correlations between the 224 CDS and GM and Ford

	Period 1 (pre-crisis) Correlations	Period 2 (crisis)		Period 3 (post-crisis) Correlations
		Correlations	Adjusted Correlations	
CDX NA IG	0.071	0.205	0.105	0.058
CDX NA HY	0.067	0.198	0.102	0.065
iTraxx Main	0.115	0.303	0.159	0.071
Autos	0.185	0.422	0.227	0.105
iTraxx Crossover	0.145	0.356	0.190	0.141
Global index[a]	0.091	0.250	0.130	0.069

Note: Period 1: from 12/15/04 to 03/15/05; period 2: from 03/16/05 to 08/24/05.

CORRELATIONS BEFORE AND DURING THE CRISIS

Indeed, the correlations between the CDS of the 224 firms and those of GM and Ford notably increased during the crisis, from 9 percent to 25 percent overall (Exhibit 40.2). Investment grade CDS have been impacted as well as the high yields. More detailed results show that this result holds on average for each sector. At a firm level, correlations with GM increased for 200 CDS out of 224, and with Ford for 179 of them. As the rise in correlations might stem from an increase in volatility, we have also calculated adjusted correlations that take into account volatility changes. Unsurprisingly, the adjusted correlations are lower than the plain ones, but they also increased during the crisis, from 9 percent to 13 percent.

Contagion hit all industries, geographical areas and categories (IG or HY) across the board. American and European firms seem equally affected. This may be due to several factors. (1) A large share of the deals on the CDS market are trades on indices, tranches of indices, or synthetic CDOs, and not on individual CDSs in these cases, positions are taken or liquidated for a whole range of CDS simultaneously. (2) The CDS market has been highly concentrated involving few large market makers and investors, especially at that time. Consequently, any difficulties supported by market participants have been likely to spread on the whole market. (3) Both distressed firms are multinationals, present in a whole range of countries, thus able to impact the world economy. European firms even seem to have been more impacted than the U.S. ones.

Let us take a closer look at other car-makers' CDS. This is possible for European firms, as the iTraxx index contains a subindex of the auto industry, whereas it is not the case for the North-American index. The increase in correlation was particularly marked, from 19 percent over the reference period to 42 percent during the crisis. If we look at the individual results, we can see that all the auto firms in the sample had their CDS premia positively correlated with those of GM and Ford during the crisis. This means that the other car-makers were hit by GM and Ford difficulties, instead of benefiting from them through a competitive effect. Moreover, the adjusted correlations between the CDS of the car-makers and GM increased for all firms in the sample (although not with Ford).

We have checked that this rise in correlations is a significant phenomenon, instead of a purely random one, by running the usual tests for comparing correlations between two periods. As a matter of fact, the GM crisis significantly affected more than half of the CDS in the sample. One hundred and twenty seven out of 224 firms had their correlations with GM increased significantly at a 90 percent confidence threshold (103 at a 95 percent threshold). Contagion from Ford is also patent, although less marked, as 49 firms were impacted with a 90 percent threshold (23 with a 95 percent threshold). However, the rise in correlations is less significant when considering the adjusted correlations. This suggests that part of the rise of correlations results from the increase in volatility during the crisis. Therefore, the simultaneous rise of most CDS spreads at that time was chiefly due to the usual co-movements within the market. In this sense, contagion has certainly occurred, but not shift-contagion.

CONCLUSION

The General Motors and Ford crisis in May 2005 affected the whole CDS market. Considering a sample of 224 CDS, we show that correlations between a majority of CDS and those of GM increased significantly during the crisis, which suggests contagion effects. Nevertheless, this does not hold when adjusting correlations for biases due to higher volatility. In other words, the usual price transmission mechanisms within the CDS market were not shifted by the crisis. The strong interdependence inside the market and the high volatility generated by the crisis were sufficient to significantly raise correlations. All industries were hit across the board, although auto-makers were particularly affected. On the whole, this study reveals the vulnerability of the CDS market to exogenous shocks.

REFERENCES

Acharya, V. V., S. Schaefer, and Y. Zhang. 2007. "Liquidity Risk and Correlation Risk: A Clinical Study of the General Motors and Ford Downgrade of May 2005." *Working Paper* SSRN.

Allen, F., and D. Gale. 2000. "Financial Contagion." *Journal of Political Economy* 108:1–33.

Baig, T., and I. Goldfajn. 2002. "Monetary Policy in the Aftermath of Currency Crises: The Case of Asia." *Review of International Economics* 10:1, 92–112.

Beinstein, E., C. Pedersen, and B. Graves. 2005. "Quantitative Strategy: Dislocations in Tranched DJ CDX.NA.IG Market May Present Opportunities." JPMorgan, *Credit Derivatives and Quantitative Strategy*, May 11.

Boyer, B. H., M. S. Gibson, and M. Loretan. 1999. "Pitfalls in Test for Changes in Correlations." *International Finance Discussion Paper* 597, Board of the Governors of the Federal Reserve System.

Coudert, V., and M. Gex. 2010a. "Contagion Inside the Credit Default Swaps Market: The Case of the GM and Ford Crisis in 2005." *Journal of International Financial Markets, Institutions and Money* 20:109–134.

Coudert, V., and M. Gex. 2010b. "CDS and Bond Market, Which Leads the Other?" *Review of Financial Stability* No. 14, Bank of France, June.

De Gregorio, and R. Valdes. 2001. "Crisis Transmission: Evidence from the Debt, Tequila, and Asian Flu Crisis." *The World Bank Economic Review* 15:2, 289–314.

Dungey M., R. Fry, B. González-Hermosillo, and V. Martin. 2003. "Characterizing Global Risk Aversion for Emerging Markets during Financial Crises." *IMF Working Paper* 03/251.

Forbes, K., and R. Rigobon. 2002. "No Contagion, Only Interdependence: Measuring Stock Market Co-Movements." *Journal of Finance* 57:5, 2223–2261.

Jorion, P., and G. Zhang. 2009. "Credit Contagion from Counterparty Risk." *Journal of Finance* 64:2053–2087.

Packer, F., and P. D. Woolridge. 2005. "Overview: Repricing in Credit Markets." *BIS Quarterly Review*, June.

Pericoli, M., and M. Sbracia. 2003. "A Primer on Financial Contagion." *Journal of Economic Surveys* 17:September, 571–608.

Venizelos, G. 2005. "Correlation Correction." *Credit in Focus* ABN AMRO, May 12.

ABOUT THE AUTHORS

Virginie Coudert holds a PhD in mathematical economics from the University of Paris I (Pantheon-Sorbonne). She works as a scientific advisor at the Banque de France and is a visiting professor at the University of Paris X (Nanterre). She is also a research associate at the Centre d'Etudes Prospectives et d'Information Internationale (CEPII) in Paris. Virginie Coudert has written many articles in the area of monetary economics, international finance, and exchange rates.

Mathieu Gex is an economist at the Banque de France. He also teaches at University of Paris X (Nanterre). Mathieu Gex is currently achieving a PhD in finance on the credit default swap market at the University of Grenoble. He has written several papers on credit derivative markets, risk aversion, and contagion effects.

CHAPTER 41

Equity Market Contagion and Comovement

Industry Level Evidence

KATE PHYLAKTIS
Professor at Sir John Cass Business School, City of London

LICHUAN XIA
Chief Economist at Cypress House Asset Management in Hong Kong

F inancial crises seem never far away from us. A series of crises were witnessed in the past 20 years: the 1992 Exchange Rate Mechanism (ERM) attacks, the 1994 Mexican peso collapse, the 1997 Asian crisis, the 1998 Russian collapse, the 1998 Long-Term Capital Markets (LTCM) crisis, the 1999 Brazilian devaluation, the 2000 technological crisis, and most recently, the 2007 U.S. subprime mortgage crisis. A striking feature of crises is that markets tend to move more closely together during volatile times than during tranquil times. Such strong comovement is usually beyond the explanation of real and financial linkages and often referred to as contagion. For example, during the Asian crisis, following the collapse of the Thai baht's peg in July 1997, the financial markets of East and Southeast Asia—in particular, Thailand, Malaysia, Indonesia, the Philippines, and Korea—headed in a similar, downward direction during late 1997 and early 1998. The closer linkage between markets during crisis episode makes it possible that external shocks are transmitted across different markets. Especially shocks from one market are propagated to the markets, which have no real or financial linkages with the market in crisis and to the markets that are in different geographic locations.

What is the driving force behind the transmission of shocks from one country to the others? Is it fundamentals driven, or is it just a case of pure contagion such as irrational, herd mentality displayed by panic-stricken investors? Understanding contagion and its origin is important for policy makers and fund managers aiming to diversify risks. For policy makers, if the crisis is mainly due to contagion, that is, due to temporary, nonfundamental factors, then short-run isolation strategies, such as capital controls, could be highly effective in reducing the effect of the crisis. On the other hand, if the crisis is transmitted mainly through permanent fundamental factors, then these short-run isolation strategies will only delay a country's adjustment to a shock (Dungey et al. 2003; Forbes and Rigobon 2001). For fund managers, if contagion prevails in times of crisis, the benefit of international diversification will be hampered when it is needed most.

The contagion on financial markets has been extensively studied. The results are, however, mixed. The early studies make use of correlation analysis and find contagion exists. The central idea is to assess whether the correlation coefficient between two equity markets changes across tranquil and volatile periods. If the correlation increases significantly, it suggests that the transmission between the two markets amplifies after the shock and thus contagion occurs. For example, King and Wadhwani (1990), find that cross-market correlations between the United States, United Kingdom, and Japan increased significantly after the 1997 U.S. stock crash. Calvo and Reinhart (1996) focus on emerging markets and find that the correlations in equity prices and Brady bonds between Asian and Latin American emerging markets increased significantly during the 1994 Mexican peso crisis. Baig and Goldfajn (1999) test for contagion in equity indices, currency prices, interest rates, and sovereign spreads in emerging markets during the 1997–1998 Asian crisis. They document a surge of significant cross-market correlations during the crisis for many of the countries.

Later studies have recognized that focusing on correlations can be misleading. For example, Forbes and Rigobon (2002) show that looking at unadjusted correlation coefficients is not appropriate, as the calculated correlation coefficient is an increasing function of the variance of the underlying asset return, so that when coefficients between a tranquil period and a crisis period are compared, the coefficient in the crisis period is biased upward as volatility rises substantially. After correcting for this bias, they find no contagion during the 1997 Asian crisis, the 1994 Mexican peso collapse, and the 1987 U.S. equity market crash. Instead, a high level of market interdependence is found during these crises periods, which reflects a continuation of strong cross-market linkages present globally. Bekaert, Harvey, and Ng (2003) avoid the above correlation analysis and develop a two-factor (global and regional) asset pricing model to examine the equity market contagion in the regions of Europe, South-East Asia, and Latin America during both the Mexican and Asian crises in the 1990s. By defining contagion as correlation among the model residuals after controlling for the local and foreign shocks, the authors show that there is no evidence of additional contagion caused by the Mexican crisis. However, economically meaningful increases in the residual correlation have been found, especially in Asia, during the Asian crisis, a result of contagion confirmed by Dungey et al. (2003) and others who have studied the contagion on Asian equity markets.

Studies on equity market contagion unanimously focus on the empirical evidence at market level and examine whether contagion exists across markets. The question they try to answer is whether idiosyncratic shocks from one particular market or group of markets are transmitted to the other markets during financial crises. In this paper, however, we take a different perspective and explore the equity market contagion at the disaggregated industry level, an issue which has not yet been examined in the previous literature. The question we endeavor to answer is whether unexpected shocks from a particular market (group of markets) or a particular sector are propagated to the sectors in other countries.

Studying the contagion effect at sector level is important for several reasons. First, studying the contagion at the market level may mask the heterogeneous performances of various sectors. Sector contagion can be asymmetric, in the sense that some sectors are more severely affected by external shocks than the other sectors within a market. Forbes (2001) shows that trade linkage is an important determinant of a country's vulnerability to crises that originate from elsewhere in the world. If this is so, sectors with extensive international trade (e.g., traded goods sectors) would tend to be more prone to external shocks than sectors with less international trade (e.g., nontraded goods sectors). Some sectors (e.g., banking) may even constitute a major channel in transmitting the shocks across markets during crises (see e.g., Tai 2004). From the point view of portfolio management, the sector heterogeneity of contagion implies that there are sectors which can still provide a channel for achieving the benefit of international diversification during crises despite the prevailing contagion at the market level. Second, there is evidence showing that in recent years the global industry factors are becoming more important than the country specific factors in driving the variation of international equity returns (e.g., Phylaktis and Xia 2006a, 2006b). Industries have overcome the cross-border restrictions and become increasingly correlated worldwide, which increases the likelihood of industries' role in propagating the global shocks and providing a channel for transmitting the contagion effect. Third, the industrial composition varies across global markets. Large, mature markets (e.g., U.S. and U.K.) comprise of more diversified industries whereas small, less mature markets (e.g., Switzerland) are usually concentrated on a few industries. It is thus interesting to know whether markets with similar industrial structures will comove more closely with each other and be more prone to contagion during crises compared to the markets with different industrial structures.

Although the exact definition of contagion is not agreed on in the literature, we define in this paper contagion as excess correlation—that is, correlation over and above what one would expect from economic fundamentals. Our paper takes an asset pricing perspective based on the methodology of Bekaert, Harvey, and Ng (2003) and examines two sources of risk: one from the U.S. equity market (proxy for the world market) and the other from the regional market, nesting an International CAPM model and a Regional CAPM model, after controlling for local fundamental factors. Essentially, our framework decomposes the correlations of sector returns into two components: the part the asset pricing model explains and the part the model does not explain. The explained part provides potential insights about sector level integration; and the unexplained part allows us to examine the correlations of model residuals, which we define as the contagion effects at the sector level. Our sample covers 10 broad sectors in 29 smaller countries across the regions of Europe, Asia, and Latin America (see Appendices 1 and 2) with a time span of January 1990 to June 2004.

In terms of sector level integration, we find that two sectors exhibited common features in the three regions: the Information Technology sector showing a global nature and the Utilities sector a local regional nature. This is not surprising as the Information Technology sector is considered more international in nature while Utilities sector is subject to local country-specific factors. However, the rest of the sectors performed variably across regions. In Europe and Latin America, those sectors are dominated by the regional factors and, as such, more strongly integrated at the regional level. Financials, General Industries, and Cyclical Services are the top three sectors with the greatest regional integration in magnitude. In contrast, in Asia those sectors are more heavily influenced by the U.S. market and more integrated at the global level. The strongest globally integrated sectors are General Industries, Financials, and Cyclical Goods.

Our finding of regional dominance in Europe is consistent with the results of other studies (see e.g., Fratzscher 2002). This regional dominance can to a large part be attributed to the drive toward EMU and in particular, the elimination of exchange rate volatility and uncertainty in the process of monetary unification after the introduction of the euro. The dominance by the regional market in Latin America is also reported in other papers as well (see e.g., Heaney et al. 2002). Similarly, the stronger connection to the U.S. market in Asia is also documented in Bekaert, Harvey, and Ng (2003).

In terms of contagion, we find an overall contagion exists over our entire sample period for most of the sectors, but the transmission channels and magnitude of contagion vary across regions. For possible transmission channels, contagion across the three regions is transmitted via global and regional shocks. But in Europe and Asia, an additional channel is identified, which is the shocks from equivalent sectors within the region. This confirms our prior expectation that contagion occurs at the sector level and sectors provide channels in propagating unexpected shocks. For the magnitude of contagion, in Europe and Latin America the most severe contagion comes from the regional shocks whereas in Asia it is mainly driven by the shocks from equivalent sectors within the region.

In this chapter, we also examined whether there is additional contagion during the periods of Mexican crisis in 1994–1995 and the Asian crisis in 1997–1998. Our results reveal the following: First, contagion is transmitted in some sectors and not in others. This explains the mixed results found in studies of contagion at the market level. Second, the results also point out that even though contagion might be prevalent at the market level, there are still some sectors that are immune from the contagion effect during a crisis. Third, in our analysis of the Mexican crisis, we found that the financial sector did exhibit additional correlation with respect to the United States in Europe and Asia, but it did not in Latin America. Meanwhile, correlations with equivalent sectors in the region were not found. This demonstrates that financial links with the United States might have transmitted the Mexican crisis in the region. This result is supported by Frankel and Schmukler (1998), who examined the behavior of mutual funds in international equity markets. They have found that the Mexican crisis spread to other equity markets in Latin America through New York rather than directly. In Europe and Asia, trade links might have been the transmission mechanism of the crisis.

In the case of the Asian crisis, the scenario is different. Our analysis indicates that contagion can only be observed in Asia. In addition, the Financials sector is among the sectors that displayed additional correlation with respect to the United States. This again confirms the financial links through the United States for the propagation of the crisis. This result is supported by Van Rijckeghem and Weder (2001, 2002), who examined shifts in portfolios of European, North American, and

Japanese banks during the Asian crisis. They found that North American banks shifted their lending amid emerging markets from Asia to Latin America and Europe, explaining our findings as to why the last two regions were unaffected. In short, our analysis lends support to the importance of financial links through a financial center, such as the United States, in propagating a crisis, at least within the region of the initial disturbance.

To conclude, by applying a two-factor asset pricing model, we examined the equity market integration and contagion at industry level. With regard to integration, we have found that the sector level integration displays a distinct pattern across regions: Sectors in Europe and Latin America have higher betas with respect to the regional market than with respect to the U.S. market, suggesting the stronger integration at the regional level. Conversely, sectors in Asia are more responsive to the U.S. market than to the regional market and thus more integrated at the global level. Our findings of regional differences are also confirmed in other papers studying the international equity market comovements. The heterogeneous performance of sectors across regions indicates that those sectors are less globally correlated than we have expected and still subject to the regional effects.

With regard to contagion, an overall contagion over our entire sample period is found for the majority of sectors in Europe, Asia, and Latin America. However, the transmitting channels and the magnitude of contagion vary across regions. Sector shocks do play a role in contagion propagation. Finally, in examining whether the Mexican and Asian crises provide additional contagion effects, we find that nearly half the sectors in the three regions were affected via the global shocks during the Mexican crisis. During the Asian crisis, no additional contagion is found in Europe or Latin America, but a worsened contagion transmitted via the global and regional shocks is found for most sectors in Asia. In reviewing the affected sectors, we note that the Financials sector exhibited additional correlation with respect to the United States in Latin America during the Mexican crisis and in Asia during the Asian crisis supporting the importance of financial links through a financial center in propagating a crisis.

Thus, our results confirm the sector heterogeneity of contagion and this has implications for portfolio managers aiming to diversify risks. On the one hand, industries sectors are found to have crossed national boundaries and become integrated with the rest of the world. This means that domestic risk factors now matter less and nondomestic factors matter more. Diversification across countries may be losing merit and diversification across industries is preferable. However, the divergence of integration across regions points to the fact that industries sectors are not as globally correlated as we expect and regional effects still play a role. Therefore, selecting portfolios across regions rather than within regions would be more efficient. However, international investors and portfolio managers are concerned with diversification in volatile times, especially during crisis periods when it is most needed. Our evidence indicates that some sectors are plagued with contagion during crises, so investors and portfolio managers should avoid choosing individual securities from those contagious sectors. However, our evidence also demonstrates that there are sectors which are immune from external shocks or contagion during financial crises. Those sectors can provide a tool to diversify risks during crisis periods and to achieve the benefits of diversification.

APPENDIX 1: FTSE ACTUARIES (SECTOR AND INDUSTRY CLASSIFICATION)

Sector	Industries Included
Basic Industries	Chemicals Construction and Building Materials Forestry and Paper Steel and Other Metals Chemicals, Construction, and Building Materials, Forestry, and Paper Steel and Other Metals
Cyclical Consumer Goods	Automobiles and Parts Household Goods and Textiles
Cyclical Services	General Retailers Leisure Entertainment and Hotels Media and Photography Support Services Transport
General Industries	Aerospace and Defense Electronic and Electrical Equipment Engineering and Machinery
Information Technology	Information Technology Hardware Software and Computer Services
Non-Cyclical Consumer Goods	Beverages Food Producers and Processors Health Personal Care and Household Products Pharmaceuticals and Biotechnology Tobacco
Non-Cyclical Services	Food and Drug Retailers Telecommunication Services
Resources	Mining Oil and Gas
Financials	Banks Insurance Life Assurance Investment Companies Real Estate Speciality and Other Finance
Utilities	Electricity Gas Distribution Water

APPENDIX 2: SAMPLE COUNTRIES INCLUDED IN THE ANALYSIS

Region	Countries Included
Europe	Belgium, Denmark, Spain, Finland, Greece, Ireland, Luxemburg, Netherlands, Norway, Austria, Portugal, Sweden, Switzerland, Turkey
Asia	Hong Kong, Malaysia, Korea, Indonesia, Singapore, Thailand, Taiwan, Philippines
Latin America	Argentina, Brazil, Columbia, Chile, Mexico, Peru, Venezuela

REFERENCES

Baig, T., and I. Goldfajn. 1999. "Financial Market Contagion in the Asian crisis." *IMF Staff Papers* 46:2, 167–195.

Bekaert, G., H. R. Harvey, and A. Ng. 2003. "Market Integration and Contagion." *NBER Working Paper* 9510. Accepted at the *Journal of Business*.

Calvo, S., and C. Reinhart. 1996. "Capital Flows to Latin America: Is There Evidence of Contagion Effects?" In G. Calvo, M. Goldstein, and E. Hochreiter, eds. *Private Capital Flows to Emerging Markets*, 151–171. Washington, DC: Institute for International Economics.

Dungey, M., R. Fry, and V. L. Martin. 2003. "Equity Transmission Mechanisms from Asia and Australia: Interdependence or Contagion?" *Australian Journal of Management* 28:157–182.

Forbes, K. 2001. "Are Trade Linkages Important Determinants of Country Vulnerability to Crises?" *NBER Working Paper* 8194, www.nber.org/papers/w8194.

Forbes, K., and R. Rigobon. 2001. "Contagion in Latin America: Definitions, Measurement, and Policy Implications." Document prepared for the World Bank Conference: "How It Spreads and How It Can Be Stopped." Washington, DC, February 2000. www.worldbank.com.

Forbes, K., and R. Rigobon. 2002. "No Contagion, Only Interdependence: Measuring Stock Market Co-Movements." *Journal of Finance* 57:2223–2262.

Frankel, J., and S. Schmukler. 1998. "Crises, Contagion, and Country Funds: Effects on East Asia and Latin America." In R. Glick, ed. *Managing Capital Flows and Exchange Rates: Perspectives from the Pacific Basin*, 232–266. New York: Cambridge University Press.

Fratzscher, M. 2002. "Financial Market Integration in Europe: On the Effects of EMU on Stock Markets." *International Journal of Finance and Economics* 7:3, 165–194.

Heaney, R. A., V. Hooper, and M. Jagietis. 2002. "Regional Integration of Stock Markets in Latin America." *Journal of Economic Integration* 17:745–760.

King, M., and S. Wadhwani. 1990. "Transmission of Volatility between Stock Markets." *The Review of Financial Studies* 3:1, 5–33.

Phylaktis, K., and L. Xia. 2006a. "The Changing Role of Industry and Country Effects in the Global Equity Markets." *European Journal of Finance* 12:627–648.

Phylaktis, K., and L. Xia. 2006b. "Sources of Firms' Industry and Country Effects in Emerging Markets." *Journal of International Money and Finance* 25:459–475.

Tai, C. 2004. "Can Bank Be a Source of Contagion during the 1997 Asian Crisis?" *Journal of Banking and Finance* 28:399–421.

Van Rijckeghem, C., and B. Weder. 2001. "Sources of Contagion: Is it Finance or Trade?" *Journal of International Economics* 54:293–308.

Van Rijckeghem, C., and B. Weder. 2002. "Spillovers Through Banking Centres: A Panel Data Analysis." *Journal of International Money and Finance* 22:483–509.

ABOUT THE AUTHORS

Kate Phylaktis is currently a professor of international finance and director of the Emerging Markets Group at Sir John Cass Business School in London. She received an MSc in economics from the London School of Economics and a PhD in banking and finance from City University. Dr. Phylaktis has held various positions at the school including head of the Department of Banking and Finance. Before joining the school, she worked at the London School of Economics. Visiting appointments include the research department of the International Monetary Fund, University of Bordeaux, the Athens Laboratory of Business Administration, and the Warsaw University.

Dr. Phylaktis has published in prestigious journals in the areas of foreign exchange markets, capital markets, and emerging markets finance. Current work focuses on microstructure issues, financial market integration, dual-listing of securities, and on international diversification. She has written three books. She is an associate editor of five journals.

Lichuan Xia is the chief economist and director of Cypress House Asset Management in Hong Kong. He received an MBA and a PhD in finance from Cass Business School U.K. and an M.A. in economics from the Graduate School of the People's Bank of China. Having worked with China's central bank and several financial and securities companies in Hong Kong and Singapore, Dr. Xia has more than 15 years of practical research experience in macroeconomics and financial markets. His numerous academic papers have been published on top journals such as *Journal of International Money & Finance* and *Financial Management Journal*.

CHAPTER 42

Price Contagion of Foreclosed Properties

ERIC ROSENBLATT
President of Credit Risk Analytics and Monitoring, Fannie Mae[*]

VINCENT YAO
Director of Economics at Federal National Mortgage Association (Fannie Mae)

Foreclosures create substantial social costs. Communities suffer when foreclosures are clustered, adding further to the downward pressure on property values. Lower property values in turn translate to lower tax revenues for local governments, and increases in the number of vacant homes can foster vandalism and crime. At the national level, the declines in house prices that result from the addition of foreclosed properties to the supply of homes for sale create broader economic and financial stress.
—Ben S. Bernanke, Chairman, Board of Governors
of the Federal Reserve System

Three recent papers find empirical support for the chairman's opinion that foreclosures lower the values of neighboring properties. (Immergluck and Smith 2006; Lin, Rosenblatt, and Yao 2007; Shlay and Whitman 2004). But before calling the matter completely settled, we would ask: What does the chairman (and others) mean when they speak of "foreclosures"? Sometimes people say foreclosure when they really mean a "foreclosed home." It is common, for instance, to advertise "foreclosures for sale." It is surely not a good sign for a community to have a large number of foreclosed homes for sale. But it is also not a good sign to have a large number of homes for sale, regardless of the reason. Foreclosure itself is actually just a legal proceeding, a process of resolving an indebtedness that is not being paid, similar to bankruptcy. It typically results in a home for sale, though this is not necessarily the case: The bank could rent the property to the owner or someone else, could keep it off the market until the market recovered, or use the land for some other purpose.

---

[*]The opinions expressed in this chapter are those of the authors alone and do not necessarily represent the views of Fannie Mae.

A large number of foreclosed homes for sale represents a problem for the local real estate market on two accounts, neither having a direct connection to the legal act of foreclosure. First of all, when supply shifts upward, prices will adjust downward. Second, and more related to the act of foreclosure, many of these homes are in poor repair, making the neighborhood look bad, and possibly making it dangerous, due to squatters, fire risk, or other similar hazards. But this is true whether the maintenance failures and nonoccupancy comes about through foreclosure, job loss, abandonment, or in some other way. Is foreclosure to blame? If we say foreclosure is to blame, when does the damage really occur: at foreclosure, or well before, when the borrower ceases investments in their property?

The issue is particularly pressing at this time because in the past few years foreclosures sales have reached rates not seen since the Depression. According to the MBA survey, in 2006 the in-foreclosure rate in the United States was 1.84 percent while in 2010Q1 it is already 4.68 percent at annualized rate. The cause of the current crisis does not seem to be borrowing (interest) rates, because these have mostly been historically low in the past decade, even for subprime loans: Rather it was the amount of debt borrowed, relative to income, which was unprecedented. Even a low interest rate cannot overcome the problem of repaying a debt 10 times one's annual salary.

Alternatives to foreclosure include short sales or deeding the home to the lender in lieu of foreclosure, which do not limit the supply shock. Another more highly publicized alternative to foreclosure is loan modification. Until about 2009, modification generally took some form of temporary forbearance. But when home values dropped sharply, accompanied by rising unemployment, this approach was deemed insufficient. With major investments from Fannie Mae and Freddie Mac, the federal and local governments, and other lenders, genuine forgiveness entered the picture through dramatically lower interest. Modification is a critical tool of public policy, reduces the suffering of many owners, and supports home preservation by keeping the borrower interested in the ultimate value of the home—but modification does not always succeed and is expensive in its own right. By lowering cash flows, the modification effectively lowers the cost of the home to the borrower, perhaps helping the homeowner to maintain the home's value; but there is obviously a wealth transfer, from the lender, or the taxpayer, to the owner. However, an additional critical benefit of modification is that it keeps a unit of supply off the market, which supports home prices.

It seems unreasonable to doubt that excessive supply hurts prices, but most papers about foreclosure externality try to demonstrate that foreclosures have an additional negative impact on home prices, even after controlling for supply and demand. Why would foreclosure have special negative externalities? The key problem is that the natural interest that homeowners have in maintaining their properties is missing. When owners sell homes for themselves, whether in distress or not, they protect and invest in the home to maximize its value. What is most value-destroying in foreclosures is that there is a period, sometimes very protracted, in which the homeowner may not have the cash or motivation to maintain the home, because he will not realize a return on any investments in the home. Unimproved, unmaintained, sometimes even unprotected, the property deteriorates and loses value. Another question is whether there occurs separately a value loss because the repossessing bank is an inefficient seller. Although the typical homeowner enjoys living in the house and must be induced to leave through a high offer, a bank owner might take a lower value to be done with it. Also, if there are widespread emotional or aesthetic biases of buyers against buying a foreclosed property, a so-called *stigma cost*, or if it is particularly difficult to buy a foreclosed home, then demand might be stifled, causing the foreclosed property to sell at a discount to its market value.

Lin, Rosenblatt, and Yao (2007) argues that whatever the cause of lower prices for a foreclosed home, these lower values themselves have a direct negative effect on the sale price of neighboring homes because they form the pool for appraisal comparables of the neighbors when they are for sale. A lower comp value leads to a lower appraisal value for the neighbor. Lin et al. (2007) then test their theory by studying 11,000 Chicago-area arm's-length sales in 2003 (when home prices were rising) and 14,427 arm's-length sales in 2006 (when home prices were falling), both groups having a substantial number of neighbors repossessed by banks through foreclosure. The authors estimate the prices of those sales (which are not themselves foreclosed properties) as a function of the characteristics of the home (lot size, square footage, age of the home), the location of the home (county), and how many foreclosures there are in the neighborhood. Modeling the price of homes based on their characteristics is called *hedonic modeling*. The paper is groundbreaking in calculating the distance from, and elapsed time since, foreclosures and using these as explanations of price. It finds large negative impacts on the price of ordinary sales from having foreclosures nearby and recent, a whopping 8 percent hit in the 2006 sample for having a recent foreclosure within 10 blocks.

Despite the state-of-the-art GIS innovations, the paper and large contagion effects can be questioned on two grounds. First, the hedonic characteristics (features of the home) are spare. There is nothing about condition, construction quality, view, and so on. Second, the location controls (apart from proximity to foreclosures) are highly aggregate. Prices within a whole county can vary enormously. If foreclosures tend to be clustered in the lower valued part of each county (as one would expect), then the near neighbors to foreclosures might be in worse condition than the average homes in the county; or the area could just have location-related features that are valued less, for example, further from work centers. In either case, the neighbors would sell for less than the county average regardless of the proximity of foreclosures. Indeed, causality might run in the opposite direction: The low values of the neighborhood might cause the higher rate of nearby foreclosures rather than the other way around. When cause and effect run in both directions, it is called *endogeneity*.

Harding, Rosenblatt, and Yao (2009) try to solve the problem of not having all the hedonic characteristics of a home by studying the price changes in repeat sales of same houses: For instance, a home at 123 Main Street might be sold from Owner 1 to Owner 2 in 2001 and then Owner 2 sells it to Owner 3 in 2006. Because it is the same house being sold twice (once in 2001 and once in 2006), the difference in sales price will mainly reflect (on average) how much local home prices have changed over the time period. Even though the home is a little older, so are the other homes in the zip code, so the general trend ought to explain differences in price, on average. Indeed, many major home price indices (S&P Case-Shiller and FHFA, for example) are constructed by examining such repeat sales: The home price trend (index) is just the path of local home prices that best explains the changes in prices of such pairs in some geographical area. Harding et al. (2009) add a twist to the usual repeat sales methodology. They calculate how many foreclosures there are near the home at each point of the sale, and what stage those foreclosures are in, and use these differences to help explain price change. The argument of the chapter is that any average change of values between the homes that exceeds or falls short of the general local trend is due to the different quantities, distance, or timing of nearby foreclosures.

The local trend considered in this chapter is at the zip code level, a much smaller level than the county control in Lin et al. By using zip code controls instead of county, the authors hope to limit the objection that foreclosures are confined to the lower valued subareas of the geography in question, calling into question whether it is the foreclosures or the subarea causing value differences. The repeat sales methodology helps with this problem as well: Different parts of the zip having different values does not confuse a repeat sales model unless the different subareas are also experiencing different overall trends. It is the change in prices that matter in repeat sales models, not the absolute price.

The findings of this chapter tell an intuitive story, one that seems to fit how people really buy homes. Foreclosures affect property values of neighbors by far the most only if they are close, within 300 feet, probably within sight, or at least within sight on any short walk. The effect on the price of a sale by a nearby foreclosure drops sharply when moving to a ring from 300 to 500 feet, drops to near insignificance when the ring extends from 500 to 1,000 feet, and there is no effect beyond 1,000 feet. Also the effect of price is small unless the foreclosures are bunched. The effect of the first foreclosure within 300 feet is about 1 percent. Second and third foreclosures in an area cause additional, not quite linear, drops in price. The foreclosure contagion effect can grow to be substantial but only where foreclosures are common.

Another finding of this chapter, which seems strikingly consistent with the story we have outlined here about why foreclosure makes a difference. The impact on prices does not really occur at foreclosure. It occurs in the year leading up to foreclosure and the impact on prices actually stops getting more negative at the time of legal foreclosure. This fits the story of owners who, once they believe they will lose their home, stop maintaining it and allow an eye-sore to develop in the neighborhood, or even a nuisance or a danger in some cases. When the bank finally gets control of the property, the deterioration ceases as they get it ready for resale. In this picture of the world, the foreclosure itself, like a bankruptcy, serves a useful public purpose for reorganizing assets and putting them in the hands of the party that can maintain their value. This is not at all to say that foreclosure is anything but a tragic situation, only that it is not the legal act of foreclosure that destroys value: It is the maintenance failure that occurs when a borrower has lost interest or means for maintenance. Moreover, the effect does not overwhelm local home values unless there is a significant cluster of foreclosures in a small area.

REFERENCES

Immergluck, D., and G. Smith. 2006. "The External Costs of Foreclosure: The Impact of Single-Family Mortgage Foreclosures on Property Values." *Housing Policy Debate* 17:1, 57–79.

Harding, J., E. Rosenblatt, and V. W. Yao. 2009. "The Contagion Effect of Foreclosed Properties." *Journal of Urban Economics* 66:4, 164–178.

Lin, Z., E. Rosenblatt, and V. W. Yao. 2007. "Spillover Effects of Foreclosure on Neighborhood
Property Values." *Journal of Real Estate Finance and Economics* 38:4.

Shlay, A., and G. Whitman. 2004. "Research for Democracy: Linking Community Organizing
and Research to Leverage Blight Policy." *City and Community* 5:2.

ABOUT THE AUTHORS

Eric Rosenblatt is the vice president of credit risk analytics and monitoring at Fannie Mae. He holds a PhD in finance from Rutgers University. Although primarily a
business economist, Dr. Rosenblatt has maintained a continuing academic interest,
publishing 13 articles in peer-reviewed journals, all in the field of mortgage finance.

Vincent Yao is a director of economics at Federal National Mortgage Association
(Fannie Mae). Prior to that, he worked as an assistant professor at the University of
Arkansas at Little Rock College of Business and Administration. He holds a PhD
in economics from the University at Albany—State University of New York and
B.A. in business from the People's University of China.

CHAPTER 43

Liquidity and Hedge Fund Contagion[*]

NICOLE M. BOYSON
Assistant Professor of Finance, the Riesman Research Professor, and the William
Conley Faculty Fellow at Northeastern University's College of Business
Administration

CHRISTOF W. STAHEL
Assistant Professor of Finance at George Mason University's School of Management
and a Visiting Fellow at the FDIC's Center for Financial Research

INTRODUCTION

The term financial contagion has often been used to describe the tendency of an
economic crisis in one economy to spread to other economies. Recent examples
include the Asian financial crisis of 1997, often referred to as the *Asian Flu*, and
the Russian financial crisis of 1998, often referred to as the *Russian Virus*. The
recent Greek debt crisis, as another example, has led to widespread concern about
the creditworthiness of related economies, such as Spain and Portugal, and even
unrelated economies, including other European countries and parts of Asia.

A more general notion of contagion, widely accepted in the financial economics
literature, defines contagion as correlation in assets, markets, or economies *over and
above* what one would expect from economic fundamentals, sometimes referred to
as *excess correlation*. To further clarify this definition, we consider an example. In
the United States, the performance of large stocks and small stocks tends to be
highly correlated (moves together). Exhibit 43.1 shows this graphically by plotting
the monthly returns on the S&P 500 index, a proxy for large stocks, along with the
monthly returns for the NASDAQ index, a proxy for small stocks, for the period
January 1996 to June 2010. It is obvious from the graph that although these returns
are highly correlated, they do not move together in perfect lockstep. For contagion
to exist between these two markets, the correlation measured at a particular point
in time would need to be higher than the expected correlation between these two
asset classes during "normal" times.

---

[*]This chapter is based on "Hedge Fund Contagion and Liquidity Shocks," by Nicole M.
Boyson, Christof W. Stahel, and René M. Stulz, forthcoming in the October 2010 issue of the
Journal of Finance.

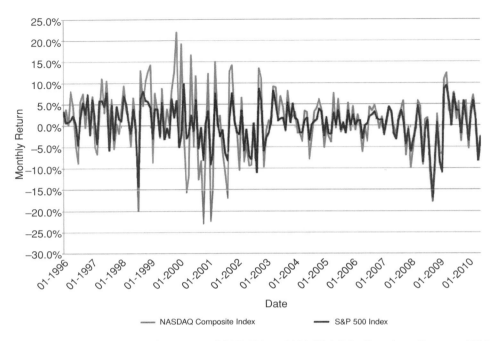

Exhibit 43.1   Monthly Performance of S&P 500 and NASDAQ Indices from January 1996 to June 2010

Using this definition of financial contagion, the focus of this chapter is to document and attempt to explain the existence of financial contagion within one particular asset class—hedge funds—and between that asset class and broad markets.

THE HEDGE FUND INDUSTRY

Hedge funds are professionally managed private investment pools generally only available to wealthy individuals and institutional investors, such as pension funds and endowments. They are usually organized as limited partnerships, with the manager(s) as the general partner(s) and the investors as the limited partners. Hedge fund managers often invest personal assets in their funds, and are typically compensated with a fixed management fee of 1 to 2 percent of assets and an incentive fee of 20 percent of profits. Because hedge funds are largely unregulated, except for SEC fraud statutes, and are not typically available to retail investors, their managers have significantly more investment flexibility than, for example, most mutual fund managers. Specifically, hedge fund managers often use leverage, take short positions in securities, and use derivative contracts such as swaps, futures, and options. This investment flexibility has led to the emergence of a number of unique investment styles, such as convertible arbitrage, long-short equity, and global macro.

By most accounts, the hedge fund industry has experienced significant growth over the past several years. Since hedge funds are generally not required to disclose their holdings or their assets, an exact estimate of the industry's size is difficult to obtain. However, a number of hedge funds voluntarily report data to data vendors, allowing a rough estimate of the industry's size. According to data from Credit Suisse/Tremont, one of the largest data vendors, the industry has grown from an estimated size of about $40 billion in total assets under management in 1990 to about $1.5 trillion in assets under management in 2010. Of course, hedge funds' use of leverage, short sales, and derivative contracts implies that their total dollar exposure is likely significantly higher.

The hedge fund industry is a particularly relevant environment in which to examine financial contagion. Because hedge funds invest in a number of markets worldwide, and are often described as liquidity providers helping to improve market efficiency, they are important players in the financial world. Further, their trading flexibility allows hedge funds to use a number of dynamic trading styles that in theory should provide significant diversification relative to broad financial markets, such as equities, bonds, and foreign currencies, and across different hedge fund styles.

HEDGE FUND CONTAGION

We begin by gathering data from a major hedge fund database vendor, Hedge Fund Research (HFR). HFR provides monthly aggregated index data for a number of hedge fund styles beginning in January 1990. Our sample extends from January 1990 to October 2008, and thus, captures a number of financial crises, including the Asian Flu, the Russian Virus, the collapse of Long-Term Capital Management in 1998, the downgrade of Ford and GM in 2005, and the recent credit crisis of 2008. We use index data for eight separate hedge fund styles, including Convertible Arbitrage, Distressed Securities, Event Driven, Equity Hedge, Equity Market Neutral, Global Macro, Merger Arbitrage, and Relative Value Arbitrage.

Convertible Arbitrage funds attempt to profit from the relative value differences between the equity and debt of a particular publicly traded firm. Distressed Securities funds establish positions in equities or debt instruments of financially distressed firms. Event Driven funds invest in companies involved in corporate transactions, such as restructurings or tender offers. Equity Hedge funds maintain both long and short positions in a wide range of equity securities, and typically maintain at least a partially hedged position. Equity Market Neutral funds are similar to Equity Hedge funds in that they take long and short positions in equities, but differ in that they generally maintain a low exposure to market movements. Global Macro funds invest in a wide range of markets, including equity, fixed income, currency, and commodity markets, predicated on movements in macroeconomic variables. Merger Arbitrage funds are a subset of Event Driven funds that invest in firms undergoing pending or expected mergers. Finally, Relative Value funds set up positions to capitalize on a value discrepancy between two or more different investment assets.

The first step in our analysis is to document the typical correlations across these eight hedge fund styles as well as between the eight hedge fund styles and main markets to establish the benchmark relationship. For the main market variables, we use the Russell 3000 Index for the stock market, the Lehman Brothers Bond Index for fixed income, and the U.S. Trade-Weighted Dollar Index published by the Federal Reserve for currencies. Data for these indices is obtained from Datastream. We estimate correlation coefficients for the entire time series of monthly returns for each of these hedge fund and broad market indices. A correlation coefficient can range from –1 to 1; a coefficient of 0 indicates that the returns for the two indexes are unrelated (do not move together), while a coefficient of 1 indicates a perfect positive correlation meaning that the two variables move in lockstep.

The correlations between each of the eight hedge fund indices and the Russell 3000 index are all positive and range from a low of 0.21 for Merger Arbitrage to 0.79 for Convertible Arbitrage. By contrast, correlations with the bond index and currency index are significantly smaller, although always positive. Turning to the correlations among the hedge fund indices, these are all positive as well, ranging from a low of 0.27 between Convertible Arbitrage and Relative Value, and 0.83 between Distressed Securities and Event Driven.

Having described the normal correlation relationship between and among the hedge fund index and main market returns, we now turn to an analysis of contagion. Our analysis follows prior literature in financial economics, and uses a quantile regression approach. This approach allows us to estimate the probability of a given hedge fund index's return conditional on the performance of all other hedge fund index returns.

The results of the quantile regression indicate a strong positive relationship in poor returns among hedge fund indices. For example, when the equally weighted average of all hedge fund indices (excluding the Relative Value index) is in the bottom tenth percentile of all returns, the Relative Value index has a 35 percent chance of its returns also falling in the bottom tenth percentile, as compared to a 10 percent probability if there were no relationship among the poor returns in hedge fund indices. Among the other indices, the Equity Market Neutral index has a 20 percent chance of falling in the bottom tenth percentile of all returns, the Event Driven index has a 55 percent chance, and the estimates for the other hedge fund indices fall somewhere in between. These results are quite impressive: Even the index with the lowest probability (Market Neutral) has twice the unconditional probability of its returns falling into the bottom tenth percentile relative to a no-dependence case. In fact, these results hold for all percentiles of returns below the fiftieth percentile (poor returns).

By contrast, there is no significant relationship between good returns across the indices. As a specific example, the probability of any specific index's returns falling in the top tenth percentile of all returns when the equally weighted average of all other hedge fund returns is also in the tenth percentile is only about 5 percent, indicating that there is no interdependence among good returns. Further, there is no relationship between extremely poor (or good) returns between the hedge fund and main market indices, implying that extremely poor return contagion is not much of an issue between main markets and hedge funds. Additional statistical tests using a logit methodology confirm the quantile regression results of contagion among extremely poor hedge fund returns, and lack of contagion between hedge fund returns and main market returns.

LIQUIDITY SHOCKS

We next attempt to explain the existence of this contagion. Recently developed theoretical models in financial economics suggest that shocks to funding liquidity (the availability of funding) force hedge funds to reduce their leverage and provide less liquidity to the markets, which reduces asset liquidity (the ease with which assets trade). When the impact of the funding liquidity shock on asset liquidity is strong, funding becomes even tighter for speculators, causing a self-reinforcing liquidity spiral in which both types of liquidity continue to deteriorate. An implication of these liquidity spirals is that they affect the performance of all assets held by hedge funds, leading to increased commonality in poor performance; that is, contagion.

Based on this theory and other related literature, we identify seven "contagion channel" variables and examine whether large adverse shocks to these variables are associated with an increase in hedge fund contagion. These variables include the difference in yield between Baa-rated corporate bonds and the 10-year Treasury bond, the Treasury-Eurodollar TED spread, the difference between overnight repurchase agreement and reverse overnight repurchase agreement volume, a stock market liquidity measure based on the average bid-ask spread, a stock index for commercial banks, a stock index for prime brokers, and finally, investment capital flows out of hedge funds.

For the two yield spreads, a widening of these spreads has been associated with a decrease in liquidity as investors prefer Treasury bonds to corporate bonds or Eurodollar deposits when liquidity is low. Repurchase agreements are a collateralized form of short-term lending among large financial institutions. When repurchase agreement volume decreases, this indicates a reluctance to lend, and thus, a potential shock to liquidity. The stock liquidity measure increases when liquidity is low as brokers charge significantly higher prices to buy stocks than they pay to sell stocks. The two stock indices, for banks and prime brokers, would presumably experience poor performance when liquidity is low as shocks that decrease the financial strength of these hedge fund intermediaries could be passed along to hedge funds through increased margin (collateral) requirements as institutions decrease their lending. Finally, hedge fund flows are calculated as the monthly change in investor outflows as a percentage of assets under management, using individual fund data from the CSFB Tremont hedge fund database. Large investor outflows could lead to a liquidity shock for the hedge fund.

Using a multinomial logit regression approach, we estimate the probability of observing either two or three hedge fund styles with simultaneous extreme negative returns (low contagion), or four or more hedge funds styles with simultaneous extreme negative returns (high contagion) conditional on our set of channel variables. We find that an extreme negative shock to the credit spread increases the probability of high contagion from 1 percent (i.e., the probability of high contagion when there is not an extreme negative shock to the credit spread) to 15 percent. A shock to the TED spread increases the probability of low contagion from 13 percent to 23 percent, and increases the probability of high contagion from 2 percent to 7 percent. For a shock to hedge fund flows, the probability of low contagion increases from 13 percent to 23 percent, while the probability of high contagion increases from 1 percent to 13 percent. Finally, a shock to bank stock performance increases the probability of high contagion increases from 2 percent to 7 percent.

CONCLUDING REMARKS

In this chapter, we document the propensity of extremely poor returns in hedge funds of different styles to cluster together at certain points in time. We show that this clustering is in excess of the normal level of correlation that would be expected, and hence, may be called contagion. There is no evidence of contagion in poor returns between hedge funds and main markets, and further, there is no evidence of contagion in extremely good returns among hedge funds or between hedge funds and main markets.

We next turn to potential explanations for the existence of this contagion. We find that contagion in hedge fund returns is linked to extreme adverse shocks to certain variables, which we denote *contagion channel variables* and are related to market and funding liquidity. These variables include yield spreads, returns on bank and prime brokerage stocks, hedge fund outflows, repurchase agreement volume, and bid-ask spreads on common stocks. Extreme adverse shocks to these variables significantly increase the probability of hedge fund contagion, suggesting a link between liquidity shocks and commonality in hedge fund performance.

Our results have important implications for investors. In particular, investors that select hedge funds for their presumed diversification benefits should recognize that while hedge funds do appear to provide some diversification benefits relative to main markets, the existence of contagion in extremely poor returns across different hedge fund styles implies significantly less downside protection for investors that diversify across hedge fund styles than a simple correlation analysis would suggest.

ABOUT THE AUTHORS

Nicole M. Boyson is an assistant professor of finance, the Riesman Research Professor, and the William Conley Faculty Fellow at Northeastern University's College of Business Administration, and has been at Northeastern since 2004. She earned her PhD in finance from Ohio State University in 2003, an MBA from Case Western Reserve University in 1998, and a B.A. in accounting from Kent State University in 1990. Prior to joining Northeastern, she was an assistant professor of finance at Purdue University. Her primary research interest is in the area of investments with an emphasis on hedge funds and mutual funds. Her teaching interests include investments and fixed income. Professor Boyson's research has been published in the *Journal of Finance, Journal of Financial and Quantitative Analysis, Journal of Empirical Finance, Financial Analysts Journal*, and *Review of Derivatives Research*. She is also a Certified Public Accountant.

Christof W. Stahel is an assistant professor of finance at George Mason University's School of Management and a visiting fellow at the FDIC's Center for Financial Research. He received his licentiate in economics in 1996 from the University of Zürich, Switzerland; an M.A. in economics from Ohio State University in 1997; and a PhD in finance from Ohio State University in 2004. His research focuses on domestic and international capital markets and investments. He has published scholarly articles in the *Journal of Finance and Empirical Economics*. He regularly teaches courses at the undergraduate and graduate level in investments and international finance at George Mason University's School of Management.

CHAPTER 44

No One Is Safe

Bankruptcy Spreads throughout an Economy

HARLAN D. PLATT
Professor of Finance and Insurance, Northeastern University

MARJORIE A. PLATT
Professor of Accounting, Northeastern University

SEBAHATTIN DEMIRKAN
Bentley University

This chapter explores the connections between financial distress or bankruptcy and other areas within the economy.[1] Though the motivation for this work is obvious, there has been little effort made to quantify how the misfortune of one agent in an economy soon becomes the hardship of another agent. Failure to understand how financial distress or bankruptcy can spread in an economy leads to poorly designed or underfunded efforts (a Keynesian view) to limit or forestall this damaging relationship. Feedback mechanisms within an economy, such as we discuss below, that spread adversity also lead to more substantial aggregate impacts as one problem causes another.

We have been working to understand the contagion of bankruptcy within an economy. Our focus is the way failure spreads between the corporate bankruptcy rate (the percentage of businesses that fail) and the personal bankruptcy rate (the percentage of families that go bankrupt). To perform our analysis, we obtain data from the 50 states over the time period 1990–2006. The primary data collected included the business bankruptcy rate (the number of business bankruptcy filings in a state divided by the number of publicly traded firms in the state) and the personal bankruptcy rate (the number of nonbusiness bankruptcy filings in a state divided by the population of the state). Additional factors in our regression model included several indicator variables (whether the state has an income tax, whether the state is a farm state, whether the state is an industrial-manufacturing state), and other economic variables such as state population, the number of people employed in the state, the average total revenue of publicly traded companies in the state, the average plant, property, and equipment of publicly traded companies in the state, the average dividend paid by publicly traded companies in the state, state level GDP, the average total retained earnings of publicly traded companies in the state, and the average total shareholder equity of publicly traded companies in the state.

Our efforts attempted to identify the possible interrelationship between these two failure rates, business and personal bankruptcy filings. Intuitively, people work and earn salaries with which they pay their normal expenditures such as mortgages, car payments, college tuition bills, and more mundane expenditures on food, gasoline, and entertainment. Discontinuation of salaries and income that result from companies filing for bankruptcy protection in the courts and then laying off or firing a portion or all of its workers puts a strain on a family's ability to make necessary payments such as described above. Families with limited wealth (i.e., accumulated personal savings) or insufficient familial or other contacts from whom supplemental funds could be borrowed in some cases file for personal bankruptcy protection themselves. Similarly, as documented by Sullivan, Warren, and Westbrook (2001), ill health and divorce frequently result in families having to resort to bankruptcy to obtain protection from unsatisfied creditors. A slowdown in personal consumption expenditures by newly bankrupt individuals or families (as quantified by the personal bankruptcy filing rate) may lead to a dramatic reduction in their future spending behaviors. This reduction in consumption level reduces corporate sales and profits and on the margin will lead to a heightened corporate bankruptcy rate.

The principle finding of our work on personal and corporate bankruptcy appears in Exhibit 44.1. The Exhibit expresses our findings with elasticities (which compares one percentage change response to a second percentage change response). We find that a 10 percent increase in the rate of personal bankruptcy is associated with a 7.33 percent increase in the business bankruptcy rate, and that a 10 percent increase in business bankruptcies results in a 3.43 percent increase in the personal bankruptcy rate. These elasticities suggest that percentage increases in either bankruptcy rate lead to positive and smaller increases in the other bankruptcy rate. For example, when a state with a 1 percent corporate bankruptcy rate and a 1 percent personal bankruptcy rate has a 10 percent increase in the corporate bankruptcy rate (rising to 1.1 percent) then the personal bankruptcy rate would also rise but by the smaller 7.33 percent rate (e.g., rising to 1.0733 percent). Similarly, a 10 percent initial increase in the personal bankruptcy rate (rising to 1.1 percent) would lead to a 3.43 percent increase in the corporate bankruptcy rate (rising to 1.0343 percent).

The astute reader no doubt wonders about the circularity between personal and corporate bankruptcies. The most important issue is whether this fundamental

Exhibit 44.1 Empirical Analysis: Does Unemployment Steer Personal and Corporate Bankruptcies?

	Change in Corporate Bankruptcy Rate	Change in Personal Bankruptcy Rate
A 10% change in Corporate Bankruptcy Rate	10%	3.43%
A 10% change in Personal Bankruptcy Rate	7.33%	10%

Source: Platt, H., and Demirkan, S. 2010. "The Contagion between Corporate and Personal Bankruptcy," *Journal of Financial Transformation.*

system is stable or explosive. An explosive system is a description of what happens successively after one individual or one company goes bankrupt. In that case, there are increasing failure rates in both categories as one type of failure leads to another type of failure and that failure itself then leads to more failures in the original category. In an explosive system, the reactive or secondary increase is larger than the original increase. Fortunately, our results indicate a stable system with both elasticities having values that are less than unitary. This is seen by noting how the secondary change in a bankruptcy rate, for example, the personal bankruptcy rate, is less than the initial increase, in that case in the corporate bankruptcy rate. A stable system has diminishing amplitudes of successive failures. So although it is true, for example, that an increase in personal bankruptcy leads to an increase in corporate bankruptcy and that increase in corporate bankruptcy leads to an increase in personal bankruptcy, each successive round of increase is smaller than the previous round. Our work shows that bankruptcies reverberate throughout the economy in diminishing waves.

A further complication is how the unemployment rate interacts with these two bankruptcy rates. That is, the unemployment rate itself may influence the two bankruptcy rates. Unlike the earlier work above, which documented a correspondence between the two bankruptcy rates, we now ask whether a change in the unemployment rate (without or before a change in a bankruptcy rate) is related to changes in either the bankruptcy rate of companies or of individuals. That is, the inquiry addresses whether a stable corporate and personal bankruptcy association can be upset by the onset of an economic slowdown that manifests itself in a rising unemployment rate. Similarly, we examine whether the two bankruptcy rates themselves influence the unemployment rate. Here the question is how can a rising tide of corporate, personal, or corporate and personal bankruptcies lead to changes in the unemployment rate. The logic behind this notion is that corporate bankruptcies are likely to result in layoffs and firings of employees, which could translate directly into a change in the unemployment rate; at the same time changes in personal bankruptcy rates, as demonstrated by the work above may lead to changes in the corporate bankruptcy rate and then possibly to changes in the unemployment rate in a similar fashion.

Our findings describe a strong positive interrelationship between unemployment, personal bankruptcy, and corporate bankruptcy. We find a contemporaneous relationship between unemployment and personal bankruptcies and a lagged relationship between unemployment and business bankruptcies. The contemporaneous portion of the relationship between these three phenomena is intuitive. A higher unemployment rate, which documents job loss and separation, occurs at the same time as when individuals or families file for personal bankruptcy. Though Sullivan, Warren, and Westbrook (2001) note the importance of sickness and family separation (divorce) as factors prompting personal bankruptcy, reductions in family income following joblessness, as personified by an increase in the unemployment rate, no doubt also contributes to personal bankruptcy. In contrast, we document a lagged effect when corporate bankruptcies increase; that is, we do not identify an immediate impact of an increase in the unemployment rate being transmitted to the business bankruptcy rate, rather this transmission occurs after a short time transpires. This suggests that the route by which the infection spreads is from corporate bankruptcies going to personal bankruptcies and then to unemployment.

Exhibit 44.2   Empirical Analysis: Does Unemployment Steer Personal and Corporate
Bankruptcies?

	Change in Lagged Unemployment	Change in Corporate Bankruptcy	Change in Personal Bankruptcy
A 10% change in Lagged Unemployment	10%	39%	30%
A 10% change in Corporate Bankruptcy	0.5%	10%	1.6%
A 10% change in Personal Bankruptcy	1.1%	7%	10%

The three-way relationship, between the unemployment rate and the personal
and corporate bankruptcy rates, was tested using data for the 50 states covering
a 19-year period. The modeling work was performed using standard OLS, 2SLS,
and 3SLS regression analysis. The latter two statistical methods are designed for
situations where there are systems of relationships, in this case among the three
factors. In addition, our statistical analysis controls for the possible effects of other
factors such as GDP, the employment level, and the level of aggregate financial
variables within a state. Our empirical findings are presented in Exhibit 44.2.

The first thing to notice from Exhibit 44.2 is the new values for the transmission of bankruptcy between the personal and corporate sectors. Our first research
effort found that a 10 percent increase in the business bankruptcy rate resulted in
a 3.43 percent increase in the personal bankruptcy rate; here in the second project,
a 10 percent increase in the business bankruptcy rate has a smaller increase, 1.6
percent, transmission affect to the personal bankruptcy sector. Likewise, a 10 percent increase in the personal bankruptcy rate, which in the previous work resulted
in a 7.33 percent increase in the business bankruptcy rate, in this work, which
includes the unemployment rate, now finds a slightly lower 7 percent increase in
business bankruptcies. The explanation for this reduced transmission effect is that
the unemployment rate is an important and necessary component to a statistical
model explaining bankruptcy transmission.

Second, Exhibit 44.2 describes a new factor, the lagged unemployment rate,
and its impact on bankruptcies. A 10 percent change in the lagged unemployment
rate results in a 39 percent change in the corporate bankruptcy rate and a 30 percent
change in the personal bankruptcy rate. These are explosive rates of transmission
since the rate of change in the bankruptcy rates exceeds the original rate of change
in the unemployment rate. This is not worrisome. The reason for this conclusion
is the secular stability in the unemployment rate. From the period 1948–2010, the
annual unemployment rate has ranged between 2.9 percent and 9.7 percent while
for the most part the rate has been between 3 percent and 8 percent. In other words,
the unemployment rate is well bounded. Increases in unemployment greater than
50 percent are unusual. All our findings report a very strong transmission of economic decline from unemployment to the two bankruptcy rates. An economy with
a 5 percent unemployment rate that suffers an economic decline that brings its unemployment rate to 6 percent, a 20 percent change, would according to our results
experience a 78 percent increase in the corporate bankruptcy rate (39 percent × 2)
and a 60 percent increase in the personal bankruptcy rate (30 percent × 2). Although
the rate of transmission of failure from unemployment to the two bankruptcy rates
is in fact explosive, the long-run stability in the unemployment rate dampens the
transmission to the two bankruptcy rates so that the system remains stable.

NEW THOUGHTS

The empirical work described earlier documents a strong transmission rate of bankruptcy between sectors of the economy. Although the likelihood that such a transmission existed was no doubt believed by most policy makers, economists, and observers, the statistically significant empirical findings of our work should quell any doubts about the existence of this relationship. Our work, which also included the unemployment rate, demonstrates an added relationship between the two bankruptcy rates and the unemployment rate, but it also notes how lagged unemployment (from the prior year) is the transmission vehicle to bankruptcy and not the current bankruptcy rate. The lagged nature of this relationship is actually beneficial for the legislative branch of government because it suggests that policy makers need not respond immediately to the possibility of an economic downturn in order to avoid future bankruptcies. They can wait and observe before enacting policies to reduce an economic decline. Of course, congressional sluggishness is well known and documented but our results suggest that the delay is not costly.

As recently as 2005, Congress enacted changes in the bankruptcy code that affected the ability and willingness of companies and people to file for bankruptcy protection. That legislation—known as the Bankruptcy Abuse Prevention and Consumer Protection Act—originally focused on a dramatic increase in personal bankruptcies but eventually incorporated additional changes affecting the ease and ability of companies to file for bankruptcy. It is well known that legislation is influenced by special interests groups and their lobbyists. Sometimes good intentions may become bad results when undue influence is exerted by special interests. The way that bankruptcy spreads across an economy like an illness or an infection should give pause to legislators being bombarded by lobbyists. The unintended consequences of legislative proposals being pushed by special interest groups may be changes that lead to increased bankruptcy either in the personal or business sectors. What makes this pernicious is the fact that those initial bankruptcies will spread between sectors and across the economy inflicting further damage and resulting in a deeper decline than might otherwise be the case.

NOTE

1. Previous research includes the following articles: Platt, Harlan, and Sebahattin Demirkan. 2010. "The Contagion between Corporate and Personal Bankruptcy." *Journal of Financial Transformation*, forthcoming; and Platt, Harlan, Sebahattin Demirkan, and Marjorie Platt. 2010. "Does Unemployment Steer Personal and Corporate Bankruptcies?" http:// ssrn.com/abstract=1524484.

REFERENCES

Platt, H. 2009. "Surprise: You Filed for Bankruptcy. Now What?" *Journal of Bankruptcy Law* (Nov./Dec.): 571–576.

Platt, H., Demirkan, S., and Platt, M. 2010. "Does Unemployment Steer Personal and Corporate Bankruptcies?" http://ssrn.com/abstract = 1524484.

Platt, H., and Demirkan, S. 2010. "The Contagion between Corporate and Personal Bankruptcy," *Journal of Financial Transformation*.

Sullivan, Teresa A., Elizabeth Warren, and Jay Westbrook. 2001. *The Fragile Middle Class: Americans in Debt*. New Haven, CT: Yale University Press.
Rauch, Jonathan. 1995. *Demosclerosis: The Silent Killer of American Government*. New York: Three Rivers Press.

ABOUT THE AUTHORS

Harlan D. Platt has achieved a national reputation as a corporate renewal expert. He is regularly quoted by the *Wall Street Journal*, *BusinessWeek*, *Forbes*, the Associated Press, and other news outlets. Dr. Platt is a professor of finance at Northeastern University in Boston. He received his PhD from the University of Michigan and a B.A. from Northwestern University. He teaches Strategies for Companies in Crisis. In addition, he was the faculty dean of the Turnaround Management Association for 10 years. He is the author of 9 books and nearly 50 academic articles. He co-authored the book *The Phoenix Effect*, which describes how to accelerate corporate performance. It was on the Amazon.com list of top 100 overall best sellers. Korean, French, and Chinese editions of *The Phoenix Effect* are available. His first book, *Why Companies Fail*, has remained in print since 1985 and in 2001 was translated into Korean.

Marjorie A. Platt is group coordinator and professor of accounting at Northeastern University. She received her PhD and M.A. from the University of Michigan, M.B.A. from Babson College, and B.A. from Northwestern University. She is a Certified Management Accountant. She publishes and consults on the prediction of corporate bankruptcy and financial distress. Her work is published in the *Financial Review*, *Journal of Business Research*, *Journal of Business Finance & Accounting*, and *Journal of Banking and Finance*. She is also a senior research fellow with the Design Management Institute. Her current design-related research focuses on how managers use financial and nonfinancial information to make decisions about new product design and development and the evaluation of design performance. Her most recent articles in this area have appeared in *Journal of Product Innovation Management*, *Advances in Management Accounting*, *Design Management Journal Academic Review*, and *Accounting Horizons*.

Sebahattin Demirkan is a faculty member in McCallum Graduate School of Business at Bentley University in Waltham, Massachusetts. Before joining Bentley, he was assistant professor in the School of Management at State University of New York Binghamton University and in the College of Business Administration at Northeastern University. He received his master's and doctorate in accounting and MBA degrees from the University of Texas-Dallas. He did his undergraduate work at Bogazici University in Istanbul, Turkey. Demirkan's research interest is in empirical and analytical capital market research. He published several articles in academic journals such as *Accounting Research Journal*, *Corporate Finance Review*, *Journal of Financial Transformation*, *Global Economics and Management Review*, *Journal of Private Equity*, *Journal of Management and Expert Systems with Applications*. He teaches managerial, cost, and financial accounting classes in graduate and undergraduate levels.

CHAPTER 45

The Contagion Effects of Accounting Restatements

A Summary

NICOLE THORNE JENKINS
Owen School of Management, Vanderbilt University

INTRODUCTION

The market's reaction to information contained in a report is predicated on the substance and quality of the contents. When the information is relevant and the quality is high, the market's response is likely to show up in an adjustment to a publicly traded firm's stock price. When the quality and content of information that has been previously impounded into prices is found to be unreliable, the market is left to reassess the stock price of the firm and the reliability of past and future reports. This reassessment generally leads to a decline in stock price, particularly when the error was an overstatement of firm performance or value.

When one firm in the market has been found to be less than credible, the natural question is, "Are there other firms in the market that are experiencing similar phenomena?" This is the fundamental issue with financial contagion—the known piece of firm-specific bad news may in fact be the tip of the iceberg for a group of firms. This appears to be the case with the restatement of previously issued financial reports. Similar to other economic phenomena, accounting restatements tend to occur in waves. However, because of materiality levels, this financial reporting failure is not as fluid as mergers, changes in capital structure, and other economic events. Rather, it is driven by specific guidelines, which after being stress tested may lead some firms to restate. However, due to immateriality, it is possible that a firm with the identical problem may not require restatement. In a paper entitled *The Contagion Effects of Accounting Restatements* (Gleason, Jenkins, and Johnson 2008) we provide evidence that accounting misstatements discovered at one firm lead to the market reassessing the content and credibility of financial reports issued by other nonrestating firms in the same industry, leading to a contagion return. The analysis performed there is summarized in this chapter.

BACKGROUND AND HYPOTHESES

In spite of Generally Accepted Auditing Standards (GAAS) and best efforts on the part of managers and auditors, material errors occur in the published financial statements. The reason for the errors vary, including manipulative accounting practices, errors in applying complex financial reporting standards, the correction of technical errors, SEC mandated adjustments, and so on. Whatever the reason, financial statements are restated because management believes that the previously published report(s) can no longer be relied on in accordance with proper application of Generally Accepted Accounting Principles. GAAS dictates that persons known to be relying on those statements must be notified. In August 2004, the SEC formalized the notification process regarding these reports by requiring firms to disclose material accounting errors requiring a restatement by filing a Form 8-K within four business days of establishing that prior financial statements can no longer be relied on. Prior to this rule, companies announced their intentions to restate in a variety of formats, including press releases, conference calls, the filing of an amended statement, and so on. Regardless of the format of the disclosure, announced restatements are accompanied by significantly negative stock price reactions on average.

When a restatement announcement occurs, the confidence that the market has in the previously issued reports is called into question. It is widely understood and expected that the stock price of a restating firm will decline significantly around the announcement of this unfavorable event. The existing literature that investigates the announcement of a restatement is vast and the findings are robust. Prior research documents large price reactions to accounting restatements, averaging a loss in market value of approximately 10 percent for all restatements, and more than 20 percent for restatements deemed as irregularities (Palmrose et al. 2004). There is substantial evidence that restatements also lead to executive turnover (Desai et al. 2006), shareholder litigation (Badertscher 2010; Griffin 2003; Palmrose and Scholz 2004), declines in sell side analysts' consensus forecast of annual earnings and increases in forecasted dispersion (Hribar and Jenkins 2004; Palmrose et al. 2004), and to an increase in the implied cost of equity capital (Hribar and Jenkins 2004).

Prior research is silent about whether restatements convey information useful to market participants in pricing the common shares of similar firms—produce a contagion return. It is possible that the act of restating is particularly idiosyncratic in that it affects the restating firm's value but leaves nonrestating peers unchanged. Our first test examines market returns for restating firms and their sample of peer firms over different time periods. An alternative explanation is that the restatement may influence peer firms because it communicates information about the industry's economic prospect. If this is the case, then we should observe downward revisions in analysts' earnings forecast for peer firms. The second analysis considers the response that analysts have to the industry as a result of a restatement. Last, our primary belief is that restatements function as a catalyst for altering an investor's perception about the financial statements issued by nonrestating firms in the industry. If this conjecture is true then contagion stock returns—those returns of peer firms over the restatement period—will be positively correlated with variables that proxy for differences in the quality of the peer firm's reporting financial information. In a follow-up analysis, we consider the effect of accounting quality and market pressures on the contagion return.

To better illustrate the phenomena that we are investigating, consider, for example, Great Atlantic & Pacific Tea Company's (A&P) $36.8 million restatement in 2002. The restatement was prompted by an internal investigation into the company's accounting for vendor allowances. A&P's stock price fell 16 percent the day the restatement was announced. A *Wall Street Journal* article on the A&P restatement quoted one industry analyst who said that vendor allowances are "a very complicated area of accounting that's only now getting a lot of [investor] attention" (Covert 2002b). Few (if any) grocery companies disclosed details of their vendor allowance accounting practices in financial statement footnotes. The article concluded by noting that two of A&P's competitors (Kroger Co. and Winn-Dixie stores) quickly confirmed their continuing use of the more conservative accounting approach just adopted by A&P. Public confirmation was presumably meant to dispel investor concern about aggressive accounting.

Two other grocery companies (Safeway and Albertson's) "didn't immediately respond to requests for comment" (Covert 2002a), leaving investors and analysts in doubt as to whether these firms' previously reported financial results were tainted. One industry analyst predicted that other (unnamed) grocery retailers would eventually restate earnings because of improper accounting for vendor allowances. Two grocery firms (Flemmings Cos. and U.S. Foodservices) did so during the ensuing nine months.

Because of situations like the above, market participants become suspicious of the financial reports of firms that are peers of restating firms. The rational response by the market would be to consider the likelihood of a similar restatement for the nonrestating peer. The more weight given to this likelihood, the larger the stock price response. We expect this market response to be more prominent for firms that have lower quality accounting as measured by high levels of accruals and on which there is significant market pressure to maintain performance levels. Last, the adverse market reaction for the peer firms will be increasing in its similarities with the restating firm.

SAMPLE SELECTION AND RESULTS

Our sample is comprised of restatement events obtained from the General Accountability Office (GAO) restatement dataset (GAO 2003), which runs from January 1, 1997, through June 30, 2002; augmented with hand-collected data from the *Wall Street Journal* from January 1, 1990, through December 31, 1996. After filtering on the availability of financial data and the existence of a nonrestating peer group, our final sample consists of 888 restatement events involving 807 firms.

Existing research has shown that financial contagion occurs when quarterly earnings are released; therefore, we eliminate all restatement events from our sample that are made simultaneously with the quarterly earnings announcements. In an effort to remove noise from the sample, we also discard all restatements that do not convey unfavorable information. Last, we eliminate all restatements involving IPR&D because they are transaction specific and clustered in calendar time.[1] Our final sample is comprised of 380 restatement events. This sample contains firms from every economic section; however, information technology firms (≈30 percent) and consumer discretionary firms (18 percent) represent the largest industries.

We construct our sample of nonrestating peer firms by using the eight digit Global Industry Classification Standard codes. The identification process that we use results in approximately 59 peer firms for each restatement event. We require each peer group to be comprised of at least five firms to diversify the impact of any idiosyncratic price movement that might otherwise confound our analysis.

First, we examine the stock price behavior of restating firms over three periods relative to the announcement date, which is day 0. The announcement period (days −1 to +1 centered on the announcement date) and two post-announcement windows (days +2 to +10 and +2 to 60) are used to capture information about share price behavior around the restatement announcement for both the restating firm and its nonrestating peer group of firms. Exhibit 45.1 summarized the returns over these windows. The average returns over all of the windows are reliably negative for the restatement firms and mostly negative for the peer firms. Restating firms experience a significantly negative market reaction within the short three-day window around the announcement date (−19.8 percent). Moreover, we document a negative drift in the two post-announcement date windows, which likely reflects the resolution of investor uncertainty about the circumstances, magnitude, and scope of the misstatement and other related bad news. Similar market reactions are

Exhibit 45.1 Abnormal Daily Stock Returns for 380 U.S. Firms That Announced Accounting Restatements from January 1990 through June 2002 and Their Nonrestatement Industry Peer Firms

	Restatement Firms			Peer Firms		
	N	Mean (%)		N	Mean (%)	
Announcement (day −1 to 1)	380	−19.8	t	22,510	−0.5	***
Pre-announcement (day −10 to +10)	380	−4.6	t	22,510	−0.8	***
Post-announcement (day +2 to +10)	380	−2.1	t	22,510	−0.7	***
Post-announcement (day +2 to +60)	380	−10.3	t	22,510	−0.2	***

Restatements announced concurrently with quarterly or annual earnings are excluded from the sample as are those where the three-day announcement period abnormal stock return for the restatement firms is equal to or greater than −1.0 percent. Restatement firms' announcement period stock returns are therefore different from zero by construction (denoted by "t" in the table) because the sample is restricted to restatements that adversely affect shareholder wealth at the restatement firm. Nonrestatement peer group firms are identified from Compustat using the eight-digit Global Industry Classifications Standard (GICS) of the corresponding restatement firm. Nonrestatement firms are discarded if: (1) CRSP stock returns for the announcement period plus the following 240 trading days are not available on the CRSP data files; (2) analysts' consensus earnings per share forecasts issued immediately before and after the restatement announcement are not available on the I/B/E/S data files; (3) the pre-announcement stock price is less than $5; or (4) the peer firm restated its own financial statements within the preceding two years. Daily stock returns are size adjusted using CRSP NYSE/AMEX/NASDAQ market capitalization decile returns and are then compounded over time to reflect a "buy and hold" return. Day 0 is the trading date of the first restatement-related press release issued by the restatement firm. A * (** and ***) denotes a statistically significant two-tailed t-test of the null hypothesis that the mean cumulative abnormal return is different from zero at the 0.10 (0.05 and 0.01) level, respectively.

documented for the nonrestating peer firms. The primary difference for these firms is that the magnitude of the market reaction is much smaller and the rank order of the return by window length is not maintained. However, these magnitudes are consistent with those documented in earlier contagion studies (Docking et al. 1997; Lang and Stulz 1992).

In our second analysis, we consider whether a restatement by one firm in the industry affects analysts' EPS forecast for peer firms and, if so, whether these forecast revisions then explain the share price behavior of peer forms. Palmrose et al. (2004) find that restatements are accompanied by a statistically significant 6.7 percent decline in analysts; consensus EPS forecasts and that this decline is associated with the corresponding share price decline in the announcement period. The change in analysts forecast may be mechanical or it may arise because analysts and investors believe the economic prospects of the announcing firm and the industry are deteriorating. We find results consistent with the notion that restatements convey some news information about deteriorating economic conditions in the industry. However, analyst forecast revisions do not explain the three-day abnormal stock return for peer firms for nonrestating firms.

In our next analysis, reported in Exhibit 45.2, we investigate whether induced contagion stock returns are correlated with measures of accounting quality and capital market pressure. Our proxy for accounting quality follows from prior studies showing that large accounting accruals predict restatements (Richardson et al. 2003) and SEC enforcement action (Dechow et al. 1996). Thus, measures that contain accruals are the best indicators of accounting quality. In our regression analysis, we consider several specifications for accounting quality, total earnings, earnings decomposed into operating cash flows, and total accruals, and a third specification that further decomposes total accruals into operating and investing accruals. We find no evidence that the contagion returns are associated with total earnings (Model 1). However, we do find a negative association between contagion returns and total accruals (Model 2) as well as the decomposition of total accruals into operating and investing accruals (Model 3). Moreover, we find a positive association between contagion returns and operating cash flows (Models 2 and 3). The implication of these findings is that contagion returns of peer firms appear to be more pronounced for firms that have lower accounting quality—more accruals. By contrast, peer firms with higher operating cash flows—higher accounting quality—experience less-pronounced contagion stock price declines. In summary, this is evidence that the contagion stock return reflects investor concern about the relative contribution of operation cash flow and accruals to report earnings rather than just a concern about earnings levels.

Within these same models we consider the capital market pressure that firms face to engage in aggressive accounting in an effort to maintain historical performance levels. These pressures, ex ante increase the likelihood of a restatement for the firm. Drawing from Richardson et al. (2003), we consider five market pressures that increase the likelihood of restatement.[2] Contagion stock returns exhibit consistently positive and significant association with three of the capital market pressure variables that we consider, earnings to price ratio (EP), book-to-market (BM), and STRING firms with small positive forecast errors in each of the prior four quarters. These results indicate that firms with higher growth expectations—EP and

Exhibit 45.2 Regression Tests for the Influence of Accounting Quality, Capital Market Pressure, and Control Variables on Contagion Stock Returns

		Model 1	Model 2	Model 3
Intercept		1.256***	−1.027***	−1.017***
Accounting quality:				
EARN	?	0.256		
CFO	?		1.384***	1.372***
TACC	−		−0.458***	
OPER_ACC	−			−0.507**
INVST_ACC	−			−0.405*
Capital market pressure:				
EP	+	0.659***	1.040***	1.072***
BM	+	0.288**	0.314**	0.318**
EPS_GROWTH	−	0.271**	0.231*	0.230*
STRING	−	0.023	−0.036	−0.036
Control variables:				
RESTRET	+	−0.256	−0.240	−0.242
REVISION	+	0.370	0.177	0.171
REST_SIZE	−	−0.077***	−0.080***	−0.080***
FIRST	−	0.243	0.252*	0.250*
DAYS_F	−	−0.003***	−0.003***	−0.003***
DAYS_L	−	−0.001***	−0.001***	−0.001***
LEV	?	−0.046***	−0.044***	−0.044***
YEAR FIXED EFFECTS		Not reported	Not reported	Not reported
Adj. R-square		2.33%	2.49%	2.48%
F statistic		12.75***	13.64***	13.14***
Sample size		12,886	12,884	12,884

The dependent variable is the size-adjusted buy-and-hold stock return for each nonrestatement peer firm cumulated over the three trading days centered on the restatement announcement date. The sample selection procedures used to identify peer (nonrestatement) firms are described in Exhibit 45.1. Variable definitions appear in Exhibit 45.2. Coefficient estimates for year fixed-effect variables are omitted for brevity. Influential observations with leverage values exceeding 2.0 are eliminated to facilitate estimation of robust regression coefficients (Belsley, Kuh, and Welsch 1980). Coefficient estimates are multiplied by 100 in the table. A * (** or ***) denotes a statistically significant two-tailed t-test of the null hypothesis that the coefficient estimate is different from zero at the 0.10 (0.05 and 0.01) level, respectively.

BM—and those with a track record of continuous quarterly EPS growth experience a larger contagion return decline than do peer firms with low growth expectations and no track records.

To recap, the evidence presented in Exhibit 45.2 is consistent with the notion that accounting restatements trigger stock price declines among peer firms that in part reflect investors' accounting quality concerns. This conclusion follows from the observation that contagion stock returns are decidedly more negative for peer firms with high accounting accruals and low operating cash flows and high capital market pressure for aggressive accounting choices.

In follow-up analyses, we consider alternative specifications and controls to ensure the robustness of our results and to provide additional insights. First we find that the majority of our results on accounting quality are driven by revenue restating firms. Also, we find some contradictory evidence on the influence of capital market pressure when we consider the reason for the restatement. Second, we find that the size of the decline in contagion returns is larger when the peer firms use the same external auditor as the restating firm. We also find that a penalty is assessed by the market for these firms when they also have higher earnings. This result is concentrated in the revenue restating portion of the sample. There are several other tests that are performed in the referenced paper and the reader is directed to the original article for a more thorough discussion of the work performed and interpretation of the results.

The paper that has been summarized here examines whether accounting misstatement discovered at one firm causes capital market participants to reassess the content and quality of financial statements previously issued by nonrestating firms in the same industry. We find that accounting restatements that adversely affect shareholder wealth at the restating firm also induce a small but statistically reliable share price decline among nonrestating peer firms. This price decline is unrelated to changes in the analyst's EPS forecasts, our proxy for restatement induced changes in investors' expectations about peer firms' future economic prospects. We also find that nonrestating firms with high industry-adjusted accruals experience a more pronounced share price decline than do low-accrual peer firms. This accounting contagion effect is concentrated among revenue-related restatements by relatively large firms in the industry. For these restatements, investors impose a larger contagion penalty on the stock prices of peer firms with higher earnings and higher accruals when peer and restating firms use the same external auditor. There are several caveats to our empirical results, which are detailed in the referenced paper. In spite of these limitations, the evidence that restatements lead to contagion in stock prices of peer firms is robust for restatements associated with revenue recognition issues.

NOTES

1. In-Process Research and Development (IPR&D) appears on the financial statements of firms through an acquisition. Generally, R&D costs are expensed as incurred; however, when a firm acquires a firm that has IPR&D, GAAP requires this intangible asset to be valued and recorded on the books of the consolidated entity. In 1998, the SEC challenged, the valuations of IPR&D of several public companies, which led to a wave of IPR&D restatements. Research has shown that IPR&D-related restatements do not have an effect on the share price of restating firms nor do they produce contagion stock price effects among peer firms (Banyi 2006).

2. Richardson et al. (2003) find that investors' perceptions of future earnings grown as measured by book-to-market (BM), and earnings to price ratios (EP) are negatively related to the probability of restatement. Peer firms that trade as substantial multiples of book value and earnings—have low BM and EP—presumably face greater pressure to adopt aggressive accounting practices to deliver the anticipated earnings growth. The authors also find that firm size (SIZE) is positively related to the probability of restatement. Larger firms are subject to lower scrutiny by market participants. This heightened scrutiny contributes to increased capital market pressure for aggressive accounting choices. Two other variables have been shown to predict future restatements, firms with increases in year over year quarterly EPS in each of the four quarters prior to restatement (EPS_GROWTH)

and firms with small positive forecast errors in each of the prior four quarters (STRING). Richardson finds that firms with high EPS_GROWTH are more likely to restate while STRING firms are less likely to restate.

REFERENCES

Badertscher, B. 2010. "Overvaluation and its Effect on Management's Choice of Alternative Earnings Management Mechanisms." *Working paper.* University of Notre Dame.

Banyi, M. 2006. "An Evaluation of Causes and Consequences of In-Process Research and Development Overstatements." *Working paper.* Oregon State University.

Belsley, D. A., E. Kuh, R. E. Welsch. 1980. *Regression Diagnostics: Identifying Influential Data and Sources of Collinearity.* New York: John Wiley & Sons.

Covert, J. 2002a. "A&P Restatement Spotlights Retailer Accounting Concerns." *Dow Jones News Service,* July 5, 2002.

Covert, J. 2002b. "A&P Restates Financial Results, Revealing Better Earnings Picture." *Wall Street Journal,* July 8, 2002.

Dechow, P., R. Sloan, and A. Sweeney. 1996. "Causes and Consequences of Earnings Manipulation: An Analysis of Firms Subject to Enforcement Actions by the SEC." *Contemporary Accounting Research* 13:1, 1–36.

Desai, H., C. E. Hogan, and M. S. Wilkins. 2006. "The Reputational Penalty for Aggressive Accounting: Earnings Restatements and Management Turnover." *Accounting Review* 81:1, 83–112.

Docking, D. S., M. Hirschey, and E. Jones. 1997. "Information and Contagion Effects of Bank Loan-Loss Reserve Announcements." *Journal of Financial Economics* 43:219–239.

General Accounting Office. 2003. *Financial Statement Restatements: Trends, Market Impacts, Regulatory Reponses, and Remaining Challenges.* Washington, DC: GAO-03-138.

Gleason, C., N. Jenkins, and B. Johnson. 2008. "The Contagion Effects of Accounting Restatements" *The Accounting Review* 83:1, 83–110.

Griffin, P. 2003. "A League of Their Own? Financial Analysts' Response to Restatements and Corrective Disclosures." *Journal of Accounting, Auditing and Finance* 18:4, 479–518.

Hribar, P., and N. Jenkins. 2004. "The Effect of Accounting Restatements on Earnings Revisions and the Estimated Cost of Capital." *Review of Accounting Studies* 9:2–3, 337–356.

Lang, L., and R. Stulz. 1992. "Contagion and Competitive Intra-Industry Effects of Bankruptcy Announcements: An Empirical Analysis." *Journal of Financial Economics* 32:45–60.

Palmrose, Z., V. Richardson, and S. Scholz. 2004. "Determinants of Market Reactions to Restatement Announcements." *Journal of Accounting and Economics* 37:1, 59–90.

Palmrose, Z. V., and S. Scholz. 2004. "The Circumstances and Legal Consequences of Non-GAAP Reporting: Evidence from Restatements." *Contemporary Accounting Research* 21:1, 139–180.

Richardson, S., I. Tuna, and Min Wu. 2003. "Capital Market Pressures and Earnings Management: The Case of Earnings Restatements." *Working paper*. University of Pennsylvania.

ABOUT THE AUTHOR

Nicole Thorne Jenkins, CPA, PhD, is an associate professor at the Owen Graduate School of Management at Vanderbilt University. She received her PhD from the University of Iowa and degrees in accounting and finance from Drexel University. Dr. Jenkins has authored several articles in the areas of stock repurchases and accounting restatements which have appeared in such leading publications as the *Journal of Accounting and Economics*, the *Accounting Review*, and the *Review of Accounting Studies*.

CHAPTER 46

Are Banks' Earnings Surprises Contagious?*

MARCEL PROKOPCZUK, CFA
ICMA Centre, Henley Business School, University of Reading, UK

INTRODUCTION

Are earnings surprises in the banking sector contagious? This question is of interest because the banking sector is of crucial importance for the entire economy. Due to the high degree of interconnection with other sectors, a crisis in the banking sector could lead to severe consequences for the economy. Thus, to prevent such crises, the banking sector is highly regulated—although, regulation takes place mainly on an individual bank level. The presence of contagion effects, which increases the risk of a systemic financial crisis, that is, the systemic risk in the financial system, calls for a regulation that takes the multiple linkages within the system into account and minimizes the risks due to spillover effects.

In this chapter, we analyze whether negative earnings surprises have contagious effects in the banking sector; that is, whether they cause the reporting bank's competitors to react on the new information. We furthermore compare the banking sector with all the other industry sectors, especially the insurance sector, to investigate the question whether the banking sector behaves differently.

Earnings announcements provide information about the true value of the company and claims on it. If market prices before the announcement are based on the earnings expectations and markets are efficient, a negative surprise will lead to an immediate devaluation of the firm's value. As earnings surprises are clear-cut firm-specific events, these are perfectly suited for the purpose of studying contagion. This is due to the fact that all public macroeconomic and sector-specific information is already reflected in the analysts' earnings forecasts.

Whether the competitor's security prices of a firm react negatively, positively, or not at all, depends on the type of information and the structure of the sector. If the information is firm-specific and if no linkages exist with the other firms, only the respective company security prices should react. However, negative information like a decrease in sales forecasts could be related to sector-specific information and thus reveal information for the entire sector, yielding adverse reactions of

---

*This chapter is a summary of the original paper Prokopczuk (2010) forthcoming in *Applied Financial Economics*. The copyrights of the main manuscript are with Taylor & Francis.

competitor security prices. This type of negative reaction is commonly referred to as *information contagion.*[1]

Additionally, a firm-specific event resulting in an adverse announcement can also have direct negative consequences for the competitors. This is the case if interfirm connections increasing the default risk of the competitors through the increased risk of the originating firm exist. The best example—which is also the motivation of our study—is the banking sector, in which strong connections exist between the institutions through the interbank lending and borrowing market. Thus, a credit event at one bank could spill over to other ones, easily leading to an increase in default risk of the entire sector; that is, an increase in systemic risk.[2]

The second major financial sector, namely the insurance sector, also engages in the interbank market. Therefore, contagion due to lending relationships seems equally likely in both sectors. The same is true for information contagion. However, a third hypothesis exists, which predicts a higher degree of contagion in the banking sector than in the insurance sector: the fire-sale meltdown theory presented by Diamond and Rajan (2005). In their model, banks are assumed to hold illiquid assets while issuing demand deposits. Diamond and Rajan (2005) then show that liquidity shortages stemming from the asset side of the banks can lead to contagion effects. As the underlying assumptions of their model are clearly more plausible for the banking sector than for the insurance sector, this theory may explain any differences between these two sectors with respect to contagion.

However, a firm-specific event could also lead to the opposite effect. As discussed in Lang and Stulz (1992) and Jorion and Zhang (2007), if imperfect competition is prevailing in the sector, problems in competing firms could allow firms to increase their prices or their market share to earn (at least temporary) an additional rent. This effect is not exclusive for operating problems, as financial problems can cause a negative reputation, which possibly causes customers to refrain from doing business with the firm, and switching to a competing producer or service provider.

Taking everything into account, when adverse events happen, the observable consequences will be the sum of the aforementioned effects. Theoretically, there is no reason why one or the other effect should be predominant.

A few papers analyzing adverse events in the banking sector do exist. Akhigbe and Madura (2001) study 99 publicized bank failures and find contagion effects on rival banks, which are stronger when the failed bank is large, a multibank holding, or publicly held. The contagion effects of dividends reductions at banks are analyzed by Slovin et al. (1999). Their main finding is that these reductions are negative events for both large super-regional banks as well as regional banks themselves, but only cuts at super-regional banks have negative consequences on stock prices of other banks.

Our study is closely related to this strand of literature. We fill the gap in the literature between studies on intra-industry contagion effects of earnings surprises and studies of the banking sector. To the best of our knowledge, this is the first study analyzing contagion effects in the banking sector due to negative earnings surprises. Furthermore, we are the first to compare the results with the average of the nonbanking sectors, and especially the insurance sector, which is a second highly regulated sector of the U.S. economy.

The main results of our study follow. We find that negative earnings surprises cause significant contagion effects in the banking sector. In contrast, the nonbanking sectors show, on average, no signs of contagious behavior. The difference between the banking sector and the nonbanking sector proves to be highly significant. When analyzing the insurance sector separately, we do not find any contagion effects, which indicates a smaller degree of systemic risk in the insurance sector. Finally, we find that contagion in the banking sector is the strongest if the originator as well as the affected institutions are important banks. These results support the need for a system-based regulation of the banking sector.

DESIGN OF THE STUDY

The goal of our study is to investigate whether contagion is present in the banking sector and whether the banking sector behaves differently compared with the other sectors of the economy. To detect possible contagion effects, we employ traditional event study methodology. We use negative earnings surprises, that is, analysts' forecasts minus realized earnings, as informational event. Negative earnings surprises are perfectly suited as all public information should already be included in the analysts' forecasts. The new negative information may be attributable to macroeconomic developments or may be company-specific. We measure the contagion effect by analyzing the reaction of the stock prices of companies operating in the same sector as the reporting company. Macroeconomic surprises are controlled for by considering abnormal returns, which are calculated as deviations from the market return.

We first analyze whether the reporting company's stock price exhibits a significant decline to make sure that the negative earnings surprise indeed is negative information for the reporting company. We then analyze the stock price reaction of companies operating in the same sector. To analyze whether the banking sector exhibits a different behavior, we compare the results with the nonbanking sector and also the insurance sector.

RESULTS

First, we analyze the effect of negative earnings surprises on the reporting companies themselves. This analysis shows whether on average the news indeed was a negative surprise, and we can verify the timing of the market responses to the new information, that is, whether the reported date was actually the date of information release to the public. If the information was available to the public, or at least to the analysts making the forecasts, before the reported event date, or the date of reported earnings were not correct, we should, on average, not observe an abnormal reaction by the reporting company. In this case, we would not expect the competitor companies to react as well.

On the event date, the average negative abnormal daily return is −0.73 percent, which is followed by −0.54 percent on the next successive day. Both values are significantly smaller than zero, with p-values very close to zero. Conditioning on more negative earnings surprises, that is, news with a bigger negative surprise, the average abnormal returns decreases, as to expect, down to −1.15 percent. The first ex-event day also shows significant negative average returns, which are, however, in absolute terms, about 30 percent smaller than the event day abnormal returns.

In the main part of the study we analyze the competitor's reaction to earnings surprises of a company operating in the same sector. We split the data into banks and nonbanks to investigate whether banks behave differently.

For the banking sector, we observe on the event date an abnormal return of −0.0843 percent, which is significantly negative, indicating the existence of contagion. On the subsequent day the abnormal return is slightly positive, but not significantly different from zero. In contrast, the nonbanking sectors show, on average, no signs of contagious behavior. The average abnormal return of competitor portfolios is −0.0015 percent on the event day and 0.0190 percent on the subsequent day; both being not significantly different from zero, and thus not showing any contagion effects. Conditioning on the degree of surprise, we find that contagion effects in the banking sector are even stronger for greater degrees of surprises. In contrast, the average abnormal returns of the nonbanking sectors are insignificant, even when conditioning on greater relative surprises.

A second highly regulated sector of the economy is the insurance sector. Similar to the banking sector, insurance companies are regulated on an individual level. However, when discussing regulating the financial sector on a systemic level, insurance companies are frequently mentioned as part of the system that should be included. To investigate the validity of this argument, we analyze the insurance sector separately in order to see whether contagion effects exist within this sector. Although the abnormal return of the reporting insurers' competitor portfolios are negative in most instances, the size is much smaller compared with the banking sector and only insignificantly smaller than the average of all sectors. Therefore, in contrast to the banking sector, no contagion effects are observable in the sample of negative earnings surprises at the insurance companies considered, providing evidence in favor of the fire-sale meltdown theory of Diamond and Rajan (2005).

Finally, we analyze whether the strength of the contagion effects differ in characteristics of the announcing banks. More precisely, we suspect that adverse events at more important banks cause stronger negative contagion effects at their competitors than adverse announcements from less important banks. The *importance* of a bank is proxied by its size, that is, its market capitalization. We use the average market capitalization of the year in which the earnings surprise was reported. Based on this criterion, we split the banking sample by the average market capitalization of the sector, which is the annual average of the year in which the event takes place. Overall, this analysis indicates that the size of the banks considered is an important factor regarding the strength of contagion effects. The highest level of contagion is observed for big competitor banks when another big bank experiences a negative earnings surprise.

CONCLUSION

In this chapter, we address the question of whether contagion is present in the U.S. banking sector, measured by stock price reaction following negative earnings surprises. To put the results into perspective, we compare the banking sector with the nonbanking sector.

Applying traditional event study methodology, we find that negative earnings surprises are contagious in the banking sector. The degree of contagion is increased by the degree of surprise. The abnormal return of the banks' competitors' portfolios is on average −0.08 percent for all negative surprises and increases up to −0.18 percent for greater earnings surprises. These results are significantly larger (in absolute terms) than the average abnormal returns for the nonbanking sectors. Earnings surprises at important (big) banks cause more pronounced reactions at competitor banks than surprises at small banks. The highest degree of contagion is found for big banks, reacting on negative news at another big bank.

Given the importance of a stable banking system for the real economy, the existence of contagion effects makes it necessary to draw the attention of the regulator to the entire system, rather than regulating on an individual bank level. Potential contagion effects could translate through the banking system, leading to a systemic crisis.

Analyzing the second highly regulated sector—the insurance sector—separately, we do not find any signs of contagion in this sector. This finding supports the notion that a systemic regulation of the insurance sector is less important compared to the banking sector. The financial supervision should therefore focus on the banking sector when aiming to implement a system-based regulation.

NOTES

1. See Bikhchandani et al. (1992) for a theoretical analysis of information contagion in general.
2. See Allen and Gale (2000) for a theoretical analysis of contagion and systemic risk due to interbank lending.

REFERENCES

Akhigbe, A., and J. Madura. 2001. "Why Do Contagion Effects Vary among Bank Failures." *Journal of Banking and Finance* 25:4, 657–680.

Allen, F., and D. Gale. 2000. "Financial Contagion." *Journal of Political Economy* 108:1, 1–33.

Bikhchandani, S., D. Hirshleifer, and I. Welch. 1992. "A Theory of Fads, Fashion, Custom, and Cultural Change as Informational Cascades." *Journal of Political Economy* 8:3, 992–1026.

Diamond, D. W., and R. G. Rajan. 2005. "Liquidity Shortages and Banking Crises." *Journal of Finance* 60:2, 615–647.

Jorion, P., and G. Zhang. 2007. "Good and Bad Credit Contagion: Evidence from Credit Default Swaps." *Journal of Financial Economics* 84:3, 860–883.

Lang, L.H.P., and R. M. Stulz. 1992. "Contagion and Competitive Intra-Industry Effects of Bankruptcy Announcements." *Journal of Financial Economics* 32:1, 45–60.

Prokopczuk, M. 2010. "Intra-Industry Contagion Effects of Earnings Surprises in the Banking Sector." *Applied Financial Economics*.

Slovin, M. B., M. E. Sushka, and J. A. Polonchek. 1999. "An Analysis of Contagion and Competitive Effects at Commercial Banks." *Journal of Financial Economics* 52:2, 197–225.

ABOUT THE AUTHOR

Marcel Prokopczuk is a lecturer in finance at the ICMA Centre, Henley Business School, University of Reading, U.K. He holds a PhD in finance from the University of Mannheim and a MSc in business engineering from the University of Karlsruhe. He is a CFA charterholder and holder of the Professional Risk Manager (PRM) designation.

Index